Career Development in Higher Education

A volume in
Research in Career Development
Grafton T. Eliason, John Patrick, and Jeff L. Samide, *Series Editors*

Research in Career Development

Grafton T. Eliason, John Patrick, and Jeff L. Samide
Series Editors

The primary purpose of *Research in Career Development* is to provide a broad look at the field of career development research including career counseling, career guidance, career education, and general career development programming, and to examine some of the field's major themes, approaches and assumptions. The series examines both knowledge from the past as well as what the future might bring. It brings together a variety of experts/authors from the area of interest and provides readers with a framework for action based on the best available research information.

Career Development in the Schools
Edited by Grafton Eliason and John Patrick

Issues in Career Development
Edited by John Patrick, Grafton Eliason, and Donald Thompson

Career Development in Higher Education

Edited by

Jeff L. Samide
California University of Pennsylvania

Grafton T. Eliason
California University of Pennsylvania

John Patrick
California University of Pennsylvania

INFORMATION AGE PUBLISHING, INC.
Charlotte, NC • www.infoagepub.com

Library of Congress Cataloging-in-Publication Data

Career development in higher education / edited by Jeff L. Samide, Grafton
T. Eliason, John Patrick.
    p. cm. – (Issues in career development book series)
Includes bibliographical references.
 ISBN 978-1-61735-508-0 (pbk.) – ISBN 978-1-61735-509-7 (hardcover) –
ISBN 978-1-61735-510-3 (e-book)
1. Career education–United States. 2. Education, Higher–United States.
3. Counseling in higher education–United States. I. Samide, Jeff L. II.
Eliason, Grafton. III. Patrick, John, 1955-
 LC1037.5.C366 2011
 378.1'9425–dc23

                                                          2011025283

DEDICATION

This work is dedicated to my wife Norma and to my daughter Rosie.
Norma's work ethic, keen intellect, enduring support and
calming influence has been central to my successes in life.
Rosie inherited all that is good from her mother
and is a distinct improvement over her old man.
—Jeff L. Samide

To my family and friends:
Trisha, Sophia, and Noah
Grafton and Zoe
Deighn, Claire, and Elle
Laurie and Mike
Mark, Jim, Ed, and Jeff
With much love and thanks,
—Grafton Eliason

To those who help others.
—John Patrick

CONTENTS

SECTION I

A COMPREHENSIVE OVERVIEW OF CAREER DEVELOPMENT IN HIGHER EDUCATION

SECTION II

THE PRACTICE OF CAREER DEVELOPMENT
IN FOUR YEAR LEARNING INSTITUTIONS

SECTION III

CAREER DEVELOPMENT IN GRADUATE LEVEL EDUCATION

SECTION IV

TECHNICAL INSTITUTIONS AND COMMUNITY COLLEGES

SECTION V

CONTEMPORARY TOPICS IN CAREER DEVELOPMENT

ACKNOWLEDGEMENTS

A work such as you are currently holding in your hand cannot be completed without a host of others who invested time, intellect and creativity into the process. We three editors had the great advantage of being surrounded by many outstanding graduate students, several with publication experience, who soon will undoubtedly experience the thrill of authorship in their own right. But until that day, they can be assured that they contributed well to a project that will advance the body of knowledge in our profession.

Marissa Fenwick—Marissa is a graduate student who is very meticulous and organized. She has a strong interest in career development, and you will see her name listed as co-author on chapter eleven. Her initial readings of chapters and insights greatly improved the final product.

Maria Grandas—Maria spent a great deal of time organizing our review process, acquiring releases from our chapter authors, and chasing down dozens of important details. An extremely talented and compassionate individual, she readily gave us her time and expertise, even when it caused her inconvenience.

Amy Issac—Amy joined our project a bit later into the process. She was responsible for compiling information about our authors, and she finalized all of our copyright releases. Her diligence and great attention to detail is appreciated.

Matt Menard—Matt offered his time over his Christmas holiday to read the entire manuscript and offer us a studied opinion on issues of organization and continuity. We truly appreciate his work and hope that his wife will for-

Career Development in Higher Education, pages xi–xii
Copyright © 2011 by Information Age Publishing

give him for the time he spent with us instead of assisting her with their two children, Nicholas, aged three, and Samuel, a newborn.

Emily Trifaro—Emily lent us solid experience in editing as well as a "can-do" attitude. When a deadline loomed, Emily could be counted upon to shoulder the burden with a smile. An experienced author and editor in her own right, Emily frequently expressed gratitude for the chance to participate in the process. It is likely that she taught us as much as she learned.

Bonnie Vatter—Bonnie signed on early to our project. She worked hard for us and needed little direction, despite her own work and job search. She always was concerned with doing her best for us and on occasion doubted her work despite its high quality. Sometimes, we editors fret that we didn't provide her with enough feedback. So, here now, "Well done, Bonnie!"

We would also like to acknowledge all of our chapter contributors whose expertise and passion for their topics bring to life the theories and practice of career development.

Finally, we wish to express our appreciation to California University of Pennsylvania, our wonderful colleagues in the Department of Counselor Education, and the administration for their strong support and encouragement. Truly, Cal U is a great place be.

FOREWORD

One significant factor that makes *Career Development in Higher Education* an excellent book is its editors and authors who are, indeed, experts in their field. I first met Jeff Samide, Grafton Eliason, and John Patrick several years ago when I became dean of the graduate school. I was immediately impressed with their work ethic, scholarship, and most importantly, their dedication to their students and the counseling profession. I can say the same for several of the authors I have known for even longer, such as Emily Sweitzer, Taunya Tinsley, Gene Sutton, and Rhonda Gifford. For those I don't know personally, after reading their manuscripts, I feel as if I already do. Everyone associated with this work offers scholarly and real-world perspectives to critical areas of higher education that *demand* our attention. They definitely got mine.

The number of relevant topics compiled here is astounding. There is also present a seamless flow of information from one chapter to another. There are many well-founded recommendations for success including topics such as mentorship and identity development and job support services for students with disabilities and mental illness. Specific strategies are presented with a focus on career development for student athletes, and the book even includes career development in the military, which quite naturally begins within the framework of postsecondary education.

Overall, the aim of the entire work is directed to the success of the students who seek to achieve the "American Dream," which because of globalization in education including distance education, is now sought by international students. Indeed, a chapter is specifically devoted to career development for students from abroad. Many of our institutions of higher

Career Development in Higher Education, pages xiii–xiv
Copyright © 2011 by Information Age Publishing
All rights of reproduction in any form reserved.

education provide a great service in assisting students with job opportunities in the region and even throughout the country. Lourens Human from the University of Pretoria goes further and provides an excellent chapter that includes discussion on how students can transfer a foreign education to a meaningful workforce experience in their home country.

I am compelled to once again mention the breadth of the subject matter in this book. For example, Kimberly Desmond and Kayla Snyder's chapter addresses issues relating to the preparation of high school students for career development activities when they go on to college. And on the other end of the spectrum, Travis Schermer and Caroline Perjessy provide interesting discussion relative to career counseling for doctoral students whose objective is often securing a tenure-track position in academia.

Moreover, what gives the book particular emphasis is its focus on contemporary needs, issues, and scholarship. For example, topics such as the applicability of the Internet and virtual learning to career counseling are addressed. Multicultural issues are presented in realistic fashion, and the unfortunate economic downturn throughout the country is discussed in relation to the serious need of retraining members of the American workforce who are seeking a second or even third career.

Our students, whether technical, community college, undergraduate, or graduate, need us now more than ever. It is one thing to provide the pure academic foundation for their future careers, but without the many aspects of specialized mentoring and counseling, students may end with nothing more than an empty promise of the American Dream. *Career Development in Higher Education* is a resource that every academic professional should have at the ready. Undoubtedly, student services provided by counselors and career advisors will improve greatly because of this scholarship. Once you begin to read this book, you will quickly see for yourself the expertise that the editors and authors bring to such challenging and contemporary issues.

—**John R. Cencich, J.S.D.**
Dean of the Graduate School
California University of Pennsylvania

INTRODUCTION

Career Counseling in Higher Education

In a 2008 survey by the National Center for Public Policy and Higher Education, Americans have reiterated their convictions that higher education is important; a college degree is necessary for better job prospects in the long run and would be better than taking a decent job immediately after high school. Additionally, the survey found that the majority of Americans believe employers are less likely to hire people without degrees even if they could do the job. As this is being written, colleges and universities are registering students for classes, having them select or change majors, completing programs of study, responding to those who are wondering what types of jobs are out there for them to pursue upon completion of their degrees, and helping students to acquire the necessary skills to find work. They are essentially assisting students who come to higher education as the means to achieve their "vision of the future" and to be in a better position to secure work that is both personally meaningful and available.

The students that higher education serves also come from exceptionally diverse backgrounds and life circumstances that reflect the rich tapestry of American and international life. They want to believe that higher education is the way and are willing to make the countless sacrifices of time, money, and effort to make it so. Despite economic woes that transcend ethnicity, geographic location, and often their own level of education, parents continue to believe in the American Dream, that is: education is the best means of securing a bright future for their children. They do this despite

Career Development in Higher Education, pages xv–xvii
Copyright © 2011 by Information Age Publishing
All rights of reproduction in any form reserved.

a rapidly changing world that brings with it great anxieties as to the future. Within this context, countless numbers of faculty, staff, and administrators are working with students daily to help them craft their "visions" into reality. But how do we assist these dedicated professionals in working with college and university students to make their career visions come true? It is with those professionals in mind that this book is designed to assist.

The book is organized into five sections. In Section I, a comprehensive overview of career development in higher education is given. The first chapter in this section is a thorough review of the literature by Rebecca Roberts Martin that highlights important resources that can be used when providing career counseling to post-secondary students. William Rullo provides insight borne of great experience into the varied influences on career decision making. Kimberly Desmond explores how to best prepare high school students to best take advantage of career development activities in higher education. Emily Sweitzer describes a process for mentorship and identity development, which, when implemented could lead to improved post-secondary career development.

In Section II, Nadine Garner describes and explores the practice of career development at the baccalaureate level in both public and private colleges and universities. In the following chapter, Gene Sutton and Rhonda Gifford examine both the components of a career counseling center and how a career counseling center may be used to facilitate career development.

Section III features the challenges of fostering career development among graduate students. In that section, Mathew Ishler explores the career development needs of master's degree students, while Travis Schermer examines the career needs of doctoral students, including finding employment in academia.

Section IV focuses on the career development needs of students attending technical institutions and community colleges. Jon Lent examines the role of career counseling in technical institutions, while Fred Redekop describes and explores the role of career development in community colleges.

Section V features contemporary topics in career development. Reflecting the diversity of students attending post-secondary institutions of higher education, several authors have written about the career needs of specific student populations. Demond Bledsoe and Eric Owens discuss multi-cultural issues in career development, whereas Lourens Human examines the career development needs of international students. Helen Hamlet provides much needed insight into the career development and counseling needs of students with disabilities and special needs. Additionally, Mark Lepore discusses how job support services at the post-secondary level can help to eliminate barriers to employment facing college graduates with mental illness. Amy Walker and Taunya Tinsley shed insight into the challenges facing student athletes as it relates to their career development. George Williams and co-contributors provide much needed information on the framework and structure of the military branches, along with a fine discussion of the career development needs of students who are in the military. Other topics include the evolution of the virtual learning environment and the Internet as it relates to career counseling, by Ray Feroz and Marissa Fenwick. And James Matta explores the career issues faced by students who are re-training or are embarking on second careers in a declining job market.

It is our hope that you will find the information contained in this book to be timely and useful as you work with students attending colleges and universities to fulfill their "career visions." Your "being there" to assist these students is very much needed and appreciated.

—**The Editors**

REFERENCE

The National Center for Public Policy and Higher Education. (2008, August). *Policy Alert: Is college opportunity slipping away?* Retrieved from http://www.higher education.org/pa_college_opp/College_Opportunity.pdf

SECTION I

A COMPREHENSIVE OVERVIEW
OF CAREER DEVELOPMENT
IN HIGHER EDUCATION

CHAPTER 1

A REVIEW OF THE LITERATURE AND IMPORTANT RESOURCES CONCERNING CAREER DEVELOPMENT IN HIGHER EDUCATION

Rebecca L. Roberts Martin
Kent State University

Selecting a career path as a young high school graduate can be an intimidating task. Students are introduced to careers as early as the preschool years; however, the college-bound student often faces overwhelming pressure and confusion when the time comes to select one specific program or pursue one specific career. As the costs of higher education continue to rise for both students and institutions, counselors face increasing pressure to provide career development services to high school and college students to increase college admissions and retention rates and prepare graduates for the world of work. The purpose of this chapter is to introduce the history of career development in higher education, including an overview of vocational guidance programs, career counseling theories and several assess-

Career Development in Higher Education, pages 3–24
Copyright © 2011 by Information Age Publishing
All rights of reproduction in any form reserved.

ments and techniques. The chapter includes examples of career counseling centers at the collegiate level, examples of how technology can be used to advance career development and the technology available to assist students with disabilities.

HOW CAREER DEVELOPMENT IN HIGHER EDUCATION BEGAN, THE FIRST PROGRAMS

Early career resources for students, before the 20th or even 19th century, were inclined to be more of a casual interaction between a faculty "mentor" and student "mentee" in a university setting, as well as leaning toward being a traditionally male communication (Herr, Cramer, & Niles, 2004; Rullo, Eliason, & Patrick, 2008). Many of these early relationships within the university were meant to assist the student in employment transition but unfortunately, due to the nature of the exclusivity between professor and student, lead to partiality for some and poor employment placement for others. This makeshift system was lacking in professional uniformity for the student, and in 1884 a more formal system utilizing university appointments boards began to develop to assist students with employment transition at Cambridge University (Watts & Kidd, 2000).

Cambridge University is one of the earliest universities documented with career assistance to students. Official approval and funding of the appointments board at Cambridge, initially called the Association for the Regulation of Teachers, was on February 27, 1902 (Waters, Chesterman, Holegate, Kirkman, Raban, & Smith, 2002). From 1884 to 1902 many University Appointment boards had sprung up in small campuses across the United States and the United Kingdom. The University Appointment Board was separated into areas that provided assistance with:

- *Working with employers,* to make the case for the employment of graduates, to elicit suitable vacancies and to assist the employers to fill those vacancies with suitable candidates from the University
- *Working with its associates* to discover their skills, knowledge, and aspirations; to match those to available opportunities, and make appropriate recommendations to employers
- *Working in partnership with others* (Waters et al., 2002).

The University Appointment Board partnered with parents of students and local businesses to help students find options after graduation. However, the one population that was not served was women. The University Appointment Boards did not have women as members until 1948, when women became full members of the University. Separate career services were provided for women for many years; although a distinct Cambridge University Women's Appointment Board (CUWAB) was developed in 1930 as a joint project between Newnham and Girton Women's Colleges (Waters et al., 2002). Other noteworthy early predecessors of career placement services have been linked to Oxford University and Yale University (Herr et al., 2004).

VOCATIONAL GUIDANCE PROGRAMS

Initial career counseling called "vocational guidance" (Pope, 2000, p. 196) was the child of industrialization. Prior to industrialization many individuals would follow in the occupational footsteps of fathers, for males, and mothers, for females (Lucas, 1986; Pope, 2000; Rullo et al., 2008). As agriculture waned and industry blossomed in the United States, the demand for urban work and those trained for the technology of urban work grew. The end of World War I also increased the need for career services as many returning veterans needed career assistance, as well as those workers who held the veterans' jobs while the military personnel were in active service (Pope, 2000).

CAREER COUNSELING, LINKING PAST TO THE PRESENT

Pope (2000) discussed the development of career counseling to include six stages, beginning in 1890 to the present time. The first stage of development was job placement. Placement services were fathered by Frank Parsons who was "heavily influenced" (Pope, 2000, p. 196) by the work of Jane Adams, a social worker who developed a settlement house in Chicago to assist immigrants in community transition (Chapter 21, n.d.). Frank Parsons was ultimately considered to be the "Father of Guidance" (Chapter 21, n.d.; Lucas, 1986) and opened the Vocational Bureau at Civic Service House in Boston Massachusetts in 1908 (Lucas, 1986; Pope, 2000; Rullo et al., 2008). Parsons created a trait and factor model of career counseling based on the ideas of, (1) understanding of one's self; (2) familiarity of conditions for success for various areas of employment; (3) and understanding the relationship between understanding of one's self and the familiarity of conditions for success for various areas of employment (Lucas, 1986; Pope, 2000).

Psychological testing became a necessary part of career assessment during this first stage. The scientific method granted career assessment an acceptance among professionals in psychology and in the burgeoning counseling field that it otherwise may not have known (Pope, 2000). While quantitative methods of testing or standardized assessment tools continued to be the norm in career counseling, qualitative assessments began to grow in popularity for more individualized career counseling in the 1990s (Young & Chen, 1999).

Stage two, according to Pope (2000), stretched from 1920 to 1939, and was largely related to vocational guidance in the schools. Pope discussed educational counseling as developing from the work of "progressive social reformers in the schools" (2000, p. 198), like Jesse B. Davis and Eli Weaver, who both promoted career development as early as 1898 and 1909 in their respective schools. Development of vocational guidance in the schools was a slower process, and it was not until President Roosevelt's New Deal and Civilian Conservation Corps (CCC) in 1933 that new life was fed in into the educational system for the unemployed youth, and again in 1935 with the Works Progress Administration (Pope, 2000).

Stage three, 1940–1959, as stated by Pope (2000), consisted of focusing resources and training on colleges and universities to produce new counselors and develop campus career assistance. After World War II and the launch of the space race post-Sputnik between the United States and the USSR, it became increasingly important to both find careers for returning veterans, and to convince others to move into the math and science professions to boost the United States technology advantage (Bourne, 1988; Lucas, 1986, Pope, 2000). The National Defense Education Act (NDEA) in 1958 was responsible for launching the Counseling and Training Guidance Institutes (Pope, 2000; Rullo et al., 2008). Bourne (1988), in an interview with Ralph Bedell, a professor who was instrumental in the development and implementation of the NDEA Training and Guidance Institutes, discussed the impact of the Institutes on the guidance profession. Bedell stated to Bourne that Bob Callis, a director of several of the Institutes, and consultant of the program reported to him that the Institutes:

> ... set a model for counseling and guidance that has not been exceeded since. They helped to standardize the counselor training programs ... A great transition occurred in counseling and guidance as a result of the Institutes. ... They also established supervision practicums in the programs. It was really a revolution in counseling. (Bourne, 1988, p. 67)

Bourne (1988) reviewed two types of career training institutes as discussed by Bedell, long-term and short-term. The long-term, or year round institutes, met the needs of novice counselors in training, while the short-term, or summer institutes, were advantageous for more seasoned counselors. Institutes were developed and funded by the NDEA at the University of Michigan and the Teachers College at Columbia University in 1958 (Bourne, 1988). In 1959 fifty more institutes were developed and funded in college and university campuses around the country. In 1967 Bedell reported there were 10,000 students who had completed a full year of counseling and guidance education at the graduate level, with an annual rate of graduation for the country at 2,000 students (Bourne, 1988).

Stage four, 1960–1974 is related to the ideas of "meaningful work and organizational career development" (Pope, 2000, p. 200). President Kennedy's vocational education consultants' panel issued a report in 1962 that recommended school counselors have an increased understanding of work and the nature of work (Pope, 2000). Eventually those recommendations became the Vocational Education Act of 1963. The legislation was followed by an expanded Vocational Rehabilitation Administration budget in 1965, with all changes meant to augment training and education and enhance vocational life. Characteristics of this stage include an increase in career counseling in the private agency and public agency arenas, as well as in governmental facilities (Pope, 2000). Young & Chen (1999) identified the need for career counselors to have an understanding of employee job satisfaction, organizational management characteristics, work relationships, and team building in order to assist the employee in finding and maintaining successful and satisfying employment. The authors also discussed ways of assisting others in establishing meaning in careers by identifying personality traits and characteristics, which may be a didactic or introspective process (Young & Chen, 1999).

The fifth stage, 1980–1989, was characterized by a transition to outplacement counseling and the private practice career counselor (Pope, 2000). Outplacement is a term used by companies that are downsizing, and outplacement counselors are those counselors used to assist those workers that have been downsized in finding new employment. The Vocational Education Act of 1963 was replaced by the Carl D. Perkins Vocational Education Act in 1984, increasing "federal authorization for vocational education programs through fiscal year 1989" (Pope, 2000, p. 204).

Stage six, according to Pope (2000), is 1990 through the present. Stage six incorporates multicultural career counseling, use of technology in career counseling, and transitioning students from school to the job through career counseling. Pope (2000) also identified the use of job partnerships in this stage, such as Welfare to Work and The Job Training Partnerships Act as examples of workforce legislation enacted to partner with career training to assist unemployed or disadvantaged individuals in gaining work or returning to work, with the training secondary to the employment. Young and Chen (1999) documented several school-to-work transition issues ranging from salary expectations, current economic conditions, future orientation of ability to find work, work attitude, gender, family financial assistance, and history of work as a teen.

DEVELOPMENT OF THE PLACEMENT OFFICE

From this rich vocational guidance background originated the distinctive college career counseling center we know today. Early career centers in the 1900s, or "Placement Offices," were often coupled with business offices, employment services, or economic departments and not related to counseling or psychology centers (Herr, et al., 2004; Lucas, 1986). After World War II, Placement Offices utilized Parson's trait and factor approach to career assessment and functioned much like an employment agency, matching a person's skills to job availability (Lucas, 1986). The NDEA vocational guidance education funding in 1958 gave rise to the number of vocational counselors in the United States, setting a foundation for the development of career counseling centers. Lucas (1986) discussed the role of the Civil Rights Movement, the Civil Rights Act of 1964, and Title VII, all of which prohibited employment discrimination, and along with the restricted labor market, the surplus of college graduates and the rise of the liberal arts major, culminated in the need to revamp the traditional Placement Office. The author reviewed the growth of the initial college career counseling offices in the 1970s that offered students, "Career education, career counseling, conferences and career days," along with "job search skills" (Lucas, 1986, p. 11).

The college career counseling center, according to Lucas (1986), had issues with organizational separation from other departments. The organizational placement of the college career center often had more to do with the center's director's philosophy of placement versus career development planning (Lucas, 1986). The author reported a few campuses housed their career counseling centers with student services, continuing to focus services on placement concerns, while others incorporated career counseling with placement for stand-alone centers that began to focus on career development. More modern college campuses frequently have career counseling centers integrated with college counseling services to create a more "holistic approach" (Lucas, 1986, p. 13).

Benefits of an integrated center, according to Lucas (1986), are increased student use and willingness to engage. Lucas discussed detriments to integration of centers, such as the fear of one of the services losing its own unique characteristics and the other dominating the center, or "overextending the staff and resources" (1986, p. 15). The author stated it is necessary for the career center to determine its own mission related to the size of the campus, be it a community college campus or a large university, and to decide how best to integrate itself and what role it has for its campus (Lucas, 1986). McMurray & Sorrells (2007) reported collaboration between student services and career services as well as other programs on campus as necessary to help students thrive on college grounds. The authors discuss how to increase collaboration by enhancing dialogue among faculty, advising departments, admission departments and career services staff. The dialogue between departments allows for increased communication regarding student- related issues and needs, such as informing students about available internships and job fairs (McMurray & Sorrells, 2007).

GROWTH OF THE CAREER COUNSELING CENTERS

Career counseling centers have developed on college and university campus settings from employment placement offices to full service career centers. Career counseling centers are found at two and four year institutions.

Kent State University in Kent, Ohio is an example of a comprehensive career services center at a four year institution (Kent State University Career Center, 2010). Kent State University has an eight-campus collegiate system and is among the largest regional organizations in the country, with more than 19,000 undergraduate students and 5,000 graduate students enrolled at the main Kent campus and over 13,888 students enrolled in the regional campus settings in 2009 (Kent State University Career Center, 2010). All of the Kent State regional campuses have a career center, with some regional campuses offering more services than others, in all probability based on campus size and student population. Each regional campus career center offers a link to the Kent State main campus Career Services Center.

The following is a review of the Career Service Center at the main Kent Campus, and does not include any of the regional campus service centers. Kent State University Career Services offers assistance to students, alumni, employers, faculty and staff, and family members of students. Housed in Career Services are: administrative staff that oversee the department, including a Director and two Associate Directors; an Academic Testing Coordinator; a Career Education Director, a Career Education Career Counselor, and a Career Education Graduate Assistant; an On-Campus Recruiting and Employer Relations Assistant Director and a Recruiting Secretary; a Student Employment Senior Personnel Assistant and a Student Employment Administrative Clerk; and a Public Relations and Operations Office Manager, and Two Public Relations Operations Receptionists (Kent State University Career Center, 2010).

Kent State University's Career Services Department's description is an example of Lucas's (1986) concept of an integrated Career Services Center, although placement of campus psychology and counseling services are outside to the Department of Career Services. Students must be referred for psychological or mental health counseling assistance.

Kent State University Career Service Center provides some unique, interactive on-campus and web-based services for patrons (Kent State University

Career Center, 2010). A unique resource offered by this institution is Interview Prep, an on-line, interactive, web-based experience where students can practice their interview skills with InterviewStream. With InterviewStream, student's can use their webcam to record and play back a mock job interview with questions tailored to their education, qualifications, desired job position, and experience (Kent State University Career Center, 2010).

An on-campus event for various majors is an interview day where the Kent State University Career Service Center invites students to the Kent Student Center Ballroom to interact with organizations and businesses in their chosen field. An example of this is the upcoming "Meet the Accountants Night," where prospective undergraduate and graduate MBA and accounting majors are encouraged to bring their resumes and dress professionally to interact with organizations that range from the government to the corporate sectors (Kent State University Center, 2010). This event allows students the opportunity to network and introduce themselves to prospective employers, as well as apply for internships if they are needed.

Stark State College of Technology is a two year college in North Canton, Ohio that offers associates degrees and professional development, and is host to a more conventional Career Development Office (Stark State College Career Development Office, 2010). Stark State College reports that as of 2010 it is the largest technical college in Ohio, with more than 12,000 credit students and approximately 4,000 non-credit students (Stark State College Career Development Office ,2010). Stark State College boasts nine satellite branches in two Ohio Counties. Stark State College does not offer career services at any of their satellite branches, only their main branch in North Canton, Ohio. But satellite students are able to have full access to the services at the main branch career center at all times. Stark State College Career Development Office staff includes a Career Development Specialist and a Director of Career Development. The Career Development Office offers services to students and alumni of the college, who can make use of on-campus information, mock interviews, job fairs, career exploration, and multiple job search links (Stark State College Career Development Office, 2010).

On-campus information through the Stark State College Career Development Office can be found in the Career Center Library, which houses books on various careers and job information, materials on cover letters and resumes, and information on interviewing. A job bulletin board is available, and jobs are posted where students can locate notices of vacancies for local businesses and part-time campus openings for students (Stark State College Career Development Office, 2010).

Stark State College offers a distinctive on-line assistance program that be found in the form of e-Discover for career planning at the Career Development Office. As a career guidance tool, e-Discover allows students to identify personality traits that impact choices, investigate skills previously learned, and find what ideal work environment fits with each student. The Stark State College Career Development Office offers e-Discover free for students to use through their offices and encourages students to take advantage of the instrument (Stark State College Career Development Office, 2010).

ASSESSMENT TOOLS USED
IN CAREER COUNSELING CENTERS

Effectual career counseling centers utilize assessment tools to explore a student's job values, personality characteristics and interests, and values toward work (Hammond, 2001). Standardized and qualitative assessment tools are used in college career counseling centers, at both two- and four-year institutions (Young & Chen, 1999). Provided is a review of many of the most frequently used assessment tools in both two- and four-year institutions; this is not, however, to be considered a complete listing, rather a highlight of representative resources available in the literature.

In review of available career assessments, the most popular is Holland's RIASEC typology. Holland's RIASEC (Realistic, Investigative, Artistic, Social, Enterprising, and Conventional) is a familiar assessment for most career centers and many vocational interests are "frequently measured and summarized" in reference to Holland (Gati, Fishman-Nadav, & Shiloh, 2006, p 26; Holland, 1997). According to Gati and colleagues (2006), individuals' affective responses lead them to choose certain types of activities that eventually become a career interest. The Self-Directed Search (SDS) inventory (Gati et al., 2006; Holland, 1997) also utilizes the RIASEC typology with a self-guided, self-scoring instrument.

Pulver and Kelly (2008) reviewed use of the Myers-Briggs Type Indicator (MBTI) in career counseling services as one of the most common personality assessment instruments utilized for career counseling. The MBTI is based on the Jungian-type theory of extraversion–introversion, sensing–intuition, thinking–feeling, and judging–perceiving (Myers, McCaulley, Quenk, & Hammer, 1998; Pulver & Kelly, 2008). The MTBI career report matches personality type with occupational choices. The authors also discussed the use of the MTBI in helping to assist in identifying career and academic goals.

Another traditional career assessment tool is the NEO-PI-R, or Five-Factor Model of Personality (Costa & McCrae, 1992; Hammond, 2001). Hammond (2001) discussed the Five-Factor Model (FFM) to include Neuroticism, Extraversion, Openness, Agreeableness, and Conscientiousness. Each of these personality types lean toward a certain occupational characteristic, and understanding of your type will lead to greater career success (Hammond, 2001).

Young and Chen (1999) list several widely used interest inventories in career counseling, including the Strong Interest Inventory, the Kuder Occupational Interest Survey, the Campbell Interest and Skill Inventory, and the Career Thoughts Inventory. Card sorts were also identified as alternatives to traditional assessments and included the Career Interest Card Sort, and Missouri Occupational Card Sort (Young & Chen, 1999).

Young & Chen (1999) again reviewed other popular career assessments such as the Career Success Expectations Scale (CSES), The Career Transition Inventory (CTI), The Pressure Management Indicator, The Decisional Process Inventory, the Decision-Making Difficulties Questionnaire (CDDQ), The Career Decision Profile, The Assessment of Attributions for Career Decision Making (AACDM), Coping with Career Indecision, Differential Aptitude Test (DAT), and Super's Career Rainbow.

Smart and Peterson (1997) reviewed use of the Adult Career Concerns Inventory (ACCI), previously known as the Career Development Inventory (CDI) in their study on Super's vocational developmental stages. The ACCI measures test takers' "level of concern with Super's four stages of career development" (p. 364), which are "(a) exploration, (b) establishment, (c) maintenance, and (d) disengagement" (p. 359). The items on the ACCI are rated on a one to five Likert-type scale, and the test offers a shortened 48-item version from the original 60-item instrument (Smart & Peterson, 1997).

The World of Work Inventory (WOWI), developed by Ripley, Neidert, and Ortman, and has more recently come to popular use in career assessment (Spies & Plake, 2005). The WOWI has five sections, identifying information (demographics), self-selected choices (two occupational choice and two academic subjects), career interest activities (136 items), career training potentials (98 items), and job satisfaction indicators (96 items) (Spies & Plake, 2005). The WOWI personalizes a profile based on personality, interest, skills, aptitude, and preference for qualities of work environment. The authors describe the WOWI as multidimensional and integrated. "Career counselors who have switched to using the WOWI indicate several reasons, including: limited staff time required for test administration, automated and immediate scoring results, completely web-based testing, ability to modify for various reading levels, and low cost to test ratio. In addition, job recommendations included in the testing results are linked to O*NET codes for additional career exploration activities with the student" (Deborah Roberts, personal communication, July 8, 2010).

Another assessment with increased use in the College Career Center is The K-State Problem Identification Rating Scales (K-PIRS), which looks at students' level of current functioning, change readiness, and presenting problems (Robertson et al., 2006). The authors described the instrument as having seven scales that measure "Mood Difficulties, Learning Problems, Food Concerns, Interpersonal Conflicts, Career Uncertainties, Self-Harm Indicators, and Substance/Addiction Issues" (p. 141). Robertson and colleagues (2006) discussed the K-PIRS as having a rating scale, rather than a check list, allowing students to identify their concerns more clearly, as well as the ability to be completed and scored quickly.

Engelland, Workman and Singh (2000) reviewed a recent revision to the rapidly increasing cache of career assessments. The authors presented a modified SERVQUAL scale, or service quality scale, "that consisted of 17 items in total and included eight of the original SERVQUAL items" (p. 240). The original SERVQUAL measured dimensions of tangibles, reliability, responsiveness, assurance, and empathy, given twice to measure service expectations and service performance perception (Engelland et al., 2000). The revised instrument consists of completely new items for the tangibles and assurance dimensions, and two new items for reliability that effectively measure service quality and service performance (Engelland et al., 2000).

TECHNOLOGY USE IN CAREER COUNSELING CENTERS

Pope (2000) acknowledged the use of technology in career counseling as the sixth stage of development, and use of technology in the career counseling center continues to flourish. Hoyt and Maxey (2001) reviewed the necessity of the career counselor in working with technology in assisting students to choose between four year and other post-secondary career oriented education. Both school counselors and college career counselors work with students in transition between high school and college and often need to help students identify if higher education will "pay" (Hoyt & Maxey, 2001). Some of the technology at their disposal that can assist with this process is the U.S. Department of Labor's website, which lists the Bureau of Labor Statistics (BLS) charts and data, based on age and educational degree. Another technological resource allowing counselors to assist students in weighing out the job predictions in a field is the Occupation Outlook Quarterly online. The document allows students to see what their potential job outlook may be for several years in advance (Hoyt & Maxey, 2001). It is available on the U.S. Department of Labor's website.

The O*Net has now replaced the traditional Dictionary of Occupational Titles (DOT) for standardized occupational information (O*Net, n.d.) for the US Department of Labor, and for many other career counseling settings due to the frequently outdated and often limited information (Dictionary of Occupational Titles, n.d.) in the DOT. The Dictionary of Occupational Titles was developed in 1939 to help match jobs with workers

(Dictionary of Occupational Titles, n.d.). It is still available online for die hard users but does offer a link to the much more user friendly O*Net. The O*Net offers the consumer detailed descriptions of their chosen job, along with the necessary skill and knowledge areas needed, the tasks the person would complete at the job, matching RIASEC code, work style and values, and wages and employment trends (O*Net, n.d.). The O*Net is useful for career counselors in assisting students to think rationally about choices of majors while in school as the list of Job Zones specifies what extensive training or post graduate work may be included in the career choice. The O*Net offers a job summary page or a more extensive detailed or custom report based on need. The O*Net is free to use.

The Occupational Outlook Handbook (OOH) is accessible through the US Department of Labor website (Occupational Outlook Quarterly, n.d.). For each job reviewed, the OOH 2010–2011 edition gives the training and education needed, earnings, job prospects, actual job duties, and job working conditions. The OOH allows the user to link to state-specific job information and employment statistics (Occupational Outlook Quarterly, n.d.).

Many states, such as Ohio and Washington, have their own interactive career information to assist college career counselors. Ohio has The Ohio Labor Market Information online for career exploration in the state of Ohio (Ohio Labor Market Information Online, n.d.). This site allows the user to enter the location in the state or the zip code, and the desired occupation or occupational field, and a report is given specifying occupational title, average wages, and projected annual job openings in different regions of Ohio. The information can easily be downloaded into an excel spreadsheet format and given to the student (Ohio Labor Market Information Online, n.d.).

Career and rehabilitation counselors in the state of Washington often use The Washington Occupational Information System (WOIS), a career information system (Washington Occupational Information System, n.d.). The WOIS is a private, non-profit career website that allows its users to purchase career profiles portfolios, assessments, and have access to job summaries and details similar to the O*Net. The WOIS serves colleges, businesses, secondary schools, libraries, counseling agencies, and government vocational rehabilitation programs," (Washington Occupational Information System, n.d.). Deborah Roberts, M.A., Rehabilitation Counselor with The Department of Social and Health Services/Division of Vocational Rehabilitation in Olympia, Washington, stated she believes the WOIS to be more user friendly than the O*Net and finds the site easier to navigate with clients (Deborah Roberts, personal communication, July 8, 2010). Roberts reported the WOIS offers her clients the advantage of media, as many of the job summaries show a short video of a person actually performing the job, and offers a student page for clients transitioning to college with preparatory assistance for the PSAT, ACT, SAT, SAT Subject Tests, AP Test, and ASVAB (Deborah Roberts, personal communication, July 8, 2010).

The state government of Ohio offers a similar service to the WOIS called The Ohio Career Information System (OCIS), which is an internet-based career system for schools, colleges, and vocational systems (Ohio Career Information System, n.d.). The OCIS is supported by the Ohio Department of Education and users can pay an annual site license fee of $450 for the period July1st through June 30th to have access to updated career, academic, and financial aid information (Ohio Career Information System, n.d.).

A review of on-line resources would not be complete without the mention of the CareerOneStop. The CareerOneStop is sponsored by the U.S. Department of Labor and has on-line employment tools to help students explore careers, find education options, identify their own interests and talents, and plan out their job search (CareerOneStop, n.d.). On the website itself are tools to assist with the development of a resume, cover letters, and job interviews. Other resources include state by state job banks, as well as the actual physical location of a Career One Stop agency in each state locale.

ASSISTIVE TECHNOLOGY USED IN CAREER COUNSELING CENTERS

The need for assistive technology on campus grows as students with special needs continue to increase their presence on college campuses with the expansion of the Americans with Disabilities Act (ADA). Norton and Field (1998) discussed the student population expansion of those with special needs to be higher in two year institutions than four year institutions. Assistive technology in college career centers is a key area for those with special needs as they focus on career exploration, job shadowing, job seeking abilities, and job readiness (Norton & Field, 1998).

Assistive technologies were identified by Thompson, Draffan and Patel (2009) to include use of:

> . . . screen reader applications for blind users' screen magnification software for users with low vision; speech recognition or other alternative input technologies for users with mobility impairments; and scan, highlight and read software solutions for users with dyslexia or other disabilities affecting their ability to read print. (p. 1)

Supplementary technologies may include captioned or transcribed video or podcasts for material being presented in these formats for students who are deaf or hard of hearing, or narration for blind students (Thompson et al., 2009). Students with learning disabilities, Attention Deficit Disorder, and Asperger's are now using these same types of accommodations that were more traditionally reserved for those with vision impairments, and with very good success (Deborah Roberts, personal communication, July 8, 2010). Computers in college career centers must be readily accessible for all students to be able to utilize irrespective of disability.

An additional assistive technology used in career counseling centers is screen reader software, such as the Kurzweil 3000 v12 (Summary Report of the Iowa Text Reader Studies 2006–2007 for Kurzweil 3000, n.d.). The software is used to convert text to computerized speech, which can then be listened to by the student. This is helpful for individuals with blindness or low vision, learning disabilities, Attention Deficit Disorder, Autism Spectrum Disorder, or even individuals with mental health barriers such as anxiety. Along with converting text to speech, the Kurzweil 3000 has study tools such as bubble charting, electronic highlighter pens and on-screen sticky notes which can be valuable for improving learning strategies.

A screen reader similar to the Kurzweil 3000 that scans text to speech through the use of an attached scanner is the WYNN Wizard. The WYNN Wizard recognizes homophones and is fairly consumer friendly. Both the WYNN Wizard and Kurzweil 3000 offer MP3 conversion for convenient listening through an MP3 device (WYNN Wizard, n.d.).

Dragon Naturally Speaking 10 Standard presents a voice to text dictation program that allows the student talk into a microphone on the computer instead of having to type on a traditional keyboard. The software then transcribes the words into text, email, forms, spreadsheets, or any other format needed. Dragon dictation is now offered for iPad™, iPhone™, iPod-Touch™. Mobile speech applications have a text-to-speech option for many cell phones. Dragon proffers multiple versions and expanded vocabularies (Dragon Naturally Speaking, n.d.).

The voice to text programs previously discussed function very well for individuals with multiple disability barriers and significant learning challenges, along with those who require simple voice to text translation. A disadvantage of using software previously discussed can be the cost-to-benefit ratio, which includes determining how many users will be authorized to use the onsite equipment or if the college is purchasing the software for the student to make use of off-site. A software version that may be more attractive and user friendly to the limited student budget, or the college career center with a restricted budget, presents itself in the version of Read-Please2003. ReadPlease2003 offers a free version which does not expire, or an enhanced version with more speech patterns and other options. This is a simple, easy to use screen reader which can be downloaded by a student onto their home computer through internet access. A student can copy and paste any electronic text into the open software window in order to have the text read aloud (ReadPlease2003, 2003).

One of the most up-to-date pieces of technology is the Livescribe Smart Pen. The Livescribe Smart Pen is an assistive technology that many parents are purchasing for their students who are going off to college. The Livescribe Smart Pen records what is written through the aid of a special notebook. The student can chose to record the audio version of the instructor's lesson at the same time they are taking notes. The student can then go back and click on the page in the notes they want to review what the instructor said at a later time (Livescribe Smart Pen, n.d.).

One of the assets college career centers can use to supplement their own resources is coordination with local government vocational rehabilitation programs for exploration of assistive technology devices (Lindstrom, Flannery, Benz, Olszewski, & Slovic, 2009). Local vocational rehabilitation counselors can offer expertise and guidance on obtaining loans or coordination grants from assistive technology resource centers such as the Oregon Office of Vocational Rehabilitation Services (OVRS), the University of Washington, Washington Assistive Technology Act Program (WATAP), or the Ohio Rehabilitation Services Commission (RSC), Bureau of Vocational Rehabilitation (BVR) (Lindstrom et al., 2009).

An illustration of coordination of services between local government vocational rehabilitation programs and college career services as discussed by Lindstrom and colleagues (2009) is evident at Stark State Technical College in North Canton. Ohio. Stark State College coordinates a program with the Ohio Rehabilitation Services Commission; Bureau of Vocational Rehabilitation (RSC; BVR) called the THEME Project (THEME, n.d.). THEME is a grant funded program that promotes the advancement of success in postsecondary education and improvement of employment outcomes (THEME, n.d.). Students who have an open case with the Ohio RSC; BVR and are receiving services from Disability Support Services at Stark State College may be eligible for developmental reading supports, mentoring, short-term mental health counseling and referral, job shadowing and skills training, career exploration, assistance with purchasing adaptive technology or equipment, and job placement support after graduation (THEME, n.d.).

USE OF OTHER TECHNIQUES IN COLLEGE CAREER COUNSELING CENTERS

Regularly identified in the literature are the use of courses, workshops and seminars in career services. Herr and colleagues (2004) discussed career education courses and their relevance to student learning in group settings. The authors reviewed several universities that provided career education with curriculum that was similar to traditional individual career investigation, such as reviewing career options, assessing individual's interests and skills, and completing a job search, although all were accomplished in a group format. They posit career classes can be successful as a career counseling intervention for advancing career or academic maturity (Herr et al., 2004).

Smart, Ethington, Umbach, and Rocconi (2009) reviewed the efficacy of Holland's typology theory for "alternative theory-based learning outcomes" and the compatibility with faculty members (p. 487). The study examined 137 four year colleges and universities with a total of 14,336 faculty ($n = 6,685$). Faculty members were assigned Holland Codes and were asked to select one course they taught for student learning outcome ratings 1 to 4 (1 "very little" to 4 "very much"). A four by two multivariate analysis of variance (MANOVA) design was used to evaluate the variables and interactions between faculty members and student learning. Smart and colleagues found that, "while not uniformly true, we believe our collective findings support the premise that the findings for consistent academic environments are more in accord with predictions derived from Holland's theory than are those for inconsistent environments." (2009, p. 496). For example, artistic environments encourage artistic activity and abilities, and investigative environments enhance scholarly and mathematic abilities (Smart et al., 2009). The applications of this study important to the college career center are in understanding how our programming affects students. The authors warn of using a "one size fits all" when designing courses and workshops for career development, and helping the student by creating a diverse learning environment.

Workshops can also be an effective way to reach students with undecided majors or to assist those with career indecision. Lepre (2007) studied the effects of a persuasive message, The Theory of Planned Behavior (TOPB), on career workshop attendance among college students. Using a pre- and post-test control group experimental four by two, Lepre studied 154 students (113 women and 41 men), 66 who were certain about career choice and 88 who were uncertain about career choice at the beginning of the study. The data was analyzed using an analysis of variance (ANOVA). The results indicated that any message targeting a student's beliefs and attitudes toward enrolling in a workshop has an impact on that student's intentions. Positive messages about enrolling in workshops were not found to be highly effective. Concerns were raised regarding students' anxieties around choosing a major and overall apathy toward career counseling in general. Lepre (2007) also encouraged career counseling centers to develop media campaigns that detail available resources to help undecided students increase attendance at workshops or career courses.

Peer counseling is discussed by Herr and colleagues as a paraprofessional trend that is growing in college and university career centers around the country. Peer counselors are often students who are involved in master's or doctoral programs at the college or university itself, or interns in the career counseling center from another college or university. Peer counselors work under supervision and offer a way for the career center to reduce its own budgetary expenses (Herr et al., 2004).

An example of a facilitated peer counseling program used in a community college setting is a specialized training entitled the Dependable Strengths Articulation Process (DSAP), through the Center for Dependable Strengths (CDS). The CDS is run through Highline Community College in Des Moines, Washington and offers an 18-hour, peer assisted training in a group format. The process allows peer trainers to then assist others in identifying their dependable strengths through storytelling and reflecting on experiences in life. This process is used to help others with career planning and job development (CDS, n.d.).

Career counselors also meet individually with students to review assessments and assist students in their career search. Individual meetings are a foundation of career counseling and continue to be one of the most frequently used interventions (Herr et al., 2004). Individual career counseling can easily become the most costly intervention, albeit the best way to build rapport and increase motivation toward change. The expense may lead many career centers to attempt to find a balance between individual career counseling and the use of career workshops or groups (Herr et al., 2004). Depending on the function of the center, the amount of staffing, and whether it is more of a traditional college employment program or a full service, integrated career center, the career staff may be asked to forgo individual career counseling in lieu of attending career days, job fairs, admissions events, or alumni activities (Herr et al., 2004).

PROFESSIONAL ORGANIZATIONS AND RESOURCES FOR COLLEGE CAREER COUNSELING CENTERS

The first professional organization for career counselors was the National Vocational Guidance Association (NVGA) developed in 1913 in Grand Rapids Michigan. The NVGA, which in 1984 became the National Career Development Association (NCDA), established the Vocational Guidance Bulletin in 1915, published by the U.S. Office of Education. Later this journal became Occupations: The Vocational Guidance Journal. Founders of the NVGA were Frank Leavitt, Jesse B. Davis, Meyer Bloomfield, and John M. Brewer. Pope discussed the change in the associations in 1951 when the NVGA became one of the founding divisions of the American Personnel and Guidance Association (APGA), which was later to transform itself into the American Association for Counseling and Development (AACD), and then on to its final conversion as the American Counseling Association

(ACA). The APGA listed its second president as Donald Super in 1953. The journal of the APGA Occupations—The Vocational Guidance Journal—soon became the Personnel and Guidance Journal, so the NVGA developed its own quarterly journal in 1952, The Vocational Guidance Quarterly. In 1966, The National Employment Counseling Association (NECA), became a charted division of ACA (Pope, 2000).

The NVGA was instrumental in the development of the National Center for Credentialing Career Counselors in 1983. In 1984 "the National Certified Career Counselor Credential became the first specialty certification area" for the National Board of Certified Counselors (Pope, 2000, p. 203). Career counseling centers have professionals that are licensed as professional clinical counselors, professional counselors, counseling psychologists, rehabilitation counselors, licensed independent social workers, and licensed social workers (NCDA, n.d.)

Certification is also available to assist in furthering education for career counselors. A Career Development Facilitator (CDF) has taken 120 or more training hours, provided by an experienced instructor (NCDA, n.d.). A Global Career Development Facilitator (GCDF) has completed at least 120 hours of training, in addition GCDFs must maintain ongoing continuing education activities (Center for Credentialing Education, n.d.).

Pope (2000) discussed additional associations linked to career counseling including: the Association for Career and Technical Education (ACTE), which was founded in 1926 for the advancement of education that prepares youth and adults for successful careers, and the American School Counselor Association (ASCA), which was created in the 1950s to advance the professional identity of the school counselor.

Further influential associations in the field are the National Association of Workforce Development Professionals (NAWDP), a professional association for individuals working in employment and training, and related workforce development systems (NAWDP, n.d.). The International Association of Workforce Professionals (IAWP) founded in 1913, formerly the International Association of Personnel in Employment Security (IAPES), is a professional organization for members whose jobs relate to employment security or workforce development systems (IAWP, n.d.). The Interstate Conference of Employment Security Agencies (ICESA) was founded in 1937 and is the national organization of state government officials who administer unemployment insurance laws, employment services, training, and labor market information programs (ICESA, n.d.). The United States Psychiatric Rehabilitation Association (USPRA) was organized in 1975 to provide psychiatric rehabilitation and recovery oriented practices through education and professional credentials, research, service outcomes, and networking (USPRA, n.d.). The American Rehabilitation Counseling Association (ARCA) is an organization of rehabilitation practitioners concerned with improving the profession of rehabilitation counseling and service to persons with disabilities (ARCA, n.d.). The National Rehabilitation Counseling Association (NRCA) was founded in 1958 and considers itself to be the largest organization representing rehabilitation counselors today (NRCA, n.d.). The International Association for Educational and Vocational Guidance (IAEVG) advocates that all people who need and want educational and vocational guidance and counseling can receive it from a competent and recognized professional (IAEVG, n.d.). The Association of Computer-based Systems for Career Information (ACSCI), developed in1978, is dedicated to the advancement of career information and the delivery of that information (ASCI, n.d.). The Association for Assessment in Counseling and Education (AACE) is dedicated to the development and use of assessment and diagnostic techniques in counseling, a division of the ACA (2010). The Society for Vocational Psychology's mission it is to promote research, teaching, practice, and public interest in vocational psychology and career interventions, Division (17) of the APA (2010).

SUMMARY

College career counseling centers have a rich and diverse history of development. Drawing from Parson's ideas of guidance (Pope, 2000), the formation of early placement centers taught guidance counselors to direct students to a world of work that was a "best fit" for individual skills instead of automatically entering into the family business. But as guidance blossomed into career development, students were opened to the concepts of meaningful and satisfying work and how their personality types may best fit into different work environments (Pope, 2000). Today the focus is on technology and how best to assist diverse populations as our college career counseling centers continue to grow and change due to the economic climate and student need. The tools of the Career Counselor are as varied as the student populations with whom they work. The career counseling center, whether at a two year community college or a four year institution, has the opportunity to make a long-term, positive impact.

REFERENCES

American Counseling Association (ACA). (2010). Retrieved from http://www. counseling.org

American Psychological Association (APA). (2010). Retrieved from http://www. apa.org

American Rehabilitation Counseling Association (ARCA). (n.d.). Retrieved from http://www.arcaweb.org/

Association for Assessment in Counseling and Education (AACE). (n.d.). Retrieved from http://www.theaaceonline.com/

Association of Computer-based Systems for Career Information (ACSCI). (n.d.). Retrieved from http://www.acsci.org/

Bureau of Labor Statistics. (n.d.) Retrieved from http://www.bls.gov/

Bourne, B. (1988). Making ideas work: Ralph Bedell and the NDEA institutes. *Journal of Counseling and Development, 67,* 136–142.

CareerOneStop. (n.d.). Retrieved from http://www.careeronestop.org/

Center for Credentialing Education. (n.d.). Retrieved from http://ccc-global.org

Center for Dependable Strengths. (n.d.). Retrieved from http://www.dependablestrengths.org

Chapter 21, Mental Health Practitioners and Trainees, Section V: Insurance for Mental Health Care. (n.d.). Retrieved from http://mentalhealth.samhsa.gov

Costa, P. T., Jr., & McCrae, R. R. (1992). Normal personality assessment in clinical practice: The NEO Personality Inventory. *Psychological Assessment, 4,* 5–13.

Dictionary of Occupational Titles. (n.d.). Retrieved from http://www.occupational-info.org/contents.html

Dragon Naturally Speaking. (n.d.). Retrieved from http://www.nuance.com/

Engelland, B. T., Workman, L., & Singh, M. (2000). Ensuring service quality for campus career services centers: A modified SERVQUAL scale. *Journal of Marketing Education, 22*(3), 236–245.

Gati, I., Fishman-Nadav, Y., & Shiloh, S. (2006). The relations between preferences for using abilities, self-estimated abilities, and measured abilities among career counseling clients. *Journal of Vocational Behavior, 68,* 24–38.

Hammond, M. S. (2001). The use of the Five-Factor Model of Personality as a therapeutic tool in career counseling. *Journal of Career Development, 27*(3), 153–165.

Herr, E. L., Cramer, S. H., & Niles, S. G. (2004). *Career guidance and counseling through the lifespan: Systematic approaches* (6th ed.). Boston, MA: Pearson.

Holland, J. L. (1997). *Making vocational choices* (3rd ed.). Odessa, FL: Psychological Assessment Resources.

Hoyt, K. B., & Maxey, J. (2001). Career counseling in the information age. *Journal of Career Development, 28*(2), 129–138.

International Association for Educational and Vocational Guidance (IAEVG). (n.d.). Retrieved from http://www.iaevg.org

International Association of Workforce Professionals (IAWP). (n.d.). Retrieved from http://www.iawponline.org.

Interstate Conference of Employment Security Agencies (ICESA). (n.d.). Retrieved from http://www.workforceatm.org/

Kent State University Career Center, Kent State University, Kent, Ohio. (n.d.). Retrieved from http://career.kent.edu/home/index.cfm

Lepre , C. R. (2007). Getting through to them: Reaching students who need career counseling. *The Career Development Quarterly, 56,* 74–84.

Lindstrom, L. E., Flannery, K. B., Benz, M. R., Olszewski, B., & Slovic, R. (2009). Building employment training partnerships between vocational rehabilitation and community colleges. *Colleges Rehabilitation Counseling Bulletin, 52*(3), 189–201.

Livescribe Smart Pen. (n.d.). Retrieved from http://www.livescribe.com/

Lucas, E. B. (1986). College career planning and placement centers: Finding their identity. *Journal of Career Development, 13*(1), 9–17.

McMurray, A., & Sorrells, D. (2007). Student services and the college classroom: Some ideas for collaboration, *College Student Journal, 41*(4), 1218–1223.

Myers, I. B., McCaulley, M. H., Quenk, N. L., & Hammer, A. L. (1998). *MBTI manual: Guide to the development and use of the Myers-Briggs Type Indicator* (3rd ed.). Palo Alto, CA: Consulting Psychologists Press.

National Association of Workforce Development Professionals (NAWDP). (n.d.). Retrieved from http://www.nawdp.org/.

National Career Development Association. (n.d.). Retrieved from http://associationdatabase.com/aws/NCDA/pt/sp/facilitator_overview

National Rehabilitation Counseling Association (NRCA). (n.d.). Retrieved from http://nrca-net.org/.

Norton, S. C., & Field, K. F. (1998). Career placement project: A career readiness program for community college students with disabilities. *Journal of Employment Counseling, 35*, 40–44.

Ohio Career Information System. (n.d.). Retrieved from http://www.ocis.org/

Ohio Labor Market Information online. (n.d.). Retrieved from http://ohiolmi.com/asp/career/jobtool.asp

O*Net. (n.d.). Retrieved from http://online.onetcenter.org/

Occupation Outlook Quarterly. (n.d.). Retrieved from http://www.bls.gov/opub/ooq/ooqhome.htm.

Pope, M. (2000). A brief history of career counseling in the United States. *The Career Development Quarterly, 48*, 194–211.

Pulver, C. A & Kelly, K. R. (2008). Incremental validity of the Myers-Briggs Type Indicator in predicting academic major selection of undecided university students. *Journal of Career Assessment, 16*(4), 441–455.

ReadPlease2003. (2003). Retrieved from http://readplease.com/

Robertson, J. M., Benton, S. L., Newton, F. B., Downey, R. G., Marsh, P. A., Benton, S. A., Tseng, W. C., & Shin, K. H. (2006). K-State problem identification rating scales for college students. *Measurement and Evaluation in Counseling and Development, 39*(3), 141–160.

Rullo, W., Eliason, G. T., & Patrick, J. Ed. (2008). The ASCA model and the educational trust. In Eliason, G. T., & Patrick, J. (Eds.) *Career Development in the schools: A volume in research in career development.* Charlotte, NC: Information age publishing.

Smart, J. C., Ethington, C. A., Umbach, P. D., & Rocconi, L. M. (2009). Faculty emphases on alternative course-specific learning outcomes in Holland's model environments: The role of environmental consistency. *Research in Higher Education, 50*(5), 483–501.

Smart, R., & Peterson, C. (1997). Super's career stages and the decision to change careers. *Journal of Vocational Behavior, 51*, 358–374.

Spies, R. A., & Plake, B. S. (Eds.). (2005). World Of Work Instrument (WOWI). *The sixteenth mental measurements yearbook.* Lincoln, NE: Buros Institute of Mental Measurements.

Stark State College Career Development Office, Stark State College of Technology North Canton, Ohio. Retrieved from http://www.starkstate.edu/?q=career-development.

Summary Report of the Iowa Text Reader Studies 2006–2007 for Kurzweil 3000. (n.d.). Retrieved from http://www.kurzweiledu.com

THEME. (n.d.). Retrieved from http://www.starkstate.edu/

Thompson, T, Draffan, E.A., & Patel, P. (2009). Survey on accessible technology in higher education. *ATHEN E-Journal, 4,* 1–12.

United States Psychiatric Rehabilitation Association (USPRA). (n.d.). Retrieved from http://www.uspra.org

University of Washington, Washington Assistive Technology Act Program, WATAP. (n.d.). Retrieved from http://watap.org/

Washington Occupational Information System (WOIS). (n.d.) The Career Information System. Retrieved from http://www.wois.org

Waters, L., Chesterman, G., Holegate, J., Kirkman, B., Raban, T., & Smith, R. (2002). *'A work worthy of the university': A centenary history of Cambridge University career services.* Cambridge Career Services, University of Cambridge, Manual.

Watts, A. G., & Kidd, J. M. (2000). Guidance in the United Kingdom: Past, present and future. *British Journal of Guidance & Counselling, 28*(4), 485–502.

WYNN Wizard. (n.d.) Retrieved from http://wynnwizard.com/

Young, R. A., & Chen, C. P. (1999). Annual review: Practice and research in career counseling and development–1998, *The Career Development Quarterly, 48,* 98–141.

CHAPTER 2

INFLUENCES ON CAREER DECISION MAKING

William S. Rullo

Selecting a career is one of the most important choices that is made during one's lifetime. The career selection process is complex and dynamic (Behrend, Thompson, Meade, Grayson, & Newton, 2007). Scholars and practitioners today consider career exploration to be a lifelong endeavor that spans across many roles in life (Bluestein, 1997; Niles, Anderson, & Goodnough, 1998; Zikic & Hall, 2009). Planned career opportunities tend to provide positive career outcomes (Zikic & Hall, 2009).

People today have more freedom in choosing a career and are better able to design their careers. According to Brown and Associates (as cited in Vianen, De Pater, & Preenen, 2009), people tend to have higher career satisfaction when they have chosen their own careers. That's why individuals need to have work volition in selecting their career choices. Work volition centers on "an individual's ability to freely make career choices" (Duffy & Dik, 2009, p. 29). However, our personalized life experiences and circumstances can deeply impact the volition of our career decisions.

Experts claim that individuals will change careers (not jobs) in their lifetimes between five to seven times (Casto, 2000). Hansen's research shows that most will change careers four to five times within their working ca-

Career Development in Higher Education, pages 25–55

reers (Hansen, n.d.). According to Bandura, Barbaranelli, Caprara, and Pastorelli (2001), the career development process is lifelong. Individuals making decisions about career opportunities are influenced by many factors (Ferry, 2006). Although there are volumes of factors that can influence individual decision-making about career choices, several of these major factors will be highlighted throughout this chapter. Factors such as birth order; parents and family; cultural values; work and educational experiences; generational experiences; religious and spiritual values; gender; role models; economic and financial values; internal and external influences; media impact; and careers of the future can greatly impact the career decision-making process.

WHAT IS DECISION-MAKING?

"Decision making is difficult. It involves a complex process of cognitive reasoning and, therefore, it costs time and effort" (Vianen et al., 2009, p. 299). According to Gelatt (1989), "decision making is the process of arranging and rearranging information into a choice or action" (p. 253). Factors such as a person's culture, the status of the economy, interpersonal roles, and basic self-structure impact the decisions made (Amundson, 1995). To help with feeling more secure and happy, there are five stages of career development that aid in making better decisions: "defining the problem, understanding the underlying mechanisms, formulating plausible alternatives, prioritizing alternatives, and evaluating the outcomes" (Vianen et al., 2009, p. 299).

In addition to the decision-making stages, researchers have identified five decision-making styles: rational, intuitive, dependent, avoidant, and spontaneous. The rational style depicts a logical and organized approach to decision-making. Intuitive style relies on feelings and influence. Needing the support of others is critical for the dependent style of decision-making. The avoidant style centers on delaying or circumventing the decision-making process; moreover, making impulsive decision-making highlights the spontaneous style (Vianen et al., 2009).

When applying these styles to career decision-making, Singh and Greenhaus (as cited in Vianen, De Pater, & Preenen, 2009) state that "a rational strategy was valuable for finding a good fit, but mostly this strategy was combined with intuitive decision-making" (p. 300). Individuals who have used both rational and intuitive styles and who have a higher self-awareness and nurturing environment claimed that it helped to make a better choice. However, "too much emphasis on rational thinking may block rather than encourage decision-making" (Vianen et al., 2009, p. 300). It is suggested that there be a combination of rational thinking and "gut feeling" as this may ultimately result in making optimal career decisions (Vianen et al., 2009).

Individuals make a decision when two conditions are satisfied. "First, a chosen option must be at least minimally attractive; second, the option must be relatively better than other options" (Vianen et al., 2009, p. 301). If these conditions are not met, it is likely that indecision will occur. In general, the decision-making process is often unclear because all plausible alternatives may not be present. Even if all alternatives are available, uncertainty and confusion may persist as to which alternative is the best strategy for making a good decision (Vianen et al., 2009).

Bacanli (as cited in Tien, 2007) states that career indecisiveness can have two types of personality characteristics associated with it—exploratory and impetuous. Bacanli's research indicates that exploratory indecisiveness stems from negative personality traits that can consist of "external locus of control, low self-esteem, and high levels of irrational beliefs, while impetuous decisiveness is more cognitively oriented and is predictable by a smaller portion of variance in personality types" (Tien, 2007, p. 122).

WHAT IS THE CAREER DECISION-MAKING PROCESS?

The career decision-making process is a proactive process. It is necessary to make time to engage in activities that will help to make correct career decisions. It is important to reflect on the information gathered from these experiences and that they align with one's personal values, interests, and skills (Northwestern University, 2009). When making a decision on career choice, it is natural for people to base decisions on options with which they are most familiar (Orndorff, 2002).

The career decision-making process requires that people not only have sufficient information about themselves, but also about the world of work and being exposed to opportunities that point them in the right direction. People need to take time to understand their motivation for engaging in the career decision-making process. It should be a process that stems from a sincere desire to engage in self-discovery (Northwestern University, 2009).

Part of the self-discovery process of career decision-making stems from addressing these questions: "What do I enjoy doing? What do I value in life? And what personality traits do I prefer in a work setting?" (Wittenberg University, 2008). After answering those questions, the next step of the career decision-making process should focus on careers that align with one's interests, values, skills, and personality. It is important to research those careers to determine which ones are the "best fit" (Wittenberg University, 2008).

Most people struggle when making a career decision around available vocational and educational options. Individuals feel insecure and unhappy because of the pressures and difficulties they face when making a career decision (Vianen et al., 2009). It is important to discern whether the pressure they face when making a career decision is internal or external. External pressure on career decision-making can be from parents and friends when considering a career choice (Northwestern University, 2009).

To make the most appropriate career decision, it is necessary to engage in the career decision-making process (Northwestern University, 2009). The key to making effective career-decisions is to evaluate career choices. "The challenge lies in blending rational and intuitive approaches, as the goal is to arrive at a decision that is consistent with your 'gut feelings' while at the same time being grounded in practical reasoning" (Wittenberg University, 2008, n.p.).

WHEN DOES THE CAREER DECISION-MAKING PROCESS BEGIN?

"The process of selecting a career begins at an early age" (Hoffner, Levine, Sullivan, Crowell, Pedrick, & Berndt, 2006, p. 5). Research supports that at the onset of childhood, career decision-making is a lifelong process (Auger, Blackhurst, & Wahl, 2005). Both Ginzberg and Gottfredson (as cited in Auger et al., 2005) claim "children go through a fantasy period in which their career choices are based solely on their interests and desires, with minimal attention paid to their abilities or selectivity of the career" (p. 322).

According to Stockard and McGee (1990), fourth grade students are already aware that different careers possess different levels of prestige and status (Hoffner et al., 2006). Cook, Church, Ajanaku, Shadish, Kim, and Cohen (1996) discovered that African American boys in the second grade from inner-cities sense that they have future career limitations and base their career aspirations on this perception (Hoffner et al., 2006). Schoon and Parsons have determined that "teenage aspirations are a good predictor of adult occupational attainment: young people with high aspirations are more likely than their less ambitious peers to enter a profession or managerial career" (Hoffner et al., 2006, p. 5).

According to life span and career development theorists, people are completely engaged in the career selection process during the early adulthood years (Pisarik & Shoffner, 2009). In addition, career decision-making occurs as people progress through educational, employment, and other experiences in their lives (Amundson, 1995). These individual experiences and differences "must be taken into account when examining the foundations of career-decision making" (Amundson, 1995, p. 13).

MAJOR CAREER DEVELOPMENT THEORIES

There are varieties of theories that explain reasons for individuals selecting certain career choices. Four key career theories highlighted in this chapter are Parson's Trait-Factor; Holland's Career Typology; Super's Life-Span/Life-Space; and Krumboltz's Social Learning Theory of Career Choice.

Parson's Trait-Factor Theory

The Trait-Factor Theory incorporates "abilities, work values, occupational stereotypes and expectations, residence, family socioeconomic status and childrearing practices, general adjustment, personality factors including needs and propensity for risk taking, educational achievement, level of aspiration, and gender" into career decision-making (Herr, Cramer, & Niles, 2004, p. 177–178). Describing the relationship between these variables and choices is a key component of the Trait-Factor approach (Herr et al., 2004). The Trait-Factor Theory has four underlying assumptions and propositions according to Klein and Weiner (1977):

- Each individual has a unique set of traits that can be measured reliably and validly.
- Occupations require that workers possess certain very specific traits for success, although a worker with a rather wide range of characteristics can still be successful in a given job.
- The choice of an occupation is a rather straightforward process, and matching is possible.
- "The closer the match between personal characteristics and job requirements, the greater the likelihood of success (productivity and satisfaction)" (Brown & Brooks, 1990, p. 17).

Holland's Career Typology

Holland's theory on careers is based on the premise of a correlation between an individual's vocational interest and a description of the individual's personality. Information about an individual's self-concept is gathered from an interest inventory; while "personality traits are identified by preferences for school subjects, recreational activities, hobbies, and work; and vocational interests can be viewed as an expression of personality" (Brown & Brooks, 1990, p. 39). Holland contends that every individual to some extent resembles one of the six personality types. The six personality types include: Realistic, Investigative, Artistic, Social, Enterprising, and Conventional. The realistic person favors responsibilities that center on systematic manipulation of machinery or tools such as a machinist. Investigative individuals are analytical, curious, methodical, and precise, such as a biologist. Artistic people are expressive, original, and nonconforming, as best represented by an artist or decorator. Bartenders and counselors are examples of individuals from the social category who enjoy working with others and refrain from order and systematic activities. People who are considered as enterprising individuals usually enjoy attaining organizational goals while manipulating others, exemplified by managers, salespeople, and lawyers. In addition, the conventional type enjoy the routine of systematically manipulating information and filing records. Financial experts, secretaries, and file clerks represent the conventional type.

Four assumptions stem from Holland's work. These assumptions include:

- In our culture, most persons can be categorized as one of six types: realistic, investigative, artistic, social, enterprising, or conventional.
- There are six kinds of environments: realistic, investigative, artistic, social, enterprising, or conventional.
- People search for environments that will let them exercise their skills and abilities, express their attitudes and values, and take on agreeable problems and roles.
- Behavior is determined by an interaction between personality and environment (Brown & Brooks, 1990).

Super's Life-Span/Life-Space

When discussing career development and career decision-making it is always important to "maintain time perspectives: the past, from which one has come; the present, in which one currently functions; and the future, toward which one is moving" (Brown & Brooks, 1990, p. 197). Super explains the career development process as "ongoing, continuous, and generally irreversible..." (Herr et al., 2004, p. 221). The premise of his theory centers on the individual serving as an organizer of personal experiences who selects careers that allow the individual to operate in a role that closely parallels the individual's self-concept (Herr et al., 2004).

Super's belief centers on the concept that humans are not static and that personal change is continuous in everyone's life. His model is "a very comprehensive developmental model that attempts to account for the various important influences on a person as they experience different life roles and various life stages" (Canadian Career Development Foundation, 2004, n.p.).

The following are some of Super's main tenets from the "Big Picture" concept according to the Canadian Career Development National Standards and Guidelines (Canadian Career Development Foundation, 2004) highlighting Super's Life-Span/Life-Space Theory on Career Choice:

- Every individual has potential. People have skills and talents that they develop through different life roles making them capable of a variety of tasks and numerous occupations.
- In making a vocational choice, an individual is expressing his or her understanding of self, or self-concept. People seek career satisfaction through work roles in which they can express themselves, implement, and develop their self-concept. Self-knowledge is the key to career choice and job satisfaction.
- Career development is life-long and occurs throughout five major life stages: Growth, Exploration, Establishment, Maintenance and Disengagement. Each stage has a unique set of career development tasks and accounts for the changes and decisions that people make from career entry to retirement.
- These five stages are not just chronological. People cycle through each of these stages when they go through career transitions.
- People play different roles throughout their lives including the role of "worker." Job satisfaction increases when a person's self-concept includes a view of the working-self as being integrated with their other life roles.

Krumboltz's Social Learning Theory of Career Choice

The Social Cognitive Career Theory (SCCT) is a comprehensive and dynamic theory that considers a variety of characteristics around career development (Tang, Pan, & Newmeyer, 2008). SCCT focuses on the reason why individuals select particular careers, why they may change careers, and why they prefer different careers at various points in their lives (Brown & Brooks, 1990). It centers on the belief that career choice can be influenced through experiential and vicarious learning (Mitchell & Krumboltz, 1985; Bosco & Bianco, 2005). "Experiential learning occurs through direct experience that affects future actions" (Bosco & Bianco, 2005, p. 168). Vicarious learning is the result of observing the actions and outcome of others. "The SCCT (Lent, Brown, & Hackett,1994) proposes that career choice behavior is shaped by outcome expectancies, career interests, and career self-efficacy, and that career self-efficacy plays a mediating role between one's background and interests and one's outcome expectancies" (Tang et al., p. 285). It has accentuated the significance of social support as a vital component in the career development process (Lent et al., 1994; Schultheiss, Palma, Predragovich, & Glasscock, 2002). The theory studies how "factors such as genetic predisposition, environmental conditions and events, learn-ing experiences, and cognitive, emotional, and performance responses and skills" impact the career decision-making process (Brown & Brooks, 1990, p. 148). Krumboltz, Lent, Brown, and Hackett (as cited in Duffy & Dik, 2009) claim that social learning and cognition theories purport that career decision making is based on "an individual's learning experiences about work and perceived ability to perform particular tasks necessary to succeed in a certain career" (p. 29).

The following summary is from the "Big Picture" concept according to the Canadian Career Development National Standards and Guidelines highlighting Krumboltz's Social Learning Theory on Career Choice:

- The four main factors that influence career choice are genetic influ-ences, environmental conditions and events, learning experiences, and task approach skills (e.g., self-observation, goal setting, and information seeking).
- The consequences of those factors, most particularly learning experiences, lead to the development of beliefs about the nature of careers and their role in life (self-observational generalizations). These beliefs, whether realistic or not, influence career choices and work-related behavior.
- Learning experiences, especially observational learning stemming from significant role models (e.g., parents, teachers, heroes), have a powerful influence on career decisions, making some occupations more attractive than others.
- Positive modeling, reward and reinforcement will likely lead to the development of appropriate career planning skills and career be-havior (Canadian Career Development Foundation, 2004).

These theories will be illustrated throughout the types of career decision influences.

TYPES OF CAREER DECISION INFLUENCES

Birth Order and Siblings

According to Pawlik-Kienlen (2007), birth order can influence one's viewpoint toward a career. Some of the latest research reveals that single children and first-born children express more of an interest in intellectual careers, while later-born children or youngest children express more of an interest in careers that are artistic and outdoors oriented.

Birth order can influence how individuals view themselves and their relationships with others. Although it can be subtle, it has established some commonalities in the order of siblings. For example, the eldest sibling assumes more responsibility (Amundson, 1995). Frederick Leong, a professor at Ohio State University, states, "parents typically place different demands and have different expectations of children depending on their birth order" (Pawlik-Kienlen, 2007). Parents treat their oldest child differently than the way they treat younger children (Bradley & Mims, 1992). Parents are more inclined to support only children or first-born children to pursue prestigious careers such as law or medicine, which require higher levels of education as well as intellectual challenges (Pawlik-Kienlen, 2007). According to Bradley and Mims (1992), "first-born children occupy higher status, higher pay, and higher power occupations" (p. 447).

Birth order may cause some siblings to assume certain roles that allow them to achieve success. This can be demonstrated when the first-born child takes on the role as a caregiver. If the first-born child is successful as a caregiver, it could influence career decision-making. Adjacent siblings demonstrate success in something different from their immediate older sibling. Many times younger siblings have not selected a career because of an older sibling already in that particular career (Bradley & Mims, 1992).

The number of family members can also influence career choices, since larger families may have less financial support for the older children in college, while younger family members may receive additional financial support because the financial burden declines when the older sibling is no longer living at home (Schulenberg, Vopndracek, & Crouter, 1984; Taylor, Harris & Taylor, 2004).

Through the life span, siblings provide a substantial amount of relational support (Cicirelli, 1995; Kenny & Perez, 1996; Schultheiss et al., 2002). Because siblings have shared values and beliefs, they are uniquely able to provide emotional support to one another (Cicirelli, 1995; Dunn, 1985; Schultheiss et al., 2002). Throughout the career exploration and decision-making process, siblings bestow support and function as role models with each other (Blustein et al., 2001; Schultheiss, Kress, Manzi, & Glasscock, 2001; Schultheiss et al., 2002). Based on developmental theory, siblings provide security and affection to each other (Cicirelli, 1995; Schultheiss et al., 2002). "Siblings share a long history of intimate family experiences that have been hypothesized to contribute to similarities in perceptions and values and, in turn, promote mutual understanding and influence decision-making." Because of having close family experiences from childhood and throughout adolescence, siblings are likely to be involved in a parallel career development process. Sibling influence provides "an important and informative view of the real-life context in which young adults explore and commit to their careers" (Schultheiss et al., 2002, p. 303).

Parental and Family Influences

Research over the past 50 years demonstrates that parents pose the "greatest influence over their children's career decisions" (Crown Financial Ministries, n.d., n.p.). Career decisions are more "an expression of the family" rather than "primarily an individual event" (Amundson, 1995, p. 12).

The study of a genogram can provide an appropriate format to talk and learn about family structure. It "can help identify family characteristics such as role, rules, and power structures" (Bradley & Mims, 1992, p. 445). Genograms provide valuable information about family issues and patterns that are important to consider when making decisions. It is important to note that family processes or interactions pass on from one generation to the next generation (Bradley & Mims, 1992).

The career genogram is a highly recognized instrument that collects data about the influence of the family (Okiishi, 1987; Chope, 2006). "The genogram allows for understanding the origin of career expectations from the family and can help pinpoint family judgments about career choices and definitions for success" (Chope, 2006, p. 185).

According to Bratcher (as cited in Chope, 2001), "A family's concepts of rules and boundaries, beliefs, values, traditions, and myths are among the most influential systemic issues likely to affect one's career" (Chope, 2001, p. 55). Adolescents are more likely to have higher goals for themselves if they perceive that their parents have high educational goals for them (Taylor et al., 2004). Parents, siblings, and other relatives are identified as support and provide role model influence in exploring careers and the decision-making process (Schultheiss et al., 2001; Schultheiss et al., 2002).

Boys and girls list their parents as having great influence on their career expectations (Paa & McWhirter, 2000). "Parents can play a significant role in helping their students make informed decisions about their future" (Orndorff, 2002). Parents should encourage their children when they are discovering careers and possible majors (Orndorff, 2002). Boys who live with both parents have higher career aspirations (Hoffner et al., 2006). Students are reluctant to pursue career options without the approval of their parents (Taylor et al., 2004). Many times parents do not realize the influence they have on their children's career choices (Crown Financial Ministries, n.d.). There are times when students "choose a major or career just to get their parents off their backs" (Orndorff, 2002). The amount of family influence is dependent upon the extent an individual can separate from the family. If there are strong ties within the family, it will be more difficult for an individual to become autonomous with the career decision-making process.

In a study analyzing elementary-aged children's aspirations and expectation, Auger, Blackhurst and Wahl (2005) noted that elementary school students are usually able to name their parents' jobs by giving the name of the business or organization instead of mentioning a specific job. About half of the children who participated in the study could not give specifics when asked to describe their parents' work, while 23 percent of 40–55 year olds made career decisions during childhood about their current career (Auger et al., 2005). However, the more indecisive an individual is about a career, the more parental involvement is found (Bradley & Mims, 1992). Parents need to offer "unconditional support" as their child explores and wrestles with one of life's major decisions (Orndorff, 2002).

Girls' interest in career choice may be the result of watching their fathers work (Parker-Pope, 2009). According to Parker-Pope (2009), fathers appear to be playing a bigger role in their daughters' career choices compared to men of previous generations. Studies conducted indicate that mothers and fathers can have varying influences on career choices for their children. According to Mickelson and Velasco (as cited in Taylor et al., 2004), mothers are more influential on career choices of their children than their fathers are. Parents who possess more education have daughters who select nontraditional careers (Bosco & Bianco, 2005). However, Bosco and Bianco (2005) state that "maternal work patterns are significantly related to life-style choices for women" (p. 165). The mother's work career influences her daughter's attitude about work (Affleck, Morgan, & Hayes, 1989; Bosco & Bianco, 2005). Female college students are more inclined to select nontraditional careers similar to their mothers' and to attend comparable colleges (Almquist, 1974; Bosco & Bianco, 2005). According to Steele and Barling, (as cited in Bosco & Bianco, 2005) "mothers' gender role beliefs affect the career choice of their daughters" (p. 169).

According to college counselors, students find it difficult to select a major that conflicts with their parent's expectations (Chope, 2001). Bowlby (1982, as cited in Chope, 2001) contends that individuals who have connected well with their own families can better connect with employment networks. When families support what is most important for the individual, they automatically support the decision-making process for that individual (Chope, 2001). When families have open and direct discussions among family members, there is a strong likelihood children will develop vocational interests and goals that are clear and stable (Johnson, Buboltz, & Nichols, 1999). Therefore, "family interactions play an important role in forming aspirations and decisions about careers" (Taylor et al., 2004, p. 3).

However, sometimes because of parental discord or divorce, the family interactions are associated with developmental struggles for the young adult family members. There is a "theoretical contention that family functioning plays a role in the career development process" (Johnson et al., 1999, p. 141). Researchers claim that the origins of family relationships are connected with the career development process of college students (Johnson et al., 1999). "Parental divorce impacts developmental tasks related to interpersonal development but may not directly affect the career process" (Johnson et al., 1999, p. 142). However, Thomas and Gibbons (2009) contend that "adolescents whose parents divorce face academic and vocational impediments that challenge their career options" (2009, p. 223). Children of divorce experience less vocationally-enhancing support and opportunities (Thomas & Gibbons, 2009). Amato and Cheadle (as cited in Thomas & Gibbons, 2009) contend that, in the course of their lifetime, children of divorce usually earn less money and obtain less education. Overall, they display "lower levels of academic and vocational attainment" (p. 223).

Cultural Influences and Concerns

When addressing career decision-making, it is important to incorporate the family's cultural views regarding work. The career decision-making process for family members is often influenced by culturally-specific factors. Based on their cultural background, some families emphasize the importance of earning money, independence, refraining from drawing attention to oneself, and/or personal achievement (Chope & Consoli, 2006).

Perceptions of work have changed as more people are influenced by other cultures (Chope & Consoli, 2006). The world of work is like a matrix; it is no long a linear world (Chope, 2000). It is a concept that greatly impacts people from cultures who do not have linear career paths. "Many immigrant families and families of color take a more rigid point of view in the career decision-making processes of their children than families who feel they have more maneuverability and privilege" (Chope & Consoli, 2006, p. 87). Multicultural parents support their children by helping them reach educational and career goals that they establish for their own children (Chope & Consoli, 2006).

However, there can be plenty of pressure for an individual to "conform to both the norms of the family and those of the culture" (Chope & Consoli, 2006, p. 87). The primary concern is the reputation of the family. Shame is brought upon the family when a child selects a major that is not approved by the family, fails to perform satisfactorily academically, or fails professionally. Children are seen as the "next generation" to bring pride to the family (Chope & Consoli, 2006). Many times the collective needs of the family or cultural group are taken into consideration when making career decisions (Amundson, 1995).

Work and Educational Experience

"Having specific, long-range, job-related goals encourage students to pursue their academic endeavors, particularly when a relationship between these endeavors and a desired future career is highlighted" (Hull-Blanks, Kurpius, Befort, Sollenberger, Nicpon, & Huser, 2005, p. 27). When a value is associated with a specific career, college students are more inclined to follow their academic pursuit (Hull-Blanks et al., 2005).

Internships are another academic experience offered to students. An internship is a great way to experience the deepest level of career exploration. Internships allow students to experience a career of interest firsthand. It is important that the internship be aligned with the student's long-range academic plan. Serving as an intern allows an individual to network with others in the work place. Networking with coworkers and supervisors helps to create a working relationship. It is from these relationships that employers recruit quality candidates for vacant positions (Orndorff, 2002). Having "personal contact with employers and people working in the field can also give you an enormous amount of information," which is helpful when making career decisions (Notre Dame, 2008).

Interviewing individuals in a career of interest can provide current and personalized perspectives. Aside from actually working in a particular career, an individual can "get a feel" as to whether or not he or she would like a certain career. College students rate informational interviewing as the most constructive activity in helping them to select careers (Notre Dame, 2008).

According to Nauta and Epperson (as cited in Tang et al., 2008), the amount of time spent in school and the amount of math and science courses taken during high school demonstrate a strong correlation with the selection of science and math as college majors. Exposure to work experiences has proven to greatly influence one's level of educational goals (Rottinghaus, Lindley, Green; & Borgen, 2002; Tang et al., 2008).

Generational Values

According to researcher and author Tulgan (as cited in Armour, 2005), the new generation of workers (Generation Y), who are not yet 30 years old, will be different from any other work generation. Tulgan states that this generation has been pampered, nurtured, and programmed with a slew of activities since they were toddlers, meaning they are both high-performance and high-maintenance. New college graduates will oversee employees who are old enough to be their parents (Armour, 2005).

New workers, "born in the early to mid-1980s," entering the workforce will select employment based on "how the job will accommodate their desired lifestyle, that is, how will they balance work with their personal life" (Bosco & Bianco, 2005, p. 166). Generation Y employees focus on making their jobs accommodate their personal lives (Armour, 2005). Making decisions about getting married, having children, and finding ways to integrate work with all aspects of their lives are some of the most critical decisions this generation of workers will make.

The new generation of employees "want jobs with flexibility, telecommuting options and the ability to go part-time or leave the workforce temporarily when children are in the picture" (Armour, 2005). Lifestyle encompasses marital status, parenthood, and being able to change career needs for the needs of the family (Bernardi & Hooks, 2000; Mash, 1978; Schroeder, Blood, & Maluso, 1992; Bosco & Bianco, 2005).

Generation Y workers don't stay with a career for very long because of scandals such as the Enron scandal. Tulgan states that Generation Y is incredulous of employee loyalty because of these types of scandals (Armour, 2005). This generation likes to multi-task, especially with the use of technology, and prefer not to stay on one assignment for too long. They prefer virtual problem solving, rather than meeting in person or discussing the problem over the phone (Armour, 2005).

Religious and Spirituality Values

Allport and Ross (as cited in Duffy & Dik, 2009), purport that faith is instrumental in the career decision-making process for those individuals with intrinsic religious and spiritual commitments. "Religious values play an important role in the career choices of many" (Chope & Consoli, 2006, p. 87). Duffy reports that it is important for career counselors to be aware of the degree to which "an individual's spirituality and religiosity shape the types of careers they decide to pursue" (Tien, 2007, p. 113). Some individuals consider career decision-making as an augmentation of discerning God's will. When a "career path is identified as consistent with God's will or plan, individuals may orient their activities in pursuing that path as a way in which they might honor God or a Higher Power" (Duffy & Dik, 2009. p. 35). Duffy and Dik (2009) refer to this as a "calling". Individuals who have experienced the calling report higher levels of general and work-specific satisfaction compared to others who have another approach to work (Duffy & Dik, 2009). Some elements of religion and spirituality affect career values and satisfaction as well as career-decision self-efficacy (Tien, 2007).

According to Constantine, Miville, Warren, Gainor, and Lewis-Coles (as cited in Tien, 2007), data obtained through semiformal interviews to explore the relationship between spirituality, religion, and career development have emerged into six themes:

1. Degree of identification as religious and/or spiritual
2. Parents' influence on religious and/or spiritual beliefs

3. Roles of religion and/or spirituality in participants' career development

4. Challenges in dealing with academic and career-related issues

5. Religious and/or spiritual strategies for dealing with academic and career-related challenges

6. Indicators of success in future careers or occupations.

To help deal with the pressure of career-related stress; individuals have relied on "spiritual and/or religious activities, such as praying, reading the Bible, and attending church" (Tien, 2007, p. 114). Religion and spirituality have impacted career choice in a similar manner in following a "calling" and passion for one's vocation (Tien, 2007).

Bloch and Richmond (1998) identify seven factors between spirituality and work. Each of these components focuses on different areas of career development:

1. *Change*: Being open to change in yourself and the world around you

2. *Balance*: Achieving balance among the activities of your life such as work, leisure, learning, and family relationships; being able to leave behind that which is no longer useful and to retain core values and useful skills

3. *Energy*: Feeling that you always have enough energy to do what you want to do

4. *Community*: Working as a member of a team or community of workers and understanding you are part of communities of companionship; communities of culture; and the cosmic community

5. *Calling*: Believing that you are called to the work you do by your particular mix of talents, interests, and values

6. *Harmony*: Working in a setting that harmonizes with your talents, interests, and values; working in a setting that permits the experience of flow, a "state of mind when consciousness is harmoniously ordered and they want to pursue whatever they are doing for its own sake" (Csikszentmihalyi, 1990, p. 6)

7. *Unity*: Believing that "the work you do has a purpose beyond earning money and in some way serves others" (Bloch, 2004, p. 347).

When an individual views work as spiritual, he/she considers the work as a contribution to the world and the creation of the universe. In addition, when a career is considered spiritual, the moral quandary of separating life from work is avoided (Bloch, 2004).

Gender Influences

Gender influences may influence career choice (Byars & Hackett, 1998; Tang et al., 2008). Early adolescents have developed two cognitive competencies that center around career development: self-concept and career perceptions. It is during this time that students possess a sound understanding of gender type and prestige level of careers and will begin to eliminate career choices based on these criteria (Tang et al., 2008). An example of this would be when "female students might avoid choosing occupations that are generally perceived as too masculine (e.g., a career as a miner) and also might consider eliminating choices that are perceived as low social prestige status (e.g., a career as a housemaid)" (Tang et al., 2008, p. 286). McNulty and Borgen (1988) state that students will "'sacrifice interest in field of work to maintain sex type and prestige' (pp. 222–223) in their career choice" (Hoffner et al., 2006, p. 5).

According to Jacobs, Chhin, and Bleeker (as cited in Tien, 2007), "parents' gender-typed occupational expectations" are "significantly related to their children's own expectations and to the children's actual career choices" (p. 99). Gender-typed careers are significantly related to career satisfaction. There is a strong correlation between parents who have early gender-typed career expectations for their children and the actual career decisions made by their adult children (Tien, 2007).

When balancing work and family, Cinamon's research (as cited in Tien, 2007) indicates that men and women handle work and family conflicts differently. Cinamon states that there are two types of work and family conflicts: work-interfering-with-family and family-interfering-with-work. Women "anticipated higher levels of both types of conflict between work and family than men. They also demonstrated lower efficacy in managing these conflicts than did men" (Tien, 2007, p. 112).

When it comes to what is most important in making long-term career choices, men place more emphasis on making money, whereas, women place more emphasis on careers that involve "working with people and contributing to society" (Duffy & Sedlacek, 2007, p. 149). Men focus more on value-related career goals and fewer job-related ones, whereas women are more inclined to focus on job-related career goals and fewer value-related goals (Hull-Blanks et al., 2005; Harrington & Harrigan, 2006). In a study of 120 undergraduate men conducted by Hogue, Yoder, and Singleton (as cited in Chope, 2008), the results indicated, "men were likely to feel entitled to pay that was higher than that afforded to women" (Chope, 2008, p. 107). The men's responses were obtained even after they were directly informed that the women outperformed them with greater competence on the same work tasks; the men still believed that they were worthy of receiving higher wages than the women (Chope, 2008).

Jome, Surething, and Taylor (as cited in Harrington & Harrigan, 2006) studied the trends of employed men's career choices in terms of masculinity and gender-nontraditional, vocational interests. Their research indicated that men who were more apt to having traditional male careers were described as "individuals who were more likely to express discomfort with gays and lesbians, were less interested in people-oriented activities, and were comfortable with expressive behavior toward other men" (Harrington & Harrigan, 2006, p. 106–107). Men in non-traditional careers exhibited less homophobic concerns and more personalized interactions, whereas men employed in female-dominated careers expressed an interest in service-oriented and personalized careers. When men make a career choice, major factors such as masculinity, gender-role attitudes and interpersonal vocations are key factors (Harrington & Harrigan, 2006).

Corrigall and Konrad (as cited in Chope, 2008) analyzed men's and women's early gender role attitudes around marriage, children, and workforce outcomes in comparison to later career outcomes (Chope, 2008). "The early gender role attitudes of women turned out to predict their later work hours and earnings: women with egalitarian attitudes worked longer hours and earned more wages than did those women with traditional attitudes" (Chope, 2008, p. 108). The results of the research indicate that gender role attitudes are influenced by subsequent behavior and can be adjusted to address relationship and family contextual demands (Chope, 2008).

According to Whitmarsh, Brown, Cooper, Hawkins-Rodgers, and Wentworth (as cited in Chope, 2008), women who were greatly influenced by their families and who were developmentally earlier in their career decision-making selected female-dominated careers in comparison to women who went into gender-neutral careers. Women who had greater career exploration opportunities and made their career decisions later entered into gender-neutral careers sooner than women who selected female-dominated careers (Chope, 2008).

Role Models

Role models can play a key role as a significant influence in helping young people with their career development skills. Mothers, fathers, and teachers can serve as role models who contribute to the development of career and educational goals. In a study conducted in a small midwestern town, 464 high school male and female students completed a survey regarding their own career decisions. The female students placed more emphasis on role models and less emphasis on income as perceived influences in their career decision-making process in comparison with the male students. The female students ranked mother, father, and female friends as their three most perceived influences. On the other hand, the male students believed that their father, mother, and male friends were perceived influences in their career decision-making process (Paa & McWhirter, 2000). The results of the survey claim that "same-sex models were perceived to be more influential on current career expectations than role models of the other sex" (Paa & McWhirter, 2000, p. 49). Young people in the process of selecting a career tend to follow same gender role models (Almquist, 1974; Bosco & Bianco, 2005; Pallone, Richard, & Hurley, 1970). Key adult figures can provide essential developmental support and encouragement throughout the career development process (Herr et al., 2004).

According to Bandura's theory, role model influences from role model similarity, meaning that the greater the role-model similarity to the protégé, the greater the influence (Paa & McWhirter, 2000). According to Super's theory, role models greatly influence a variety of aspects of career development for young people (Paa & McWhirter, 2000). Providing individuals with appropriate role models can help with career decision-making. "Models can both demonstrate the task approach skills of decision-making and cause persons to consider occupations they would previously have rejected" (Brown & Brooks, 1990, p. 189). However, simply having exposure to role models is not enough to influence career decision-making. According to Nauta, Epperson, & Kahn (as cited in Perrone, Zanardelli, Worthington, & Chartrand, 2002), key characteristics such as support and relationship qualities can contribute to career decision-making.

Economic and Financial Influences

The current socioeconomic status on a global scale has greatly influenced many individual's career choices (Vianen et al., 2009). Given the status of the global economy, the concentration of careers has drastically changed in the last 40 years. The new economy has led to a decrease in the amount of high-paying, blue-collar careers (Carnevale & Desrochers, 2003). Half of the college students participating in a 2008 Student Loan Survey preferred a job with higher pay and less job satisfaction to repay their student loans. The results of the Student Loan Survey indicate that almost one-third of college students decided to select a particular career because of their student loans, while two-thirds of the college students report "they are more likely to accept a job that offers loan assistance and/or repayment" (Experience, Inc., 2008).

Parents' career statuses along with their educational background and income affect the career choices of their children (Hotchkiss & Borow, 1985; Bosco & Bianco, 2005). According to Lemkau's (1979) research, (as cited in Bosco & Bianco, 2005), the "social economic status and having a mother in the workforce were associated positively with females' choice of a non-traditional occupation" (p. 168). Interest in pursuing further education is related to family income (Bosco & Bianco, 2005).

The most significant sign that the economy demands highly educated employees is demonstrated by the increased wages of college graduates in comparison to high school graduates. Current earnings trends depict disparities among the most and least educated workers, which illustrates the financial advantages associated with education. For example, an associate degree usually provides a wage increase of approximately 20 to 30 percent more than that of a high school diploma. Employees with an associate degree in academic subjects receive fewer earnings than career programs such as engineering, business, health, or computer science (Carnevale & Desrochers, 2003).

Individuals with bachelor's degrees typically earn an additional 10 to 20 percent increase above an associate degree. According to Grubb, individuals who hold a bachelor's degree and who specialize "in occupational fields such as engineering, computer science, business, and health generally have higher returns than those workers with degrees in education, social sciences, and humanities" (Carnevale & Desrochers, 2003, p. 232). Therefore, employees with associate degrees benefit financially from a more specialized education (Grubb, 1996; Carnevale & Desrochers, 2003).

Internal and External Influences and Social Support

An individual's career decision making can be impacted by either internal or external influences. Internal influences center on an individual's satisfaction as the main motivation (Duffy & Dik, 2009). Careers are most vibrant when they are in agreement with one's values, purpose, and passions. This helps individuals to connect with their 'calling' which ultimately allows them to express who they are to the outside world (Matthews, n.d.). However, the primary motivation that influences an individual's career decision-making stems from outside sources. The postulation is that everyone appeals to varying degrees of internal and external factors when making career decisions (Duffy & Dik, 2009).

For example, adolescents "perceive their career expectations to be influenced by personal, background, and environmental factors" (Paa & McWhirter, 2000, p. 38). Perceived ability is a better indicator of career interests rather than actual ability (Barak, 1981; Paa & McWhirter, 2000). Lent and Brown (as cited in Paa & McWhirter, 2000) claim that "differential reinforcement by parents, teachers, and peers can influence the formation of career interests and eventually career choices" (p. 38–39).

Although few career development models incorporate social support as an integral component, Schultheiss (2003) claims that it is a relational element that is a critical piece of career development. Social support can come in many forms from parents, siblings, significant others, and extended family who serve as support and assistance toward career decision-making. According to Packard and Nguyen (2003), mentor relationships help to provide direction with career decision-making. Youth mentoring demonstrates a sound approach for career development that allows for continuous opportunities for the youth to develop resilience and academic encouragement. This also allows the youth the chance to connect with role models who can promote the development of self-efficacy, self-esteem, and career exploration skills (Perry, 2009). Tieger & Barron-Tieger (1995), (as cited in Miller, n.d.), claim that to experience career satisfaction, it is paramount to know yourself, what your goals are, and how to go about achieving these areas. Past research endorses the concept that important relationships can have great impact in developing the autonomy of following career aspirations (Perry, 2009). To provide further support to this notion, the research of Ali, McWhirter, and Chronister (as cited in Perry, 2009) indicates that "sibling and peer support, but not parental support, predicted vocational / educational self-efficacy among low-income youth" (p. 492).

Career Exploration Programs

According to Baker and Taylor (1998) and Evans and Burck (1992) (as cited in Perry, 2009), the most effective career exploration programs for school-age students are those "programs that impact academic achievement at the greatest level, occur over an extended period of time (averaging 2 years), are delivered consistently with a large 'dosage' effect (150 to 200 hours of direct exposure), and complements language arts or math" (p. 493).

Watts and Sultana (as cited in Perry, 2009) state that "international research has made it abundantly clear that career education and guidance are directly tied to lifelong learning, the labor market, and social equity" (p. 493). Simply having a 'taster' course or a one-day career fair will not be effective enough to make an impact on career development. Programs such as School-To-Work cannot be marginalized; they need to be securely linked to the community in a comprehensive manner for the career development program to be effective (Perry, 2009).

Larson's research (as cited in Perry, 2009) promotes career education programs as enhancers of school success, self-efficacy, and an autonomous approach to help students achieve their goals. A successful program focuses on developmental assets commonly connected with positive youth development (Perry, 2009). Career fairs and field practice projects are two types of career learning activities that help to heighten students' career-related knowledge bases. The career fair will allow students to gain an awareness of a broad spectrum of career options (Tang et al., 2008). According to the American School Counselor Association's National Standards (2002), career fairs that engage students in learning about careers and the people in those careers help the students to achieve the development of "career awareness, employment readiness, and career information acquisition skills and understand how their education, the world of work, and personal qualities coexist" (Kolodinsky, Schroder, Montopoli, McLean, Mangan, & Pederson, 2006, p. 166). The field practice will provide the students with a more specific perspective on detailed particulars of a career (Tang et al., 2008).

College students who participated in a career development course reported, "significant gains in career decision-making self-efficacy and vocational identity" (Scott & Ciani, 2008, p. 263). Based on a dissertation by Smith (1971) (as cited in Bradley & Mims, 1992), "freshman and sophomore university students who participated in a five-week group vocational guidance treatment advanced further in vocation developmental stages than did students participating in an individual counseling treatment" (p. 446). Osborn, Howard, and Leierer (as cited in Chope, 2008) also support this concept, as their research centered on a career course offered to racially and ethnically diverse college freshmen. The course was six weeks long and focused on "understanding of the work world, recognizing and reframing negative thoughts about work, understanding career decision making; and identifying personal interests, skills, abilities, and values, and relating these to career and educational goals" (Chope, 2008, p. 122). The students had the opportunity to create an action plan that was also part of the course. Because the course was being offered to college freshmen, there was a reduction in dysfunctional career thoughts. The students who originally demonstrated the highest levels of dysfunctional career thoughts had the greatest reduction in dysfunctional thinking (Chope, 2008).

Colleges offer career-mentoring programs in which the alumni and parents agree to be career mentors. This allows students to gain direct information about their career of interest. Internships and volunteering are some of the best ways for students to learn about careers of interest (Orndorff, 2002). Individuals' career goals are affected when they experience positive performance with activities that are career related (Ginzberg, Ginsburg, Axelrad, & Herma, 1951; Super, Savickas, & Super, 1996; Hull-Blanks et al., 2005). Huang (as cited in Chope, 2008) discovered that students whose jobs were related to their college major and career goals were positively influenced in their studies. Huang also stated that it is important for universities to offer term-time employment to further assist students as they develop their career interests and encourage employers to offer positions to college students that are related to their college major (Chope, 2008).

De Cooman, De Gieter, Pepermans, Du Bois, Caers and Jegers (as cited in Chope, 2008) analyzed the relationship between the reason for choosing a particular career and selecting a major. Their research indicated how selecting a college major could be greatly impacted by job motives and values (Chope, 2008).

Choosing a Major

Choosing a major in college can be a difficult decision. It is one of the most important decisions to make as a student. Selecting a major "involves careful consideration and a serious time commitment" (Florida State University, 2009, n.p.). According to Hansen, a college student should not rush into a decision about a major immediately upon entering college. "A majority of students in all colleges and universities change their major at least once in their college careers; and many change their majors several times over the course of their college career" (Hansen, n.d., n.p.). As students begin the journey of discovering their career path, it is important to know that "your major in college is important for your first job after graduation" (Hansen, n.d., n.p.).

Graunke and Woosley (as cited in Harrington & Harrigan, 2006) studied college students during their sophomore year, the expected year to select a major. Their research indicates, "sophomores were more likely to report choosing a major or a career as their major concern" (p. 101–102). Graunke and Woosley observed that "commitment to a major and faculty/staff interactions were significantly correlated with grade point average in fall and spring semesters, whereas commitment to a major and activity involvement were positively correlated only in the spring" (Harrington & Harrigan, 2006, p. 102). The selection of a major promotes academic performance and a connection with an academic department and its faculty (Harrington & Harrigan, 2006).

Media Influences on Career Choice

Television is "one of several important sources of occupational information for young people" (Hoffner et al., 2006, p. 3). Mass media provides information about careers in the workplace that center on work-related socialization. This supports the social cognitive approach to career development that people learn by watching others (Bandura, 1986; Bandura 2001; Hoffner et al., 2006). Through watching the work-related experiences of others, the work values and attitudes of young people are shaped (Signorielli & Kahlenberg, 2001, Hoffner et al., 2006). "Much evidence shows that young viewers learn from the values, beliefs, and behaviors exhibited by TV characters" (Hoffner et al., 2006, p. 4). Television can be a great learning tool about work; however, it depicts a somewhat limited and distorted perspective about the workforce. It often transmits inaccurate and stereotypic images about how co-workers communicate and behave (Hoffner et al., 2006).

According to Signorielli (1993), individuals who are heavy television viewers, yearn for careers that are prestigious, well paid, not demanding, and provide long leisure and vacation time. While Wright and colleagues (Whright, Huston, Truglio, Fitch, Smith, & Piemyat, 1995) claim that people who watch a plethora of television especially and those who believe that television is realistic, desire careers that closely resemble those on television (Hoffner et al., 2006). King and Multon's research (as cited in Hoffner et al., 2006), indicates that younger viewers demonstrate a higher propensity to be influenced by the careers of their favorite characters.

Feilitzen, Linne, and Hoffner use the term *wishful identification,* as a key phrase to explain the psychological process that one goes through in attempting to be like someone else (in Hoffner et al., 2006). There is a strong likelihood that "the depiction of characters' occupations and workplace experiences should contribute to young people's wishful identification and thus affect their occupational aspirations" (Hoffner et al., 2006, p. 7). The more that people watch television, the higher the wishful identification with a favorite character; whereas, wishful identification is lower with parents who possess more education. In addition, the predictability of wishful identification is dependent upon the amount of time watching television (Hoffner et al., 2006). Therefore, the amount of income and level of education for the heavy television viewer's dream jobs "are positively correlated with these attributes of the characters' jobs" (Hoffner et al., p. 3).

Wishful identification also serves as a predictor with respect to intrinsic and extrinsic rewards of a character's favorite career. People are more inspired with the extrinsic rewards of a character's job such as a high salary, respect, character, and excitement. In contrast, intrinsic rewards are not desired as much by a character's job that requires intelligence, ability, and decision-making skills (Hoffner et al., 2006).

Future Careers and Fastest Growing Careers

Every day new careers are being established (Northwestern University, 2009). According to DeFillippi and Arthur (1994) because of changes in the job market, traditional linear careers will not be in high demand. The market centers more on rapid adaptation of knowledge and skills. Because of changes in work activities, jobs, and occupational areas, careers in the future will no longer follow a conventional path of career development. It will require lifelong learning and change (Vianen et al., 2009).

Not only are future job markets going to look for individuals who are confident in completing tasks that enhance earlier work experiences, but they will also expect employees to work on strengthening their role breadth self-efficacy. Parker (as cited in Vianen et al., 2009), defines role breadth self-efficacy as individuals who feel "confident about carrying out tasks that expand on their earlier experiences" (p. 305). Role breadth self-efficacy centers on an individual's confidence in performing job responsibilities and interpersonal tasks that go beyond traditional boundaries (Parker, 1998).

Hecker (as cited in Carnevale & Desrochers, 2003), states that the fastest-growing careers are going to require an associate degree, followed by an increase in careers that require a bachelor's degree. According to the United States Bureau of Labor and Statistics (2005), the following is a list of the Ten Fastest Growing Occupations from 2004–2014:

- Home health aides
- Network systems and data communications analysts
- Medical assistants
- Physician assistants
- Computer software engineers, applications
- Physical therapist assistants
- Dental hygienists
- Computer software engineers, systems software
- Dental assistants
- Personal and home care aides

According to Bhattacharyya (2010), it has become more of a challenge to select a career that fulfills personal needs while realizing your goals and ambitions. Because of the financial difficulties the United States has been experiencing, it is important to consider careers that provide stability as well as a generous income. The following careers will be in high demand over the next ten years and will help provide income and stability (Bhattacharyya, 2010):

- Physician assistant
- College professor
- Nurse practitioner
- IT project manager
- Certified Public Accountant

- Geoscientist
- Physical therapist
- Computer or network security consultant
- Anesthesiologist
- Gynecologist
- Psychiatrists
- Nurse anesthetist
- Sales director
- Lawyer
- Veterinarian
- Senior financial analyst
- IT business analyst
- Software developer and software quality assurance technician
- Technical writer
- Occupational therapist

Implications of Career Development and Career Decision-Making

According to Tinto (1993), individuals with career goals are more inclined to stay in school (Hull-Blanks et al., 2005). Students with career goals are more likely to graduate or remain in school than individuals who are without career goals (Farmer, Wardrop, Anderson, & Risinger, 1995; Hull-Blanks et al., 2005). Altmaier, Rapaport and Seeman (1983), found that students who are on academic probation did not have certain career goals, which greatly influenced their academic performance. Ting (as cited in Hull-Blanks et al., 2005) stated that long-term career goals significantly influenced academic performance.

Self-esteem and educational self-efficacy have been linked to career goals. Bandura (as cited in Hull-Blanks et al., 2005), defined self-efficacy as "an individual's belief in his or her ability to complete a set of tasks to obtain a specific outcome" (Hull-Blanks et al., 2005, p. 17). Adolescents who have specific career goals display a higher level of self-esteem compared to adolescents without career goals (Chiu, 1990; Hull-Blanks et al., 2005).

Career exploration is a lengthy process in which one can become more aware of his or her likes and dislikes as well as focus on exploration of a specific domain or area. According to Jordaan (as cited in Zikic & Hall, 2009), "career exploration shapes the way in which one thinks about oneself, influences one's self-concept, and shapes the way one thinks about the world of work" (p. 187).

REFERENCES

Affleck, M., Morgan, C. S., & Hayes, M. P. (1989). The influence of gender role attitudes on life expectations of college students. *Youth & Society, 20*(3), 307–319.

Almquist, E. (1974). Sex stereotypes in occupational choice. *Journal of Vocational Behavior, 54*(1), 13–21.

Altmaier, E., Rapaport, R., & Seeman, D. (1983). A needs assessment of liberal arts students on academic probation. *Journal of College Student Personnel, 24*(3), 266–267.

American School Counselor Association. (2002). *Ethical standards for school counselors.* Retrieved from: http://www.schoolcounselor.org/

Amundson, N. E. (1995). An interactive model of career decision making. *Journal of Employment Counseling, 32*(1), 11–21.

Armour, S. (2005). *Generation Y: They've arrived at work with a new attitude.* Retrieved from: http://www.usatoday.com

Auger, R. W., Blackhurst, A. E., & Wahl, K. H. (2005). The development of elementary aged children's career aspirations and expectations. *Professional School Counseling, 8*(4), 322–329.

Baker, S. B., & Taylor, J. G. (1998). Effects of career education interventions: A meta-analysis. *Career Development Quarterly, 46*(4), 376–385.

Bandura, A. (1986). *Social foundations of thought and action: A social cognitive theory.* Englewood Cliffs, NJ: Prentice Hall.

Bandura, A. (2001). Social cognitive theory of mass communication. *Media Psychology, 3*(3), 265–299.

Bandura, A., Barbaranelli, C., Caprara, G. V., & Pastorelli, C. (2001). Self-efficacy beliefs as shapers of children's aspirations and career trajectories. *Child Development, 72*(1), 187–206.

Barak, A. (1981). Vocational interests: A cognitive view. *Journal of Vocational Behavior, 19*(1), 1–14.

Behrend, T. S., Thompson, L. F., Meade, A. W., Grayson, M. S., & Newton, D. A. (2007). *Gender differences in career choice influences.* Paper presented at the 22nd Annual Meeting of the Society for Industrial and Organizational Psychology, New York.

Bernardi, R. A., & Hooks, K. L. (2000, January). *The relationship among lifestyle preferences, attrition, and career orientation: A three-year longitudinal study.* Paper presented at the midyear meeting of the AAA's Auditing Section, San Diego, CA.

Bhattacharyya, M. (2010). *Best careers for the next ten years.* Retrieved from: http://www.buzzle.com/articles/best-careers-for-the-next-ten-years.html

Bloch, D. P. (2004). Spirituality, complexity, and career counseling. *Professional School Counseling, 7*(5), 343–350.

Bloch, D. P., & Richmond, L. J. (1998). *SoulWork: Finding the work you love, loving the work you have.* Palo Alto, CA: Davies-Black.

Blustein, D. L. (1997). A context-rich perspective of career exploration across life roles. *The Career Development Quarterly, 45*(3), 260–274.

Blustein, D., Fama, L., White, S., Ketterson, T., Schaefer, B., Schwann, M., Sirin, S., & Skau, M. (2001). A qualitative analysis of counseling case material: Listening to our clients. *The Counseling Psychologist, 29*(2), 240–258.

Bowlby, J. (1982). *Attachment and Loss (Volume 1) Attachment* (2nd ed.) New York: Basic Books.

Bosco, S. M., & Bianco, C. A. (2005). Influence of maternal work patterns and socio-economic status of Gen Y lifestyle choice. *Journal of Career Development. 32*(2), 165–182.

Bradley, R.W., & Mims, G. A. (1992). Using family systems and birth order dynamics as the basis for a college career decision-making course. *Journal of Counseling & Development, 70*(3), 445–448.

Brown, D., & Brooks, L. (1990). *Career choice and development* (2nd ed.). San Francisco: Jossey–Bass.

Byars, A. M., & Hackett, G. (1998). Applications of social cognitive theory to the career development of women of color. *Applied & Preventive Psychology, 7*(4), 255–267.

Canadian Career Development Foundation. (2004). *Canadian career development national standards and guidelines.* Retrieved from: http://ccdf.ca/ccdf/New-Coach/english/ccoache/e4a_bp_theory.htm

Carnevale, A. P., & Desrochers, D. M. (2003). Preparing students for the knowledge economy: what school counselors need to know. *Professional School Counseling, 6*(4), 228–236.

Casto, M. L. (2000). *The six stages of modern career development.* Retrieved from: http://www.quintcareers.com/career_development.html

Chiu, L. (1990). The relationship of career goals and self-esteem among adolescents. *Adolescence, 25*(99), 593–597.

Chope, R. C. (2000). *Dancing naked: Breaking through the emotional limits that keep you from the job you want.* Oakland, CA: New Harbinger.

Chope, R. C. (2001). Influence of the family in career decision-making: Identity development, career path, and life planning. *Career Planning and Adult Development Journal,* 54–64.

Chope, R. C. (2006). Assessing family influence in career decision making. In G. R. Walz, J. Bleuer & R. K. Yep (Eds.), *VISTAS: Compelling perspectives on counseling, 2006* (pp. 183–186). Alexandria, VA: American Counseling Association.

Chope, R. C. (2008). Practice and research in career counseling and development–2007. *The Career Development Quarterly, 57*(2), 98–173.

Chope, R. C., & Consoli, A. J. (2006). *Multicultural family influence in career decision making.* Austin, TX: Pro-Ed.

Cicirelli, V. G. (1995). *Sibling relationships across the lifespan.* New York: Plenum.

Cook, T. D., Church, M. B., Ajanaku, S., Shadish, W. R., Kim, J. R., & Cohen, R. (1996). The development of occupational aspirations and expectations among inner-city boys. *Child Development, 67*(6), 3368–3385.

Crown Financial Ministries (n.d.). *Parents influence career decisions.* Retrieved from http://www.crown.org

Csikszentmihalyi, M. (1990). *Flow: The psychology of optimal experience.* New York: Simon & Schuster.

DeFillippi, R. J., & Arthur, M. B. (1994). The boundaryless career: A competency-based perspective. *Journal of Organizational Behavior, 15*(4), 307–324.

Duffy, R. D., & Dik, B. J. (2009). Beyond the self: External influences in the career development process. *The Career Development Quarterly, 58*(1), 29–43.

Duffy, R. D., & Sedlacek, W. E. (2007). What is most important to students' long-term career choices. *Journal of Career Development, 34*(2), 149–163.

Dunn, J. (1985). *Sisters and brothers.* Cambridge, MA: Harvard University Press.

Evans, J. H., & Burck, H. D. (1992). The effects of career education interventions on academic achievement: A meta-analysis. *Journal of Counseling and Development, 71*(1), 63–68.

Experience, Inc. (2008). *Half of college students polled would choose salary over career satisfaction.* Retrieved from http://www.experience.com

Farmer, H., Wardrop, J., Anderson, M., & Risinger, R. (1995). Women's career choices: Focus on science, math, and technology careers. *Journal of Counseling Psychology, 42*(2), 155–170.

Ferry, N. M. (2006). Factors influencing career choices of adolescents and young adults in rural Pennsylvania. *Journal of Extension, 44*(3).

Florida State University. (2009). *Choosing a major or occupation.* Retrieved from http://www.career.fsu.edu

Gelatt, H. B. (1989). Positive uncertainty: A new decision making framework for counseling. *Journal of Counseling Psychology, 36*(2), 252–256.

Ginzberg, E., Ginsburg, W. W., Axelrad, S., & Herma, J. L. (1951). *Occupational choice: An approach to a general theory.* New York: Columbia University Press.

Grubb, W. N. (1996). *Working in the middle: Strengthening education and training for the mid-skilled labor force.* San Francisco, CA: Jossey-Bass.

Hansen, R.S. (n.d.). *Choosing a college major: How to chart your ideal path.* Retrieved from http://www.quintcareers.com

Harrington, T. F., & Harrigan, T. A. (2006). Practice and research in career counseling and development–2005. *The Career Development Quarterly, 55*(2), 98–167.

Herr, E. L., Cramer, S. H., & Niles, S. G. (2004). *Career guidance and counseling: Through the lifespan.* New York, NY: Pearson.

Hoffner, C. A., Levine, K. J., Sullivan, Q. E., Crowell, D., Pedrick, L., & Berndt, P. (2006). TV characters at work: Television's role in the occupational aspirations of economically disadvantaged youth. *Journal of Career Development. 33*(1), 3–18.

Hotchkiss, L., & Borow, H. (1985). Sociological perspectives on career choice and attainment. In D. Brown & L. Brooks (Eds.), *Career choice and development* (pp. 137–168). San Francisco: Jossey-Bass.

Hull-Blanks, E., Kurpius, S.E., Befort, C., Sollenberger, S., Nicpon, M.F., & Huser, L. (2005). Career goals and retention-related factors among college freshmen. *Journal of Career Development, 23*(1), 16–30.

Johnson, P., Buboltz, W. C., & Nichols, C. N. (1999). Parental divorce, family functioning, and vocational identity of college students. *Journal of Career Development, 26*(2), 137–146.

Kenny, M. E., & Perez, V. (1996). Attachment and psychological well-being among racially and ethnically diverse first-year college students. *Journal of College Student Development, 37*(5), 527–535.

Klein, K. L., & Wiener, Y. Interest congruency as a moderator of the relationship between job tenure and job satisfaction and mental health. *Journal of Vocational Behavior, 70*(1), 92–97.

Kolodinsky, P., Schroder, V., Montopoli, G., McLean., Mangan, P., & Pederson, W. (2006). The career fair as a vehicle for enhancing occupational self-efficacy. *Professional School Counseling, 10*(2), 161–167.

Lent, R.W., Brown, S. D., & Hackett, G. (1994). Toward a unifying social cognitive theory of career and academic interest, choice, and performance. *Journal of Vocational Behavior, 45*(1), 79–122.

Mash, D. J. (1978). The development of lifestyle preferences of college women. *Journal of National Association for Women Deans, Administrators, and Counselors, 41*(2), 72–76.

Matthews, V. (n.d.). Coaching career development strategies for competitive advantage: Finding freedom from within. *Career Planning and Adult Development Journal.* Retrieved from http://www.careertrainer.com

McNulty, W. B., & Borgen, W. A. (1988). Career expectations and aspirations of adolescents. *Journal of Vocational Behavior, 33*(2), 217–224.

Miller, N. (n.d.). Career portfolios: Their evolution and current revolution. *Career Planning and Adult Development Journal.* Retrieved from http://www.career-trainer.com

Mitchell, L. K., & Krumboltz, J. D. (1985). Krumboltz's learning theory on career choice and counseling. In D. Brown & L. Brooks (Eds.), *Career choice and development* (pp. 235–280). San Francisco, CA: Jossey-Bass.

Niles, S. G., Anderson, W. P., & Goodnough, G. (1998). Exploration to foster career development. *The Career Development Quarterly, 46*(3), 262–275.

Northwestern University. (2009). *Career decision-making process.* Retrieved from http://www.northwestern.edu

Notre Dame. (2008). *Career decisions: informational interviews.* Retrieved from http://www.ucc.nd.edu

Okiishi, R. W. (1987). The genogram as a tool in career counseling. *Journal of Counseling and Development, 66,* 139–143.

Orndorff, R. (2002). *Helping your student make informed career decisions.* Retrieved from: http://www.collegeparents.org

Paa, H. K., & McWhirter, E. H. (2000). Perceived influences on high school students' current career expectations. *The Career Development Quarterly, 49*(1), 29–44.

Packard, B. W., & Nguyen, D. (2003). Science career-related possible selves of adolescent girls: A longitudinal study. *Journal of Career Development, 29*(4), 251–263.

Pallone, N., Richard, F., & Hurley, R. (1970). Key influences of occupational preference among black youth. *Journal of Counseling Psychology, 17*(6), 498–501.

Parker, S. K. (1998). Enhancing role breadth self-efficacy: The roles of job enrichment and other organizational interventions. *Journal of Applied Psychology, 83*(6), 835–852.

Parker-Pope, T. (2009). *More dads influence daughters' career path.* Retrieved from http://well.blogs/nytimes.com/2009/02/23/more-dads-influence-daughters-career-path/

Pawlik-Kienlen, L. (2007). *New insights about birth order: Being first or last born affects your career, health, & personality.* Retrieved from http://www.behavioural psychology. suite101.com

Perrone, K. M., Zanardelli, G. Worthington, E. L., & Chartrand, J. M. (2002). Role model influence on the career decidedness of college students. *College Student Journal.* Retrieved from http://findarticles.com/p/articles/mi_m)FCR/is_1P36/ai_85007774/

Perry, J. C. (2009). Career counseling with secondary school-aged youth: Directions for theory, research, and practice. *South African Journal of Higher Education, 23*(3), 482–504.

Pisarik, C. T., & Shoffner, M. F. (2009). The relationship among work possible selves, socioeconomic position, and the psychological well-being of individuals in early adulthood. *Journal of Career Development. 35*(3), 306–325.

Rottinghaus, R., Lindley, L. D., Green, A., & Borgen, F. H. (2002). Educational aspirations: The contribution of personality, self-efficacy, and interests. *Journal of Vocational Behavior, 61*(1), 1–19.

Schoon, I., & Parsons, S. (2002). Teenage aspirations for future careers and occupational outcomes. *Journal of Vocational Behavior, 60*(2), 262–288.

Schroeder, K. A., Blood, L. L., & Maluso, D. (1992). An intergenerational analysis of expectations for women's career and family roles. *Sex Roles, 26*(7–8), 273–291.

Schulenberg, J. E., Vopndracek, F. W., & Crouter, A. C. (1984). The influence of the family on vocational development. *Journal of Marriage and the Family, 46*(1), 129–143.

Schultheiss, D. (2003). A relational approach to career counseling: Theoretical integration and practical application. *Journal of Counseling and Development 81*(3), 301–310.

Schultheiss, D., Kress, H., Manzi, A., & Glasscock, J. (2001). Relational influences in career development: A qualitative inquiry. *The Counseling Psychologist, 29*(2), 214–239.

Schultheiss, D., Palma, T. V., Predragovich, K. S., & Glasscock, J. M. (2002). Relational influences on career paths: Siblings in context. *Journal of Counseling Psychology 49*(3), 302–310.

Scott, A. B., & Ciani, K. D. (2008). Effects of an undergraduate career class on men's and women's career decision-making self-efficacy and vocational identity. *Journal of Career Development, 34*(3), 263–285.

Signorielli, N. (1993). Television and adolescents' perceptions about work. *Youth & Society, 24*(3), 314–341.

Signorielli, N., & Kahlenberg, S. (2001). Television's world of work in the nineties. *Journal of Broadcasting & Electronic Media, 45*(1), 4–22.

Stockard, J., & McGee, J. (1990). Children's occupational preferences: The influence of sex and perceptions of occupational characteristics. *Journal of Vocational Behavior, 36*(3), 287–303.

Super, D. E., Savickas, M. L., & Super, C. M. (1996). The life-span, life-space approach to careers. In D. Brown, L. Brooks, & Associates (Eds.), *Career choice and development: Applying contemporary theories to practice* (3rd ed., pp. 121–178). San Francisco, CA: Jossey-Bass.

Tang, M., Pan, W., & Newmeyer, M.D. (2008). Factors influencing high school students' career aspirations. *Professional School Counseling, 11*(5), 285–295.

Taylor, J., Harris, M. B., & Taylor, S. (2004). Parents have their say...about their college-age children's career decisions. *National Association of Colleges and Employers Journal.* Retrieved from http://www.jobweb.com

Thomas, D. A., & Gibbons, M. M. (2009). Narrative theory: A career counseling approach for adolescents of divorce. *Professional School Counseling, 12*(3), 223–229.

Tieger, P. D., & Barron-Tieger, B. (1995). *Do what you are: Discover the perfect career for you through the secrets of personality type.* Toronto, Canada: Little, Brown & Company.

Tien, H. L. (2007). Practice and research in career counseling and development–2006. *The Career Development Quarterly, 56*(2), 98–140.

Tinto, V. (1993). *Leaving college and rethinking the causes and cures of student attrition.* Chicago, IL: University of Chicago Press.

United States Bureau of Labor and Statistics. (2005). *10 fastest growing occupations from 2004–2014.* Retrieved from http://www.bls.gov/news.release/history/ecopro_12072005.txt

Vianen, A. E., De Pater, I. E., & Preenen, P. T. (2009). Adaptable careers: Maximizing less and exploring more. *The Career Development Quarterly, 57*(4), 298–309.

Wittenberg University. (2008). *Tips on making career decisions.* Retrieved from http://www4.wittenberg.edu

Wright, J. C. Huston, A. C., Truglio, R., Fitch, M., Smith, E., & Piemyat, S. (1995). Occupational portrayals on television: Children's role schemata, career aspirations, and perceptions of reality. *Child Development, 6*(6), 1706–1718.

Zikic, J., & Hall, D. (2009). Toward a more complex view of career exploration. *The Career Development Quarterly, 58*(2), 181–191.

CHAPTER 3

PREPARING HIGH SCHOOL STUDENTS FOR CAREER DEVELOPMENT ACTIVITIES IN HIGHER EDUCATION

Kimberly J. Desmond, PhD, LPC, NCC
Indiana University of Pennsylvania

Kayla Snyder, MEd
Punxsutawney Area School District

The American School Counselor Association (ASCA) provides a valuable resource for counselors seeking to implement career development standards for students. The ASCA National Standards for Career Development are designed to help students acquire the necessary skills, attitudes, and knowledge to successfully transition into the world of work (ASCA , 2005). The career content standards for students are used as a foundation for the career development activities described in this chapter. The content standards describe what students should know and be able to do within the career education curriculum in a school system (ASCA, 2005). Within each of the three career content standards are competencies that outline specific expectations for students. Finally, indicators under the competencies de-

Career Development in Higher Education, pages 57–73
Copyright © 2011 by Information Age Publishing
All rights of reproduction in any form reserved.

scribe the knowledge, skills, and abilities students will demonstrate to meet the competencies and standards.

INVESTIGATION OF THE WORLD OF WORK

Developing organizational skills, setting goals, making decisions, working cooperatively, and developing hobbies may start as early as elementary and middle school. It is important to begin exploring these areas in the early stages of career development. However, a more in depth examination of career choice should occur during high school (Capuzzi & Stauffer, 2006). Standard A of the ASCA National Standards for Career Development states, "Students will acquire the skills to investigate the world of work in relation to knowledge of self and to make informed career decisions" (ASCA, 2005, p. 104). Table 3.1 provides the competencies and indicators listed under this standard.

TABLE 3.1 ASCA Career Development

Standard A: Students will acquire the skills to investigate the world of work in relation to knowledge of self and to make informed career decisions (ACSA, 2005).

C:A1 Develop Career Awareness (Competency)
C:A1.1	Develop skills to locate, evaluate and interpret career information (**Indicator**)
C:A1.2	Learn about the variety of traditional and nontraditional occupations
C:A1.3	Develop an awareness of personal abilities, skills, interests and motivations
C:A1.4	Learn how to interact and work cooperatively in teams
C:A1.5	Learn to make decisions
C:A1.6	Learn how to set goals
C:A1.7	Understand the importance of planning
C:A1.8	Pursue and develop competency in areas of interest
C:A1.9	Develop hobbies and vocational interests
C:A1.10	Balance between work and leisure time

C:A2 Develop Employment Readiness
C:A2.1	Acquire employability skills such as working on a team, problem-solving and organizational skills
C:A2.2	Apply job readiness skills to seek employment opportunities
C:A2.3	Demonstrate knowledge about the changing workplace
C:A2.4	Learn about the rights and responsibilities of employers and employees
C:A2.5	Learn to respect individual uniqueness in the workplace
C:A2.6	Learn how to write a resume
C:A2.7	Develop a positive attitude toward work and learning
C:A2.8	Understand the importance of responsibility, dependability, punctuality, integrity and effort in the workplace
C:A2.9	Utilize time- and task-management skills

Source: ASCA, 2005.

Career Awareness

While career development will change and progress over time, it is hoped that by the time students reach the secondary level they are actively involved in gathering information and planning for their future. To assist with career awareness, school counselors and teachers can work collaboratively to build a curriculum that aids a student's ability to gain information and knowledge about various careers (Gewertz, 2010). For example, exploring both traditional and nontraditional occupations can offer extremely beneficial information to all ages. It is common for students to pursue similar careers as their parents or guardians; however those careers may not necessarily be the best fit for the individual, based on skills and interests. Having the opportunity to explore careers outside of the family or community system can broaden students' horizons. Specifically, guest speakers from a variety of fields can present information in class to secondary students. This provides face to face interactions allowing a dialogue to occur between the professional and the student. Students also have the opportunity to explore pros and cons of a particular field (Capuzzi & Stauffer, 2006). Perhaps most helpful would be the availability of the professional to answer questions such as the amount of schooling required, job opportunities, income, job location, job security, and cost of training.

Career centers are another way to provide high school students with career and college readiness activities. One example is a program titled START (Student, Teacher, and Adult Research and Technology Center) that was adopted in the state of Mississippi to expand the current traditional career center role (Bock, 2010). These types of programs emphasize the importance of American high schools reinventing career exploration activities to 21st century career centers. This particular 21st century career center offers a variety of support services including "academic enrichment, college and career preparation, counseling, access to online courses, adult education, research and information literacy skill development, technology access, lending library, and other services to students as needed" (Bock, 2010, p. 1). Because this program reaches out to all stakeholders, primarily parents, it encourages and allows them to be engaged in helping plan for their student's future.

Knowledge of self also helps students make informed career decisions (ASCA, 2005). In order to develop awareness of personal abilities, skills, and interests, students need to continually assess their own strengths and weaknesses as well as likes and dislikes. This can be difficult for young adults since this often isn't part of the typical educational curriculum. Measurements such as interest inventories can serve as a guide that will draw out particular fields and areas where these strengths and interests can be applied in higher education and future careers (Grande, 2008). Ways students can learn about self include assessments, such as the Strong Interest Inventory (SII) or the Differential Aptitude Test (DAT). The SII provides specific career areas related to individual interest, while the DAT measures abilities related to specific careers. Other tools include the use of classroom guidance lessons. Not only are guidance lessons used to reach all students, but they are also a helpful means to career related discussions, sharing various perceptions and ideas about the career process. Box 3.1 is an example lesson plan used to draw out students' individuality and uniqueness. Accepting the differences amongst individuals and focusing on self allows an individual to pave their own career.

BOX 3.1
THE TREE OF LIFE GUIDANCE LESSON

Goals/Objectives
1. To identify components in life that contribute to individual similarities and differences
2. To demonstrate an understanding and level of acceptance among those similarities and differences

Materials
- oranges
- napkins
- basket
- tree
- cutouts (leaves, orange circles, roots, bark)
- tape

Motivation/Introduction
1. Give one orange to each child, asking them to "get to know your orange." Students will examine their oranges—smell them, touch them, toss them in the air, and roll them around. Notice marks or characteristics that make their orange different from other oranges.
2. After a few minutes, collect the oranges in a basket, and discuss ways that students are going to be able to find their orange (what are they looking for?). Go around to each child asking him or her to find their orange in the pile. Ask questions like "How did you know that was your orange? What gave it away?"
3. Talk about how people, too, come in different sizes, different shapes, different shades of color, different "dents and bruises."

These aspects influence who we are, the paths we take, the goals we set, the motivation we have, and the careers we pursue.

4. Now ask students to peel their orange. Once everyone has peeled their orange ask them to look around and compare their orange with the others. Ask, "If we were to put our oranges back into the basket how easy or difficult do you think it'd be to find your orange this time?" (Explain similarities/differences and how it relates to people: We are all different in many ways. However, we're also very similar in many ways. These similarities and differences make up who we are—in other words, our individuality.) "Today, we're going to work on uncovering our individuality and how it relates to choosing a career. To do so, we're going to look at the journey of our oranges—how they got here and how it relates to us." So where do oranges come from? Answer: A tree. Show large cutout of a tree.

LESSON BODY
Roots:

1. Start by explaining the roots of the tree (analogy for our cultural/ethnic background, gender, and the past). "Can anyone think of an example that would fall into the root category that we just mentioned?" (One example might be our own cultural/ethnic background).
2. "Break into groups of two or three with the people next to you. Have a discussion with each other and come up with more examples of our roots, either about yourself or in general. Write each idea on the pieces of paper that we're passing out."
3. Ask one person from each group to stick the ideas that they wrote down on the roots of the tree. Once all the pieces have been stuck on the tree, reflect on the ideas, and have a brief discussion about the students' reactions and how it may or may not influence individuality and career choice.

Trunk:

4. Talk about moving up the trunk. It represents the foundation, which comprises our values, morals, and beliefs. "Can anyone think of an example that would fall into the trunk category?" (Give examples of our own values).
5. "In the same groups have a discussion with each other and come up with more examples of the trunk, either about yourself or in general. Write each idea on the pieces of paper that we're passing out."

6. Ask one person from each group to stick the ideas that they wrote down on the trunk of the tree. Once all the pieces have been stuck on the tree, reflect on the ideas, and have a discussion about the students' reactions, again tying them into individuality and career choice. Also focus on where the values, morals, and beliefs come from and whether the values tie us together or cause conflict (knots in the tree).

Branches/Leaves:

7. Talk about moving up the tree to the branches and leaves. "The branches represent our roles within school and society. The leaves represent personal characteristics. What are some examples of our roles and our personal characteristics?"
8. "In the same groups, discuss with each other more examples of roles and characteristics. Write down the roles on the brown paper, and our characteristics on the leaves."
9. Ask one person from each group to stick the ideas that they wrote about roles on the branch of the tree and attach the leaves to the branches. Once all the pieces have been stuck on the tree, reflect on the ideas, and discuss how each section influences the other.

Orange:

10. Summarize the various parts already discussed and how they lead to the growth of the orange, which represents each student as an individual.
11. Each person writes his or her name on the orange paper circle as well as their career choice (with the consideration of all the other parts of the tree) and sticks it on the tree.

Closure:

Relate to the similarities and differences discussed in the introduction. Explain how these similarities allow us to connect and the differences make us unique (use these individual characteristics to pursue careers that are best for us as individuals). Through these, we are able to work together to contribute to society, just as oranges are squeezed to make orange juice.

Source: Adapted from Stern-LaRosa, C. M. (2001).

Career awareness and development encompasses a great deal of planning, decision making, and goal-setting. This ongoing process can be taught through the interactions of guidance lessons and individual advising meetings with the school counselor or other school personnel. Classroom guidance lessons can be used to facilitate learning on the topics of self discipline, teamwork, and career goal planning to facilitate a student's success-ful transition into higher education. Individual advisement meetings can be used to develop a personalized career plan to help determine areas of interest, areas needing further investigations, and career goals. Strategies like team building activities can be incorporated into nearly every lesson, while individual career plans can be reviewed and reassessed regularly as the student gains knowledge of self and career information (ASCA, 2005).

While the activities previously discussed are important elements of ca-reer decision-making, areas of interests and hobbies also help to inform students. Without enthusiasm and enjoyment in a given field, the chance for success decreases (Grande, 2008). With that, job interest is directly cor-related to job satisfaction (European Foundation, 2007). High school is the perfect time for exploration of job interests and can influence the develop-ment of career choice. New experiences introduce areas of exploration that can inform a student's interests and hobbies. Helping students investigate how their interests and hobbies may relate to the world of work may influ-ence job satisfaction. Ways to facilitate this investigation may include career exploration classes or field visits to specific career settings. Participation and investigation during the high school years allows students to explore and change their minds without the loss of credits and/or semester costs at the higher education level (Capuzzi & Stauffer 2006).

Similar to exploring interests and hobbies, it is also important to help students examine their ability to work and incorporate leisure activities. Sometimes this process is left out by students, parents, teachers, and many other adults. However, it can be one of the most important elements of career planning. Finding time for leisure activities goes hand in hand with the overall wellness of individuals. Caring for oneself is essential to making quality decisions, producing excellent work and progressing effectively. En-couraging students to set up self-reward systems supports the need to care for self. For example, time and effort invested into schoolwork can merit an equal amount of time doing something relaxing or enjoyable like a hobby. Helping students manage personal wellness at the high school level can limit their anxiety at the present time, demonstrate the importance of self-care and transcend healthy habits into future work settings (ASCA, 2005).

Employment Readiness

Employment readiness skills are essential when examining career de-velopment activities in higher education. Employment readiness encom-passes activities such as applying for a job, writing a resume, having a posi-tive attitude toward work and learning, understanding the importance of professionalism in the work place, and using time management skills

(ASCA, 2005). Many employment readiness activities are learned through on-the-job training. More specifically, job responsibilities and norms differ from place to place. High school students need to be flexible and open to learning the requirements of the workplace. School personnel can assist students with learning organizational skills and tools, writing resumes and cover letters, and practicing interviewing skills. Focusing on resume writing and mock interviews in high school creates a dialogue about possible responsibilities, individual uniqueness and attitudes, and the importance of organization (Capuzzi & Stauffer, 2006).

Many of the activities mentioned foster students' career awareness and employment readiness skills by providing tools to investigate the world of work and gain knowledge of self. It is essential that school counseling programs provide a career development curriculum that promotes access to career information and facilitates opportunities for students' personal growth. According to Niles and Harris-Bowlsbey, "Today, perhaps more than ever, systematic career development interventions are needed to help young people advance in their career development" (2009, p. 359).

FUTURE CAREER GOALS

ASCA also encourages students to begin formulating and identifying career goals. Standard B of the ASCA National Standards for Career Development states, "Students will employ strategies to achieve future career goals with success and satisfaction" (2005, p. 104). Table 3.2 provides the competencies and indicators listed under this standard. Many parents of students may be struggling to manage their own careers, so schools have a responsibility for providing adolescents with the competencies they need to begin career planning (Niles & Harris-Bowlsbey, 2009). It is here that a career curriculum within the school can have the greatest impact.

Acquire Career Information

With the increased use of technology, computer-assisted career counseling programs are now available for purchase that enable students to develop a comprehensive plan of career development. Through the use of these programs in schools, students have access to up-to-date career-related information. Some of these programs include Kuder Career Planning System, Career Cruising, Career Noodle, DISCOVER, and SIGI. While a thorough explanation of those resources is beyond the scope of this chapter, each program is designed to help students develop a career portfolio that identifies interests, values, strengths, and skills, with the intent to empower students to make

TABLE 3.2   ASCA Career Development

Standard B: Students will employ strategies to achieve future career goals with success and satisfaction.

C:B1 Acquire Career Information (Competency)

C:B1.1   Apply decision-making skills to career planning, course selection and career transition (**Indicator**)

C:B1.2   Identify personal skills, interests and abilities and relate them to current career choice

C:B1.3   Demonstrate knowledge of the career-planning process

C:B1.4   Know the various ways in which occupations can be classified

C:B1.5   Use research and information resources to obtain career information

C:B1.6   Learn to use the Internet to access career-planning information

C:B1.7   Describe traditional and nontraditional career choices and how they relate to career choice

C:B1.8   Understand how changing economic and societal needs influence employment trends and future training

C:B2 Identify Career Goals

C:B2.1   Demonstrate awareness of the education and training needed to achieve career goals

C:B2.2   Assess and modify their educational plan to support career

C:B2.3   Use employability and job readiness skills in internship, mentoring, shadowing and/or other work experience

C:B2.4   Select course work that is related to career interests

C:B2.5   Maintain a career-planning portfolio

Source: ASCA, 2005.

decisions regarding career planning (Dollarhide & Saginak, 2008). The ultimate goal is to assist students in the career planning process, recognizing that career exploration is essential to informed decision making.

Acquiring career related information also occurs for those students planning to attend college through campus visits and interviews. Schools must have in place policies that allow for absences to visit campuses, attend open house programs, visit with university representatives, and attend receptions sponsored by the college or university. Educating parents about the admission process and encouraging parents to get involved in post-secondary planning can also help students to think critically about future career goals (Poznanski, 2009). College nights at the high school in which students and parents are provided information related to financial aid, application procedures, available resources, and frequently asked questions can help solidify the partnership for school planning between the student, school, and family members. The school counselor can also follow-up with classroom guidance lessons that reinforce the information presented during college nights. One example is for school counselors to help students learn to navigate

The Occupational Information Network (O*NET), a website developed by the U.S. Department of Labor that allows for the exploration of career and educational requirements in a particular field. Another example is to assist students with learning how to find admission criteria and procedures for various colleges and universities online including navigating education websites (see the included list of websites at the end of this chapter).

Identify Career Goals

After gaining information about careers, students may begin identifying career goals. Setting career goals can be a daunting task for students. School personnel, including the school counselor, can help students engage in activities that promote career development. A sample activity that assists with goal setting is provided in Figure 3.1.

The School to Work Opportunities Act of 1904 supports schools as they develop opportunities for students to set and work toward career goals. More specifically:

> This legislation provides money to schools to develop instructional programs based on both academic and occupational standards; to provide opportunities to all students to engage in work-based learning; including work experience, mentoring, and apprenticeships; and to provide what are termed connecting activities, which develop links between the workplace and schools. (Brown, 2007, p. 238)

School-To-Work opportunities may involve collaboration with local businesses or agencies for students to learn about a particular career or trade. For example, Lapan (2004) describes a situation where a social studies teacher's curriculum included lesson plans on monetary policy. Through the School-To-Work program the teacher arranged structured student visits to the Federal Reserve Bank and Small Business Association. One of the benefits of that experience was students' learning about the career possibilities available to them. Career exploration and counseling is a substantial portion of the School-to-Work programming. Brown (2007) recommends that students choose a career path no later than 11th grade, thus helping schools meet the ACSA standard of identifying career goals.

RELATIONSHIP BETWEEN THE PERSON AND CAREER PLANNING

The ASCA National Model Standard C states, "students will understand the relationship between personal qualities, education, training and the world

Grade Level(s):	9–12
Title:	This Is My Life
Summary:	Students identify tentative life and career goals and relate these to future occupational choices.
Procedure:	1. At the start of the session, have students wad up a piece of paper. Pull a wastebasket or other container up to the front of the room and have students try to lob the wad of paper into the wastebasket from where they are sitting. As advisor ask, "What was the goal of that activity?" (to get the wad of paper into the basket), "Who reached the goal?" 2. Continue with the discussion, "Why didn't some of you reach the goal?" (no skills, not enough effort, aimed in the wrong direction, too far away from the goal, couldn't see the goal, etc.). 3. Explain to students that this simple exercise is not unlike students who look toward their future careers. Some students can't see the goal; some aren't aimed in the right direction. Others don't have enough skills or don't want to put any effort into it. 4. Explain to students that determining career goals is not a one shot (one time) activity. It is a continual process, and it is not always easy. Tell students that the process has to begin somewhere even if they have no idea about what career or careers they would like to have. 5. Give students "This Is My Life" handout. Ask them to take time to answer the questions honestly. 6. Ask students to share answers (if they feel comfortable doing so). Connect student questions with elements requested on the student's career plan. **This Is My Life Handout** 1. The best thing I have done in my life so far is . . . 2. When I graduate from high school I would like to . . . 3. If I could do anything as an adult it would be . . . 4. If I could have a career doing what I really enjoy doing most it would be a job in . . . 5. The three things I would most like to achieve in my life are . . .

Figure 3.1 Sample activity. *Source*: Adapted from the Indiana Department of Education Academic Standards & Resources, 2010.

TABLE 3.3   ASCA Career Development

Standard C: Students will understand the relationship between personal qualities, education, training and the world of work.

C:1 Acquire Knowledge to Achieve Career Goals (Competency)

C:C1.1   Understand the relationship between educational achievement and career success **(Indicator)**

C:C1.2   Explain how work can help to achieve personal success and satisfaction

C:C1.3   Identify personal preferences and interests influencing career choice and success

C:C1.4   Understand the changing workplace requires lifelong learning and acquiring new skills

C:C1.5   Describe the effect of work on lifestyle

C:C1.6   Understand the importance of equity and access in career choice

C:C1.7   Understand that work is an important and satisfying means of personal expression

C:2 Apply Skills to Achieve Career Goals

C:C2.1   Demonstrate how interests, abilities and achievement relate to achieving personal, social, educational and career goals

C:C2.2   Learn how to use conflict-management skills with peers and adults

C:C2.3   Learn to work cooperatively with others as a team member

C:C2.4   Apply academic and employment readiness skills in work-based learning situations such as internships, shadowing and/or mentoring experiences

Source: ASCA, 2005.

of work" (2005, p. 105). Table 3.3 provides the competencies and indicators listed under this standard.

Knowledge to Achieve Career Goals

In a school system, activities can be incorporated that offer knowledge and give information, skills, and strategies for career development. From those, students can make choices and judgments that best suit their personal preferences. According to Niles and Harris-Bowlsbey (2009), engaging in broad career exploration enables students to know which educational and career paths make the most sense for them within the context of accurate self-understanding. In order to gain an accurate understanding of self related to career planning, effective and appropriate activities for all students at the high school level must be incorporated. Unlike elementary and middle school counselors, high school counselors are suggested to spend 25–35% of their time completing individual student planning (ASCA, 2005). Therefore, counselors are able to meet a large portion of the career standards set by ASCA within individual student planning. Some of these activities include:

- individual student academic program planning;
- interpreting cognitive, aptitude and achievement tests;
- analyzing grade-point averages in relationship to achievement;
- interpreting student records (ASCA, 2005, p. 56).

Skills to Achieve Career Goals

School personnel must also emphasize the importance of incorporating guidance activities that are both psychoeducational and experiential in nature to help develop the skills needed to work toward career goals (Niles & Harris-Bowlsbey, 2009). It is nearly impossible to create accurate, everyday, real life job simulations; however, assisting students to see snapshots of typical days will help guide them to see pros and cons of chosen paths. Exploration can be done on a variety of levels including school-wide activities, classroom activities, and individual consultations also known as individual student planning.

School-wide activities are a resourceful way to reach all students. Since all high school students must transition into the "real world" at some point, reaching all students is an essential part of the career planning process. School staff can implement activities such as career fairs, job shadows, interviews with professionals, and classroom guest speakers to assist in the transition. Career fairs should include a range of occupations for a more accurate representation of all the possibilities. Community connections are essential in setting up job shadowing opportunities, helping students interview professionals, and bringing professionals into the classroom (Tang, Pan, & Newmeyer, 2008). In addition to those activities, school counselors can provide students with ideas and resources to help guide the conversations with professionals in order to have insightful discussions and gain useful information. A brief set of questions to consider when meeting with a professional (based on the ASCA standards) is provided below. The purpose of these questions is to guide students in their interactions and discussions with professionals in the field.

Questions to Guide Discussions with Professionals

1. What academic subjects connect to your field?
   (Standard C:C1.1—Educational achievement)

   2. What are the most fulfilling/satisfying aspects of your job?
(Standard C:C1.2—Personal success & satisfaction)
   3. What is it that made you gravitate toward this field?
(Standard C:C1.3—Interests influencing career choice)
   4. How do you stay up-to-date in your field?
(Standard C:C1.4—Professional development/lifelong learning)
   5. How does this career impact your lifestyle?
(Standard C:C1.5—Effect of work on lifestyle)

Classroom level activities allow the school counselors to team up with classroom teachers and align subject content with career options. Researching information, completing projects, and giving presentations can connect the two areas in order to assist in the exploration process. Research and other critical thinking activities incorporate in-depth information—for example comparing and contrasting educational/career paths and achievement rates (i.e., job security, salaries, promotion opportunities, job descriptions). Classroom guidance lessons can also be delivered to explore areas of self in relation to specific paths. These activities may include discussions of students' interests, abilities, self-efficacy, and outcome expectations. Tang, Pan, and Newmeyer (2008) conducted a study with 141 midwestern public high school students. Participants were given a three-part questionnaire that asked about demographic information, paid work experience, and family activities related to career awareness and exploration. Through factor analysis the authors identified learning experiences and self-efficacy as two critical factors influencing high school students' career development. More specifically, helping students see their fullest potential allowed them to believe and identify their own abilities and expectations, thus leading to greater satisfaction in career planning. In addition, students were intrinsically motivated to seek out additional learning experiences which built upon their belief in self and their abilities.

Recently, the importance of individual counseling has been tied to the pursuit of successful career counseling (Capuzzi & Stauffer, 2006). That could mean going back and reassessing the interest inventories and ability tests given throughout earlier stages of the career development curriculum. Integrating the psychoeducational and experiential aspects of the career development curriculum empowers students to make informed decisions about their future career goals.

Resources for Students and School Personnel

There are countless resources on the Internet that provide information for students, families, and school personnel. In Table 3.4 is a list of websites

TABLE 3.4 Internet Resources for Students, Families, and School Personnel

Organization	Website	Description
Adventures in Education	http://www.aie.org/	Resources for students, families, and educators related to college planning, financial aid, career guidance, and money management.
American Council on Education	http://www.accnet.edu	Information about services available to support higher education of youth from underserved communities is provided.
American School Counselor Association (ASCA)	http://www.schoolcounselor.org/	The leading school counseling organization that supports school counselors in career development planning for students.
American School Counselor Association National Model	http://www.ascanationalmodel.org/	This website provides an overview and identifies the components of the ASCA National Model.
Boomer Career	http://www.boomercareer.com/	Information is provided about resume writing, job opportunities, and government jobs.
College Board	http://www.collegeboard.com/	This website has resources for students, parents, and professionals to assist with higher education planning.
Counselor's Room	http://www.counselorsroom.com/	Lesson plans for career development activities are provided by grade level.
EduPASS	http://www.edupass.org/	This website provides information for international students desiring to pursue higher education.
Fastweb	http://www.fastweb.com/	This is a scholarship search engine.
FinAid	http://www.finaid.org/	Financial aid resources are searchable through one website.
Minority Online Information Services	http://www.molis.org/	Financial aid information and data related to diverse groups at institutions is available through this organization.
National Career Development Association	http://www.ncda.org	This organization promotes career development awareness and activities.
PA Career Education and Work Standards	http://www.pacareerstandards.com/	Resources for parents and teachers regarding career education are provided.
United States Department of Labor	http://online.onetcenter.org/	This website allows for exploration of occupations, skills, and job information.
United States Government Employment Opportunities	http://www.usajobs.gov/	Federal jobs and employment information is available at this website.

that the authors of this chapter have found particularly useful. Readers of this chapter are encouraged to keep an ongoing list, as websites and resources are ever-changing.

SUMMARY

The ASCA National Model provides a framework for integrating career development into the learning activities of students. School personnel are encouraged to create career exploration opportunities for students in high school so they can expand their knowledge of self and career to plan for the future. School personnel must also be involved in providing career development interventions for students, as these activities prepare them for the tasks they may encounter as adults. More specifically, students must be able to make connections about how current school activities are related to their future (Niles & Harris-Bowlsbey, 2009). Students are then able to apply the skills and knowledge they are obtaining by setting and working toward goals. The activities described in this chapter can assist students with developing the skills, knowledge, and awareness for successful transition into the world of work. Career planning and decision making can be an overwhelming time for students. When students are equipped with the necessary tools for effective career planning it can also be an exciting and positive time in their development. Competence in career decision making is an indication of a positive education outcome as defined by society (Dollarhide & Saginak, 2008). Developing students' career competence throughout high school provides them with the tools they need for a successful transition from students into contributing members of society.

REFERENCES

American School Counselor Association. (2005). *The ASCA national model: A framework for school counseling programs* (2nd ed.). Alexandria, VA: Author.

Bock, S. (2010). Twenty-first century career center. *National Career Development Association.* Retrieved from http://www.associationdatabase.com

Brown, D. (2007). *Career information, career counseling, and career development.* Boston, MA: Pearson.

Capuzzi, D., & Stauffer, M. (2006). *Career counseling: Foundations, perspectives, and applications.* Boston, MA: Pearson.

Dollarhide, C.T., & Saginak, K.A. (2008). *Comprehensive school counseling programs: K–12 delivery in action.* Boston, MA: Pearson.

European Foundation for the Improvement of Living and Working Conditions. (2007). *Measuring job satisfaction in surveys: Comparative analytical report* [Data file]. Retrieved from http://www.eurofound.europa.eu/ewco/reports/.../TN0608TR01.pdf

Grande, M. (2008). Using dialogue journals and interest inventories with classroom volunteers. *Teaching Exceptional Children, 41*(2), 56–63.

Gewertz, C. (2010). College and the workforce: What 'readiness' means. *Education Week, 29*(17), 24–25.

Indiana Department of Education Academic Standards & Resources. (2010). Retrieved from http://dc.doe.in.gov/Standards/AcademicStandards/index.shtml

Lapan, R. T. (2004). *Career development across the K–16 years: Bridging the present to satisfying and successful futures.* Alexandria, VA: American Counseling Association.

Niles, S., & Harris-Bowlsbey, J. (2009). *Career development interventions in the 21st century* (3rd ed.). Upper Saddle River, NJ: Pearson.

Poznanski, B.R. (2009, Fall). Average students need *not* apply. *ASCA School Counselor Magazine,* 4–6.

Stern-LaRosa, C. M. (2001). *When life hands you a lemon, peel it.* Talking to Your Child About Hatred and Prejudice, Anti-Defamation League. Retrieved from http://www.adl.org/issue_education/hateprejudice/Prejudice7.asp.

Tang, M., Pan, W., & Newmeyer, M. (2008). An explorative study to examine career aspiration of high school students. *Professional School Counseling, 11*, 285–295.

CHAPTER 4

PRE- AND POST-SECONDARY CAREER SELECTION

A Process for Mentorship and Identity Development

Emily M. Sweitzer
California University of Pennsylvania

Post secondary career selection is a process that is comprised of many concrete and hypothetical variables that are not only influenced by the external world, but also by the internal cognitions of the adolescent. This chapter examines both Erikson's (1968) and Marcia's (1980) theories of identity attainment with respect to the qualitative cognitive and social processes through which the adolescent transitions. This chapter also explores the applicative and conjunctive use of Baumrind's (1971) Parental Style Theory when combined with the basic premises of identity formation. Specifically, Baumrind's (1971) authoritative parenting style is discussed within the context of career mentor characteristics. The union of these theories holds particular promise for the development of career strategies and activities that uniquely and simultaneously address the distinct identity changes of adolescent and the emotional and behavioral patterns of the authoritative mentor.

Career Development in Higher Education, pages 75–88
Copyright © 2011 by Information Age Publishing
All rights of reproduction in any form reserved.

CAREER SELECTION

Career selection, in and of itself, is a challenging and demanding task for any age. It is a wide ranging entity that requires a comprehensive and complex analysis of oneself, as well as an awareness of the dynamic changes that transpire in the current workplace. Successful selection occurs only after one employs critical investigation, active discovery, considerable evaluation, and practical identification. Essentially, one must engage in a critical investigation of existing career opportunities, decisively evaluate one's current strengths and weaknesses, consider one's likes and dislikes and simultaneously identify professional and educational opportunities that can provide means for training and knowledge acquisitions. It is also crucial that one considers such factors as present ability, future potential, and interpersonal skill and preference.

Adolescence, in comparison to adulthood, poses unique challenges as career selection occurs in the midst of identity development and role model/mentor selection. Identity development is central to the process of career selection and can be explained as a developmental transition from egocentrism to objective self awareness, a time for critical self evaluation and the simultaneous selection of an employment match (Elkind, 1978). It is also crucial that a distinction be made between the development of the self and the development of an identity.

Whereas the self incorporates a broad understanding of one's capabilities, perceptions gained from others, and recognition of one's unique characteristics (Harter, 2006), identity formation encompasses multiple experiences, reflects teleological thoughts, and emerges from numerous roles and self appraisals (Kroger, 2007). Identity can be likened to a paint mixture that requires many tints to obtain one resulting and unifying color. In addition, identity is comprised of many interpersonal and diverse components that reflect specificity as well as uniqueness. One's unique and overarching identity is constructed from smaller identities that emerge from career paths, political affiliations, religious identification, relationships, culture and ethnicity, and physical characteristics (Orbe, 2008). One's identity is comprised of experiences, perceptions, and beliefs that reflect intensity, demonstrate frequency, and exemplify duration. For instance, one may consider the amount of passion with which they hold a belief or cause. They may also reflect on the regularity with which this belief or attitude emerges, and simultaneously contemplate the length of time that they have held this belief. More often than not, identity is a life-long process of which development can be explained in terms of the richness of its hue, rather than its resulting and identifiable color.

The following will examine the period of adolescent identity development from two theoretically related yet distinct theorists, Erik Erikson

(1950) and James Marcia (1966). Each conceives of adolescence as an optimal time for the emergence of identity, but they differ with respect to the number of qualitative variations that an adolescent may choose with respect to a conflict or decision.

Erik Erikson

Identity, as a concept, gained initial recognition from Erik Erikson (1950). The self and its interaction with others are central to Erikson's Psychosocial Theory of development. His theory is based upon the successful resolution of eight psychosocial conflicts that originate at specific developmental and age levels. He was one of the first developmental theorists to address the strains of adolescent identity development. He coined this strain as identity versus role confusion.

In regard to adolescence, Erikson proposed that between the ages of twelve and twenty individuals begin to question their existence as well as their basic meaning in life. Thus, he designated this time period as "identity versus role confusion." It is during this stage of development that adolescents engage in both self and career experimentations. These trial and error experimentations can occur within several contexts and require the adolescent to formulate evaluations, judgments, and decisions, in regard to gender identification, political affiliations, sexual status, and so on. Essentially, Erikson proposed that adolescents are enclosed within a labyrinth where they must traverse many paths before discovering the correct path that reaches their goals. Erikson chose the term "psychological moratorium" to describe the challenges that adolescents face. This term describes the delicate interplay between the successive stages of childhood dependence and adult independence. Thus, according to Erikson, personal responsibility and accountability play significant roles in adolescent development (Erikson, 1968).

Erikson posited that initially adolescents will identify with various roles that reflect the confusion that they experience as they transition into adulthood. These roles may be displayed in their clothing choices, friend selections, and career ideations. Whereas one day they may dress conservatively and express an interest in a traditional career, the very next day they may dye their hair purple and declare a bohemian lifestyle. Erikson viewed this vacillation, although intense at times, as normal and healthy. He posited that a healthy and strong identity will emerge for those who successfully reconcile and unify their experimentations, while role confusion will result for those who are unable to fuse their experiences. A successful outcome often depends upon the successful resolution of conflicts from other stages; our identity is thus built from these earlier resolutions. What was once described as specific and succinct components of the self during early and middle childhood emerges in adolescence as an assorted toolkit, capable of handling an array of self tasks.

Erikson's conception of adolescent development has influenced theorists such as Elkind (1978) and Marcia (1987) to extend his theoretical premises into more complex models of identity formation. Furthermore, Erikson's psycho-social theory of adolescent development has provided researchers with an avenue from which they can explore the fundamental reasoning and decision making patterns of early and late adolescence.

James Marcia

Building upon Erikson's (1950) theory, James Marcia's (1994) theory extends the psychosocial stage of adolescence into four courses of action that one's identity can transition through and/or undergo. Instead of using the terms conflict or crisis, Marcia describes the adolescent's identity transitions as explorations. The difference in terminology posits a more optimistic outlook for the adolescent as he/she experiments with an array of roles and experiences. According to Marcia, the explorations then assist the adolescent in the development of a sense of commitment. As adolescents transition through Marcia's four courses of identity formation, they engage in diverse, but logical thought patterns that appear to reflect their complex and dynamic state of identity.

Career investigation and exploration can be uniquely applied and explained within Marcia's theory of adolescent identity. The process of career development is closely aligned with the development of one's individual identity and can easily be thought of as a component of one's over-arching identity. The four stages represented in Marcia's (1966) theory are as follows:

Identity diffusion: Identity diffusion can be characterized as the initial search for and experimentation with identity (Marcia, 1999). Essentially, adolescents representing ages ten through thirteen dominate this stage. During this stage, young adolescents are not concerned with the development of a career path, nor are they interested in exploring the skills and abilities associated with the development of a career identity (Waterman, 1999). In essence, their behaviors can be likened to a 1970s pin ball machine where the ball is thrust forward, bounces off many pegs, and rebounds to be thrust in an entirely different direction than expected or planned. It is at this stage that most young adolescents adamantly pronounce one day that they are going to be rock stars, astronauts, movie and sports stars, and super models and the very next day declare their interest in astronomy, biology, ice skating, and so on. Their attitudes and behaviors are likely indicative of the vast amount of information that they are observing in their given culture and media circle. Cognitively, it is as if they are attempting to assimilate all of their respective skills (despite their level of accuracy or quality) with their vivid imaginations of the hypothetical. At this stage, there is clearly no exploration or commitment.

Identity moratorium: In contrast to the haphazard identity approach employed by the adolescent in the previous stage, identity moratorium is proposed to give rise to the slightly older adolescent. Within this stage adolescents begin a process of trial and error with regard to career exploration and identity. They begin to actively evaluate their observable world in terms of its match to them. Their ideas, reflections, and choices begin to align more closely with their definitive and tangible skills and abilities (Marcia, 1999). However, the adolescent represented in this stage is void of commitment and lacks a definitive plan for reaching a steadfast goal (Cote, 2006). Interestingly, despite the heavy concentration of young adolescents at this stage, Waterman and Waterman (1971) assert that college age students are also more likely to be represented within this stage, as they begin to actively challenge their steadfast beliefs and value systems within a culture that is defined by diversity, investigation, and evaluation.

Identity foreclosure: In general, this stage of development exemplifies the adolescent who readily commits to a career path without engagement in the processes of investigation and discovery (Marcia, 1999). The adolescent, in contrast to those represented in the stages of identity diffusion and moratorium, willingly and consciously chooses a defined identity and career path. The assumed identity and career path often resembles that held by a parent or another authority figure. One could also apply this particular stage and its level of commitment to the behaviors and admirations displayed by a young child who imitates the career behaviors of his/her parent or teacher. Literature commonly describes this level of commitment and void of exploration as negative (Kroger, 2003; Phinney, 2000). However, Phinney (2000) also asserts that this negative response may in part be reflective of cultural value systems that regard strong displays of independence and exploration.

Identity achievement: Waterman and Waterman (1971) concluded that identity achievement is most represented by those within the 19 to 21 age range. This stage of identity can be defined as the culminating stage at which the adolescent has successfully transgressed through critical exploration and has intentionally made a commitment and selected a career path that is based upon self-evaluation of their individual values, abilities, and characteristics. However, despite being significantly represented by the age range of 19 to 21, identity achievement for the most part is more indicative of the college student, rather than the non-college adult (Kroger, 2003).

Marcia's (1966) theory of adolescent identity formation represents distinct qualitative changes through which the adolescent progresses. These changes are indicative of their vast cognitive, social, behavioral, and inter-personal experiences and consequent internal evaluation of these expe-riences. Marcia's theory is unique in that his proposed stages inherently provide for interpersonal interaction, discourse, modeling and exchange. Essentially, it holds promise for mentorship that is either real or received vi-cariously by the adolescent and/or young adult. This additional facet lends tremendous possibility for the establishment and procurement of quality career mentorship that can not only facilitate the adolescent's successful transition to identity achievement, but can also assist with one particular aspect of identity attainment: career selection.

PARENTING STYLES AND IDENTITY DEVELOPMENT

In consideration of the significant role that interpersonal relationships have upon the various developments of the adolescent, several studies have documented the distinct value of family in regard to adolescents' success-ful transition to identity achievement (Cooper, Behrens, & Trinch, 2008; Schacter & Ventura, 2008). The family, and in particular, parents facilitate the skill development that is required in the search for a well-rounded and secure identity. Specific parental patterns in particular have been shown to enhance independent thinking, foster evaluation, and promote perspective taking. Cooper and Grovtevant (1989) noted that an optimal balance for identity engages the adolescent in dialogue that simultaneously encourages self declaration and fosters individuality and uniqueness. They furthered their assertion, stating that the parent-adolescent relationship should also promote deference, tolerance, and receptiveness for others' viewpoints.

Parental Patterns

The poignant familial variables and characteristics that are associated with the development of identity achievement in adolescence can be linked to the variables that are associated with particular parental styles in early childhood: authoritative, permissive, authoritarian, and disengaged. These infancy and early childhood parental styles are typically discussed with regard to fostering attachment, trust, and independence. These styles essentially define our interpersonal interactions (Baumrind, 1971; Steinberg, 2001).

The goals of parenthood, in general, assume two basic functions. The first is to develop high standards. High standards encourage children to excel to the best of their abilities. Creating standards aids children in de-veloping problem solving abilities and prepares them for the trials and suc-cesses of everyday life. A second aim is to be responsive to the needs of our children. It is crucial for healthy cognitive, physical, social, and emotional development to identify children's needs and provide for them. Responsiveness is, however, defined as recognizing and acting in ways that provide support, protection, and most importantly, personal growth for our children (Baumrind, 1971).

In essence, the development of a parenting style is the outcome of applying high standards and reflecting responsiveness. There must be a crucial balance between these two variables for successful parenting to develop. A successful parenting style is also highly individualistic; it depends on the varied conditions, personalities, and circumstances of a particular family. What works for one family may not work for another (Baumrind, 1971; Steinberg, 2001).

It is crucial to review these styles, as research is well documented in terms of their direct impact on adolescent behavior and future interpersonal relationships. The four specific styles are discussed in the following section (Baumrind, 1991a, 1991b; Collins, Laursen, Mortenson, & Ferreira 1997; Spera, 2005).

Authoritative Parenting

The behaviors that authoritative parents display provide for a balance between the adoption of high standards and the application of responsiveness. These parents are demanding, but yet responsive. They are aware of their children's strengths and weaknesses. They provide opportunities for their children to capitalize on their strengths and develop strategies that address or remediate their weakness. Authoritative parents are also keenly aware of how much is too much, how far to push, and what experiences will benefit their children with parental support. Fairness and consistency are the dominant characteristics displayed by authoritative parents.

As a result, adolescents raised in an authoritative environment are generally confident and able to accept and meet new challenges. In summary, this parenting style isn't too hot or too cold, but just right.

Authoritarian Parenting

In contrast, authoritarian parents demand high standards, but generally demonstrate minimal responsiveness to the needs of their children. This parenting style values obedience and rejects individuality. Although children are taught what is right and wrong, they are not taught to comprehend the social and personal implications of why particular actions are right or wrong. Instead, a regimented code of values that reflects that parent's personal belief system is dictated to the children. Furthermore, these children are not taught to problem solve. Thus, when a confusing situation arises, and the parents are absent, these children are often left confused, anxious, and scared. These emotions arise because the children either lack the practice and skill in making decisions, or are fearful of making the wrong choice because the parents will not agree. Anger and resentment are two additional emotions that characterize children of authoritarian parents. These children, and eventual adolescents, may resort to complete rebellion of a parent's ideology or become withdrawn and uncertain about their role and function in society (Baumrind, 1971).

Permissive Parenting

In contrast to the restrictiveness of the authoritarian parent, the permissive parent is characterized as overly tolerant. This parenting style is indicative of high responsiveness with low demands or standards. Total acceptance and tolerance of individuality are the rules, not the exceptions. Permissive parents tend to be "one of the group." Although many parents and children possess strong friendship-like relationships, the permissive parent, in contrast, is more indicative of the immature, risk-taking friend, who lacks responsibility for one's self, others, and the larger community. Permissive parents are highly responsive to the needs of their children. They are typically overly indulgent with respect to providing their children with materialistic comforts, lenient with respect to rules, and very tolerant of misbehavior and disrespectful actions directed toward others and themselves. Adolescents reared in a permissive environment tend to develop such characteristics as dependence, immaturity, impulsivity, and a carefree attitude. Essentially, they, like those reared in an authoritarian environment, have not been given the opportunity to develop problem solving skills. Unlike adolescents reared in an authoritarian environment who have a specific model to emulate, adolescents of permissive parents often don't encounter challenges. They are often sheltered from challenges, or they frame challenges for selfish outcomes (Baumrind, 1971).

Disengaged Parenting

Disengaged parents can be characterized as apathetic. Their apathy is evident in both their expectations/demands and in terms of their responsiveness. Sternberg, Lamborn, Darling, Mounts, and Dornbusch (1994) comment that this parental style in particular may be associated with midlife parents who may invest their interests and energies to their own indulgences, rather than to the needs and activities of their children. School absences and delinquent behaviors often typify the conduct displayed by adolescents from disengaged parents. In essence social competence, self control and maturity are skills that are void in these parent-adolescent interaction patterns (Baumrind, 1971).

Clearly, parental styles greatly influence the behavioral patterns displayed by adolescents. As adolescents begin their search for an identity, the requisite skills and interpersonal interaction patterns have already been rehearsed. Knowledge of these parental styles should then facilitate our understanding of the decision making patterns displayed by adolescents in terms of their career selections. They should also contribute to our knowledge and selection of optimal career mentors. In effect, mentors can be likened to surrogate parents who assist with the adoption of requisite skills and behaviors that enable adolescents to affirm a successful identity and evaluate career selections in accordance with their distinctiveness.

MENTORSHIP

Mentorship, as a process and as an activity, is typically defined within the context of graduate education and work-related, job skill training opportunities (Allen, Eby, Poteet, Lentz, & Lima, 2004; Kennedy, 1997; Lyons & Scroggins, 1990). However, if one considers the characteristics and skills that are attributed to positive and productive mentoring, it can easily be viewed as a process that is of particular value for the emerging adolescent and young adult.

Qualitatively defined and with respect to employment, a mentor is a professional colleague who takes an interest in helping a junior colleague develop into a successful and effective professional. A mentor is someone who provides guidance, experience, and support as the new colleague transitions through the course of his/her professional development (Johnson, 2007). Morris Zelditch of the American Council of Graduate Schools (1990) is often quoted with regard to the diverse and experiential roles that a mentor displays:

> Mentors are advisors, people with career experience willing to share their knowledge; supporters, people who give emotional and moral encouragement; tutors, people who give specific feedback on one's performance; masters, in the sense of employers to whom one is apprenticed; sponsors, sources of information about and aid in obtaining opportunities; models, of identity, of the kind of person one should be to be an academic. (p. 4)

Cognitively, successful mentors can be perceived more as facilitators and role models, rather than supervisors or evaluators. They share more than simply skill based information; they share value development and behaviors that contribute to fundamental interpersonal relationship patterns. An effective mentoring relationship is characterized by the following interpersonal characteristics: trust, respect, understanding, and empathy. Effective mentors are also willing and able to share life experiences, wisdom, and professional expertise. They should strive to assist the mentee with various interpersonal networking opportunities and skills. Mentors are good listeners, good observers, and good problem-solvers. They invest time and effort into understanding the individual goals of their mentees, while being respectful of diverse perspectives and cultural mores (Eby, 2007).

Cohen (1995) identified specific mentor behaviors that produce qualitative changes for both the mentee and mentor as they transition through specific stages. The stages begin with a definitive focus on interpersonal relationship building and evolve into a comprehensive self analysis. These behaviors parallel the behaviors displayed by the authoritative parent. Cohen's model (1995) prompts the mentor to be available, be flexible, engage in active listening, provide constructive criticism, ask and clarify questions and statements, be flexible, model appropriate behaviors, and demonstrate respect for diversity in opinion and thought.

In recognition of a similar premise, as described by Cohen (1995), Forehand (2008) discussed the possibilities for utilizing mentoring for psychology students within the context of Baumrind's Parenting Model (1971). He proposed that a model (borrowing from Kram, 1983 and Noe, 1988) could be developed to incorporate both psychosocial and instrumental assistance for the mentee. Essentially the mentor would provide for specific developmental and interpersonal needs, as well apply distinct behaviors that foster the acquisition of pertinent and relevant behaviors for the mentee (Forehand, 2008). Therefore, if one were to consider the aforementioned theories of Erikson (1968), Marcia (1966), and Baumrind (1971), it would be feasible and beneficial to match specific adolescent developmental processes with specific mentor characteristics. The authoritative parenting style appears to best emulate the characteristics of successful mentoring. The authoritative parenting style, for instance, (because of its balanced approach to responsiveness and expectations) provides the most opportunities for instilling an atmosphere of secure experimentation with diverse roles and characteristics. Furthermore, within this style the adult assumes the role of facilitator and/ or guide, rather than dictator or authority figure. Using Marcia's (1966) four identity statuses, the next section discusses the potential psychological and cognitive influences that the introduction of an authoritative career mentor may have upon career investigation and selection.

Identity Diffusion and Mentoring

The young adolescent who is encompassed by many media images and who is just beginning to enlarge his/her social network is especially vulnerable to the identity status of diffusion. Within this stage, the authoritative mentor can contribute guidance and support that complements the adolescent's zest for experimentation, but yet provides structured direction for the adolescent to begin to consider unique abilities and strengths in conjunction with various career opportunities. The career mentor may, for example, engage the adolescent in an examination of the characteristics and qualities that a person in a particular field and/or disciplined professional must possess. That exercise would enhance the adolescent's perspective taking skills and complement the adolescent's meta-cognitive transition, as described by various researchers (Damon & Hart, 1988; Piaget 1952). In essence, the career mentor, at this stage of development, would serve as a guide, encouraging the adolescent to consider the various attributes of others in particular roles, prompting and encouraging them to begin a process of self analysis with regard to their "fit" for various roles.

Identity Foreclosure and Mentoring

The authoritative mentor role is especially significant for the adolescent who is within Marcia's (1980) foreclosure stage. The adolescent within this stage is comfortable with accepting the roles and characteristics of an authority figure without engaging in self trial and error. Thus, he or she readily commits to a predetermined and perceived career outlook (Marcia, 1980). The role of authoritative mentor would focus on the adolescent's engagement in career experimentation and understanding of the self. Whereas the typical adolescent quest for autonomy is grounded in parental reactions to their novel assertions for independence (Collins & Steinberg, 2006), the adolescent with the foreclosure status has typically experienced an authoritarian parent who directs, rather than guides (Baumrind, 1971). The mentor's role would be to provide opportunities for the adolescent to engage in activities that facilitate discovery and autonomy, such as career shadowing, apprenticeships, and completing career inventories. Mentoring relationships at this phase should encourage adolescents to consider their likes, dislikes, strengths, and weaknesses.

Identity Moratorium and Mentoring

The adolescent represented by identity moratorium is fully engaged in career exploration, but can be said to lack a career plan or outlook. This adolescent readily recognizes his or her unique attributes and characteristics, but appears to be in the midst of trying everything without establishing a timeframe for completion or commitment (Marcia, 1980).

The authoritative career mentor's role may be to facilitate a timeline for accomplishments and assist in the development a clear plan for action. It is as if the adolescent, within the status of moratorium, is capable of thinking abstractly, but not concretely. They are able to reason hypothetically, as defined by Piaget (1952), but lack the self discipline to recognize and define parameters for their future commitments. The career mentor may assist with resume building, defining and building upon specific academic themes, assisting with the preparation of applications for college entrance examinations, job applications, and facilitating the development of a personal timeline for completion of a task.

Identity Achievement and Mentoring

The authoritative mentor's role becomes simplistic as the adolescent approaches the identity achievement stage of development. Essentially, the mentor's role is to provide support and continued guidance. Cooper and Grovtevant (1989) contend that adolescent identity is enhanced by a familial environment that displays cohesiveness and encourages uniqueness and autonomy. Specific mentor behaviors may consist of social support, active listening, and modeling problem solving.

CONCLUSION

Both Marcia's (1980) Identity Status Model and Erikson's Psychosocial Identity Theory (1968) hold particular value to practitioners and parents alike when used to understand emerging adolescents and their respective cognitions. The theories are also noteworthy as one begins to utilize them as a means to guide in the analysis of an adolescent's career-related thoughts and eventual career selections. Marcia's (1980) and Erikson's (1968) theories hold both unique and specific promises when applied within the context of Baumrind's (1971) Parental Style Theory. As the workplace evolves and new vocations are created, adolescents become faced with increasingly difficult questions and decisions. In addition to their quest for identities that are representative of the self, they must also extend the self to consider its relation to the ever-changing world economy its employment opportunities.

Baumrind's (1971) Parental Style Theory, and in particular, its authoritative parent style, possesses specific behavioral patterns that can be adopted and modeled by a career mentor. As the authoritative parenting style is used in conjunction with the premises comprised within the formation of adolescent identity, career mentoring becomes both an emotionally supportive and behaviorally dynamic process capable of problem solving and adapting to meet developmental specific challenges and decisions.

REFERENCES

Allen, T.D., Eby, L.T., Poteet, M.L., Lentz, E., & Lima, L. (2004). Career benefits associated with mentoring for protégés: A meta-analysis. *Journal of Applied Psychology, 89,* 127–136.

Baumrind, D. (1971). Current patterns of parental authority. *Developmental Psychology Monographs, 4*(1, Pt.2)

Baumrind, D. (1991a). Effective parenting during early adolescent transition. In P.A. Cowan & E. M. Hetherington (Eds.), *Advances in family research* (Vol. 2). Hillsdale, NJ: Erlbaum.

Baumrind, D. (1991b). The influence of parenting style on adolescent competence and substance use. *Journal of Early Adolescence, 11*, 56–95.

Cohen, N.H. (1995). *Mentoring adult learners: A guide for educators and trainers.* Malabar, FL: Krieger Publishing Company.

Collins, W.A., Laursen, B., Mortenson, N., & Ferreira, M. (1997). Conflict processes and transitions in parent and peer relationships: Implications for autonomy and regulation. *Journal of Adolescent Research, 12*, 178–198.

Collins, W.A., & Steinberg, L. (2006). Adolescent development in interpersonal context. In W. Damon & R. Lerner (Eds.), *Handbook of child psychology* (6th ed.). New York, NY: Wiley.

Cooper, C.R., Berens, R., & Trinch, N. (2008 in press). Identity development, In R.A. Shweder, T.R. Bidell, A.C. Dailey, S.D. Dixon, P.J. Miller, & J. Model (Eds.), *The Chicago companion to the child.* Chicago, IL: University of Chicago Press.

Cooper, C.R., & Grovtevant, H.D. (1989, April). *Individuality and connectedness in the family and adolescent's self and relational competence.* Paper presented at the meeting of the Society for Research in Child Development, Kansas City.

Cote, J.E. (2006). Emerging adulthood as an Institutionalized moratorium: Risks and benefits to identity formation, In J.J. Arnett & J.L. Tanner (Eds.), *Emerging adults in America.* Washington, D.C: American Psychological Association.

Damon, W., & Hart, D. (1988). *Self-understanding in childhood and adolescence.* Cambridge: Cambridge University Press.

Eby, L.T. (2007). Understanding problems in mentoring: A review and proposed investment model. In B.R. Ragins & K.E. Kram (Eds.), *Handbook of mentoring.* Thousand Oaks, CA: Sage.

Elkind, D. (1978). Understanding the young adolescent. *Adolescence, 13*, 127–134.

Erikson, E.H. (1950). *Childhood and society.* New York, NY: W.W. Norton.

Erikson, E.H. (1968). *Identity: Youth and crisis.* New York, NY: W.W. Norton.

Forehand, R.L. (2008, November). The art and science of mentoring in psychology: A necessary practice to ensure our future. *American Psychologist, 68*(8), 744–755.

Harter, A. (2006). The self. In W. Damon & Learner (Eds.), *Handbook of child psychology* (6th ed.). New York, NY: Wiley.

Johnson, W.B. (2007). *On being a mentor: A guide for higher education faculty.* New York: Erlbaum.

Kennedy, D. (1997). *Academic duty.* Cambridge, MA: Harvard University Press.

Kram, K.E. (1983). Phases of the mentoring relationship. *Academy of Management Journal, 26*, 608–625.

Kroger, J. (2003). Identity development during adolescence. In G. Adams & M. Berzonsky (Eds.), *Blackwell handbook of adolescence.* Malden, MA: Blackwell.

Kroger, J. (2007). *Identity development: Adolescence through adulthood.* Thousand Oaks, CA: Sage.

Lyons, W., & Scroggins, D. (1990). The mentor in graduate education. *Studies in Higher Education, 15*, 277–285.

Marcia, J.E. (1966). Development and validation of ego identity status. *Journal of Personality and Social Psychology, 3*, 551–558.

Marcia J.E. (1980). Ego identity development. In J. Adelson (Ed.), *Handbook of adolescent psychology.* New York, NY: Wiley.

Marcia, J.E. (1987). The identity status approach to the study of ego identity development. In T. Honess & K. Yardley (Eds.), *Self and identity: Perspectives across the lifespan.* London: Routledge & Kegan Paul.

Marcia, J.E. (1994). The empirical study of ego identity. In H.A. Boama, T.L.G. Graafma, H.D., & D.J. De Levita (Eds.), *Identity and development.* Newbury Park, CA: Sage.

Marcia, J.E. (1999). Representational thought in ego identity, psychotherapy, and psychosocial development theory. In I.E. Siegel (Ed.), *Development of mental representation: Theories and applications.* Mahwah, NJ: Erlbaum.

Noe, R.A. (1988). An investigation of the determinants of successful assigned mentoring relationship. *Personnel Psychology, 41,* 457–479.

Piaget, J. (1952). *The origins of intelligence in children.* New York, NY: International Universities Press.

Phinney, J.S. (2000, March). *Identity formation among U.S. ethnic adolescents from collectivist cultures.* Paper presented at the biennial meeting of the Society for Research on Adolescence, Chicago.

Orbe, M.P. (2008). Theorizing multidimensional identity negotiation: Reflections on the lived experiences of first generation college students. *New Directions for Child and Adolescent Development, 120,* 81–95.

Schacter, E.P., & Ventura, J.J. (2008). Identity agents: Parents as active and reflective participants in theory of children's identity formation. *Journal of Research on Adolescence, 18,* 449–476.

Spera, C. (2005). A review of the relationship among parenting practices, parenting styles, and adolescent school achievement. *Educational Psychology Review, 17,* 125–146.

Steinberg, L. (2001). Presidential address: We know some things. *Journal of Research on Adolescence, 11,* 1–19.

Sternberg, L., Lamborn, S., Darling, N., Mounts, N., & Dornbusch, S. (1994). Over-time changes in adjustment and competence among adolescents from authoritative, authoritarian, indulgent, and neglectful families. *Child Development, 65,* 754–770.

Waterman, A.S., & Waterman, C.K. (1971). A longitudinal study of ego development at a liberal arts college. *Journal of Youth and Adolescence, 5,* 361–375.

Waterman, A.S. (1999). Issues of identity formation revisited: United States and the Netherlands. *Developmental Review, 19,* 462–479.

Zelditch, M. (1990). Mentor roles. In Proceedings of the 32nd Annual Meeting of the Western Association of Graduate Schools. Tempe, AZ.

SECTION II

THE PRACTICE OF CAREER DEVELOPMENT IN FOUR YEAR LEARNING INSTITUTIONS

CHAPTER 5

THE PRACTICE OF CAREER DEVELOPMENT IN PRIVATE AND PUBLIC COLLEGES AND UNIVERSITIES

Nadine E. Garner, Cathy E. Rintz, and Brielle E. Valle
Millersville University of Pennsylvania

INTRODUCTION

Career services professionals in public and private colleges and universities have the tremendous potential to become significant allies for students as they transition from college to career life. They design creative and innovative ways to deliver their courses, internships, personal counseling, and other services. In their quest to provide quality support to as many students as possible, these professionals face common challenges: engaging students to become active participants in their own career development journey and encouraging them to enlist the assistance of their institution's career services. The career counseling and development literature and the best practices in the field clearly demonstrate the positive impact that career services professionals are having in the lives of their students.

Career Development in Higher Education, pages 91–117
Copyright © 2011 by Information Age Publishing
All rights of reproduction in any form reserved.

91

In response to difficult economic conditions, and as more students and their parents question whether college is about getting an education or getting a job, colleges and universities are under pressure to improve career services and to be accountable for the transition that students make from the college and university setting to the world of work. They are also expected to take an active role in assisting the students in placement (Lipka, 2008).

Career services professionals are also at the forefront of helping students conceptualize how to function as employees in a global economy. Globalization has created a new type of work life for today's graduates. They will need to embrace the idea that they will work in an environment that will change rapidly; they will need to continually update their skills to be current in the marketplace; and they will have to be flexible and collaborative (Coutinho, Dam, & Blustein, 2008). Graduates will need to have empathy and an open mind for diverse cultural norms, values, and traditions. They will be required to function outside of their usual environments and navigate the expectations of other cultures (Di Iorio, Cerotti, & Richardson, 2009). Chickering and Braskamp (2009) consider the development of a global perspective to be a personal and social responsibility of college students.

ENGAGING STUDENTS TO UTILIZE THEIR SCHOOL'S CAREER SERVICES

The Underutilization of Career Services

The college-to-career transition is a unique, demanding, and stressful time for students, one that requires much careful thought and planning. It is a process that is present from the time a student begins contemplating what his or her major will be. With current economic conditions, and the need for students to understand the impact of globalization on their future work life, students should ideally be tapping into the myriad of career counseling and development assistance that is available. However, the undergraduate student body, as a whole, typically underutilizes one of its greatest potential allies in this journey—the campus career services office. Although this resource is free, readily accessible, and provides a wide variety of career development assistance, there is a growing body of evidence demonstrating that one of the common challenges for career services professionals at the college and university level is engaging student interest and participation in the career development services offered. Only 8.4% of graduating seniors in Sidelinger and Banfield's (2007) study reported visiting their campus' career center as part of their career planning strategy. Similarly, Fouad and others (Fouad, et al., 2006) noted that only 6.3% of students use career services.

Lisa DeLuca, Assistant Director of Career Services at Drexel University's LeBow College of Business Undergraduate Career Services, Philadelphia, commented that about six students a day come to the career services office but wished that more students would use the services. She critiques a number of student resumes on a daily basis, mostly by student appointment. "We have 2,500 undergrads; however our days are not as full as we would like them to be" (L. DeLuca, personal communication, March 30, 2010). Similarly, Diane Fleishman, Director of Experiential Learning and Career Management at Millersville University of Pennsylvania, shared "We have all of the resources for students, but our office is quiet a lot more than we would like it to be" (D. Fleishman, personal communication, March 19, 2010).

John Bau, Associate Director of the Domestic Internships Program in Undergraduate Career Services at Yale College, New Haven, CT, discussed the same phenomenon:

> I'm sure career offices everywhere bemoan that they might be underappreciated but the truth is, if we're doing our job well, and engaging students to get out into the real world, they succeed, and ultimately whatever programs we develop in the office, the larger challenge is actually getting the students engaged in the first place. Most career centers in the country are working hard and doing terrific work with whatever resources they have, but it's trying to engage the students. (J. Bau, personal communication, March 23, 2010)

Why Do Students Avoid Using Career Services?

To gain an understanding of why career services are underutilized, Fleishman and DeLuca initiated a process of inquiry on their respective campuses. DeLuca created an undergraduate advisory council to help answer such questions as, "What do students need help with? What are their strengths?" One of DeLuca's 2010 calendar goals is to analyze which times of the day are the busiest and which services are the most requested (L. DeLuca, personal communication, March 30, 2010). Fleishman enlisted the research assistance of Valle and Aguilera (2010) to conduct focus groups with students on their perceptions of the campus' career services office. "I want to know why students don't come to Career Services. Whether it is a bad experience or lack of awareness, we want to know so that we can change" (D. Fleishman, personal communication, March 19, 2010). Focus group participants responded to questions regarding their awareness of the career services office, knowledge of the services provided, reasons for not using the services, and suggestions for improvement (Valle & Aguilera, 2010). Fleishman is considering the creation of a student questionnaire based on the results of the research.

Ludwikowski, Vogel, and Armstrong (2009) examined the stigma that college students have associated with using career services. The role of stigma is powerful, in that students who respond to one or more of the three levels of stigma may sabotage taking the initiative to utilize career services because of the negative connotations associated with individuals who seek help. They discovered that students may be less likely to seek career assistance if they are concerned about public stigma, the general societal view that there is something wrong with an individual who seeks help (rather than viewing seeking help as a positive decision). Students who are concerned that family or friends will have a negative reaction to them seeking help are influenced by personal stigma. Students are also susceptible to self-stigma when they have negative self-perceptions, believing that they are somehow unacceptable if they are in need of counseling or other services (Ludwikowski, et al., 2009). A student in Valle and Aguilera's (2010) focus group discussed having a negative connotation with having to go to the building where career services is located, as that is where the financial aid office and tutoring centers are also housed. The student felt that the presence of those offices gave the impression that the building is only for when students have problems or issues.

Valle and Aguilera (2010) discovered that the students in their focus groups had minimal knowledge of the range of services offered at the career services office. They also described the lack of students' knowledge about the location of the office on campus.

Interventions to Engage Students

The career counseling and development literature has suggested several types of interventions to positively influence students to utilize career services.

Lepre (2007) discovered that using a positive persuasive message was more appealing than a negative one when reaching out to students. Lepre (2007) designed both a positive and negative persuasive message and used them in conjunction with a form of mass media to examine which type of message would best encourage students to participate in a career counseling workshop. Written in the voice of a student, the messages appeared in a college student newspaper opinion column. The positive message described the benefits of signing up for the workshop, such as "reducing career plan confusion, not wasting money on the wrong major, and creating a support network." Conversely, the negative message discussed the negative outcomes that could result from not attending the workshop, with statements such as, "If you do not attend a workshop you will not be able to get on track for selecting the right major early." While both messages concluded with urging students to sign up for and attend a career counseling workshop, the undergraduate students who were exposed to the positive persuasive message were more likely to report that they intended to subsequently enroll in a workshop.

Whitaker, Phillips, and Tokar (2004) discovered that students' expectations about career counseling can be changed by using a videotape intervention. Students often have an unrealistic expectation about the counseling relationship, mistakenly believing that the counselor will play the role of the expert and tell the student what to do, and that the student will not have to assume much personal responsibility for the process. Students who viewed a nine minute videotape simulating an initial career counseling session scored higher on the Personal Commitment factor and lower on the Counselor Expertise factor, demonstrating that the use of an informational videotape can influence students to have an accurate understanding of what to expect from a career counseling experience.

Ludwikowski, Vogel, and Armstrong (2009) provided suggestions to reduce the stigma of seeking career assistance, thereby normalizing career counseling as something that could be seen as "a sign of courage rather than a sign of weakness" (p. 415). They recommend informing students and their parents about the benefits of using career services using outreach efforts such as placing posters on campus, holding a class about career counseling at freshman orientation, and making announcements in classes.

Valle and Aguilera's (2010) focus group participants offered a number of ways for the university to better engage students to utilize career services:

> Marketing efforts were discussed among the participants mainly in ways that they felt would be more beneficial and likely to get their attention. Yard signs are useful and attention grabbing—if they knew more about the services offered, they felt they would be more likely to use the services. They also want a more centralized location. The office should be closer to the Student Memorial Center because it would be more convenient. A link on Blackboard would help as a reminder for announcements so students are more aware of upcoming events, such as mock interviews and practice exams. They felt interactive activities at information tables with freebies to hand out would be an attraction. An activity could be a raffle to get students' attention. E-mails are not effective because the participants just disregard them. They advised to rely less on e-mails and put more lawn signs up to advertise the services offered. Some participants brought up working on customer service. (p. 13)

EXPERIENTIAL OPPORTUNITIES FOR STUDENTS: INTERNSHIPS, COURSES, AND OTHER ACTIVITIES

Institutions of higher education support their students' career development by offering multiple creative ways to participate in experiential opportunities, including internships, courses, online systems, and programs with business partners. The variety of methods currently in use reflects the career development professionals' commitment to providing students with numerous approaches for them to manage the college-to-career transition with increased confidence and insight.

Internships

An internship experience can be an ideal venue for students to enrich their educational experience and to make progress in their transition from college life to career life. Internships allow students to synthesize what they have learned in their academic courses and to apply that knowledge to professional situations, under the mentorship of their supervisors. Students also benefit by becoming visible in professional settings and can take advantage of networking opportunities with potential employers and colleagues.

For example, the Career Center at the University of Oregon, Eugene coordinates the Career Development Internship Program (CDIP), which gives interested students a chance to gain real-world experience in a structured internship while earning credit. Intended to provide opportunities for upper division students (those who have at least 85 credits completed prior to enrollment), the CDIP is project-based, where interns take on new and challenging projects at their site. The students can either create an internship themselves or use one that is already implemented. Interns document their career development in written assignments and receive substantial feedback from both their site supervisors and campus advisors. The CDIP helps students discover if that particular career path is what they really want to pursue (D. Chereck, personal communication, April 1, 2010). At some schools, most students take advantage of the internship experience. All but approximately 15 out of 800 undergraduate students participate in an internship, called a "Co-op," at Drexel University's LeBow College of Business (L. DeLuca, personal communication, March 30, 2010).

Hergert (2009) found that students place a high value on the internship experience, especially when it directly relates to their future career goals and if the experience is structured to match the way the student learns best. Brielle Valle, a Speech Communication major with a Public Relations focus at Millersville University of Pennsylvania, described the benefits of participating in her spring 2010 semester internship experience in the Office of Academic Advisement at Millersville University of Pennsylvania, under the supervision of Dr. Michelle White:

> My internship was based on event-planning and revolved around the organization and implementation of the Carnival of Majors. The Carnival of Majors

is an annual event that allows students to investigate the majors and minors offered. It is especially helpful for undecided students, and it allows for representatives from many different departments to discuss their field and the job possibilities within it. I knew I enjoyed the field of Public Relations, but I did not know which avenue within PR I wanted to pursue. With this internship I was trying to investigate what event-planning on a professional level required. I am a very self-motivated and self-driven person, and this was the type of internship where I had a lot of autonomy. The office I worked for made it clear during the interview that I wouldn't be told what to do day-to-day, but that I could make my own schedule to accomplish the project. I thrive on being independent but also having the reassurance that I could go to my supervisor for guidance and approval. There was a timetable from previous years, and although I referenced it, I was allowed to work at my own pace, which for me meant working more quickly through the process than the previous intern. I met with my site supervisor, Dr. Michelle White, once a week. Dr.White set the time aside for questions and reviewed what I had accomplished up to that point. She was friendly; she genuinely cared about how I was doing and how my semester was going. Dr. White was supportive and gave me feedback, which is something that I really value. She always made it clear that I could come to her with questions. The internship helped me realize that I really do enjoy event planning! It was helpful for me to see that I organized an event and that it was a successful. Not only did I receive positive feedback but I know that I did well. In terms of my career goals and aspirations, this internship helped me realize that this is an avenue that I feel I could pursue.

The internship experience also presents a unique opportunity for schools to forge relationships with businesses. One benefit to schools is that the intern supervisors of today may well be the employers of those students tomorrow, an important selling point to the growing number of prospective students and their parents who evaluate whether to apply to a particular college or university depending on the school's ability to assist with employer connections and job placement. Businesses can benefit from the internship relationship as well. Students bring fresh ideas and new perspectives to the business setting. An internship also allows a business to evaluate the student's appropriateness as a potential employee within the organization over a long period of time, giving the business the added advantage of mentoring and grooming the student to be a good fit for the company. In addition, the business' presence on campus at career fairs and other events provides visibility to thousands of potential consumers.

In this complex relationship among the school, the internship student, and the business, it is vital that the student arrive at the internship site academically and interpersonally well-prepared to meet the performance expectations of the business. Sapp and Zhang (2009) studied the written evaluations of off-campus internship supervisors, who were asked to give their perceptions of their interns' performance in a variety of areas. The students all were attending a private university in the northeast. The trends in their feedback revealed that while supervisors felt that the interns met their expectations in areas such as attitude, interaction with others, dependability, computer skills, quality of work, and the ability to contribute, the interns did not meet their supervisors' expectations in the areas of time management, spoken communication skills, professional skills, initiative, and writing skills. Sapp and Zhang (2009) suggested that it would be valuable for colleges and universities to gather this type of feedback from internship supervisors in order to help students strengthen the connection that they are able to make between their academic and professional worlds. They also suggested that this feedback can be used by schools and employers to dialogue about "what constitutes realistic expectations regarding the abilities and performances of new college graduates" (Sapp & Zhang, 2009, p. 275).

To address the concern of the business majors' employment readiness at Griffith University, Queensland, Australia, a program called the Professional Development Program (PDP) was created. The PDP is intended to close the gap between what students believe they need to know and do to prepare for a career and what employers are actually looking for in a successful candidate (Freudenberg, Brimble, & Cameron, 2009). To build greater professional identity, skills, and awareness, the PDP is incorporated into the requirements for the degree itself. The program is presented sequentially over three years before the beginning of each trimester in a type of continuing orientation. Students work with faculty members as well as professionals in the field and receive skills, knowledge, mentoring, and networking opportunities. As a result of the project, students demonstrated improvement in their levels of confidence and professional identity (Freudenberg, Brimble, & Cameron, 2009).

The following is an interview with John Bau, Associate Director of the Domestic Internships Program in Undergraduate Career Services at Yale College. The Career Services office is ranked one of the top ten schools in the nation for "best career services" by The Princeton Review (The Princeton Review, 2010), based on students' rating of campus career/job placement services. Bau discusses the impact of tapping into the powerful resource of alumni contacts, which has resulted in the creation of numerous internships for students both domestically and abroad, as well as the unique opportunity for students to develop important professional relationships. Bau is interviewed by Cathy Rintz.

> **JB:** I think the things that we've done here in the office that make us unique are the structured internship programs. A lot of these are relationships that have been leveraged through alumni contacts. The Paul Block Journalism Internship, for example, has come about because Block Commu-

nications is a Yale alumni family that happens to own a few
newspapers across the United States. So we have positions
there. The original one is Bulldogs across America. This
program was founded in 1999 by an alum from Louisville,
KY, who was tired of the brain drain in his hometown. In the
ten years from 1989–1999, exactly zero Yalies moved to Louisville after graduation. So he leveraged relationships he had
with community and civic leaders and other Yale alums and
developed an internship program, which in the summer of
1999 brought 33 students to Louisville. His model was, they
solicited internship postings from local for-profit and non-
profit companies, some were alumni, and some were not.
He raised money, and they put on a program that includes
paid internships for all students in the program and the pay
is approximately $2700–2800 and free housing. And this is
not Yale paying, it is local Yale alumni raising the money.
They typically live on college campuses. This program was
very successful in 1999, 2000, 2001. In 2002 some alumni
from Cleveland picked up on the idea and started their own
similar program. The first program was called Bulldogs in
the Bluegrass, and the Cleveland one is Bulldogs in the Cuyahoga. It became a successful enough model in Cleveland
that other schools joined in, and they now have four, five, or
maybe six colleges participating in the program, and they've
had as many as 80 students a summer in their program, and
the vast majority of them are not Yalies, they're from other
schools. Summer on the Cuyahoga is their website, and you
can read more about it there.

Roundabout Summer of 2003, 2004, I forget, my director,
Philip Jones, who is originally from the UK, thought "Maybe
I can do this back in London, where I know a few people."
He flew to London a couple of times, and conferred with a
few colleagues, referrals, and old friends, and he developed
a program known as "British Bulldogs" with maybe a dozen
postings. We lined up different opportunities and had them
posted, and they were being held for Yalies only, they were
a mix of paid and unpaid. We reserved the housing, but we
didn't fund the housing, so it was essentially "Hey, we've
identified these dozen opportunities that are being held for
you, but you have to pay your own way and figure out how to
get there."

Piggybacking on the success of that program, we went
next to Beijing, of all places. Yale has had a longstanding

relationship with China. The first Chinese nationals that came to the United States to go to college went to Yale, and the Yale-China association is 150 years old. So there were relationships there that could be leveraged. And then suddenly in the summer of 2004 or 2005 President Levin of the University said "I want every Yale student to have the opportunity to go abroad at some point." Essentially he handed my director a credit card and said "Go build me a program." Although we had to contract it over the past year or two, at its peak we were in something like 13–15 countries across the globe with internships that were held specifically for Yalies; some were paid, some were unpaid, and they were all housed together.

While this was going on, and clearly this was very exciting, the Bulldogs Across America program, which was following a slightly different alumni model, grew to nine cities, where it is now. I think we're at 13 internationally this year. So, there are a few things in here. First of all, again, I'm not a Yalie, I'm a state school kid myself, and I so appreciate all that is Yale. But, Yalies have good friends. So over the past several years, we've historically had three positions in the English Parliament being held for Yalies, and five in the Parliament of Uganda held for Yalies. The first westerner to hold a summer internship position in the Forbidden City palace museum in Beijing was through our program. We are able to leverage these kinds of relationships. And then we have had donors give money to something called the International Summer Award, which is essentially if a student were to go on a summer program through Yale University, they would receive a percentage of aid towards the cost of that program analogous to their financial aid package. So if my child went to Yale, because I certainly earn less than whatever their cap is, they would have essentially a free ride, so that if it would cost $4000 to do a summer in Buenos Aires, then they would get that.

CR: "I'm assuming this is an unusual type of program?"

JB: Absolutely, the money piece is, but the overwhelming thing here is, that leveraging alumni relationships helps to develop opportunities that allow shared experiences for students. So at this point my office is putting somewhere in the neighborhood of 400 internships in front of students that are all being held for Yalies.

CR: Do you have a Yale contact for each of them that they are responsible to report to or keep in touch with?

JB: Each employer has some tenuous relationship with us either as an alum or friend of the office, or just an employer that somebody reached out to. On the international Bulldog side, the students all live together. Additionally, in each of the international cities there is sort of a Yale person on the ground, either an alum or someone who we've contracted with to look after the students, so that if you break your ankle in Hong Kong, there's somebody who will see you through the process.

CR: What has been the response from the campus community and from the students to this program?

JB: Oh, they absolutely love them! As well they should. And, the international ones are terribly exciting, because they're in Buenos Aires, they're in Athens, and so they get a lot of attention. Sadly, I don't run those programs! The big difference is when you look at the domestic programs in these nine cities, where internationally, I think this year we've offered around 200 positions on the international front, where we'll be somewhere around 130–140 on the domestic front. Now these are different in that in almost every city, the students are paid and/or receiving free housing. So you go from a negative cash of flow of five grand and up if you're in London or Hong Kong, to actually ending the summer with money in your pocket if you go to Cleveland or Louisville, or Denver, domestically.

CR: Does that sway people's decisions one way or the other?

JB: Well, you never know. I think as the demographics of the college change, it can. Certainly with difficult economic times, with the fact that Yale has more and more students receiving aid, students are looking towards this as an opportunity to get good experience. All of this is tempered with the fact that that Bulldogs across America cities are largely off the radar screen. We have a problem here in that we're terribly close to New York and a lot of our students only want to do these sorts of traditional, exciting cities, be it Boston, New York, or Washington, and sometimes it's a stretch to get students to think about Chicago, or get excited about Cleveland. It can be difficult at times, but there are pockets that have developed, like a few years ago, an undergrad student from New Orleans said, "I want to have my city. I want to have Bulldogs in the Big Easy." So she got together with some alums there, and that program still offers free housing for the students who go, but there's no pay for the vast majority of positions. In San Francisco there's a mix of paid and unpaid positions but the Bay Area is so widespread we simply can't centralize housing. So we've been able to adapt the model in each city. But, the domestic programs don't exist because the office said, "Boy, we need a project in Minneapolis," but rather, the program worked so well because of the one in Louisville, other alumni have said "We want one of those," and the guy who started this in Louisville actually goes around to other cities and helps them grow programs.

CR: What future developments do you see in either one of these programs? Do you envision anything in the next few years coming about that is unique or exciting?

JB: I'm looking to continue the development of the programs that are in place, but my alumni office has identified major cities in the United States that have the most Yale alumni, and so I'm looking to model programs that dovetail with where our alums are. Now I will never be able to provide free housing for students in New York City, but by the same token, my students don't need to be encouraged to go to New York either. But having said that, there may be ways I can help them get there.

   We're piloting a program this year with the unfortunate name of "Notable Internships." It's called that because we couldn't think of anything else, but it will be packaged in a better way going forward. It's under Independent Internships on the website; it's the first link there. This is a far more sustainable model for us because, number one, it costs us essentially nothing, but rather this is a way to leverage Yale alumni and employers who have had success with Yale interns in the past and continue to post with us. It's a few steps back, it's almost like a "Bulldogs Lite," so essentially these employers are not holding positions for Yalies, but yet they're very keen on hearing from Yalies.

CR: Do you see yourself moving more towards that model in the future?

JB: I think given the present economic conditions, and clearly Yale is more fortunate than most institutions, but the reality is we can't keep subsidizing more and more cities, and on some level we need to look at other relationships we have out there. And, in this way, help teach each student the value of developing personal contacts and networking. Some of these are simply coming about through a student saying "Wow, this is a really cool organization, let's see who

we know and through LinkedIn see if we can connect to
them." Now what we're doing here is simply culling internships, putting them in our database, and attaching that label
of "notable" to them, to sort of sift them up to the top, so a
student can see very quickly "Oh, here are 50 internships in
Washington, DC either with alums or with employers who
have posted with Yalies in the past, who would like to see my
application."

CR: What percentage of Yale students do you think take advantage of internship opportunities that you offer?

JB: The short answer is, I don't know. The long-winded answer
is, Yale College, the undergraduate population, is approximately 5,000 students. So, pull a quarter of them out
immediately as the senior class. So then we're looking at
3700, and from that group, we can say that in any given year
approximately 100 will go off to Wall Street or the consulting firms, so we can pull them out, and we know that 200
or so will go to International Bulldogs, and another 200 to
domestic cities, so there are approximately 400–500 interns
that will be sent out through our direct efforts. And then
there are students who pick up internships on their own, or
who we teach to do networking and they go to LinkedIn and
make contacts, and then you ask them how they got their
internship, and they'll say "I did it myself!"

CR: What sort of unexpected benefits have you seen from this
program, things that you've seen that have kind of surprised you?

JB: One of the wonderful things about our structured programs, whether it be the Bulldogs program or Paul Block
internships, is that it provides a safe forum for students to
do things they might be hesitant to do, which is develop a
real human relationship with an adult who is not a professor
or a family member, and maybe it's the alum, a supervisor,
or maybe they're colleagues, but this is an opportunity that
allows them to engage in that sort of professional relationship development that instinctively they may not know
about, and it helps get them there in a way that seems non-
threatening. To pick up the phone and dial a stranger is one
thing, but to say "You know what, we've got this wonderful
program, and we've done a little bit of the pre-work for you.
Now you have to go there and work hard and do a good
job. While you're there, go have coffee with the alum, or if
your supervisor says, let's go out and get some dessert, take

advantage of that, and ask people how they got where they are. Ask people about their stories, and that will be the time when you really learn how people navigate their own lives." As a liberal arts college, Yale has very few degrees that offer a direct transition to a career path, like production or engineering. The vast majority of our students are the more traditional sort of major—history, economics, political science, things like that—so that you can't get a marketing degree here, you can't get a business degree here as an undergraduate. You have to gain those things through internship experience or through campus work, and when they get into the workplace and they meet professionals, then they really get an understanding of what that job looks like. I think it's actually that kind of learning that is really productive for them (J. Bau, personal communication, March 23, 2010).

Courses

Both the career counseling and development literature and the best practices from career development professionals demonstrate that the use of college courses in career education is a powerful medium to support students in various aspects of career development. Career education courses allow students to gain specialized knowledge about career development; reflect on their own personal and academic development and how it relates to their future in the world of work; take tangible steps to transition from college to career; practice valuable skills in an environment where they can receive formative feedback; and receive support from peers and instructors by learning and sharing in a group setting.

Deb Chereck, Director of the Career Center at the University of Oregon, described the Career Connections course:

> Career Connections is a one-credit class that focuses on developing job search skills and networking, and it also allows students to have two informational interviews with members of the Career Center's Professional Network. The class meets once a week, for ten weeks, for fifty minutes. Students write or revise a resume and learn how to write a cover letter. The class also covers important interview questions and helps the students prepare answers. (D. Chereck, personal communication, April 1, 2010)

Lisa DeLuca, Assistant Director of Career Services at Drexel University's LeBow College of Business Undergraduate Career Services, Philadelphia, teaches the LIFEfolio Course, which uses an online portfolio system called **My LIFEfolio** (LeBow Integrated Focused Experience). The program began in 2006. Students initiate the LIFEfolio during their first year at Drexel, and they continue to add to it as a work in progress throughout their entire program. The My LIFEfolio is an electronic portfolio intended to showcase a student's professional as well as personal accomplishments and can be used when interviewing for employment. This online document consists of the four electronic portfolios of career, business concentration, writing and quantitative reasoning. Students use the My LIFEfolio to store information, reflect upon their learning, and understand its impact on their development (L. DeLuca, personal communication, March 30, 2010).

Lisa uses the career component of the portfolio when teaching the LIFEfolio class during its ten week term and also sits in on presentations. Some students get job offers after employers observe the students giving their presentations. In some cases, those who view presentations end up teaching the class because they are so impressed with the program (L. DeLuca, personal communication, March 30, 2010). Lisa further described the course:

> We created a course they need to take their senior year. They present their LIFEfolio to their peers, their instructors, and some of the sections have outside reviewers (other instructors, possible employers, alumni)—they present the portfolio and present their five year career plan. They're pretty powerful [the LIFEfolio and the presentations]. We have had students go into the class kicking and screaming and come out telling me they feel the experience was great and are now able to articulate what it is they want to do with their careers. At the end of the course, they love it. Very few are bitter that they had to take it after all is said and done. Through presenting these career portfolios students are getting a chance to get hired from prospective employers. It's a win-win for everyone. We are always trying to make the program better; it's still very new and we are trying to iron out any loose ends; you normally don't hear the word "no." (L. DeLuca, personal communication, March 30, 2010)

To impress upon students the value of networking as a tool to support their career growth during college and beyond, Segrist and Pawlow (2007) used a visual portrayal of a networking process during a Careers in Psychology course. Using a student in the class to portray a person seeking contacts, and involving other students to act as potential contacts in the student's network, the activity not only demonstrated to students the variety of contacts that can make up a network (professor, relatives, hair dresser, etc.), but also how the reach of networking can quickly increase job leads (Segrist & Pawlow, 2007). After the experience, students were able to identify more people in their lives with whom they could engage as part of their networking process. They also reported an increase in how much attention they would give to networking as a job search tool.

Malott and Magnuson (2004) incorporated the use of genograms into a one-credit, 15-week career development course at a state university. During five class meetings, students diagrammed and analyzed genograms that depicted their family themes regarding occupational patterns, in order to better understand the impact of family on career decision-making. Students found the visual appeal of the genogram to be helpful, as well as the opportunity to express thoughts and feelings about their families. Students reported gaining insight into their family dynamics regarding decision-making and work values in addition to gaining insight into their own influence from family. They were challenged to confront their family patterns and influences. They reflected on whether these dynamics led to behaviors and attitudes within the students themselves that were valuable and worth maintaining or to ones that they wanted to change (Malott & Magnuson, 2004).

To provide students with a comprehensive orientation to the psychology major, the West Virginia University Psychology Department requires pre-psychology majors to pass Psychology as a Profession, a one-credit course taught weekly for 50 minutes (Macera & Cohen, 2006). To assist students with their short-term goals, the course is designed to help students decide whether or not to major in psychology, and to understand the psychology courses and related opportunities that the university offers. For their long-term goals, students learn about career prospects, graduate school, and the knowledge and skills that are needed to realize their career aspirations. In addition to lectures and out of class assignments, students have a four-year plan assignment, in which they map out all of the courses that they will need to take to fulfill the graduation requirements for a Bachelor of Arts or Bachelor of Science psychology degree. As a result of the course, 93% of the students reported that they had either changed their plans or felt more confident about their plans (Macera & Cohen, 2006).

Osborn, Howard, and Leierer (2007) found that a short, six-week, one-credit course in career development was effective in reducing dysfunctional career thoughts in college freshmen. Dysfunctional career thoughts have been compared to Ellis' concept of *irrational beliefs*:

> They often are absolute statements that include words like *should*, *must*, or *ought* and take the form of overarching generalizations with words such as *always* and *never*. Examples of dysfunctional career thoughts are 'I get so overwhelmed with making a career decision that I just can't get started' and 'I'm never good at making decisions' (p. 366).

> Dysfunctional career thoughts are noteworthy, as they are considered to be a strong indicator of career indecision, which hinders students from making progress in their career development. A component of the course included teaching students to recognize their negative career thoughts and to reframe their negative career statements into more positive language. Instructors also reinforced the reframing of students' use of negative language during class meetings (Osborn et al., 2007).

Reed, Reardon, Lenz, and Leierer (2001) also examined the dysfunctional career thoughts in college students; although this study was different from the Osborn, Howard, and Leierer (2007) study in that students were enrolled in a semester-long career exploration course with a sample that included all levels from freshman through senior year, both Reed and colleagues (2001) and Osborn and colleagues (2007) found that students with higher levels of negative thoughts at the beginning of the course significantly and dramatically reduced their levels of negative thoughts at the end.

Grier-Reed and Conkel-Ziebell (n.d.) discovered that a constructivist approach to career development, by means of an Orientation to Self and Career course, was also effective in significantly increasing students' career decision self-efficacy and significantly decreasing students' dysfunctional thoughts. The course used a constructivist approach to career development by engaging students in the process of meaning-making. A variety of course components were activated in a classroom atmosphere of collaborative inquiry, including having students tell their own story and using their personal interpretations of the self to bring greater awareness to their career direction.

Using research findings that students who have social skills problems—such as difficulty being assertive—are also more indecisive than their more assertive peers, Nota and Soresi (2003) designed an assertiveness training program for indecisive students in their final year of high school in Italy, to assist them in their transition to the university the following year. The assertive/indecisive connection is important, as a student's successful career development journey from school to career requires the student to be assertive when approaching and networking with people regarding academics and careers, gathering necessary information, and managing family pressures related to their educational and career choices, especially if the student's choice is not well-supported by the family. Students selected for the study had a high degree of social discomfort and a low level of decisiveness about their academic and career futures. During the training, students received specific instruction and coaching on a number of topics related to the construct of assertiveness, such as how to express wishes and emotions, and how to manage aggressiveness and pressure from others. After the training program, students were able to decrease their levels of discomfort, increase their ability to make decisions, and increase their ability to gather information that would lead them to make decisions (Nota & Soresi, 2003).

The following is an interview with Katharine Brooks, Director of Liberal Arts Career Services at the University of Texas at Austin and author of the 2010 book "You majored in what? Mapping your path from chaos to career" published by Penguin Group. The Career Services office at the University of Texas is ranked one of the top five schools in the nation for "best career services" by The Princeton Review (2010), based on students' rating of campus career/job placement services. Brooks describes her "Major in the Workplace" courses, including the use of chaos theory and her creation of a "wandering map." Brooks discusses how she guides students to both maximize the unique attributes of their particular major and to discover the relevant themes in their lives, and how to translate this newfound awareness into a career. Brooks was interviewed by Cathy Rintz.

KB: 1996 was the first time I taught this course, and that was back when I worked at Dickinson. At Dickinson I taught the Liberal Arts in Business class. It was a standard three-credit class and it was based on the idea of helping students understand that what they learn in a liberal arts classroom has direct application to the workplace, because so often I would hear students say things like "I'm taking this really interesting class, but it really doesn't have any value" or "There's nothing I can do with it." The class at Dickinson was team taught with an accounting professor, and we basically included classic liberal arts texts like "Death of a Salesman," for example, and then we would include with that a case study from the Harvard Business Review on a human resources issue at a business, and then we would talk about the overlap between what you might read in literature and how could a human resources officer have helped Willie Loman.

So that was sort of the genesis, in terms of thinking about this, and when I got to the University of Texas they had an option to teach a one-credit class, which at UT means it is a one hour class that meets for approximately 15 hours. It allows for a rather short but intensive experience and again, I teach them in all different subjects, so there's the English Major in the Workplace, the Economics Major in the Workplace—it just depends on which semester we're in. The idea then is that we hone in on those majors, have the students essentially be the experts in that major, and they educate me in everything they're learning, and then throughout the course we look for the parallels between that and the parallels they might encounter in the workplace, and most importantly, how to articulate that to an employer.

CR: I see on the website you have a list of what you cover in the course. One thing listed is a wandering map. What is a wandering map?

KB: A wandering map is based on Tony Buzan's concept of a mind map. It's really just a brain dump, where you put ideas in your head on paper without worrying about the logical order of things. I shaped that to create this wandering map, which was essentially for the students just to put everything on a piece of paper that's important to them in their lives. It could be the classes they've taken, the dog they had when they were five years old, a school play they were in, it could be a paper they wrote—anything in their life that was significant. We then have an analysis of that, where first they look at the obvious connections, like "These are all the things I did in high school," or "These are all the vacations we took" —those types of superficial sorting. The next level of sorting is to look for the threads or themes through your life. A student might discover that in elementary school they wrote this little play for their classmates to do, and then in junior high school they were on the student newspaper, and maybe writing's a thread we see going through there. Often students find a thread of leadership, or maybe a thread that they're always the person that solves problems, or is the mediator. You start to see all sorts of threads that run through students' lives, and while that may not lead directly to a job, it's a clue to an element that comes naturally and might be something they will always bring to whatever job they eventually get. A student may always end up being the mediator in any work setting, regardless. So that's the wandering map.

CR: Do students actually get a grade for this course, or is it pass/fail?

KB: They get a grade, and the reason I do that is that otherwise I'd never see some of them, but the way I grade is that they get a certain number of points just for showing up in class, because so much of it is interactive. About 60% of the points are earned just for showing up each class. Then, because I do so many interactive exercises, they are forced to participate, and I don't have to worry that they're just sitting in the back with their baseball cap on backwards pretending to be working. Then when they do the assignments, they get points for turning it in. I don't give them a grade on the content, per se, I'm not going to grade their life, and I wouldn't grade a resume. So, they get points just for turning assignments in, and then ultimately they get their grade.

CR: What has been the response of the campus community to these courses?

KB: The classes are very popular, and they fill up every time. For UT it's a relatively small class, because I only allow a maximum of 25 students in the class. For a school like this, it's virtually one-on-one instruction, and so it is very popular.

CR: Do you see anything in the future that you plan to change or improve, or do you like it the way it is now?

KB: I'll always change my classes—if you look at my syllabi, they change every single semester because I come up with new ideas, or I'm always adding something. If something bombs I take it away for the next time around. I think the next step is that we're working with Continuing Education to create an on-line web-based class that students could take independently. If we run it through Continuing Ed, it would be open to any student across the country who would want to take it.

CR: Do you have other schools within University of Texas that offer something similar to this?

KB: There are more traditional career classes that are offered. I believe our Educational Psychology Department offers a general Career Development Course that any student can enroll in.

CR: Anything that's come out of this course that has surprised you, or has been an unexpected benefit?

KB: I wouldn't say I've had unexpected benefits, but the students have had unexpected benefits. Students are usually looking at me a little oddly during the first two classes, because I think they expect a very traditional career class—one week I'm going to come in and lecture on resumes, and then the next week lecture on how to do an interview. The wandering map is the first day, and that throws them off a bit. I also talk a little about the theoretical basis, which is chaos theory, and how it in general applies to the career process. One of the things I emphasize in that part of chaos theory is the "butterfly effect," the notion that an event which at the time doesn't seem like anything can actually have career implications. I tell them during the first class that they should always be watching for that butterfly effect in the next few weeks of the class, because I actually run the class in about a seven week block for a two hour chunk of time each week. I tell them "in the next seven weeks, look for the butterfly," and then I often have a student that will come up and say, "You know, last week I was at the roller derby, and I saw this table about a women's health initiative, and I've always been interested in women's health, and so I went over and chatted with them, and they've offered me an internship, and if I do well it could lead to a job." You don't necessarily expect the roller derby to produce a job, particularly for an English major, but that's exactly what happens. I spend a lot of time encouraging students to "craft small experiments." Find things that you can do that only take an hour. So many students don't participate in the career development experience or career search process because they think it takes too long. They'll say, "I want to get into advertising, but I don't have 20 hours a week to do an internship." And I'll say, "Well, do you have an hour to go to the library and read or skim through an Advertising 101 text book, so you could at least get an idea what the key words and concepts are, and what you need to be thinking about?" Well, yeah, they have an hour. One of the days we do the "Crafting Small Experiments Day," where they do some goal setting on what they want to do, and then I have them craft and brainstorm a list of the things they could do that would take less than an hour, but could move them one step closer to a career.

I think the key successful element here, or the reason it's so unique, aside from some of the exercises we do, is the fact that a lot of traditional career courses don't necessarily emphasize the value of the specific education. It's more like "OK you've got your bachelor's degree, now here you go." And, for example, they might give a little tip of the hat to an English major, like "You're probably a good communicator" or "You're probably a good writer," but they really don't help the student examine in greater depth what it is about the major they've selected that could be used and could be thought about in terms of a kind of job. I was talking to a group of English majors yesterday, and I said, "Did you guys know that English majors can make really good therapists?" They looked at me kind of funny, and I said, "Because you understand the human condition," and we talked about Emily Dickinson's poetry, and the fact that Emily Dickinson was such a loner, and lived much of her life alone, and her poems have a way of reaching adolescents who feel alone a good deal of the time. So that someone with an English degree might do very well to pursue a career in social work or psychology or something like that later on. Again, it's the idea of how you do take what they already have as natural themes or threads or interests running through their lives and parlay that into a career (K. Brooks, personal communication, April 1, 2010).

Other Experiential Activities.

InterviewStream. In use for three years at Drexel University's LeBow College of Business Undergraduate Career Services, InterviewStream is an online interactive simulation program that helps students build confidence in their communication skills. With a webcam, microphone and Internet access, students record themselves responding to any of the 1500 extremely detailed questions, which can either be generated randomly or compiled from a list from the library that are specific to interview needs. Students observe how they present themselves to potential employers, and they also receive a critique from Lisa DeLuca, Assistant Director of Career Services. Students can repeat the process, refining their skills, and then participate in a mock interview, which allows them to perfect their skills. DeLuca is constantly promoting the InterviewStream opportunity and believes that more students should take advantage of it (L. DeLuca, personal communication, March 30, 2010).

Career Center Partners Program. The Career Center at the University of Oregon maintains a Career Center Partners Program. In this program, the partners are employers dedicated to recruiting students and supporting them in their job exploration. The partners assist the UO Career Center in providing programming and services to develop each student's professional knowledge about the world of work. Career Center Partners have a history of hiring UO students and helping them achieve career success. As Deb Chereck, Director of the Career Center, explained, "We work very closely with our partners to assure they receive visibility on campus and students know their names. Career Center Partners are advocates for our UO students. The partners (if possible) are present at our career fairs" (D. Chereck, personal communication, April 1, 2010). The Career Center organizes three major career fairs and a Career Week, which engage students in multiple opportunities to network with employers.

The Walgreens Wrangle. A multi-university example of connecting students and businesses to advance students' experiential career development is the Walgreens Wrangle (Clark & White, 2010). A business strategy competition sponsored by the Students in Free Enterprise at Southern Arkansas University, the Wrangle brings together business students from twelve universities and the managers of several major corporations for a three-day event. The task of the student teams is to design a winning presentation that offers a new business strategy action plan to improve the company. Before working on their presentations, students meet with the company executives to get acquainted with the essential facts of the company, such as its history and culture, financial data, and vision for the future (Clark & White, 2010).

The Wrangle has made a tangible impact on both corporations and students. As a result of the business strategies presented by the students, businesses have changed their website designs, marketing campaigns, trade show booths, and exterior paint colors on buildings. Students have a unique opportunity to interact both professionally and socially with corporate executives. They identify mentors, build networks, and apply their knowledge from classes to a real-world situation. A number of students have even been offered job and internship positions within the organizations (Clark & White, 2010).

The National College Advising Corps. The National College Advising Corps (NCAC) is an innovative program that bridges the gap between college and career. It provides a unique employment opportunity for recent graduates to better prepare them for either graduate school or more permanent work. Graduates who are seeking a short-term and service-oriented job can spend the first two years after college serving as college advisers in high schools.

The mission of the National College Advising Corps is to identify and assist low-income, first generation students to make the transition from high school to post-secondary education. The advisers are given intensive training the summer before they embark on their placements in a high school. Founded in 2004 at the University of Virginia, the National College Advising Corps currently has programs in 11 states across the country, serving over 30,000 students nationwide (R. Freund, personal communication, January 23, 2009).

Robert Freund is the Program Director of the National College Advising Corps, Keystone Region, located at Franklin and Marshall College in Lancaster, PA. The NCAC-Keystone Region is a consortium among Dickinson College, Franklin and Marshall College, Gettysburg College, Millersville University, and Shippensburg University. Freund provided the following update on the program:

> I am pleased to report that we are approaching the completion of an extremely successful second year in the 17 high schools that we serve. Our original eight advisers are all planning the next steps in their careers. Three will be attending graduate school (University of Pennsylvania, University of North Carolina at Chapel Hill, University of Illinois) and the others are seeking employment in education. All indications are that all five of our first year advisers are excited to return for a second year. We received over 60 applications for adviser positions for next year and I interviewed 20 excellent candidates. So far we have hired five in the first round and expect to hire four more by mid-June. We have added two new high schools for next year. With the addition of these schools we will be serving over 13,000 students in 19 high schools. Our national office has applied to become a national AmeriCorps program and is in the midst of applying for a very large federal grant. A team from Stanford University is working on a comprehensive evaluation of the National College Advising Corps that will provide information about the efficacy of our program and its impact on the college going culture in the communities we serve. (R. Freund, personal communication, April 26, 2010)

The following is a reflection from Katie George, College Advisor for the National College Advising Corps, Keystone Region, on the value of participating in the program:

As I was approaching graduation during my senior year at Millersville University, I was unsure of what I wanted to do next with my life. I was currently working with young adults who had dropped out of high school and helping them to get their GED and talk about the option of college. I decided to talk to the Career Services center to see if they had any suggestions or knew of any job opportunities. I was going to graduate with a Bachelors degree in Psychology and I knew I wanted to go to graduate school, but I wasn't ready to go right away. The career counselor told me about a new job that was connected with Franklin and Marshall College. It was called the National College Advising Corps.

Working for the Advising Corps has been an educational and enriching experience for me. I have had the privilege of working in three different high schools in the past two years. I have had the opportunity to be a part of the first group in Pennsylvania along with eight other advisers. During my first year I was working at two different high schools. It was a new transition for me, because I had to move to a new area that I had never been to before and be the first person to have this position in the high school. I had to learn how to stand on my own and bring new ideas with me, but I also didn't want to interfere with the jobs of the counselors that were at the high schools. One school I was in had a graduation class of around 60 and the other had around 180 students. This year I have been working in a much larger school with close to 600 seniors and there are six counselors at the school. I have met with hundreds of students from all different backgrounds in grades 7–12. I am in the school to encourage post-secondary education and to help students realize that no matter who they are or where they come from, college can be an option for them.

Activities that I have done at the schools include: helping students with SAT registration, filling out college applications, talking about scholarships and financial aid, helping students fill out the FAFSA, and numerous meetings with parents and students. I have also conducted a number of group presentations on careers and the college process. There are many activities that go on in a high school and I was able to organize a college fair and a "Preparing for College Night." I have spoken at two financial aid nights and I organized an activity called "Decision Day" where I have fun activities in order to acknowledge the accomplishments of the seniors who have plans for their next stage in life.

Throughout the past two years of the program, I feel as though I have grown more as a person than during any other time period in my life. I have been able to find a new sense of confidence and drive, and it has created a passion in me on the importance of post-secondary education. I grew up in suburban Pennsylvania and attended a high school with a high rate of students going to college. After this experience I have realized not to take a college education for granted. There are so many students that do not have support and I want to show them that someone is on their side. Working in a rural high school setting I have realized that many of my students have not even had the opportunity to step onto a college campus. It is important to create an early awareness so they can prepare for the future.

All three of the schools I have worked in are very different. This has allowed me to see what different school systems are like and I have learned how to adapt to my surroundings. Being able to have a firsthand experience working in a high school counseling office has allowed me to see and experience things that are crucial to the learning process of becoming a School Counselor. Originally, I wasn't even considering a career in education. This experience has opened my eyes to how important a counselor's role in a school is and has made me realize that the education field is where I belong. I feel as though the National College Advising Corps has had a large impact on my life and has prepared me for my graduate work in School Counseling and for my future career in the field. (K. George, personal communication, March 30, 2010)

CONCLUSION

Career development professionals in public and private colleges and universities utilize a variety of methods in the practice of career development for their students. These professionals also consider the variety of current issues impacting the practice of career services today, including globalization and engaging students to participate in services. Current career counseling and development literature and the best practices from professionals in the field provide numerous examples of how innovative career development programs are responding to the needs of students and promoting their successful transitions from college to career life.

REFERENCES

Chickering, A., & Braskamp, L. A. (2009). Developing a global perspective for personal and social responsibility. *Peer Review*, 27–30.

Clark, J., & White, G. W. (2010). Experiential learning: A definitive edge in the job market. *American Journal of Business Education, 3*(2), 115–118.

Coutinho, M. T., Dam, U. C., & Blustein, D. L. (2008). The psychology of working and globalisation: A new perspective for a new era. *International Journal for Educational & Vocational Guidance, 8,* 5–18.

Di Iorio, A., Cerotti, P., & Richardson, J. (2009). The preparation of students for a global career: An innovative study tour program that provides an equitable and inclusive learning experience for students that advances the development of their 'global passport.' *The International Journal of Learning, 16*(4), 89–104.

Fouad, N. A., Guillen, A., Harris-Hodge, E., Henry, C., Novakovic, A., Terry, S., & Kantamneni, N. (2006). Need, awareness, and use of career services for college students. *Journal of Career Assessment, 14,* 407–420.

Freudenberg, B., Brimble, M., & Cameron, C. (2009). The building of a professional: Creating greater career identity within a degree. *The International Journal of Learning, 16*(10), 253–266.

Grier-Reed, T. L., & Conkel-Ziebell, J. L. (n.d.). Orientation to self and career: Constructivist theory and practice in the classroom. *The Learning Assistance Review, 14*(1), 23–36.

Hergert, M. (2009). Student perceptions of the value of internships in business education. *American Journal of Business Education, 2*(8), 9–13.

Lepre, C. R. (2007). Getting through to them: Reaching students who need career counseling. *The Career Development Quarterly, 56,* 74–84.

Lipka, S. (2008). In tight employment market, career services gain clout. *Chronicle of Higher Education, 54*(36), 1.

Ludwikowski, W. M. A., Vogel, D., & Armstrong, P. I. (2009). Attitudes toward career counseling: The role of public and self-stigma. *Journal of Counseling Psychology, 56*(3), 408–416.

Macera, M. H., & Cohen, S. H. (2006). Psychology as a profession: An effective career exploration and orientation course for undergraduate psychology majors. *Career Development Quarterly, 54,* 367–371.

Malott, K. M., & Magnuson, S. (2004). Using genograms to facilitate undergraduate students' career development: A group model. *Career Development Quarterly, 53,* 178–186.

Nota, L., & Soresi, S. (2003). An assertiveness training program for indecisive students attending an Italian university. *Career Development Quarterly, 51,* 322–334.

Osborn, D. S., Howard, D. K., & Leierer, S. J. (2007). The effect of a career development course on the dysfunctional career thoughts of racially and ethnically diverse college freshmen. *The Career Development Quarterly, 55,* 365–377.

The Princeton Review. (2010). The Best 371 Colleges. Academics/Administration: Best Career Services. Retrieved from http://www.princetonreview.com/schoollist.aspx?type=r&id=685&RDN=1

Reed, C. A., Reardon, R. C., Lenz, J. G., & Leierer, S. J. (2001). A cognitive career course: From theory to practice. *Career Development Quarterly, 50,* 158–167.

Sapp, D. A., & Zhang, Q. (2009). Trends in industry supervisors' feedback on business communication internships. *Business Communication Quarterly, 72*(3), 274–288.

Segrist, D. J., & Pawlow, L. A. (2007). Who do you know? Demonstrating networking in a Careers in Psychology course. *Journal of Instructional Psychology, 36*(4), 352–356.

Sidelinger, R. J., & Banfield, S. R. (2007). Planning for life after college: An analysis of career planning, proactivity, motivation, and locus of control. Paper submitted to the Student Division for presentation at the 2007 meeting of the National Communication Association, Chicago, IL.

Valle, B. E., & Aguilera, S. (2010). *Students' perception of career services.* Unpublished manuscript, Millersville University of Pennsylvania.

Whitaker, L. A., Phillips, J. C., & Tokar, D. M. (2004). Influencing client expectations about career counseling using a videotaped intervention. *Career Development Quarterly, 52,* 309–322.

CHAPTER 6

CAREER COUNSELING CENTERS AT THE COLLEGE LEVEL

Gene Sutton and Rhonda Gifford

The role of the career center has evolved over the years from being a placement center that places students into full-time jobs to a fully comprehensible college and career planning center catering to freshmen through alumni in all aspects of career development. From the early 1900s to the late 1970s, most offices fell under the name of career planning and placement (Herr, Rayman, & Garis, 1993). When it came to on-campus interviewing, students would be hand-selected to interview for positions, usually by one of their professors. "This was primarily a male activity, an old boys' network, by which a faculty member would speak on behalf of a student or persons of importance who might employ him as a favor to, or out of respect for, the professor" (Herr et al., 1993, p. 1).

With the advent of the G.I. Bill, it became apparent that soldiers returning home from World Wars I and II needed support. As a result, career placement offices began to open up on campuses across the country. In addition, employment associations also began to open. The first placement

Career Development in Higher Education, pages 119–136
Copyright © 2011 by Information Age Publishing
119

organization was established in February 1924 in Chicago—the National Association of Appointments Secretaries, named after the British equivalent of a placement director in the United States (Giordani, 2006). The name of the organization has since changed and is now the American College and Personnel Association. The goals of the organization now place more emphasis on professional development and job placement.

There have been many regional placement offices throughout the U.S. over the years. In 1956, a group at Lehigh University approved a constitution for a new national advisory council and named it the College Placement Publications Council. In later years, the name changed to the College Placement Council and again changed to the National Association of Colleges and Employers (NACE) in 1995. The mission of NACE was to support the goals of equal employment opportunities at the college level.

The goal of the Equal Employment Opportunity Commission (EEOC), established in 1956, was eliminating illegal discrimination from the workplace. In 1972, Congress gave the commission the ability to litigate enforcement in their jurisdiction. As equal employment opportunities began to change with the times, it became evident that the placement process was unethical. In the 1980s, many offices began to change their name to "Career Services" and made the interviewing processes available to all students. Due to concern with the hiring process, NACE developed the Principles for Professional Practice:

> The principles presented here are designed to provide practitioners with three basic precepts for career planning and recruitment: maintain an open and free selection of employment opportunities in an atmosphere conducive to objective thought; maintain a recruitment process that is fair and equitable to candidates and employing organizations; and support informed and responsible decision making by candidates. Adherence to the guidelines will support the collaborative efforts of career services and employment professionals while reducing the potential for abuses. (NACE, 2010c)

In the late 1980s and early 1990s, the offices began to expand their services to work with students throughout their college careers. Today, career services work with students from their freshman year through graduation. Most schools refer to this as the "four-year plan" or the "four-year timeline." California University of Pennsylvania (CalU of PA) places a heavy emphasis on their four-year plan called the Career Advantage Program. This program specifies the activities that students should be doing each year to ensure that in addition to pursuing their degree, they also obtain the soft skills employers seek (e.g., communication, leadership) to successfully market themselves as job candidates (California University of Pennsylvania, 2010).

CAREER CENTER FRAMEWORK

College and university career centers on different campuses can vary in their structure. Some have centralized offices, others have decentralized offices, and some have both. Campuses with a centralized office tend to work with all majors in all aspects of career development, from working with undecided majors to helping soon-to-be graduates with the job search process. Decentralized offices tend to be located within a specific college or major and work solely with those students (e.g., business or pharmacy department). Some campuses, whether centralized or not, will have a separate office that works with undecided students. One such campus is Oregon State University that has the office of university exploratory studies program. This program advises all undecided students through their sophomore year to guide them in to the degree that will fit their interests and goals (Oregon State University, 2010).

The name and size of career centers vary depending on a number of factors. These might include the size of the school, the budget, and the belief of upper administration regarding the importance of a career center. There are many different names for a career center, including Career Services, Career Life Planning, and Career Development.

Staffing the career center also varies with each institution. In an ideal situation, the office will have the following staff members: director, associate director, career counselors/advisors, alumni career counselor/advisor, employer development coordinator, employer relations coordinator, receptionist, and graduate assistant(s). In addition to these positions, some offices will also host graduate-level practicum and internship students. The office of Career Services at CalU of PA is one such office that offers these opportunities to graduate students. Most of these students come from the Community and Agency Counseling program with the goal of working in a career center at the collegiate level.

As for the roles of the positions, the director oversees all aspects of the center and typically reports to the dean of student affairs, the dean of academic affairs, or occasionally the provost. In addition to overseeing the department, some directors will also take student appointments, hold leadership positions with organizations related to the various industries at the state, regional, and national levels, and assist with employer development. The director also collaborates with various departments on campus to develop new programs, such as alumni relations and university development. The associate director assists the director in the operations of the center, takes student appointments, and takes on various leadership roles similar to the director. This position usually entails heading programs and events that occur on and off campus such as job fairs and conference planning. The career counselors generally work mostly with student appointments, from working with undecided students in their freshman and sophomore years to helping them find a full-time job as they near graduation. They also work with alumni who are seeking employment for a variety of reasons. Ideally, the career center would have a counselor specifically working with alumni. The employer development and employer relations coordinators are ideally separate, yet often combined positions. The development coordinator is in charge of creating relations with various companies in the region as well as nationally, going on company visits and bringing those companies to campus. They will also attend the Association of Colleges and Employers Conference at the state, regional, or national level, job fairs, chamber of commerce events, industry events, and Human Resource Association events. The relations coordinator generally is in charge of handling the recruiters from established organizations that are working with that particular college. The responsibilities can include coordinating on-campus interviews for internships and full-time jobs, setting up classroom presentations, and assisting with job fairs. The receptionist generally answers the phone, schedules student appointments, and assists the director as needed. Graduate assistants' responsibilities can range from working with students on all career-related matters to taking on projects and, in some cases, supervising student interns.

MISSION

The mission of most career centers is to help guide students through their college career. This may include working with undecided freshmen and sophomores to ensure they find a career path that is a best fit for them. Additionally, career centers help juniors and seniors gain experience in their fields so that they develop all the soft skills employers seek such as communication and problem solving. They may also help seniors seek full-time employment by assisting them with resume and cover letter writing, interviewing skills, job search strategies, or with the application process for graduate school. The mission statement of the office of Career Services at CalU of PA is the following:

> The office of Career Services supports the mission of California University of Pennsylvania in building character and building careers by providing services and resources that facilitate the lifelong career development process. Using the Career Advantage Program as a framework, we partner with our stakeholders: students, alumni, employers, university faculty and staff, and parents to provide these mutually beneficial services. (CalU of PA, 2010)

CAMPUS AND COMMUNITY RELATIONS

Depending on the particular career service office, many different relationships will develop with employers, faculty and staff, and advisory boards. "Career planning and placement services must maintain relations with relevant campus offices and external agencies, which necessarily requires regular identification of the office with which such relationships are critical" (Herr et al., 1993, p. 91). In addition to employers, CalU of PA has developed relationships with many of the faculty and staff, and has at least one professor from each department who serves as the Career Advantage Program liaison (CalU of PA, 2010). These individuals are responsible for keeping their department up to date with the CalU of PA Career Advantage Program.

CalU of PA has also created an advisory board with employers, faculty and staff, and students as part of the membership. The advisory board was set up with the intention of staying current with the field, as well as generating new ideas and programs to offer to both employers and students (CalU of PA, 2010). CalU of PA also works with the community members assisting them in all aspects of the job search. Developing relationships with all of the various stakeholders is a key component of a successful career center.

SERVICES PROVIDED/DELIVERY METHODS

The services offered by a four-year college or university career center varies based on its mission, scope, structure (centralized vs. decentralized), and staff size. Many career centers are comprehensive, offering a full range of services that includes career development and career needs. Career center services are grouped into four broad categories:

1. Career counseling
2. Job search services
3. Career information
4. Programming and outreach

Career Counseling Services

The core services of a career center is career counseling. Herr, Rayman, and Garis (1993) noted that providing counseling services enables the career center to emphasize the developmental process approach to career choice and empowers clients with the knowledge and skills to clarify and implement career plans throughout their lifetime. Career centers that do not provide individual or group counseling services run the risk of being seen as merely a job or placement center whose effectiveness is evaluated primarily by the number of organizations recruiting on campus and the number of students and graduates finding internships and jobs.

The most common ways to provide career counseling services include individual counseling sessions by appointment, intake or "drop-in" counseling, group counseling (including career classes for credit), assessment, and online counseling (NACE, 2010a).

Individual Counseling Sessions by Appointment

Individual counseling sessions by appointment typically last from 30–60 minutes and may address any of the following career issues (Herr et al., 1993):

- Career indecision
- Choice of major
- Exploring career options related to the client's major, interests, skills, and values
- Assistance in identifying opportunities for experiential education (i.e., job shadowing, cooperative education, internships, etc.)
- Assistance with the job search and/or graduate or professional school application process.

Confidential individual counseling session notes should adhere to ethical standards for Career Services as outlined by the Standards and Guidelines for Student Services/Student Development (Council for the Advancement of Standards, 1986).

Herr, Rayman, and Garis (1993) point out that client expectations of career counseling are varied and complex, requiring the career center to clarify its philosophy and practices regarding the following questions:

- To what extent does the counselor serve as educator or provide information in career counseling?
- How much follow-up and how many career counseling sessions are available to clients?
- To what extent is assessment used in the career counseling process?
- To what extent are personal issues addressed and dealt with in career counseling?

Some clients may expect, seek, and be satisfied with one or two visits to the career center; others may require multiple counseling sessions. Client expectations of the career counseling process should be clarified in the early stages of the counseling appointment (Herr et al., 1993).

Demand and use of individual career counseling typically varies depending on the type of client. For example, upperclassmen are typically more likely to seek out career center services because they need assistance in developing a resume or finding a job, whereas freshmen and sophomores may need to be encouraged to become engaged in the career planning process early in their college career. For example, all CalU of PA freshmen enrolled in the University's First Year Seminar complete the Strong Interest Inventory. Career services staff members then visit each class section to help students interpret their inventory results and plan next steps as part of the University's Career Advantage Program (CalU of PA, 2010).

Because the connection between academic programs and career options are less defined in the liberal arts and humanities, students in these majors may be less likely to seek out career counseling and other services than vocationally-oriented majors such as business or engineering (Herr et al., 1993). Career centers with a counseling component are better able to engage and serve these populations than career centers with a focus only on "placement."

Intake/"Drop-In" Counseling

Many clients prefer individual counseling but also want quick service and the convenience of dropping in the career center without an appointment. Increased demand for this type of service has prompted many career centers to provide intake or "drop-in" counseling services at least several hours per week or more often, depending on available staff. Most often, an appointment is not necessary for intake counseling, and the sessions are brief and information based (10–30 minutes maximum).

The primary purpose of the "drop-in" session is for the intake counselor to address client questions quickly and screen or refer clients to appropriate career center services or programs. Topics discussed during an intake counseling session include resume and cover letter reviews, brief interview, job search, or graduate school application questions, and questions about services or programs (Herr et al., 1993).

Full-time or part-time staff, graduate assistants, and/or peer counselors may serve as intake counselors. Because of the wide variety of career questions that clients attending intake sessions may have, all staff serving as intake counselors should be carefully trained and need to be familiar with all of the services provided by the career center, as well as able to refer clients to appropriate resources outside of the career center.

Two advantages of intake counseling are that it allows individual counseling appointments to focus on more in-depth career issues such as career choice or exploration while allowing the career center to provide immediate assistance to clients without an appointment. Intake counselors can also refer clients to other career center programs and services, potentially increasing the number of clients taking advantage of those programs and services (Herr et al., 1993).

Group Counseling

Group counseling is an alternative means to engage clients in career planning. Group counseling typically focuses on a specific topic common to all members such as self-assessment, career exploration, internship search, job search strategies, or graduate and professional school search and application. The most effective groups ideally range from five to fifteen clients, meet for multiple sessions, and are interactive in nature. They may be offered as a series of non-credit workshops or as a credit-bearing class (typically one credit, but sometimes up to three credits).

Advantages of group counseling include efficiency as well as opportunity for sharing and modeling among members of the group (Herr et al., 1993). Group sessions tailored to specific populations such as undecided freshmen, graduating seniors, minority students, returning adult students, academically at-risk students, or arts-related majors may be especially effective in creating an atmosphere of interaction and understanding. Disadvantages of group counseling, especially of non-credit offerings, are that group members may not feel compelled to attend and may not feel that their specific career concerns are adequately addressed in the group setting (Herr et al., 1993).

Assessment

Career assessment should be offered through the career center because it supports the broader counseling and career exploration mission of the career center, and when used appropriately, it provides an additional source of information as part of the career exploration process during individual counseling appointments (Herr et al., 1993).

Career assessments should not be used strictly as a diagnostic tool by clients or counselors (i.e., "tell me what I should be or do"), but rather as a launch pad for further reflection, discussion and exploration of the client's interests, values, abilities, personal qualities, or beliefs. Career counselors must be well versed in the effective use of career assessments and assist their clients in how to effectively interpret and use the information gleaned from the assessment in the career planning and exploration process.

Career assessments can be classified as follows: assessment of the client's personality type, interests, values, and abilities; computer-assisted career guidance systems (CACG); and diagnostic measures of the client's career maturity, progress, or satisfaction in the career planning process (Herr et al., 1993). Some common career assessments include:

- Myers Briggs Type Indicator (MBTI). I. G. Myers and K. C. Briggs. Consulting Psychologists Press, Inc. (personality type)
- Strong Interest Inventory (SII). E. K. Strong, Jr., J. C. Hansen, and D. P. Campbell, Consulting Psychologists Press, Inc. (interests)
- FOCUS (CACG)
- eDISCOVER (CACG)
- Career Development Inventory (CDI). D. E. Super, A. S. Thompson, R. H. Lindeman, J. P. Jordaan, and R. A. Myers. Consulting Psychologists Press. (career maturity)
- My Vocational Situation (MVS). J. L. Holland, D. C. Daiger, and P. G. Power. Consulting Psychologists Press. (career planning, knowledge and process)
- Career Beliefs Inventory (CBI). J. D. Krumboltz. Consulting Psychologists Press. (work-related behavior or beliefs)

Online Counseling

Computer-assisted career guidance systems may be used effectively without the guidance of a career counselor (Garis & Bowlsbey, 1984; Sampson & Stripling, 1979). Career assessments commonly used during an individual counseling appointment such as the MBTI and SII require professional interpretation by a career counselor. The assessments that provide diagnostic measures of client career maturity, progress, or satisfaction in the career planning process are not commonly used in the career exploration process, but may be used to evaluate career center services such as individual career counseling or credit career planning courses (Garis & Bowlsbey, 1984).

Job Search Services

Herr, Rayman, & Garis (1993) noted that job search services provided by a career center might vary widely depending on the following factors:

- College/university size and enrollment
- Geographic location (urban, rural)

- Centralized or decentralized model
- Academic programs offered

Regardless of these factors, job search services (historically referred to as "placement") should be considered part of a process. This process would include a range of services to assist clients in the implementation of career plans throughout their academic career, not just an event that occurs at the end of the senior year.

Job search services at the career center typically include the following:

- On-campus recruiting
- On-campus and regional job fairs
- Alumni career network
- Credential files

On-Campus Recruiting

On-campus recruiting provides an opportunity for career centers to connect student and alumni clients with representatives of business, industry, and government. These services also keep the career center in contact with employers and create a high profile for the career center. Career centers should have a well-organized system in place to notify and provide clients access to opportunities for on-campus interviews (Herr et al., 1993). Many centers use computerized systems to manage the on-campus interview process, including employer information and candidate notification and selection. Interviews can be "open" (first-come, first-serve basis) or "prescreened" (employer selects specific interviewees from the applicant pool). The physical setting for on-campus interviews should be quiet, private, and professional. The career center should maintain the professionalism of on-campus recruiting by providing clients with adequate interview preparation and by providing an orientation to recruiters (Herr et al., 1993).

On-Campus Job Fairs and Regional Job Fairs

Career and job fairs may be sponsored by the career center or a combination of organizations (a consortium). Some larger colleges and universities host a number of career and job fairs on campus, while other smaller colleges and universities may be more likely to participate in regional consortium fairs, whereby a number of partners collaborate to coordinate and host the fair. For example, a group of 44 colleges and universities in western Pennsylvania collaborate to host the biannual WestPACS Job & Internship Fair.

Employer and organization attendance at fairs varies widely depending on a variety of factors that include size and location of the campus, range and quality of academic offerings, and the recruiting organization's budget. Because of declining recruiting budgets, the increase in online applications and other "virtual" recruiting mechanisms has forced employing organizations to be selective in the number of colleges and universities at which they choose to recruit.

One disadvantage regarding on-campus recruiting and job fairs is that the types of employers and positions for which they are recruiting may be narrow in scope and may not represent the wide variety of majors offered at the college or university. Therefore, in order to accommodate the career exploration and job search needs of all majors, it is best for the career center to host a job fair that provides a broad range of employment options.

Alumni Career Network

Most career centers offer online job postings, referral of candidate resumes to employers, and resume books. A variety of vendors provides systems to manage these services electronically. Because it is widely held that at least 75% of job seekers find jobs through personal networking, many colleges and universities have established alumni career networks to assist their students and job-seeking alumni. These networks can be offered online for ease of access and may be sponsored through the career center or the alumni association.

Credential Files

Some employers (i.e., school districts) and graduate schools often prefer confidential recommendations to be managed and stored by the career center. With the increase of online portfolio management systems, many career centers have reduced or eliminated their credential file management service.

Career Information

The career center is well positioned to serve as a source of career information because it bridges the gap between academia and business, industry and government (Herr et al., 1993). Every career center should gather and maintain career information accessible to clients and stakeholders (including faculty, prospective students, and parents) for use in career exploration and planning. Because employment and organizational information is widely available on the Internet, many career centers have reduced or eliminated the traditional "career library" shelves of books and periodicals. Rather, they market their websites for easier access to resources. Career information offered by the career center could include:

- Academic information
- Self-assessment and career exploration information
- Internship and summer job information
- Career/occupational information
- Graduate/professional school information
- Job search information regarding resumes, cover letters, interviewing, networking, etc.
- Company/organization information
- Career-related periodicals and web sites
- Job posting sites

Programming and Outreach

Because it is not mandatory in most cases for clients to use the services of the career center, programming and outreach efforts are crucial. Career outreach programs typically are brief (one to three hours) and are primarily information-oriented. The goals of career outreach programs may be to provide an opportunity for the career center to promote its services and programs, to introduce clients to the career planning or job search process, and to provide information about a specific career planning issue to a group (Herr et al., 1993). Tailored to each audience, outreach program topics may include:

- Career center orientation
- Self-assessment of skills, interests, and values
- Exploring linkages between majors and careers
- How to find an internship or cooperative education position
- Resume and cover letter preparation
- Interview skills
- Job search strategies, including networking
- Professional business etiquette
- Orientation to on-campus recruiting
- Graduate/professional school admission
- Transition from school to work

Herr, Rayman, & Garis (1993) noted that outreach programs allow the career center to gain access to students and can be offered in a variety of settings, including:

- Academic classes
- Student clubs and organizations, including Greek organizations
- Residence halls
- Campus events (i.e., orientation, activity fair)
- Faculty and student leader training/orientation programs (i.e., new faculty orientation; or training sessions for campus tour guides, peer mentors, and resident assistants)
- Community organizations

Outreach programs can be more successful when the career center partners with specific offices and groups on campus such as the student orientation office, alumni relations, international student services, support centers for student athletes, returning adult student services, disabled student services, admissions, honors program, and so on. For example, CalU of PA's office of Career Services is partnering with the student orientation office to host a "Major Dilemma" fair where both prospective and current students can speak with upperclassmen and faculty to explore academic majors and career options (CalU of PA, 2010).

Some colleges and universities offer a career planning and implementation course for credit, taught by career center staff or a faculty member. Such courses offer several advantages, including enhancing the professional credibility of the career center and its staff, enhancing decision-making skills, and facilitating the student career-planning progress (Bartsch & Hackett, 1979; Garis & Niles, 1990). Some career courses are focused on freshmen and sophomores, with the goal of facilitating the self-assessment and career exploration process, while other courses are focused on juniors and seniors, with the goal of facilitating the career implementation process.

ADDITIONAL SERVICES

Experiential Education Support Services

With the increased focus on the value of experiential learning, many career centers provide support services to clients interested in obtaining professionally relevant experience. These services may range from assistance with resume preparation and interview skills, to assistance in identifying and applying to appropriate internship sites.

Herr, Rayman, and Garis (1993) noted that experiential education programs may include any of the following:

- Internships—semester or summer experience; typically includes academic credit; may be paid or unpaid
- Cooperative education—typically an alternating work-study program where students rotate semesters in the classroom and in the work environment; includes both credit and pay
- Externships/job shadowing—brief exposure (one day to two weeks); usually not for credit and not paid
- Summer jobs

Benchmark studies show a steady increase in the number of career centers providing students with internship and co-op assistance. In 1975, just 26% of offices said they provided this service. In 2004, more than 85% of offices said they did so (NACE, 2005).

Alumni Career Services

Students are the primary clients of career centers; however, some colleges and universities are experiencing increased demand from their alumni for assistance with career change or job search assistance. This requires that a career center develop a well-defined policy regarding response to alumni inquiries, including service content and fees, if applicable (Herr et al., 1993).

Due to decreased funding for higher education, some colleges and universities facing budget cuts have realized that an investment in providing career services to alumni may result in alumni engagement with the university. For example, CalU of PA, as part of the "CAL U for Life" initiative, provided funding for an alumni career counselor and an employer development coordinator, housed in the office of Career Services, to provide lifelong career services at no cost to alumni (CalU of PA, 2010).

Some career centers have expanded their services to alumni by collaborating with the alumni office or by charging alumni for services. Career services for alumni typically may be provided through the alumni office, through the career center, or through a combination of offices. Herr, Rayman, and Garis (1993) noted that alumni career services can include:

- Individual counseling
- Career planning and job search workshops offered on-site, regionally, or online
- Online job postings, career planning, and job search resources
- Newsletters

- Computer-based networking and resume referral
- On-site and regional career and job fairs and networking opportunities

TOP TRENDS AND ISSUES

According to the Future Trends Survey conducted by the National Association of Colleges and Employers (NACE) Future Trends Committee in 2009, career services professionals reported that they believe budget changes will be the most influential trend in the near future. Following is a summary of the top three trend rankings by college and university career centers (NACE, 2009).

Trend	% Ranked 1 or 2	% Ranked #1
Budget changes	49.6%	32.5%
Technology	46.3	23.0
Assessment metrics	37.7	15.4

Responses differed among respondents from private versus public colleges and universities, and four-year versus two-year colleges. Private colleges ranked technology as the highest-ranking trend, while public universities ranked budget changes as the highest-ranking trend.

Budget Changes

According to the NACE (2009), more than half of career centers faced a decrease in their 2009–2010 operating budgets. Career centers are finding they need to do more with less. In response to funding cuts, many career centers have adopted fees for employers (i.e., for career fairs or advertising). A minority of centers have adopted fees for students and alumni (i.e., for administration of assessments).

Technology

According to career services practitioners who responded to the NACE 2009 Future Trends survey, social networking sites such as Facebook® and LinkedIn®, and communication media such as YouTube® and Twitter®, are the most important technologies that will affect career centers in the near future.

Technology can be used to reach alumni who are outside the campus' geographic reach. For example, the University of Illinois Alumni Association's Alumni Career Center uses e-mail and the phone for advising, conference calls, and webinars for workshops; it has also enhanced an online virtual career center for alumni (NACE, 2010b).

Online and virtual recruiting will grow in popularity, especially in the early stages of recruiting, resulting in direct interaction between employers and students (NACE, 2009). There is not a clear consensus regarding how this will affect college recruiting and the role of the career center. Some respondents are concerned that career centers will be by-passed in the recruiting process and that there will be fewer employers recruiting on campus and at job fairs, while others see a continued need for high-touch, face-to-face recruiting after the initial interview (NACE, 2009).

Balancing high-tech and high-touch methods is perhaps the most challenging issue related to technology. It is important for career services professionals to stay abreast of changes in technology and to understand the sophisticated use of electronic tools and resources.

Assessment Metrics

Assessment metrics, or measuring the results of career center programs and services and demonstrating the value of the career services function, is a critical issue for career centers. It can be challenging for career services professionals to identify and implement measures that demonstrate their value because there is no simple way that will accurately demonstrate the value of the career center's services.

For example, placement statistics (i.e., the number of new graduates employed within a certain period of time after graduation) is not a reliable measure of the effectiveness of a career center's programs because there are many factors outside the circle of influence of the career center that have an impact on whether graduates find employment. Such factors may include the economy, quality of and demand for the graduate's academic program, and the graduate's willingness to relocate to find employment.

As a result, more career centers are focusing on assessing student learning outcomes: what are students learning because of using the services and attending the programs offered through the career center? For example, to assess student learning in a career development course at Barry University, an instructor designed resume, cover letter, and interviewing rubrics, or "grids." The instructor used the rubrics to determine whether the students' level of knowledge and skill has improved by comparing resumes, cover letters, and interview quality before and after students have completed the career development course (NACE, 2006).

OTHER TRENDS

NACE (2005) provides further insight into the issues and trends identified by career center staff. These trends include strengthening the image of the career center within its institution, branding the institution and career center to employers, understanding risk management and legal issues related to the recruiting and hiring process, and working with faculty and other campus stakeholders (such as university development and alumni relations) to assist students, alumni, and employers with job search and recruitment.

According to career center respondents, collaborating with other groups to promote or facilitate the work of career services is increasingly important (NACE, 2009). Partner options, ranked in order of the number and percentage of respondents choosing a particular partner option, include:

- Alumni relations
- Faculty
- Academic Advising
- Development
- Multi-school consortium
- Professional or trade association
- Another college career center
- For-profit counseling center

Collaborating with employers, alumni, and parents to provide experiential education opportunities such as job shadowing, co-op, and internships is a trend that will continue to grow. Employers want employees who are fully trained and ready to work, and increasingly utilize experiential programs as a means for identifying and hiring candidates.

Career centers will continue to be seen as important partners in the hiring process if they are adaptable and if they work in conjunction with other stakeholders in the campus community to meet the needs of both recruiters and students (NACE, 2009).

REFERENCES

Bartsch, K., & Hackett, G. (1979). Effects of a decision making course on locus of control, conceptualization and career planning. *Journal of College Student Personnel, 20,* 230–235.

California University of Pennsylvania. (2010). *Career services.* Retrieved from http://www.calu.edu/current-students/career-services/career-services/index.htm

Council for the Advancement of Standards. (1986). *CAS standards and guidelines for student services/development programs.* Washington, DC: Council for the Advancement of Standards.

Garis, J. W., & Bowlsbey, J. H. (1984, December). DISCOVER and the counselor: Their effect upon college student career planning progress. *ACT Research Report.* (85).

Garis, J. W., & Niles, S. G. (1990). The separate and combined effects of SIGI or DISCOVER and a career planning course on undecided university students. *Career Development Quarterly, 38*(3), 261–274.

Giordani, P. (2006). *National Association of Colleges and Employers through the years: The history and origins of the association.* NACE Journal. Retrieved from http://www. naceweb.org/Journal/2005october/National_Association_of_Colleges_and_ Employers_History_Origins/

Herr, E. L., Rayman, J. R., & Garis, J. W. (1993). *Handbook for the college and university career center.* Westport, CT: Greenwood Press.

National Association of Colleges and Employers. (2005). Into the future: Top issues and trends for career services and college recruiting. *NACE Journal, 66*(1), 27–32.

National Association of Colleges and Employers. (2006). *Rubrics cubed: Three rubrics to help you determine student learning outcomes in career development courses.* Retrieved from http://www.naceweb.org/Publications/Journal

National Association of Colleges and Employers. (2009). Looking ahead: Highlights from the future trends survey. *NACE Journal, 70*(1), 22–28.

National Association of Colleges and Employers. (2010a). *What does the typical career center offer?* Retrieved from http://www.naceweb.org/Publications/Spotlight_ Online/2010/0120/What_Does_the_Typical_Career_Center_Offer_.aspx

National Association of Colleges and Employers. (2010b). *How to handle the increase in alumni seeking career services.* Retrieved from http://www.naceweb.org/ spotlightonline/121008c/Alumni_Seeking_Career_Services/?referal=knowl edgecenter&menuid=0

National Association of Colleges and Employers. (2010c). *Principles for professional practice.* Retrieved from http://www.naceweb.org/principles/

Oregon State University. (2010). *University exploratory studies program.* Retrieved from http://oregonstate.edu/uesp/

Sampson, J. P., & Stripling, R. O. (1979). Strategies for counselor intervention with a computer-assisted career guidance system. *Vocational Guidance Quarterly, 27,* 230–238.

SECTION III

CAREER DEVELOPMENT
IN GRADUATE LEVEL EDUCATION

CHAPTER 7

USING CAREER DEVELOPMENT THEORY AND PRACTICE TO MEET THE NEEDS OF MASTER'S STUDENTS

Matthew W. Ishler
Pennsylvania State University

The career development needs of master's level students are diverse and broad. In an era of increasing enrollment in master's level programs (Bell, 2010; Kim, 2005), what are the career development needs of this population of students and how are educational institutions and career services staff meeting these needs? There is not a great amount of research on the career development needs of master's level students (Conrad, Duren, & Haworth, 1998; Luzzo, 2000). This chapter will introduce some of the common career development concerns of master's level graduate students, highlight strategies to address those needs, and offer a context of career development theory within which master's students and career counselors can work together to address and resolve career development questions.

Career Development in Higher Education, pages 139–156
Copyright © 2011 by Information Age Publishing
All rights of reproduction in any form reserved.

CAREER DEVELOPMENT AND IDENTITY

The development of a career identity is rooted in the constantly evolving self-concept (Super, 1990). Master's degree students, by definition, are making an investment in their career identity. Students typically enroll in a master's degree program with specific expectations regarding what the master's program will add to their career identity or career development (Luzzo, 1999). Acknowledging the hopes and goals that students hold while pursuing their master's degrees will enable career counselors to collaborate with the students to design a plan to reach those goals. Part of this planning process should include identifying and developing strategies to address perceived barriers to career development. Ninety percent of master's level students who obtain their degree terminate their education with the master's degree (Conrad et al., 1998). A starting point for providing career services to master's level students is to understand each student's expectations, goals, beliefs, experiences, and questions that have led them to pursue a master's degree.

Rationale for Master's Degree Study

Individuals enroll in a master's degree program for a variety of reasons, often including the following:

- To change careers and career direction
- To attain a career goal which requires a master's degree as a minimum educational standard
- To build field-specific knowledge
- To attain a level of leadership or authority within a field of study or work
- To develop professionally and enhance one's base of knowledge, skill, and experience
- To increase potential income and job security by advancing one's education
- To increase knowledge and skills, and learn to apply recent developments in a field, continuing one's education.

Understanding the rationale for master's level study informs career development work, enabling the student and the career counselor to identify goals for their work together. The goals may often relate to the range of career development needs expressed by master's level students.

CAREER DEVELOPMENT NEEDS

The career development needs of master's students, however, cannot be easily summarized. For example, Galles, Lenz, and Keller (2010) indicate that career counselors may perceive graduate students as having fewer career development needs than undergraduate students, because master's students are older than traditional college undergraduate students, and graduate students are presumed to have made an informed and intentional decision to pursue a specific career through earning a post-bachelor's degree. Luzzo (2000) notes that graduate students may be as open to career exploration as undergraduate students are presumed to be, adding that many students come to a master's program because of perceptions about the economy or the challenge of earning a job with a bachelor's degree.

Not all master's level students present the same career development questions, or address those questions and develop career goals at the same pace (Luzzo, 2000). In a study comparing the career development needs of graduate students to the career development needs of undergraduate students, McCaffrey, Miller, & Winston (1984) noted that although graduate students pursue a graduate degree to acquire specialized knowledge and training, they possess career development concerns and questions that are similar to undergraduate students. Master's students have a need to clarify and explore a range of career goals (Busacca & Wester, 2006; Luzzo, 1999). An assessment of graduate student needs conducted by Rimmer, Lammert, and McClain (1982) found that the greatest need that graduate students identify is for career planning and placement assistance.

From my experience providing more than nine years of career counseling to undergraduate and graduate students, master's students have certain career development needs:

- Understanding oneself—identifying interests, values, abilities, motivation, and goals;
- Occupational and career information—accessing resources that contain information about careers, industries, employment options, and career paths;
- Examining decision-making—reviewing the process used to make decisions, and exploring any hesitancy, fear, or perceived barriers to making decisions;
- The translation of academic focus areas to career possibilities— questioning how master's program curriculum, research topics, or practical and field experiences open a range of employment and career options, as well as how one can apply what may be extremely focused master's level academic training to a very broad range of career possibilities;

- Identifying and addressing career barriers—exploring the perceptions about oneself, about careers, and about the process of career development that may inhibit the exploration or pursuit of career goals;
- Building experience and competence—pursuing practical experiences designed to approximate future possible career directions, gaining "real world" experiences;
- Creating and managing a professional network—establishing one's identity in a field of study or work through connection with professionals possessing similar interests, experiences, and goals who can provide mentorship, open professional opportunities, and can form a base of support throughout one's study and career;
- Strategic job search plans—the development of a plan to achieve short and long-term employment goals, utilizing a variety of job search strategies and techniques;
- Creating and refining application materials—drafting a resume, curriculum vitae, cover letter, and related application materials that can introduce one's career goals and relevant education, experience, and accomplishments;
- Interviewing strategies—intentionally communicating and demonstrating relevant skills, experiences, accomplishments, and goals while highlighting one's interest, skill, and personality as related to the desired career goal;
- Negotiation strategies—developing an approach to negotiating employment offers, to understanding the offer and advocating for oneself from the time that the offer of employment is made. This includes learning how to ask for relocation assistance, a specific start-date, or a higher starting salary;
- Personal and career goal integration—resolving conflicts that emerge between personal goals and career-related goals. Conflicts may arise related to personal goals such as the desire to live in a specific location or relationships with family, friends, and significant others, and may necessitate compromises between personal and career goals;
- To Ph.D. or not to Ph.D.? —experiencing success as a master's level student can open opportunities to further pursue one's education. Master's level students benefit from reflecting upon the commitment, opportunities, and sacrifices related to the pursuit (or decision not to pursue) a doctorate degree.

To address how career counselors and career services centers address such diverse needs, the remaining portion of the chapter will be broken into two areas: Career counseling theories and approaches that are applicable to these needs, and Career Counseling Services capable of meeting the career development needs of master's level students.

CAREER COUNSELING THEORIES AND APPROACHES

Caple (1995) identified approaches to providing counseling to graduate students that emphasize attending to students' emerging autonomy, intellectual development, activity in creating meaning in their life, and addressing conflicts of values and expectations that may arise during graduate study. Presented here are several theories and approaches that offer a general framework for conceptualizing career development needs of master's students.

Super's Life Span and Life Stage Career Development Theory

Investigating the life role and life stage of master's level students enables counselors to understand the salience and value attributed to the roles that students perform while progressing through career development stages (Sharf, 2002). Master's level students may occupy a number of different roles and may aspire to add new roles. Roles such as student, employee, volunteer, parent, leisurite will be of varying degrees of importance to master's level students. Counselors can measure the importance of these roles through inquiring about role participation, commitment, knowledge, and value expectations (Sharf, 2002). Master's level students may have modified or concluded their participation in one or several roles to assume their graduate study. Graduate study may apply pressure and stress to the pursuit or attainment of specific life roles. While completing a master's degree, graduate students may be engaged in the process of identifying their preferred balance of multiple life roles, and graduate program participation can lead to a re-orientation of role priorities.

Super (1990) outlined and described the career development stages of growth, exploration, establishment, maintenance, and disengagement. Common stages experienced during a master's degree program may include the exploration, establishment, and maintenance stages. The precise stage will depend on the student and may be related to the rationale for graduate program participation. It is also important to note that individuals may cycle or recycle through multiple stages during their career development and master's degree programs, as new opportunities and career directions are discovered, investigated, and selected. For example, McCaffrey, Miller, and Winston (1984) found that graduate students continue to be involved in self assessment (of interests, values, and abilities), career decision-making, and career exploration. Within exploration, students reflect upon their interests, abilities, and values as related to career and educational opportunities and goals. One of the objectives of this exploration is to apply self information toward specific career goals. While specifying career goals, students may confirm academic and career choices that have been made through gaining field specific experience, increasing career knowledge, or expanding the array of identifiable career options. As career goals are identified, plans to achieve these goals will be constructed and implemented.

Master's level students may also be experiencing the establishment stage—getting established in one's selected field of work. This stage carries a connotation of career decisions being somewhat stable across time, the focus of career development becoming more specific, and individuals feeing secure within a career focus and maybe seeking advancement options. While career counselors may assume that master's students are frequently in this stage, research indicates that they may continue to explore self-information as well as career options, even after enrolling in a master's program (Luzzo, 2000; Rimmer et al., 1982).

Master's level students may often seek reassurance from faculty, peers, and from career counselors, among others, to determine whether their academic and professional goals are attainable (Busacca & Wester, 2006). Advancement interests may draw many students to master's degree programs with goals of enhancing one's knowledge, skill, and experience in order to open up a new level of career opportunities. Career counselors working with students focused upon career advancement would be wise to explore with students the likelihood of advancement, its benefits, and its potential risks or costs. Finally, through the maintenance stage, master's degree students may be updating their skills and knowledge to maintain their position or increase their capacity to contribute to an employer. Similarly, the maintenance stage can include an innovation stage where one may generate and make new contributions to a professional field. Master's students in the maintenance stage may be motivated by perceived threats to their position, including a threat to fail to achieve a certain goal or level of accomplishment.

Existential Theory

Cohen (2003) identified four stages of an existential career development process that can be applied to the career development frame of master's level students. The four stages are responsibility, evaluation, action, and re-evaluation. In the responsibility stage, master's students become aware of the need to create a plan from a vast amount of options and possible career directions. Existential anxiety and career indecision may appear when students grapple with the struggle to take ownership of career decisions, or choose to avoid the need to make a career choice. Recognizing that responsibility for vocational choices rests with the student is an important component of the career development process: owning the need to make career decisions. In an existential framework, the need to make career decisions is connected to an individual's definition of meaning and purpose in the world.

In the evaluation stage, individuals measure and compare identified career options against their definition of a meaningful and purposeful existence. This necessitates an exploration of master's students' perceptions of meaning and purpose in their own lives. Meaningful work also connotes an authentic existence—acknowledging the reality of one's identity and examining the individual that one can become—further extending the potential to live according to one's intrinsic values, interests, abilities, and motivations. The action stage involves taking ownership of career decisions, examining the decision-making process, closely looking at the factors that lead one to make or to avoid decisions, and communicating decisions to others as a means of expressing one's authentic career identity. The re-evaluation stage involves examining whether selected career directions and opportunities provide authentic existence, personal meaning, and purpose. Master's level students may question whether their academic and career goals connect to their definition of life's meaning and purpose, or they may have experiences during their graduate program which make them question or redefine life's meaning and purpose. At these points, career counselors can assist students in clarifying their definition of an authentic, meaningful, and purposeful career and life.

Career counselors working with master's level students may recognize the signs of an existential vacuum (Cohen, 2003), which include frustration or inability to identify meaning and purpose in one's career. Students may come to a master's program with goals of living a more authentic life and moving closer to their potential. Career counselors can fulfill an important need in this student population by providing counseling during moments where academic and career goals are not aligning with one's definition of a life of meaning and purpose. Existential career counseling involves working with clients to understand their own picture of their potential, and helping students to recognize whether they are fulfilling their potential or not, and what can be done to reconcile any differences. An existential counseling approach to providing career counseling to master's level students recognizes the choice and freedom that these students have to develop their own life purpose and career path. This freedom leads into the next theory, which emphasizes the idea of constructing a life and career.

Narrative Career Counseling Theory

Graduate students are committing to their own intellectual development through their degree programs. Along with this intellectual development, graduate students are also experiencing an emerging sense of autonomy within their field and within their lives (Caple, 1995). Throughout a graduate program, students are involved in the process of creating meaning by applying their learning to broader themes of purpose and achievement in their lives. Graduate students also must negotiate their own internal expectations of themselves with the expectations placed upon them by others (peers, advisers, family members, supervisees, students, and supervisors). Narrative approaches to career counseling can provide a strategy to focus on the meaning and experience of career and life development, through the experience of the student (Caple, 1995).

The narrative approach offers an extension of this theory through examining how individuals come to perceive themselves and their career experiences (Young & Valach, 2004). The sharing of the narrative can take the form of counseling dialogue, written life-stories or biographies, or the identification of key life turning points—moments when life options were opened or closed (Byars-Winston & Fouad, 2006). Narrative approaches to career development provide a vehicle for discussing and understanding the inception and evolution of individual needs and goals (Savickas as cited in Bujold, 2004). The presence of an established life narrative can serve as a biographical bridge to maintain continuity and a sense of self amid challenges like starting a master's level academic program, starting a new job, or losing a job. Within the client and counselor partnership, the client's life story is shared. This sharing allows for both client and counselor to define the central themes of meaning, purpose, challenge, relationships, and choices.

Within narrative career development theory, counselor and client collaborate to investigate how beliefs and values were created through the stories of past experiences, decisions, life roles, role models, relationships, daydreams, and sacrifices. Narrative approaches involve asking the client to identify the stories that have shaped his or her definition of self. This sense of the interconnection of past, present, and future will provide clients with the chance to define and live a more authentic life (Brott, 2005).

A narrative approach to career counseling can serve master's students through examining their perceptions of how work contributes to individuals' sense of life satisfaction (Blustein, Schultheiss, & Flum, 2004). Placing emphasis on the interdependence of career with other life roles, needs, and behaviors can offer a much deeper context for exploring career anxiety, indecision, and transition (Blustein et al., 2004). Building upon the theoretical foundations of Glasser, Adler, and Super, career and life narratives strive to understand individuals' sense of meaning and life goals as applied through various roles.

As these stories are shared and discussed, an opportunity exists for the counselor to offer a new perspective, to question, to challenge, and to ultimately re-construct the meanings and interpretations of events, with the goal of recognizing themes and patterns. With these themes (such as service, leadership, and belonging) and patterns of action, the client and counselor construct a new conceptualization of self, a future-story (Brott, 2005). Bujold (2004) emphasizes the relevance of narrative approaches in instilling a sense of creativity as a means to address career challenges, barriers, and unanticipated events. Severy (2008) added to this concept by examining how individuals narrate their own meaning through the definition of career—reflecting on the entirety of life experience and identifying long-established role models, themes, patterns, ways of interacting, and ways of seeking and finding fulfillment. Authenticity and life themes are investigated as master's students reflect upon their own life stories as they make career choices. Exploring with clients how they prioritize and meet their own needs for survival, love, belonging, power, freedom, and fun can lead to understanding the clients' sources of motivation, as well as how clients can act to construct and live a more desirable life story (Brott, 2005). Brott (2005) also encourages the application of narrative counseling with particular attention to role expectations as developed and reinforced through gender, cultural stereotypes, and negative self-thoughts.

Solution Focused Theory

The solution focused approach to career counseling is an extension of the constructivist theory in that it uses a strengths-based approach to develop and attain future career goals. Rather than focusing on past experiences and challenges, the solution focus involves discussing current challenges while examining specific strengths that the student possesses and demonstrates that they can be applied to specific challenges. For example, master's students may perceive that they have made a significant career planning error if they believe that they do not match the passion and commitment level of their peers, or perhaps if their interests do not align with a specific faculty member or adviser. A solution focused approach to career counseling can normalize these perceptions as part of the developmental growth that occurs during graduate study, and the counselor and student can identify strengths to apply toward overcoming these perceptions. Solution Focused Therapy also involves examining exceptions or circumstances where a specific problem is not occurring. For example, if a master's student believes that he or she is not motivated or intelligent enough to be in a master's level program, the career counselor operating from a solution focus may ask about instances when the student feels positive about his or her own intelligence or motivation level (Burwell & Chen, 2006). This collaborative process leads the counselor and client to discover and discuss alternative attitudes, thoughts, or approaches to a career problem or challenge; ultimately, a new perspective and attitude emerges toward oneself and one's graduate study.

A solution-based approach can be used to broaden and expand the number of career alternatives available to a master's student. Counselors encourage and compliment the skills that a master's student is using in career development, even if the student is not recognizing these skills. Skills such as organizing a research project, serving as a teaching assistant, evaluating peer or undergraduate student work, and networking within professional conferences can be transferred to the career exploration and job search process. The counselor can play a vital role in helping the master's student broaden and explore career goals by affirming, complimenting, and building a bridge between the specific work completed within a master's program and the skills that will lead the student to securing and succeeding in a career. Master's students may perceive their skills as too specific or narrow to seek work with a variety of employers in a wide array of industries. Recognizing the strengths and attributes as well as asking questions about what clients would choose if perceived barriers did not exist leads to a sharper focus and optimistic outlook that clients can author and take control over, enacting solutions to their own career challenges and barriers (Basham & Buchanan, 2009).

These specific theories can be integrated to meet the diverse needs of the master's student. Utilizing more than one theoretical approach will provide career counselors with a more holistic view of the expectations, goals, and perceived barriers that the student is addressing. Career counselors can apply a narrative approach to investigate and explore existential themes from the perspective of the student. Similarly, a solution focused approach provides an opportunity for the student to acknowledge strengths and apply them toward career exploration and career development tasks. What, if any, are the past work experiences of the master's level student, and how did this experience (or lack thereof) influence current thoughts and attitudes about careers, career possibilities, and career decision-making? How have career alternatives been explored, and what process of decision-making was used to activate career plans? As students move through Super's stages, counselors can understand how the student experiences developmental tasks and how the student is hoping to develop the self concept through the pursuit of a master's degree. Building upon these theories, specific services can assist master's students in their career development.

CAREER COUNSELING SERVICES

Careers counselors and career services professionals must take an active role in communicating that they intend to provide career counseling services specifically to master's students. Career counselors should ensure that website information and marketing materials indicate resources and services for master's students, highlighting the relevance of career counseling, educational workshops and programs, and recruiting opportunities. Career reference library material and career information sources should also reflect the diverse career exploration and decision-making needs of master's level students (Galles et al., 2010). Furthermore, career development workshops, placement services, and career exploration activities can be designed and targeted to address the diverse career development needs of master's students.

For some students, the completion of the master's program may be the first time that formal education programs will not be the immediate next step toward reaching a goal. This introduces a question of how a student transitions from being successful in an academic environment to being successful in a career and work environment. Meeting with a career counselor who is trained in counseling and career development can offer the master's level student the opportunity to reflect upon experiences, to create and communicate goals and objectives, and to strategically build a plan to achieve goals.

Master's level students direct graduate education toward a specific and narrow focus (Basham & Buchanan, 2009). Career counselors can play an important role in assisting master's students in examining and understanding how students can apply their experience and accomplishments to a broad array and wide range of career goals. Career assessment instruments such as the Strong Interest Inventory, the Self Directed Search, and Values Card Sort, among others, afford the chance for the counselor and client to collaborate on identifying career themes and preferences. With these preferences and themes, counselors and clients can begin to tentatively identify areas for career investigation. Soliciting input and inquiring about the meaning that clients attribute to career assessment results can help the counselor to understand the perspective of the student, and can allow the student to give voice to possible career directions that may confirm earlier interests and thoughts or may introduce new areas of exploration. Given the life experience, specialized education, and motivation for pursuing graduate study, it is important that career counselors respect the autonomy of master's level students in interpreting and acting upon career assessment results.

Group career counseling is another approach that is available to provide career development to master's level students. Through psychoeducational and career development process groups, graduate students work within a group of peer students to define and pursue their career goals. In a group format, students experience the benefit of sharing their experience and questions with others, recognizing that they are not alone in questioning or pursuing a specific path. Groups can be focused around career exploration strategies or job search strategies, and can be organized around career interest area such as social and human service, entrepreneurship, consulting, education, or fine arts. Groups can serve to reduce the isolation that master's students may feel within their department or cohort when each individual group member shares and receives input from others. The group counseling modality can add a level of accountability as students hold each other accountable and facilitators introduce questions for reflection and discussion. Assigning homework to the group such as writing about possible career directions or identifying networking sources can allow for independent career development work between group meetings. Ultimately, groups serve as a mode to enhance students' career maturity and capacity for career decision-making (Pyle, 2007).

Workshops specifically tailored to the needs of master's level students can further serve students in a group setting. Workshops commonly include topics such as: Resume and Curriculum Vitae (CV) writing, Interviewing Skills, Job Search Strategies, and Networking Guides. With understanding of the career goals of master's students, these workshop topics can be tailored to address the specific and common questions that master's students will present. Workshops can address specific areas of the career development process, such as how to begin a self assessment of career interests, values, and abilities; how to transfer experiences, abilities, and specialty areas to a broad array of career goals; or how to schedule and execute a job search plan. Workshops should also include and reference the variety of career services available to graduate students, which may include individual or group career counseling, as well as options to attend career fairs and campus recruiting activities. Career counselors can formalize workshop offerings by creating a credit-bearing elective course for master's students focused on the career development process of self-assessment, occupational information gathering, integration of self and career information, and development of a plan to revise and pursue tentative career goals.

Recruiting activities offer an opportunity for career counselors to advocate for the needs of master's level students. Encouraging employers to include examples of opportunities for master's level students and making these examples visible to them can increase the array of career options that master's students will consider. Master's students often perceive that recruiters who are visiting campus may only have opportunities for bachelor's degree holders and may need encouragement to participate in recruiting events such as career fairs or on-campus interviewing programs. Galles and colleagues (2010) encourage career counselors to consider planning a graduate student-focused career fair, involving recruiters with a specific interest in master's and doctoral students. Career counselors can serve an important function by addressing misconceptions and fears about whether employers are interested in candidates with master's degrees. Career counselors can rehearse with master's level students how they can present their education, their experience, and their goals while asking about available or emerging opportunities. This type of activity may not lead to an immediate employment offer, but it may lead to the type of incidental contact and conversation that can create a networking contact, a point of reference, or an advocate within an organization who can provide further information about opportunities and needed/desired skills.

For master's students, approaching recruiting events with questions about positions that can utilize a specialized knowledge or experience will open up a chance for students to describe their degrees and experiences in ways that are relevant to employers. Career counselors can enhance the likelihood of these conversations by educating employers who frequently recruit students on campus about the variety and content of master's degree programs, perhaps scheduling specific networking or information sessions for students and employers to learn about each others' goals, opportunities, and experience.

Furthermore, tracking data related to where master's students earn employment can lead to being able to offer evidence of the range of career options available to master's level graduates. Offering this type of information to master's level students, faculty members, and advisers enhances the connection among the career services staff and the students, faculty, and administrators within master's programs. While students should not be encouraged to base their career decisions on this data, it can provide a sampling of how graduates of specific master's programs have transferred their educational experiences and previous work experiences into a variety of career opportunities. Career counselors are in a prime position to bring employers and students together, through informal networking sessions as well as classroom presentations. Giving master's students the chance to hear about the post-graduation experiences of professionals in a variety of fields can help students recognize how others transition from school to work.

Career counselors play a role not only in educating students about how to network, but also in working with students to identify networking contacts. Networking involves creating and sustaining relationships based upon shared interest, commitment, and a desire to collaborate or share information and resources. Career counselors assist students in examining their skills and accomplishments and how they could be applied across multiple positions, organizations, and industries. For example, master's students may have experience managing projects and supervising the work of others. This could be applied to settings as diverse as retail management, consulting, employee training and development, or sales. Career counselors can help students to recognize that pursuing employment is not an instant process, but rather takes time and a strategy to communicate with people who may be in a position to offer information, advice, mentorship, or referrals.

Networking can be enhanced through membership and participation in professional organizations, which are often identifiable by field of study or career interest area. Attending regional and national conferences provides a forum for learning how academic interests can connect to professional employment opportunities and careers. Conferences also provide a venue to build relationships, discuss potential collaborations, and present master's student accomplishments. Ultimately, networking may lead to opportunities for master's students to pursue specific internship or field experiences, which increase students' exposure to career opportunities.

Master's level internships and field experiences provide opportunities for students to apply what they are learning and experiencing to a variety of career settings and challenges. Through experience, students can transfer the specialized knowledge, theories, and experiences associated with being master's students to the varied and complex challenges that a short-term career commitment can present. Discussing goals for field and internship experiences, preparing students for what to expect, and reflecting with them after the experience are meaningful interventions to utilize with master's students. Career counselors should prepare to assist students in seeking experiences that may not traditionally or historically be related to their specialized field of study. Connecting students' motivations for graduate study with their internship and field experiences can be some of the ways that conversations about goals and career paths are opened. Internships afford students the opportunity to apply their similar academic paths in very diverse environments. Master's students report that "real world" experiences in a variety of settings provide a powerful learning and professional development opportunity for students (Conrad et al., 1998).

Additionally, career counselors can enhance the career development experience of master's level students through forming collaborative relationships with faculty members who advise master's level students. Master's level faculty advisers provide formal as well as informal mentoring, which includes conversations about career development, career choices, and career decision-making. Advisers may offer field specific resources, knowledge of organizations that have employed graduates, and possible sources of internships and full-time employment options. Career counselors working with faculty advisers can present the benefits of master's students meeting with career counselors, such as looking broadly at career options and goals, developing a comprehensive job search and career development plan, and rehearsing and refining the application materials and interview strategies that students will use.

The benefits that career counselors can offer to master's students include confidentiality and objectivity. Master's students may feel pressured by faculty advisers to pursue a course of study or career path, and career counselors can offer an objective perspective on the career decisions that students are facing, exploring the factors influencing the decision as well as reflecting and inviting the student to share thoughts, feelings, and reactions to the various options. Career counselors provide master's students with the mental and physical space to confidentially explore career questions, discuss perceived barriers, and plan to take action necessary to enhance career development. Career counselors can contribute to departmental programs, including orientations for incoming master's students, meeting with prospective master's students, and meeting with students as they progress through their program, highlighting the importance of early career planning and encouraging students to take initiative in their career development activity.

Including master's students in the delivery of career services programs can also enhance the connection between students and career counselors. Working closely with graduate student organizations, providing workshops during graduate club meetings, and hosting orientations where career counseling activities can be introduced to groups of graduate students can inform students about career counseling services while opening dialogue between career counselors and master's students. Increased dialogue and campus-specific research may be necessary to refine and identify the exact career development needs of master's students. Surveys may identify a need for targeted programs focused upon building career-related experiences, networking skills, interviewing strategies, and resume development, as well as how assessment activities can help students organize interests, values, and abilities, and how career counseling can offer students the chance to reflect upon their experiences and education as related to their goals. Career counselors must be proactive in reaching out to master's students, going to areas within the campus community where master's students gather rather than expecting them to visit career services. Taking the first step to reach out to students can make students more aware and more likely to visit career counselors and career services. Providing an introduction of career development and career questions to master's students early in their educational program (perhaps during a new master's student orientation) can serve to normalize the questions and barriers students may encounter. With increased awareness of how career counselors can assist master's level students, these students may increase their level of participation in career counseling and career development activities.

Master's students receive information and referrals from their peers. As services are provided to individual and groups of master's students, these students will share their experiences with others, leading to increased awareness of upcoming programs and career counseling opportunities. Outreach and marketing materials from the career counseling and career services office should specifically note the relevance of counseling, programs, and recruiting events for master's level students, as many master's students will assume that career services primarily serves undergraduates. Addressing this concern and providing messages that speak to master's level students' experience levels, specific academic foci, career expectations, and emerging career goals will send a message to master's students that their career goals are valued by the career counseling and career services staff.

Organizationally, career counselors should prepare to offer services during evening and weekend hours to meet the complex and demanding schedules of master's level students. Master's level students who are balancing work and family commitments with their graduate programs may only be able to access career counseling services during these times.

FUTURE RESEARCH OPPORTUNITIES

Career counselors and all faculty, administrators, and student affairs professionals who are interested in the career development needs of master's students are encouraged to continue to investigate and document the career development needs of this population. Surveying master's students' career needs on campus provides data to support new career counseling initiatives with master's students. Surveys can be subcategorized by academic area (education, business, science, other) to identify ways to tailor career development programming, career counseling, and outreach efforts. Qualitative and quantitative approaches to investigating the career development needs of master's level students can contribute to filling this gap in career development research. Empirical research on the intersection of cultural identity and master's level study is also needed and would be a welcome addition to what is known about master's students and their career development process.

CONCLUSION

As more individuals from a variety of career and educational backgrounds consider master's level programs as a means to strengthen their knowledge and experience and achieve employment goals, it is important to continue to examine and document the career development needs of this population of students. Evaluating the impact of specific programs and career counseling interventions, such as those described in this chapter, can provide further evidence of best practices in career counseling master's students. These practices could include examining students' motivation for pursuing a master's degree, identifying the career development needs and perceived barriers of the student, and providing comprehensive career development and education that involves faculty as well as students.

The career development needs of master's students are diverse, and attention should be paid to understanding the career goals and career development concerns of students pursuing master's degrees. Master's students may present concerns ranging from understanding self, exploring career information, integrating personal and career goals, as well as developing strategies to reach defined career goals. Through an approach that is focused on the career development themes, the construction of a life story that includes career development and a focus on transferable skills, career counselors can provide a framework for master's students to embrace the multitude of options and possible life directions ahead of them.

REFERENCES

Basham, R. E., & Buchanan, F. R. (2009). A survey comparison of career motivations of social work and business students. *Journal of Social Work Education, 45,* 187–208.

Bell, N. (2010). *Graduate Enrollment and Degrees: 1999 to 2009.* Washington, DC: Council of Graduate Schools. Retrieved from http://www.cgsnet.org/portals/0/pdf/R_ED2009.pdf

Blustein, D. L., Schultheiss, D. E. P., and Flum, H. (2004). Toward a relational perspective of the psychology of careers and working: A social constructionist analysis. *Journal of Vocational Behavior, 64,* 423–440.

Brott, P. E. (2005). A constructivist look at life roles. *The Career Development Quarterly, 54*(2), 138–149.

Bujold, C. (2004). Constructing career through narrative. *Journal of Vocational Behavior, 64,* 470–484.

Burwell, R., & Chen, C. P. (2006). Applying the principles and techniques of solution-focused therapy to career counseling. *Counselling Psychology Quarterly, 19*(2), 189–203.

Busacca, L. A., & Wester, K. L. (2006). Career concerns of master's-level community and school counselor trainees. *The Career Development Quarterly, 55,* 179–190.

Byars-Winston, A. M., & Fouad, N. A. (2006). Metacognition and multicultural competence: Expanding the culturally appropriate career counseling model. *The Career Development Quarterly, 54*(3), 187–201.

Caple, R. B. (1995). Counseling graduate students. *New Directions for Student Services, 1995*(72), 43–50.

Cohen, B. N. (2003). Applying existential theory and intervention to career decision-making. *Journal of Career Development, 29,* 195–209.

Conrad, C. F., Duren, K. M., & Haworth J. G. (1998). Students' perspectives on their master's degree experiences: Disturbing the conventional wisdom. *New Directions for Higher Education, 1998*(101), 65–76.

Galles, J., Lenz, J., & Keller, B. (2010, July). *Meeting the career development needs of graduate students: Building bridges through campus connections.* Symposium conducted at the meeting of the National Career Development Association, San Francisco, CA.

Kim, E. A. (2005, February). *Career services for graduate students: A case study.* Paper presented at the Academy of Human Resource Development International Conference, Estes Park, CO.

Luzzo, D. A. (1999). Identifying the career decision-making needs of nontraditional college students. *Journal of Counseling and Development, 77,* 135–140.

Luzzo, D. A. (2000). Career development of returning-adult and graduate students. In D. A. Luzzo (Ed.), *Career counseling of college students: An empirical guide to strategies that work* (pp. 191–200). Washington, D.C.: American Psychological Association.

McCaffrey, S. S., Miller, T. K., & Winston, R. B. (1984). Comparison of career maturity among graduate students and undergraduates. *Journal of College Student Personnel, 25,* 127–132.

Pyle, K. R. (2007). *Group counseling: Principles and practices.* Broken Arrow, OK: National Career Development Association.

Rimmer, S. M., Lammert, M., & McClain, P. (1982). An assessment of graduate student needs. *College Student Journal, 16,* 187–192.

Severy, L. E. (2008). Analysis of an online career narrative intervention: "What's my story?" *The Career Development Quarterly, 56*(3), 268–273.

Sharf, R. S. (2002). *Applying career development theory to counseling* (3rd ed.). Pacific Grove, CA: Brooks/Cole.

Super, D. E. (1990). A life-span, life-space approach to career development. In D. Brown, L. Brooks, & Assoc. (Eds.), *Career choice and development: Applying contemporary theories to practice* (2nd ed., pp. 197–261). San Francisco, CA: Jossey-Bass.

Young, R. A., & Valach, L. (2004). The construction of career through goal-directed action. *Journal of Vocational Behavior, 64,* 499–514.

CHAPTER 8

CAREER COUNSELING FOR DOCTORAL STUDENTS AND RESEARCH INSTITUTIONS

Travis W. Schermer and Caroline Perjessy
Kent State University

Patrick cups his forehead in his palms, his elbows on the table. He breathes in and exhales a sigh, staring at the keyboard of his computer. He's writing an application letter for an assistant professor position. Some of his peers have pursued and attained such positions in universities, while others are still working and waiting. The latter work as part-time instructors, trying to stay connected to academia. A number of his former classmates have moved away from teaching and into community and business settings. They are now working in areas that none of them could have imagined just a couple years earlier.

In reflecting on those early years in school, Patrick recalls that in the beginning, many of his peers wanted to teach at a university. Research was a priority for everyone and they never imagined their futures without being on the cutting edge of inquiry. When he applied for the doctoral program, none of the professors shared with him or his colleagues that not all graduates would go into academic positions. It just seemed logical that they would all graduate and go on to be the next generation of faculty. It wasn't until they advanced in their studies and started looking for jobs that they came to see the limitations of the academic job market.

Career Development in Higher Education, pages 157–182
Copyright © 2011 by Information Age Publishing
All rights of reproduction in any form reserved.

The lack of teaching positions was not the only reason that members of his cohort left the academy. Some of his fellow graduates realized that while they loved their research, they hated teaching. Others found the opposite to be true. Still others realized that they did not care for the politicking they encountered in academia. In turn, they each discovered interests and skills that drove them in a multitude of directions. Initially many struggled with the decision to leave but ultimately found a lot of satisfaction in forging their own career paths.

Patrick has never wavered from his desire to be a professor, despite his struggles in finding a full-time position. He often imagines himself as a tenured professor and having his own teaching assistants. These hopeful thoughts keep him writing letters of application to academic postings and keep him teaching whatever classes he can find at local universities. "Maybe this will be my year," he thinks to himself as he sets back to typing.

Patrick's experience is not uncommon for doctor of philosophy (PhD) graduates seeking a tenure-track professor position. Often doctoral students will enter into their studies with intentions of working in academia as part of the professorate. These career goals will sometimes shift over the course of study or after graduation, as they become more aware of their career options both inside and outside of academia. The low rate of unemployed PhDs suggests that there are ample non-academic opportunities for PhDs in the market place (Shettle, 1997). Many of these positions are not always readily evident to job seekers or their advisors. Thus, career counselors have a unique opportunity to assist this population in exploring multiple vocational choices and easing their potential career transitions.

To date, there is limited literature on career counseling with PhDs. What is available provides suggestions for applying to and succeeding in faculty positions (e.g., Barnes, 2007; Heiberger & Vick, 2001; Sadler, 1999). Their insights into the process can be invaluable and may help applicants hone their curriculum vitae, application letters, and interviewing skills. For those seeking careers outside of academia, there are decidedly fewer texts available. As a result, many PhDs may think/believe they are doing something wrong or they are abnormal in some way. Career counselors are in a unique position to provide assistance in normalizing this process and scaffolding their job hunt.

The present chapter seeks to provide career counselors with information about working with PhDs on making vocational decisions. Consideration is given to PhDs who are pursuing work in either academic or non-academic careers; however particular significance is given to the latter. This is due, in large part, to the emphasis that doctoral programs typically place on finding positions within the professorate. As Basalla and Debelius (2007) observed:

> The biggest difference between academic careers and post-academic careers
> is that the road is almost too well lit in academia—you don't even need your

headlights. The path is excruciatingly clear for humanists and social scientists. You look for a job at the same time everyone else does, and if you don't find work, you simply wait until next year to repeat the process. (p. 34)

We agree with their sentiment and believe it is especially important for career counselors to be able to provide support to those seeking to leave the academic world. This chapter conceptualizes career decision making for this population and provides suggestions for working with them from a constructivist perspective. Common assumptions about this population are highlighted and activities for counselors to suggest to PhDs are provided.

THE DOCTOR OF PHILOSOPHY

Doctoral education is comprised of several different types of degrees with varying emphases. The two most notable groups are professional doctorates and the doctor of philosophy (PhD). The professional doctorate (e.g., MD, JD) is oriented toward the practice of a particular profession. These degrees commonly emphasize the clinical application of knowledge and require some form of internship. Perry (2007) noted that this type of advanced practitioner training has become increasingly common with growing numbers of doctorates for particular professions (e.g., Doctor of Psychology, Doctor of Business Administration). The distinguishing feature between the professional doctorate and the PhD is the role of research. The professional doctorate works to apply the knowledge gained from research, while the PhD works to develop knowledge through conducting research.

The PhD is both unique and universal. It is unique to each specific discipline and program, adhering to the standards set forth by the particular department. The PhD is offered in social sciences, humanities, education, engineering, life sciences, and mathematics, among other fields. Each department creates its own set of criteria for the degree, often adhering to standards established by professional organizations or the university. The PhD is also universal in its emphasis on research and its shared milestones across academic programs. The PhD in the United States (U.S.) is largely distinguished from its international counterparts by its inclusion of coursework. In the U.S., for example, the PhD typically consists of three parts, 1) coursework, 2) comprehensive examination of coursework, and 3) the completion of a dissertation or thesis (Gardner, 2009). Many institutions outside of the U.S. do not have the same coursework requirements and emphasize research through a mentorship process (Nerad, 2008). The present chapter focuses on working with PhDs in the U.S. but may be of equal assistance to career counselors working internationally.

PhD Demographics

The composition of PhDs has changed over the past several decades, becoming more diverse in gender, race, and nationality. The overall number of PhDs has increased, and the representation of minorities has increased in turn (Burns, Einaudi, & Green, 2009). The increasing diversification of this population requires that career counselors be prepared to provide culturally competent services. Not only is it beyond the scope of this chapter to provide individual attention to each cultural subgroup in the larger PhD population, but there is also very little information about culturally competent career counseling (Brown, Yamini-Diouf, & Ruiz de Esparza, 2005; Flores, 2008).

Universities in the United States graduated 48,079 doctoral students in 2007 (Welch, 2008). It took doctoral students an average of 7.8 years to graduate with the degree, with women taking an average of six months longer than men to complete. The median age for completion of the PhD varies by discipline with a range of 30 to about 42 years old, with an overall median of 33 (National Center for Educational Statistics, 2009). Males have comprised the majority of total doctoral recipients, but women have been increasing in numbers. In 1977 women were 24.8% of graduates, compared to 2007 where they comprised 45.5% of graduates (Welch, 2008).

Across varying disciplines, female doctoral students are at greater risk for not completing their doctoral degree than men, with attrition rates for women being higher. According to the national study "Completion and Attrition: Analysis of Baseline Demographic Data from the PhD Completion Project," which analyzed over 19,000 doctoral students from 24 universities, 55% of women versus 58% of men finished their doctorates after ten years (Schmidt, 2008). Researchers from the project noted that women lagged more than three percentage points behind men in completion rates prior to the ten-year mark, but persevered considerably to completion. Although increasing numbers of women enroll in doctoral programs, there continues to be gender differences in time to degree, influencing retention and attrition. Time to degree from baccalaureate to doctoral award has increased from a median of 12.6 years in 1975 to a median of 19.4 years for both men and women in 2000 (Hoffer, Dugoni, Sanderson, Ghadialy, & Rocque, 2001). Although somewhat dated, one study found that men took an average of 1.2 years less to complete their doctoral degree than females (Abedi & Benkin, 1987). Extensive time spent in school correlates with high attrition rates and limits contributions that women can offer their profession (Bair & Haworth, 1999). Depending upon the field of study, the percentage of women shifts. Women have the most PhDs awarded in education (67.4%) and the fewest in engineering (20.7%). Women's experiences of PhD education have received significant attention in the literature (e.g., Collins, Chrisler, & Quina, 1998; Dean, Bracken, & Allen, 2009; DiGeorgio-Lutz, 2002).

In 2001, those who earned their doctorate in science and engineering were 80% White, 15% Asian/Pacific Islander, 2% Black, and 3% Hispanic (National Science Foundation, 2004). The numbers are similar for all PhDs in 2004 and 2005, with 80.4% being Caucasian, 6.5% Black, 5.8% Asian, 5% Hispanic, 0.5% American Indian/Alaska Native, and 1.8% other (National Science Board, 2006) Overall, PhDs earned by Black Americans hav increased to 7% in 2007, the largest proportion being earned in the field of education (National Opinion Research Center, 2008). PhD programs remain predominately White, but the above data depicts an increasingly diversified student population. In many programs, this racial diversity is accompanied by an increasing internationalization.

In the 2005–2006 class of graduating PhDs, 36% were non-U.S. citizens (National Center for Educational Statistics, 2009). In 1995, 27% of all doctoral degrees granted in the U.S. were not to U.S. citizens (Young & Bae, 1997). Of these graduates, 53% were from five countries: the People's Republic of China, Korea, Taiwan, India, and Canada. These graduates had a diverse set of intentions after graduation, often dependent upon their area of specialization. This group was largely male, with women comprising roughly one third of the temporary residents receiving a doctoral degree (National Opinion Research Center, 2008). The areas of study were most commonly in the science and engineering fields, in contrast to U.S. citizens who were twice as likely to pursue a degree in a non-science or engineering field. Just over 60% of those in the natural sciences and in computer sciences intended to stay in the U.S. after completing their degree. Of the top five foreign countries represented at this level, the People's Republic of China and India had the largest percentages of students intending to stay in the U.S. (92% and 89%, respectively). Of all PhD graduates, 9.4% had intentions to work outside the U.S. after graduation (National Center for Educational Statistics, 2009).

As student populations become more diverse, the number of students with family commitments increases. It is common for students at this level to have a spouse, children, or be caring for an older parent. A family is most commonly thought of as being two or more people living together, joined by marriage or by family of origin. However, according to Miller (1986), a family can also exist when two or more people are joined by a shared future that requires they consider one another when making career choices. Recent graduates from doctoral programs cite family responsibilities (41%) and a spouse's employment (38%) as the greatest restriction on their job searches (National Science Foundation, 2004). According to a 2005 study by Davis, 34% of surveyed PhDs in post-doctoral appointments had one or more children. As such, the pursuit of a degree or a career change needs consideration in the context of the multiple roles that individuals play throughout life. Helping them balance their family and career is an important aspect of career counseling for this population.

It appears from demographic data that PhDs are becoming more diverse in gender, race, and nationality. Employment data suggests that there is also a diversification of post-graduate employment. Many PhDs are continuing to seek out and find academic postings; however many more are taking on positions outside academia. While the pursuit of faculty positions is still the norm within PhD culture, there are some salient shifts occurring that are providing new opportunities to PhDs. An overview of the traditional academic path for PhDs and other non-traditional non-academic sources of post-graduate employment is provided.

Employment Opportunities for PhDs

The PhD degree is viewed as a training ground for new generations of professors (Basalla & Debelius, 2007; Nerad, 2008). Due to recent changes in retirement patterns and restrictive university hiring practices (Nerad, 2008), many PhDs have to find jobs other than traditional full-time faculty positions. In the past, doctoral students wanting to enter the academy could find tenure track appointments. However, in recent years there have been increasing numbers of graduates who spend years in adjunct, post-doc, or part-time positions (Bataille & Brown, 2006; Taylor, 2006). As a result, many graduates go on to find careers in the private sector. Several editorials have suggested that PhDs making these transitions to non-academic careers face significant difficulties (e.g., Gonzalez, 1999; Newitz, 1998). They attribute these difficulties to an academic culture that views non-academic work as shameful or as a professional failure. Basic information about these different career paths is outlined, starting with an examination of the traditional academic route.

Academia. In 1989, Bowen and Sosa predicted that due to vacancies left by retiring Baby Boomers, there would be a significant shortage of PhDs in academia. Their projection indicated an increase in the production of PhDs to fill positions as late as the middle part of the 1990s. Unfortunately, for many PhDs with goals of academic work, theses predictions were incorrect and the inverse occurred. Since mandatory retirement ended in the mid 1990s, many older professors are staying on in tenured positions for longer periods, thus leaving fewer positions available for new hires (Conn, 2010).

There are not enough jobs in academia to employ all PhD graduates as full-time faculty (Taylor, 2006). As such, many graduates who wish to enter academia spend years serving in post-doc or part-time positions. Taylor (2006) suggested that PhD students should be informed about potential careers at the beginning of their training. Because many PhD programs are oriented towards creating graduates who will go on to careers in academia, students are left without many options.

Scholars have identified the doctoral degree as preparation for entering the professorate (Nerad, 2008; Taylor, 2006). These positions involve research, teaching, and administrative duties (e.g., advising students, serving on committees). When recent graduates from PhD programs evaluated their training, 94% felt an adequate training in research, 72% felt they had an adequate training in teaching, and 44% felt they had adequate training in management or administrative skills (National Science Foundation, 2001). The number of faculty at universities has increased by 46% over a period spanning from 1981 and 1999 (Anderson, 2002). According to a 1998 study by the U.S. Department of Education, full-time tenured/tenure-track faculty comprised only 38% of all instructional faculty members at U.S. institutions. In comparison, 49% of faculty members were part-time instructors at these institutions. While this does not reflect total number of hours teaching, it is noticeable that most jobs available at universities appear to be part-time postings.

Most doctoral students seek tenure-track faculty positions at research universities; however, only 25% of faculty positions are at research universities (Golde, 2004). The reality of the job market is that many more will receive job offers at small liberal arts colleges and community colleges, where the expectations for teaching and service may be greater than, or equal to, the need for scholarship. In general, academic jobs are decreasing as the number of doctoral degrees awarded increases, creating an overall shortage of academic positions (Lapidus, 1995). Despite the fact that most doctoral students expect to have academic careers (Golde & Dore, 2001), approximately 50% of doctoral recipients accept nonacademic positions (Lapidus, 1995).

In their study of four thousand doctoral students from eleven disciplines, Golde and Dore (2001) discovered the disparity within doctoral student training, doctoral student career desires, and the realities of the job market. The goals of most doctoral programs are to develop researchers within a particular field, but many graduates find they are ill-prepared for the expectations required of them after graduation, which includes a more balanced role between researcher, teacher, and service provider (Golde, 2004; Levin, 2008). In addition, most doctoral students who pursue doctoral degrees enjoy teaching and envision being a full-time faculty member (Golde & Dore, 2001). Approximately 70% of doctoral students look forward to teaching lecture courses as future faculty, but only 36% of these students feel they were adequately prepared by their program to do so (Golde, 2004).

A large number of graduate students reported not obtaining enough help in the job search process during their doctoral program (Gaff, 2002).

Of these students, 41% wanted help preparing for an academic job interview but never received it, and one third sought advice on how to prepare curriculum vitae or locate job openings, but did not receive it (Gaff, 2002). In one study of Marriage and Family Therapist (MFT) doctoral students, 57% of respondents reported a career goal of becoming a college professor but did not feel adequately prepared to do so (Miller & Lambert-Shute, 2009). At the University of Kansas History Department, both present doctoral students and alumni believed they were inadequately prepared for a career at college or teaching institutions, as well as in nonacademic careers (Levin, 2008). As a result, doctoral students would benefit from career services that assist in identifying a variety of career options.

Graduates from PhD programs are expected to have a high level of scholarly experience, a history of procuring funding, and demonstrated excellence in teaching (Walker, Golde, Jones, Bueschel, & Hutchings, 2008). In turn, they are expected to be effective at collaborating, leading, and scaffolding others' work. The expectations for PhD students and graduates are increasingly demanding and largely centered on skills and activities oriented towards academic work. As Walker and colleagues (2008) noted, "Already high expectations are escalating every year." (p. 61). It is common for PhD students to be performing the duties of a faculty member prior to completing the degree, with publications and teaching experience being the norm for many graduate programs (Newitz, 1998).

Departmental advisors or mentors typically aid PhDs in the academic job hunt. This may include the preparation of curriculum vitae (CV or Vita), cover letters, and the location of potential job openings. There are three predominant sources for academic job postings: scholarly associations, national and local publications, and network of people (Heiberger & Vick, 2001).

Scholarly Associations. These organizations are often field-specific at the local, state, and national level. Many PhD students are expected to join their respective professional organization during their academic study. As such, they may have access to the organizations' members only webpages, newsletters, and other publications. Within each of these domains, there may be job postings or useful, field-specific advice for the job search. Additionally, many such organizations will have some type of a career guidance at conferences. These may include job postings, impromptu interviews, or career guidance from professionals in the field. Encouraging PhDs to explore the resources these professional organizations have to offer can provide a significant starting point for the academic job hunt.

National and Local Publications. An increasing number of academic job sites are making their way onto the Internet. For years, *The Chronicle of Higher Education* (www.chronicle.com) was the standard for the academic job hunt. However, additional sites have been added to the roster of potential sources of job information, including *HigherEdJobs* (www.higheredjobs.com), *PhDs.org* (www.phds.org), *Inside Higher Ed* (www.insidehighered. com), *Top Higher-Education Jobs* (www.tedjob.com), and *New England Higher Education Recruitment Consortium* (www.newenglandherc.org). These sites are easy to navigate and can provide a quick glimpse into a particular field's job market.

Network of People. The old adage, "It's not what you know, it's who you know" holds true in academic circles as well as is in business. Utilizing a network of professionals in the field can help candidates gain information about openings or upcoming searches. PhDs can consult with fellow program alumni, advisors, and other professional connections made through conferences or professional service (e.g., serving on professional boards or committees). Heiberger and Vick (2001) suggested making direct contact with departments when looking for part-time, nontenure-track instructor positions. These are less likely to have formal postings and may be more dependent upon geographic location. While this aspect of the job search may not yield immediate results, it can provide opportunities over the long term.

Full-time, tenure-track faculty work remains the chosen career path for many PhD graduates. While it has become increasingly difficult for graduates to find such work, there are still many opportunities for both full-time and part-time work. Helping to facilitate the job hunt for PhDs will entail learning about any field-specific nuances that may exist. Encouraging them to consult with others in the field about such nuances will aid in strengthening their applications and their knowledge of the job market. Not all PhDs who stay in academia after graduation are working as faculty members. A great number of graduates will continue to do research in a postdoctoral position.

Postdoctoral Position. A postdoctoral position (postdoc) has traditionally been utilized to continue research training after the completion of the PhD. According to Regets (1998a), an increasing number of PhDs view a postdoc as a form of employment until an academic posting becomes available. While this view does not reflect the majority of postdocs, it is suggestive of the changing post-graduate job market. While postdoc appointments can be both educative and financially sustaining, it is not a guarantee for a later academic posting. Of those who had a postdoc appointment in science and engineering from the 1960s to the 1980s, only 35% held a tenure-track faculty position in 1995 (Regets, 1998b).

Postdoc appointments were largely uncommon during the latter part of the last century. It was shortly after World War II when they started to increase in prevalence, and their popularity grew steadily into the 1970s. This growth was followed by a sharp increase in the number of postdoc positions in the latter part of the 1980s and 1990s. Davis (2005) suggested that this expansion of postdocs was not an intentional decision, but rather a reaction to economic factors. He observed that these positions were created in response to increasing numbers of PhDs and decidedly fewer faculty positions.

Research on postdoc demographics by Davis (2005) described the population present at 28 universities across the United States. His results depicted the typical postdoc as being from another country (54%), male (58%), between the ages of 30 and 35 (58%), and married (69%) without children (66%). For those from another country, China was the most common, followed by India, Germany, South Korea, and Japan. Amongst U.S. citizens, women were the majority (51%) and the racial demographics were White/ Caucasian 75%, Asian 17%, Hispanic/Latino 4%, and Black/African American 4%. Overall, these postdocs felt satisfied with their experience (70%). The largest fraction of those surveyed expected to find an academic posting at a research institution (38%). This group did not even consider taking on the role of a faculty member at a four-year college. Davis compared these expectations with the recent data on postdocs. He concluded that very few of those who wanted to become faculty at research institutions would ultimately find those positions. While some would find such positions, others would go to four-year colleges to teach, or find careers in educational and industrial settings.

During their tenures as postdocs, members of the sample were most commonly making $38,000 per year. This was less than a similarly aged individual with a bachelors or masters degree and roughly $10,000 more than a person with his or her high school diploma. On average, full-time postdocs spent 51 hours per week working and, surprisingly, part-time postdocs worked on average 45 hours per week. While Davis noted that many postdoc appointments do not come with health benefits, 97% indicated that they were offered through their university (it was not assessed whether the postdocs had to pay for all or part of the benefits).

The National Research Council (1998) indicated that the length of time spent in these positions has increased over the past several decades. Ultimately, this is beneficial for universities who are able to hire highly educated and highly motivated people frugally. While this option is helpful in building experience, it is not a guarantee that there will be an academic position on the other side of the appointment. Many students are going into these appointments for longer periods and not finding tenure-track positions. Instead, they are moving into non-tenure or part-time appointments. The postdoctoral experience enables PhDs to stay in the academic environment.

Working Outside of Academia. Because many PhDs start their education with the expectation that they will enter the academy, there may be some struggles as they transfer into different fields. Often there are certain associations about working in academia. There is a prizing of knowledge for sake of knowledge, of liberal inquiry, and the tradition of the academy. It is often assumed that those who are the brightest stay and those who are not find work elsewhere (Gonzalez, 1999). As such, leaving this environment can feel like a failure or a deficiency.

Some will feel like they are abandoning their ideals by working outside of their chosen area. By going against the ideals of their younger selves, they may feel as if they are losing an important aspect of themselves. Some will feel like they are turning their back on their identity by making such changes. Basalla and Debelius (2007) highlighted some common concerns of PhDs leaving the academic world. Most prominent are the thoughts that they have wasted their time, are losing their identity, and have no skills to offer outside academia. Career counselors are in a unique position to challenge these types of thoughts and to help construct a positive future with vast amounts of potential.

It is becoming more common for those with a PhD to look for work outside of the academy. For many PhDs who move beyond the walls of academia, there is both an internal and an external struggle. Built into the culture of PhD academia is the assumption that newly minted PhDs will move into faculty positions. When people move away from this norm they can experience admonishment from peers and advisors, as well as from their own internal assumptions about success. When providing career counseling to PhDs leaving the academy, counselors need to help in both the preparation for the job hunt as well as assistance in overcoming the person's own beliefs and the beliefs of others.

The standard for this level of education is the completion of a dissertation, which requires that an individual hone in on a particular topic. Lapidus (1995) noted that this process can create excellent scholars but can restrict their overall perspective. In practice, this can mean that graduates are overly focused on research, resulting in difficulties teaching in academia or focusing on the problems of companies in the larger marketplace. According to Taylr and Beasley (2005), many universities are incorporating more generic skills into their training programs in order to increase the employability of graduates in the private sector. This type of move in the academic community signals a greater understanding that PhDs are graduating and pursuing a myriad of career paths.

It has not been uncommon for PhDs in engineering and science to move outside of the academy into the private sector (Jones, 2002–03). For those in other disciplines (e.g., the humanities and social sciences), there has only been movement in this direction over the past several decades. There have been many suggestions for these PhDs looking for careers outside of academia. It has been suggested that PhDs could find a fruitful career through teaching at private high schools (Bradley, 2000a), nonprofit work (Bradley, 2000b), university administration (Koch-Gibson, 2001), museums (Sanford & Sheffer, 2002; Wagner, 2000), and business consultation (Montell, 1999). However, there is no one particular path that will be best for any one PhD graduate. With this in mind, it is important to provide PhDs with space to find their own unique career paths.

INFORMED CAREER DECISION MAKING FOR PHDS

Making a decision to stay in academia after graduation, to move into a non-academic career, or to transition between careers is a significant life decision. It is one that requires people to attend to both personal and professional factors. Carney and Wells (1999) posited seven stages to making an informed career decision that can easily be applied to the concerns of PhDs. In helping PhDs to navigate these stages, career counselors provide solid bedrock upon which individuals can make the choice that is most appropriate for them.

The career decision starts with an *awareness* (stage one) that something is amiss in plans for the future. There might be a sense of an incongruence or dissatisfaction with the current career situation. When career awareness develops for PhDs, it might be the result of 1) an awareness that there are no jobs available in their field of choice, 2) an awareness that their career of choice is not satisfying for them, 3) an awareness that they will need to leave a current position for unrelated reasons (e.g., relocation for family reasons), or 4) a complete field change (e.g., moving from finance to counseling). This awareness can be accompanied by an increase in anxiety or feelings of uncertainty. Often this accurately reflects the uncertainty of making any type of career transition, which is never a guaranteed success. These feelings will often lead to an assessment of the current nature of the experience, trying to understand how to find the correct way to move forward. Often the best path forward is one that starts by taking a self-assessment of what can be given up and what from the past can inform the future.

The *self-assessment* (stage two) has two components; first, people need to examine who they are and how they want to live their lives. Essentially, one's perception of self needs to be compared to one's goals or plans. PhDs taking stock of themselves can examine their attitudes and beliefs about the different types of work they are doing. What do they find rewarding? What do they find most tedious? They need to evaluate what they might be willing to sacrifice for a career. Would they be willing to sacrifice financial security, geographic location, or prestige? The second component of this stage is to delve into the past for clues about interests and dreams. By drawing from the past, a potentially more meaningful future trajectory can be established. This process is best facilitated by a constructivist approach outlined below.

After taking the self-assessment, an *exploration* (stage three) of what is possible needs to be undertaken. During this stage, information is collected about different career paths and opportunities that may be available. Cost and benefits are weighed in regards to choosing a particular path (e.g., *what are the consequences for changing my mind if I pursue this job in the private sector and decide to leave in a year?*). For PhDs, this process may begin by exploring the literature on what positions other graduates in their field have obtained. Other sources of information include former classmates, former professors, and alumni from other institutions. Interviewing these individuals about their experiences and career choices could provide hitherto unknown opportunities for graduates in the field. For a career counselor, it is not necessary to know all the potential avenues that a PhD could explore. Rather, the goal is to assist the PhD in his or her process of exploring what might be possible. Once information is gathered, the counselor can provide support in sorting through what has been collected. After several options have been identified, the PhD can begin to narrow his or her scope by removing the least attractive options and explore which of them are most attainable.

The information that is collected requires *integration* (stage four) into the PhD's concept of what is desired and what is possible. One factor to consider at this stage is whether the nature of the work is congruent with one's own self-assessment. Is this work in line with qualities and skills the PhD possesses and enjoys? Does this work align with the PhD's ideas about desirable work environments? Does the PhD have the proper background, credentials, or experience? Another factor in integration is the consideration of the restrictions imposed on the PhD's current situation. Depending on the responsibilities in the person's life, some options might be more feasible than others. As noted previously, the most prominent restriction is often family commitments to a certain area or lifestyle. Family members are frequently tied to a location because of their own work, school, or extended familial commitments. Leaving a job that is important to them, at the benefit of the PhD, might not be feasible or desirable. Sometimes the family in an area might need personal care provided by the PhD or the PhD's spouse. If a parent or other relative requires support in daily living activities, it might be necessary to remain in the same area. Finally, the PhD's current employment might be supporting the family through the income it provides, the health insurance, or the education benefits. These types of considerations need to be made as the potential options gathered through exploration are integrated into the current self-concept and nature of the individual's limitations.

After individuals examine how well different options integrate into their self-concept and into their responsibilities, it is likely that several options have become more desirable than others. At this point, the PhD needs to make a *commitment* (stage five) to testing out one of the options. The PhD might decide to commit because he or she is no longer willing to wait, is tired of the uncertainty, or genuinely feels that this is the correct choice. Regardless, the commitment needs accompaniment with the awareness that the choice made does not have to be a life-long decision. This choice can be altered and other paths explored, if so desired. However, making such a commitment is a movement into action and into finding out whether this potential fit can become an actual fit. With any change, there is a certain amount of risk and sacrifice; however through the process of self-assessment, exploration, and integration the risk may be anticipated. Once there is a commitment, a new type of action can begin as the choice becomes implemented.

Implementation (stage six) requires putting the commitment into action by following through on the decision. This often involves looking for jobs and marketing oneself in the chosen arena. When implementing the career decision, PhDs want to ensure that they prepare themselves for difficulties, as they will inevitably arise. If the preceding stages were engaged in thoroughly, any difficulties that come about should not come as too great a surprise. There may be blocks that present themselves that delay forward movement for an indefinite period. Being disappointed at such setbacks is to be expected. Because this implementation will be difficult, PhDs need to take care of themselves and seek out moral support in order to stay dedicated to this change.

After locating a position and becoming adjusted to the new environment and responsibilities, the decision can undergo *reevaluation* (stage 7). During this stage, the goals for change are revisited and compared with the reality of the new experience. Highlighting any discrepancies can be important in evaluating whether this new experience is a good fit. This can lead to a new process of exploration, depending on the quality of the new experience. It could be that during the time it took to attain this change, a more desirable opportunity came up.

As Carney and Wells (1999) noted in the closing of their section on informed career decision, change is the one constant throughout this process. The most informed of career decisions is still going to change over time. After all, it is based on information that was pulled from the past. After the decision is made, it may quickly become obsolete. We encourage PhDs to remember that their attitudes, experiences, and goals will alter over the course of time. In this way, the changes that they make will need to be revisited and compared with the new criteria they have for their lives. It is not a static state of existence, rather one that is in constant flux and growth. For these reasons, PhDs need to integrate such decisions into a larger construction of themselves and their careers over time. For this reason we recommend utilizing a constructivist approach when assisting this population.

CONSTRUCTIVIST CAREER COUNSELING

Today, mid-career adults return to school, change careers and follow other less traditional paths of employment than previously (Savickas et al., 2009).

Graduate students, in a similar style, may embark on a career, only to return for their masters or doctoral degree in later years after several years in the workforce and raising a family. As a result, students pursuing a PhD may feel added pressure to balance work and family life. Career counseling requires interventions that view the career client as part of their environmental-social system and involved in lifelong career development (Patton & McMahon, 1999). Career construction counseling answers that call.

"Constructivism focuses on meaning making and the constructing of social and psychological worlds through individual, cognitive processes" (Schultheiss, 2005, p. 382). As a result, it is a strong departure from antiquated vocational models that focused on "choosing a vocation" (Parsons, 1909). These approaches typically involved the use of trait and factor approaches, or person-environment fit (Patton & McMahon, 1999). Client "traits," including personality style, abilities, values, interests, were matched with the "factors" needed to perform a particular job (Campbell & Ungar, 2004). These types of approaches are less effective when working with PhDs because they have already chosen fields of inquiry that reflect their "traits." Instead, PhDs are often looking for ways to take their acquired skills and knowledge and apply it meaningfully to their work.

Constructivist career theories involve narratives (stories about oneself), construction (constructing an identity in relation to society), action (exploring one's values and beliefs), and interpretation (creating meaning out of life events) (Grier-Reed, Skaar, & Conkel-Ziebell, 2009). Career planning involves striking a balance among the four aspects of life: work, health, intimacy, and play (Peavy, 1993). Trying to separate these distinct areas is not possible and requires an approach that is holistic and client centered in nature (Amundson, 2006; Peavy, 1993). Constructivist career counseling answers this challenge by addressing these areas through a meaning-centered construction. Career interventions from the constructivist perspective emphasize meaning making and empower individuals to construct career identities through life-planning skills and through the co-creation of knowledge (Grier-Reed, Skaar & Conkel-Ziebell, 2009). Career construction fits work into life, rather than people into work (Savickas, 2005).

The identification of career themes is a key aspect of career construction (Savickas, 2001, Super, 1954). Career themes represent the unique needs and desires of the individual. These themes represent what the person has been struggling with throughout his or her life. Exploring these themes assists in revealing early preoccupations. As Savickas (2001) notes, "An individual realizes his or her potential when work implements a self-concept and allows the person to develop his or her theme(s) in the occupational arena." (p. 54). The underlying philosophy of this approach is what helps shape its use in practice.

Philosophical Assumptions of Constructivist Career Counseling

Constructivist career counseling is more of a philosophical framework rather then a set of prescribed techniques (Peavy, 1996). Meaning making is a key aspect of constructivism and relates to how individuals interpret events to make sense of their lives (Hoskins, 1995). Some of the most important assumptions include (1) a person's life is more like a story than a set of scores; (2) individuals need to make meaning for themselves; (3) counselor and client are co-constructors of the client's world; (4) no one truth exists—everyone sees their reality differently from anyone else; (5) the client must feel emotionally safe within the therapeutic relationship; (6) the counselor works with the client's perceptions through the use of stories and metaphors; and (7) career is just one theme of a person's life (Peavy, 1996).

Career construction also provides a means of integrating three viewpoints of vocational behavior (Savickas, 2005). The psychology of individual differences is used to study how people differ in what they choose to do. The psychology of development is used to examine how individuals navigate their work lives by meeting developmental milestones, and managing occupational transitions. Narrative psychology is used to examine why individuals choose the work that they do, and how they fit work into their lives. By integrating these three views, the constructivist approach utilizes a more comprehensive and adaptable philosophical framework.

Assessment in Constructivist Career Counseling with PhDs

In constructivist career counseling, counselor and client participate in a collaborative and co-participatory dialogue (Peavy, 1993). This type of relationship is most advantageous when working with PhDs who often bring a great amount of information about their particular field of study. Additionally, because of the specificity that is required in doctoral study, it is unlikely that career counselors can be abreast of all potential options available to particular PhDs. As such, honoring the information that they bring with them and providing a space for them to share that information is invaluable. This open discourse between counselor and client is the foundation for any work that will be done together.

Constructivist career counseling utilizes stories as a means of self-expression (Savickas, 2005). Client stories are recurring ideas, tend to weave themselves into patterns, and are a construction of personal schemas that can help one understand vocational behavior (Savickas, 2005). The primary focus is on language, the "stories" clients choose to tell, and how they tell them. Exploring unique phrases used by the client, the use of metaphors, and the details of stories assist in developing alternative ways of thinking about the stories (Hoskins, 1995; Peavy, 1993). Using co-construction (i.e., to reveal), deconstruction (i.e., to unpack), and construction (i.e., to re-author) during the telling of stories result in the counselor and client creating a new reality for the client (Brott, 2001). Co-construction helps the client reveal his life stories from experiences in their past and present. These stories span beyond the academy and the doctoral degree into the entirety of the person's life. Deconstruction's purpose is to see the stories from different angles. These might include the perspectives of advisors, family members, or other close relationships. They might also span into perspectives pulled from other people's experiences or even pop culture (e.g., movies, books). Construction helps the client "re-author stories in a future orientation" (Brott, 2001, p. 306), giving the sense of momentum to move temporally. Throughout this process, it is important for the counselor to use active listening skills, ask facilitating questions, and show a desire to become interpersonally involved with the client (Brott, 2001; Peavy, 1993).

During the telling of these stories, experiments can help a client figure out what they would truly like in their lives (Peavy, 1993). These experiments can include drawings, role-playing, writing, conversation, and undertaking new life experiences (Peavy, 1993). Self-realization activities can occur through written activities such as the "earliest career fantasy essay," "career genogram," and "who am I experiential exercise and reflective writing," (Grier-Reed, Skaar, & Conkel-Ziebell, 2009, p. 292). Other writing activities include keeping a journal (Rico, 1991) and letter writing (White & Epston, 1990). Writing helps the career client explore career related feelings, dreams, and hopes that they may otherwise not have the opportunity to explore. Conversely, the counselor can write a letter to the client about how they experience their sessions together and hopes they have for the client. These letters can also serve to reinforce the emerging, more preferred story the client wishes to have for him or herself. Other creative career interventions involve the use of drawings, which may challenge clients to metaphorically depict important concepts or moments in their lives. In conceptual word mapping (Peavy, 1996), the career client is asked to use a colored pencil to draw a map that depicts them in the center of a circle. They are encouraged to fill in the surrounding space with relationships, experiences, and activities that encompass their world. The process of mapping "consists of linking ideas and experiences, significant others and activities into patterns and relationships" (p. 7). Each of these interventions is oriented to helping clients meaningfully explore their career development over time and give a sense of forward movement. PhD clients are well suited to this type of exploration because it pulls on the qualities that are common across disciplines: metaphorical and critical thought (Koch-Gibson, 2001).

Savickas' (1989) career style interview embodies the comprehensive theory of vocational choice and adjustment that addresses the what, how, and why of a career decision. The career style interview utilizes specific questions that engage the counselor and client in a dialogue about the client's priorities, preferences, and values. Life themes help explain the construction of careers. These life themes emerge during the stories the client shares. Stories reveal patterns (life themes) and disclose the "why" of a career decision. The career counselor using the career style interview asks several questions that help the client understand the what, how, and why. These questions include:

1. How may I be of use to you? This question takes some of the pressure off the counselor, who doesn't need to be right, only useful.
2. Who was your role model growing up? Who did you admire? Who would you like to pattern your life after? Why? For this question, it is best to avoid parents. Growing up, we face several life situations and problems. Role models represent those people who have solved the problems we are facing, which is why we are drawn to them to begin with. These role models provide the blueprint for solving problems.
3. Which magazines do you read regularly? What do you like about these magazines? Do you have any favorite TV shows? Magazines and TV shows represent the environments in which we prefer to be.
4. What do you like to do in your free time? What are your hobbies? What do you enjoy about these hobbies? Hobbies represent the time we are freest to be ourselves. What we cannot fulfill during work, we attempt to fulfill during our free time.
5. What is your favorite saying or motto? Favorite sayings represent the advice that we need to hear ourselves at a particular point in time.
6. What are/were your favorite subjects in school? Why? What subjects did/do you hate? Why? Similarly, this question identifies interests and values.
7. What are your earliest childhood memories? Early recollections may differ from time to time, but they represent the stories we need to hear at a specific point in time.
8. What would you say has been your major preoccupation over the last three to five years? This question can help identify how your preoccupation will become your occupation.

There are no right or wrong answers to these questions, nor are there any answers that warrant a specific career path. Rather, these questions catalyze a discourse about meaning from the perspective of the client. Through this process the PhD client can also begin to detach specific skills (e.g., research, critical analysis) from field-specific content. These skills can be integrated into potential future careers that are in line with the constructed career story.

The PhD clients who identify a mismatch between their career goals, academic training, and realities of the job market may consider leaving their program of study (Nerad & Miller, 1986). To keep this from occurring, career construction techniques could help a doctoral student envision a career that most fits with their interests, goals, and values, and without sacrificing their desire to pursue academic work. The following case scenario illustrates how career construction can assist a doctoral student who is in need of career guidance.

Case Scenario

Eva is a 34year-old Latina PhD student in education. She enrolled in an education PhD program after teaching high school for almost seven years. Eva enjoyed teaching high school students, but felt a desire to reach higher levels of leadership within education and believed a doctoral degree could help her. Specifically, she was interested in improving curriculum for students from underprivileged backgrounds who struggled with low levels of self-efficacy related to academics. She is interested in working as a professor of education within a higher education setting, and in educating teachers on how to incorporate a social justice lens into their teaching. Eva enjoys writing and research-related activities. Her hope is to establish a line of inquiry stemming from her efforts at promoting social justice within education. Eva's years of teaching showed her how much the system was failing these students. She vowed to do something about it.

Since entering her doctoral program, Eva has become confused about her professional goals. Her original goal of entering academia has lost some of its desirability, especially as she learns more about the academic job market, which is competitive and requires relocation. Eva is quite close to her family and is the caretaker of her elderly father who has Alzheimer's disease. This poses unique challenges for her, especially as she considers her employment options. In addition, Eva, as the only Hispanic female in her PhD program, feels marginalized. She wishes there were others in her program who were as passionate about social justice issues as she is but has not found that to be the case. At this point, Eva is seeking career guidance on her options within higher education, while also pursuing her dream of working with future educators responsible for educating underprivileged youth.

Eva comes to you with these career concerns. As a career counselor using a constructivist approach, you might spend some time exploring Eva's career concerns, her values and preferences, and her personal and professional goals. Although Eva comes to you with primarily career-related concerns, you soon come to uncover the more personal reasons for her interest in working with underprivileged youth. You discover the story of how Eva herself was one of those students. In your collaborations with Eva, you explore the stories of her life, her interpretation of those stories, and challenge her to view the stories in a more preferred way. This requires knowledge of who she is and what drives her.

To help her explore these various aspects, you assign Eva the task of journaling at home or writing an essay about her earliest career fantasy. These activities help shed light on those things that are most meaningful to her. Journaling gives Eva the freedom to explore herself and identify what truly makes her happiest. Eva's earliest career fantasy essay demonstrates her desire to be a teacher. In session, Eva participates in activities such as the career genogram, where her family career tree reveals themes and commonalities. These themes demonstrated how her family struggled to persevere through harsh economic times. These lessons were passed down to Eva, who continues to believe that people, if given the opportunity, can persevere through the most difficult of circumstances.

Finally, in using the career construction interview, further clarification on her values and preferences emerge. The interview reveals new insights and patterns for Eva, such as her love of politics. Eva never realized how her drive for social justice issues connects with policymaking. Early role models included her 3rd grade teacher, who was fair and caring with all her students, and her aunt, who was the family matriarch. Throughout this conversation, Eva begins to see the themes throughout her life that connect her to issues related to justice, education, and empowerment. As her counselor, you begin to see her sense of idealism, her desire to work hard, and her willingness to take responsibility for others.

These career construction exercises help Eva see the limitless possibilities she has for herself. In creating a more holistic view of herself, Eva is able to see beyond the limits of her academic career and was able to see how her strengths as an educator and belief in advocacy work coexist. In working with her and using a career constructionist approach, a new world full of possibilities exists and she is eager to explore career options related to educational consulting and policymaking.

CONCLUSION

Shifts in the economy and the employment practices of universities are altering the job prospects for PhD graduates. As traditional career paths become less common, PhDs will seek out the assistance of career counselors with greater frequency. Many universities are creating special positions to provide such services; however there are many more who are not. As a profession, we need to be prepared to scaffold their career exploration and advocate for their needs on university campuses.

There are particular difficulties that PhDs face as the product of the system in which they exist. One of the greatest limitations to the current system of career planning is that a student's faculty advisor often provides career guidance. The advisor has commonly worked in academia for most of his or her professional life. Therefore, he or she may view the ultimate goal of such a degree as finding an academic posting. While the advisor may be very knowledgeable about undergoing an academic job search, he or she may be unaware of possibilities outside of academia. Career counselors need to be able to step into that gap and provide assistance to this population as they adapt to an ever-changing job market. Taking on the role of advocacy, counselors can help to inject new perspectives into university departments. Through engaging faculty in discussions about career planning for graduates, a new discourse can occur to change the archaic notions that a PhD is only for professors. Counselors can meet with departments to discuss what types of career information might be pertinent for current students and alumni. Catalyzing this conversation to occur within departments can take the form of offering informational brochures or brief presentations.

Much work has been done to date on the career counseling needs of those receiving their doctorate in a professional degree (e.g., Borges, Gibson, & Karnani, 2005; Gibson & Borges, 2009; Hojat & Zuckerman, 2008). However, there has been scant work done on the career counseling needs of those with research doctorates. Other authors have given this topic some attention (e.g., Gardner, 2009; Lapidus, 1995; Vick & Furlong, 2005), but the discourse on this topic is very limited to date. This chapter reflects the first significant attempt at addressing this issue in a comprehensive fashion. We have two hopes for this chapter. First, we hope that it has provided you with some insight into the struggles of PhDs and useful ideas for working with them. Second, we hope that it as a foundation for a larger discourse about this topic. There is an increase in the interest in this topic due to the changes in the economy and the academic job market. There is scant research beyond descriptive information, and the literature is lacking on providing assistance to this population. Therefore, the profession needs to promote a discourse of this issue on university campuses and amongst the counseling profession. To that end, we hope that this tome has furthered the discussion and enhances the dialogue as we move forward.

RESOURCES FOR FURTHER INQUIRY

There are multiple books available for PhDs looking to find employment inside or outside academia. Exploring these texts for yourself and then offering them to PhD clients is an easy way to help empower them on the job hunt. The *Chronicle of Higher Education* also provides a wealth of information for PhDs on the job hunt.

Book Suggestions for Academia Jobs

Barnes, S. L. (2007). *On the market: Strategies for a successful academic job search.* Boulder, CO: Lynne Rienner Publishers.
Goldsmith, J. A., Komlos, J., & Gold P. S. (2001). *The Chicago Guide to your academic career: A portable mentor for scholars from graduate school through tenure.* Chicago, IL: University of Chicago Press.
Hume, K. (2004). *Surviving your academic job hunt: Advice for humanities PhDs.* New York: Pelgrave Macmillan.
Reis, R. M. (1997). *Tomorrow's professor: Preparing for academic careers in science and engineering.* New York: Institute of Electrical and Electronics Engineers, Inc.

Book Suggestions for Non-Academic Jobs

Basalla, S., & Debelius, M. (2007). *"So what are you going to do with that?": A guide to career-changing for M.A.'s and PhD's.* New York: Farrar, Straus, and Giroux.
Kreeger, K. Y. (1999). *Nontraditional careers in science.* Philadelphia, PA: George H. Buchanan, Co.
Robbins-Roth, C. (2005). *Alternative careers in science: Leaving the Ivory Tower* (2nd ed.). San Diego, CA: Academic Press.

REFERENCES

Abedi, J., & Benkin, E. (1987). The effects of students' academic, financial, and demographic variables on time to the doctorate. *Research in Higher Education, 27*, 3–14.
Amundson, N. (2006). Challenges for career interventions in changing contexts. *International Journal for Educational and Vocational Guidance, 6*, 3–14.
Anderson, E. L. (2002). *The new professorate: Characteristics, contributions, and compensation.* Washington DC: American Council on Education.
Bair, C. R., & Haworth, J. G. (2004). Doctoral student attrition and persistence: A meta-synthesis of research. In J. C. Smart (Ed.), *Higher education: Handbook of theory and research* (Vol. XIX, pp. 481–534). Dordrecht, Netherlands: Kluwer Academic.

Barnes, S. L. (2007). *On the market: Strategies for a successful academic job search.* Boulder, CO: Lynne Rienner Publishers.

Basalla, S., & Debelius, M. (2007). *"So what are you going to do with that?": A guide to career-changing for M.A.'s and PhD's.* New York: Farrar, Straus, and Giroux

Bataille, G. M., & Brown, B. E. (2006). Introduction: Conventional assumptions and the realities of contemporary faculty life. In G. M. Bataille & B. E. Brown (Eds.), *Faculty career paths: Multiple routes to academic success and satisfaction* (pp. xiii–xvii). Westport, CT: Praeger Publishers.

Borges, N. J., Gibson, D. D., & Karnani, R. M. (2005). Job satisfaction with congruent versus incongruent specialty choice. *Evaluation and the Health Professions, 28(4),* 400–413.

Bowen, W. G., & Sosa, J. A. (1989). *Prospects for faculty in the arts and sciences.* Princeton, NJ: Princeton University Press.

Bradley, G. (2000a, March 17). Careers for PhD's at private schools. *The Chronicle of Higher Education.* Retrieved from http://chronicle.com/article/Careers-for-PhDs-at-Priv/46265/

Bradley, G. (2000b, September 15). Careers for PhD's in the nonprofit world. *The Chronicle of Higher Education.* Retrieved from http://chronicle.com/article/Careers-For-PhDs-in-the-/46376/

Brott, P. (2001). The storied approach: A postmodern perspective for career counseling. *The Career Development Quarterly, 49,* 304–313.

Brown, M. T., Yamini-Diouf, Y.,& Ruiz de Esparza, C. (2005). Career interventions for racial or ethnic minority persons: A research agenda. In B. W. Walsh & M. L. Savickas (Eds.), *Handbook of Vocational Psychology: Theory, Research, and Practice* (3rd ed.), (pp. 227–242). Mahwah, NJ: Lawrence Erlbaum.

Burns, L., Einaudi, P., & Green, P. (2009). S&E graduate enrollments accelerate in 2007; Enrollments of foreign students reach new high. *Science Resources Statistics Info Brief* (NSF 09-314). Retrieved December 6, 2009, from http://www.nsf.gov/statistics/infbrief/nsf09314/

Campbell, C., & Ungar, M. (2004). Constructing a life that works: Part 1, blending postmodern family therapy and career counseling. *The Career Development Quarterly, 53,* 16–27.

Carney, C. G., & Wells, C. F. (1999). *Working well, living well: Discover the career within you* (5th Ed.). Pacific Grove, CA: Brooks/Cole Publishing Co.

Collins, L. H., Chrisler, J. C., & Quina, K. (1998). *Career strategies for women in academe: Arming Athena.* Thousand Oaks, CA: Sage Publications.

Conn, P. (2010, April 4). We need to acknowledge the realities of employment in the humanities. *The Chronicle of Higher Education.* Retrieved from http://chronicle.com/article/We-Need-to-Acknowledge-the/64885/

Davis, G. (2005). Doctors without orders. *American Scientist, 93,* 3, Supplement. Retrieved April 6, 2010, from http://postdoc.sigmaxi.org/results/

Dean, D. R., Bracken, S. J., & Allen, J. K. (2009). *Women in academic leadership: Professional strategies, personal choices.* Sterling, VA: Stylus Publishing.

DiGeorgeio-Lutz, J. (2002). *Women in higher education: Empowering change.* Westport, CT: Praeger.

Flores, L. Y. (2008). Career development research and practice with diverse cultural and gender groups. *Journal of Career Development, 34(3),* 215–217.

Gaff, J. (2002). Preparing future faculty and doctoral education. *Change, 34,* 6.

Gardner, S. K. (2009). *The development of doctoral students: Phases of challenge and support.* San Francisco, CA: Jossey-Bass.

Gibson, D. D., & Borges, N. J. (2009). Aligning career expectations with the practice of medicine: Physician satisfaction. *Journal of Career Development, 35*(4), 331–351.

Golde, C. (2004). *The responsibility of doctoral programs for the career preparation of future faculty* (*PeerReview,* an Association of American Colleges and Universities Publication).

Golde, C.M., & Dore, T.M. (2001). At cross purposes: What the experiences of doctoral students reveal about doctoral education. A report prepared for The Pew Charitable Trusts. Retrieved from http://www.phd-survey.org/report%20 final.pdf

Gonzalez, J. S. (1999, March 29). Four steps to succeeding outside the Ivory Tower : A former academic offers lessons in joining the "real world." *Salon,* Retrieved December 6, 2009, from http://www.salon.com/it/career/1999/03/29career. html

Grier-Reed, T., Skaar, N., & Conkel-Ziebell, J. (2009). Constructivist career development as a paradigm of empowerment for at-risk culturally diverse college students. *Journal of Career Development, 35*(3), 290–305.

Heiberger, M. M., & Vick, J. M. (2001). *The academic job search handbook.* Philadelphia, PA: University of Pennsylvania Press.

Hoffer, T., Dugoni, B., Sanderson, A., Sederstrom, S., Ghadialy, R., & Rocque, P. (2001). *Doctorate recipients from United States universities: Summary report 2000.* Chicago: National Opinion Research Center. Retrieved: http://www.norc.org/ NR/rdonlyres/C6973633-DC3E-4596-9B87-2181C83A1A78/0/sed2000.pdf

Hojat, M., & Zuckerman, M. (2008). Personality and specialty interest in medical students. *Medical Teacher, 30*(4), 400–406.

Hoskins, M. (1995). Constructivist approaches for career counselors. ERIC document. ED401505

Jones, E. (2002–03, Winter). Beyond supply and demand: Assessing the PhD job market. *Occupational Outlook Quarterly, 46*(4), 22–33. Retrieved January 14, 2010, from http://www.bls.gov/opub/ooq/2002/winter/art03.htm

Koch-Gibson, J. (2001, June 15). A PhD's road to university advancement. *The Chronicle of Higher Education.* Retrieved from http://chronicle.com/article/ A-PhDs-Road-to-Universit/45488/

Lapidus, J. B. (1995). Doctoral education and student career needs. In A. S. Pruitt-Logan & P. D. Issac (Eds.), *Student Services for the Changing Graduate Student Population* (pp. 33–42). San Francisco, CA: Jossey-Bass Inc.

Levin, E. (2008). Career preparation for doctoral students: The University of Kansas history department. *New Directions for Teaching and Learning, 113,* 83–97. Doi: 10.1002/tl.

Miller, J., & Lambert-Shute, J. (2009). Career aspirations and perceived level of preparedness among marriage and family doctoral students. *Journal of Marital and Family Therapy, 35*(4), 466–480. Doi: 10.1111/j.1752-0606.2009.00150.x

Miller, J. V. (1986). Helping adults balance career and family roles. In J. V. Miller & M. L. Musgrove (Eds.), *Issues in Adult Career Counseling* (pp. 45–58). San Francisco: Jossey-Bass.

Montell, G. (1999, November 12). Another career choice for PhD's: Management consulting. *The Chronicle of Higher Education.* Retrieved from http://chronicle.com/article/Another-Career-Choice-for-P/45638/

National Center for Educational Statistics. (2009). *Doctorate Recipients From United States Universities, 2006.* Retrieved April 9, 2010, from http://nces.ed.gov/programs/digest/d09/tables/dt09_320.asp

National Opinion Research Center. (2008). *Survey of earned doctorates fact sheet.* Chicago, IL: Author. Retrieved December 6, 2009, from http://www.norc.org/nr/rdonlyres/b40e56ec-9a4f-4892-b871-e330b689cd9/o/sedfactsheet.pdf

National Research Council (1998). *Trends in the careers of early life scientists.* Washington, DC: National Academy Press.

National Science Board (2006). *Science and engineering indicators 2006.* Arlington, VA: National Science Foundation. Retrieved: http://www.nsf.gov/statistics/seind06/pdfstart.htm

National Science Foundation. (2004). *Doctoral scientists and engineers: 2001 profile tables* (NSF 04–312). Arlington, VA: Author. Retrieved December 6, 2009, from http://www.nsf.gov/statistics/nsf04312/secta.htm

Nerad, M. (2008). United States of America. In M. Nerad & M. Heggelund (Eds.), *Toward a global PhD? Forces and forms in doctoral education worldwide* (pp. 278–299). Seattle, WA: University of Washington Press.

Nerad, M., & Miller, D. S. (1996). Increasing student retention in graduate and professional programs. In J. G. Haworth (Ed.), *Assessing graduate and professional education: Current realities, future prospects* (pp. 61–76). San Francisco, CA: Jossey-Bass Publishers.

Newitz, A. (1998, November 6). Out of academia: Why do we think that PhDs are only good for making someone into a professor? *Salon,* Retrieved December 6, 2009, from http://www.salon.com/books/it/1998/11/06/career

Parsons, F. (1909). *Choosing a Vocation.* Boston, MA: Houghton Mifflin.

Patton, W., & McMahon, M. (1999). Career development and systems theory: A new relationship. Pacific Grove, CA: Brooks/Cole.

Peavy, V. (1993). Constructivist counseling: A prospectus. *Guidance & Counseling, 9,* 3–10.

Peavy, V. (1996). Constructivist career counseling and assessment. *Guidance and Counseling, 11,* 8–14.

Perry, S. (2007). *Disciplines and doctorates.* Dordrecht, The Netherlands: Springer.

Regets, M. C. (1998a). *Has the use of postdocs changed?* National Science Foundation: Division of Science Resources Studies Issue Brief. Retrieved December 6, 2009, from www.nsf.gov/statistics/issuebrf/sib99310.pdf

Regets, M. C. (1998b). *What follows the postdoctorate experience? Employment patterns of 1993 postdocs in 1995.* National Science Foundation Division of Science Resources Studies Issue Brief (NSF 99-307). Retrieved December 7, 2009, from www.nsf.gov/sbe/srs/issuebrf/sib99307.htm

Rico, G. (1991). Pain and possibility: Writing your way through personal crisis. Los Angeles, CA: Jeremy P. Tarcher, Inc.

Sadler, D. R. (1999). *Managing your academic career: Strategies for success.* St. Leonards, Australia: Allen & Unwin.

Sanford, B., & Sheffer, H. (2002, March 11). Careers for humanities PhD's in museums. *The Chronicle of Higher Education,* Retrieved from http://chronicle.com/article/Careers-for-Humanities-PhD/45975/

Savickas, M. (1989). Career-style assessment and counseling. In T. Sweeney (Ed.), *Adlerian counseling: A practical approach for a new decade* (3rd ed.). Accelerated Development.

Savickas, M. (2001). A developmental perspective on vocational behaviour: Career patterns, salience, and themes. *International Journal for Educational and Vocational Guidance, 1,* 49–57.

Savickas, M. L. (2005). The theory and practice of career construction. In S. D. Brown & R. W. Lent (Eds.), *Career development and counselling: Putting theory and research to work* (pp. 42–70). Hoboken, NJ: Wiley.

Savickas, M., Nota, L., Rosser, J., Dauwalder, J., Duarte, M., Guichard, J., et al. (2009). Life designing: A paradigm for career construction in the 21st century. *Journal of Vocational Behavior, 75,* 239–250.

Schmidt, P. (2008). Longer road to Ph.D.'s for women and minority members. *Chronicle of Higher Education, 55*(4), Retrieved: http://chronicle.com/article/Longer-Road-to-PhDs-for/36532/

Schultheiss, D. (2005). Qualitative relational career assessment: A constructivist paradigm. *Journal of Career Assessment, 13*(4), 381–394.

Shettle, C. F. (1997). S&E PhD unemployment trends: Cause for alarm? *Division of Science Resources Studies Issue in Brief* (NSF 97-318). Retrieved December 6, 2009, from http://www.nsf.gov/statistics/issuebrf/sib97318.htm

Super, D. E. (1954). Career patterns as a basis for vocational counseling. *Journal of Counseling Psychology, 1,* 12–20.

Taylor, C. (2006). Heeding the voices of graduate students and postdocs. In C. M. Golde, G. E. Walker, & Associates (Eds.), *Envisioning the future of doctoral education: Preparing stewards of the discipline* (pp. 46–64). San Francisco, CA: Jossey-Bass Publishers.

Taylor, S., & Beasley, N. (2005). *A handbook for doctoral supervisors.* New York, NY: Routledge Press.

Vick, J. M., & Furlong, J. S. (2005, October 7). Career counseling for PhD's. *The Chronicle of Higher Education,* Retrieved from http://chronicle.com/article/Career-Counseling-for-PhDs/44938/

Wagner, R. (2000, October 13). Careers for PhD's in museums. *The Chronicle of Higher Education,* Retrieved from http://chronicle.com/article/Careers-for-PhDs-in-Museums/46302/

Walker, G. E., Golde, C. M., Jones, L., Bueschel, A. C., & Hutchings, P. (2008). *The formation of scholars: Rethinking doctoral education for the twenty-first century.* San Francisco, CA: Jossey-Bass.

Welch, V. (2008). *Doctorate recipients from United States universities: Selected tables 2007.* Chicago, IL: National Opinion Center.

White, M., & Epston, M. (1990). *Narrative means to therapeutic ends.* New York: Norton.

Young, B. A., & Bae, Y. (1997). *Issue in brief: Degrees earned by foreign graduate students: Fields of study and plans after graduation.* National Center for Education Statistics. Retrieved December 6, 2009, from http://nces.ed.gov/pubs98/web/98042.asp

SECTION IV

TECHNICAL INSTITUTIONS
AND COMMUNITY COLLEGES

CHAPTER 9

POSTSECONDARY CAREER AND TECHNICAL EDUCATION STUDENTS AND CAREER DEVELOPMENT

Jonathan Lent
John Carroll University

Maryann Meniru
The University of Akron

Approximately 9,400 postsecondary institutions offer career and technical programs. Institutions offering such programs include community colleges, technical institutes, skill and career centers, and other public and private two-year and four-year colleges. Career and technical institutions offer students an opportunity to increase workforce prospects through a shorter and more practically-focused education. Most individuals enter a four-year college thinking it will amount to a better chance in the job market. Teens and parents often maintain that a college degree is the ticket to a college-level job. However, this may not necessarily prove to be true. The reality is that at least one in three four-year college graduates will take a job that he or she

Career Development in Higher Education, pages 185–209

185

could have obtained directly out of high school (Gray, 1999). Despite the perceived notion of college equaling job success, students need to consider other methods of obtaining education and securing employment. This is especially true for students who overlook the opportunities provided by career and technical education. Counselors can be important resources for those seeking clarification in the career exploration/decision-making process. All counselors should be knowledgeable and aware of each of the postsecondary options that are available for students graduating from high school.

Every year, high school graduates ask themselves: "What's next?" There are a variety of options for graduates to consider when pondering this question. These options range from directly entering the workforce to attending one of the types of postsecondary institutions. When thinking of postsecondary options, people often think of four-year bachelor's degree programs. However, this is simply one route for those seeking postsecondary education.

The common argument for pursuing a bachelor's degree is the lifetime earnings advantage over someone who solely obtains a high school degree. The truth is both more complicated and less favorable for going directly to college. Even when a student earns a degree, the major area of concentration is important since in some cases, one with a two-year degree or certification may obtain a higher-paying job than some with certain four-year degrees.

For individuals interested in professions that require bachelor's degrees, four-year degrees may be the only option. However, for individuals who have struggled academically, are not interested in an occupation requiring a bachelor's degree, or have completed a secondary career and technical program, seeking a bachelor's degree may be either unnecessary or unrealistic.

Career and technical institutions offer students an opportunity to improve their prospects in the workforce through a shorter and more practically-focused education. Counselors should be interested in benefitting the individual, and doing so requires an assessment of skills, abilities, interests, and goals. Through an assessment of these areas, a counselor may be able to provide options for the student that includes alternatives to four-year colleges, such as community college or vocational education. An honest discussion about both the positive and negative aspects of each of these options will be most beneficial when working with students who are attempting to decide which type of institution would best meet their needs. Students and parents alike continue to invest time and money in courses of study that are not aligned with students' skills and aspirations (Gray, 1999). Students must be prepared to successfully transition to the next level. Those exploring postsecondary options must possess the skills and competencies necessary for the chosen education option (Hughey & Hughey, 1999).

One option often discounted and overlooked is pursuing a postsecondary pre-bachelor's degree. Most parents urge their children to attend four-year degree programs with little attention to other options. Career and technical schools, as well as community colleges, often take on the mission of educating students who decide on an alternative postsecondary option (Gray, 1999). While postsecondary career and technical enrollment had declined in previous years, postsecondary enrollment has been increasing (NAVE Independent Advisory Panel, 2004). Of 39 states surveyed, 70% reported an increase in enrollment since 1990 (Husain, 1999). However, career and technical education continues to suffer from a negative image among students, parents, and educators (Wonacott, 2000). Gray and Herr (2006) explain the "one way to win" mentality. This concept conveys a three-part message directly to teens. The basic premise of this message is that all teens should pursue a four-year college degree because it is the only sure way to obtain a high paying, professional job. This message tends to ignore the reality that very few students entering postsecondary institutions have taken the time to reflect on the details of this goal. Additionally, many fail to consider the reality of the situation that the economy may not generate enough positions in order to gain employment. This reality is something that needs to be conveyed to the future workforce. For many students entering higher education, it is simply not reasonable for them to pursue a four-year degree when a one or two-year training program will better meet their needs.

Students graduating high school are immediately confronted with the difficult task of making a decision that may shape their entire future. Since traditional methods of education alone may no longer be sufficient to ensure that students entering the workforce possess the necessary skills to navigate the complex economic environment, it is essential for students to evaluate all available postsecondary options. Postsecondary education options include four and two-year colleges, universities, technical schools, apprenticeships, trade schools, liberal arts colleges, institutes of technology, and other collegiate-level institutions (Miller & Mupinga, 2006). A student enrolled in any institution of higher education may be awarded academic degrees or professional certifications upon completion of the work required by the institution.

A COMMON QUESTION: "WHAT IS CAREER AND TECHNICAL EDUCATION?"

Career and technical education is a large and diverse activity in the United States (National Center for Education Statistics, 2008). Career and technical education spans both secondary and postsecondary education. Students may begin their careers and technical educations at the high school level and continue onto postsecondary education in order to gain more skills and knowledge. Many students pursue career and technical education during high school and continue on to attend a career and technical school at the postsecondary level.

These specific types of educational programs are primarily concerned with providing occupational preparation. Career and technical education at the postsecondary level is defined as a postsecondary school which trains students in a variety of skills, most commonly in the areas of business (e.g., office administration and entrepreneurship), trade (e.g., skilled trades, automotive technician, carpenter, and computer numerical control technician), health occupations (e.g., nursing, dental, and medical technicians), agriculture (e.g., food and fiber production and agribusiness), family and consumer sciences (e.g., culinary arts, family management, and life skills), marketing (e.g., merchandising and retail), and computer technology (e.g., computer-based careers). The Perkins Act (1998) defines career and technical education as:

> Organized educational programs offering a sequence of courses directly related to preparing individuals for paid or unpaid employment in current or emerging occupations requiring other than baccalaureate or advanced degree. Programs include competency-based applied learning, which contributes to an individual's academic knowledge, higher-order reasoning, problem solving skills, and the occupational-specific skills necessary for economic independence as a productive and contributing member of society. (Apling, 2003, p. 101)

Career and technical institutes offer programs that differ in length. Lengths of these programs are generally one year, eighteen months, or two years. Degree and certificate programs are also offered by career and technical institutions. These institutions attempt to respond to labor market needs and, in turn, offer programs tailored to meet requirements of specific workplaces. The intention of career and technical education is to prepare students for work and to equip them with the necessary skills to excel in the workplace. Career and technical education is commonly associated with "blue-collar" professions (e.g., mechanic, electrician, civil engineer). This may imply that career and technical education is not as rigorous or demanding as many four-year degree programs (U.S. Department of Labor, 2001). However, this could not be further from the truth. Many of the most in-demand careers and programs at technical schools may be just as rigorous and demanding from students as those offered by four-year programs.

Postsecondary career and technical education and training may be viewed in terms of two systems. First are the formal systems which include technical or vocational schools and community colleges. Second are non-formal systems which include workplace training and apprenticeships. This chapter is most concerned with addressing the formal systems of career and technical education which is delivered within technical or vocational schools.

Administration of Career and Technical Education

Snedden (1910) identified three different aspects in the pedagogy and administration of career and technical education: practical studies, technical studies, and general vocational studies. Practical studies provide concrete and specific experiences in the tasks required of the specific occupation. Technical studies contribute information and principles from other fields that underlie the practice of the occupation. General vocational studies cover the history of the occupation and the industry in which the occupation is practiced, variations in the occupation around the world, and related topics. Besides receiving the preparation for work inside and outside of the home, career and technical education students receive a concrete context for learning and applying academic skills and concepts. It aims to build upon, strengthen, and enhance skills learned in the academic curriculum as well as teaching concrete, definable skills.

Training in Career and Technical Education

The Committee on Post-Secondary Education and Training for the Workplace examined postsecondary career and technical systems and found that three kinds of work-related training are observed in career and technical institutions: qualifying or initial training, skills improvement or upgrading training, and retraining, which are often intended for displaced workers (Hansen, 1997). Each of these types of work-related training serves different functions. Qualifying or initial training is geared toward individuals who are preparing to enter into a new field. Skills improvement or upgrading training is often utilized by those who are already established in a field and wish to learn new skills to apply to their current position, or to advance to a higher position. Retraining for displaced workers focuses on preparing those who are unable to find jobs congruent with their preparation. This teaches them the skills necessary to find a more suitable occupation. It is necessary that these career and technical institutions are assessing student needs and preparing students with workplace training that is directly related to the world of work, as well as the individual's career needs.

Career and technical schools offer expert technical staff to deliver the curriculum. This curriculum can be identified as a combination of classroom instruction, hands-on laboratory work, and in some cases, on-the-job training, which is augmented by an active network of student organizations.

It is necessary to view career and technical preparation in accordance with the needs of both society and the individual. While meeting the demands of the economy, individual abilities must be utilized to the fullest. Career and technical education also posits that it is important to meet the internalized job needs of individuals.

Overall, career and technical education is a form of education that is underutilized and often under appreciated. It is necessary for counselors working with students transitioning to postsecondary education to be aware of the unique contributions career and technical education can provide to the work environment. Additionally, knowledge about how these particular institutions can be of benefit to students and adults is important.

History of Technical Institutions

Career and technical education systems in America can be followed back to the apprenticeship system prior to the Industrial Revolution. Since that time, the decline of handwork and the specialization of occupational functions have forced society to develop institutions of career and technical education. Manual training, involving general instruction in the use of hand tools, developed in Scandinavia in response to the doctrines of Friedrich Froebel and Johann Pestalozzi. The concept became popular in U.S. elementary schools after 1880. Initially, the object of this training was not vocational. It gradually developed into extended courses in industrial training. Other early forms of vocational education consisted of bookkeeping, stenography, and allied commercial work in public and private institutions (Calhoun & Finch, 1976).

In 1862, the Morill Act, which established land-grant colleges, was the first effort by the federal government to ensure vocational education. However, nothing further in this area was done until the Smith-Hughes Act (1917). The Smith-Hughes Act provided federal financing for industrial, home economics, and agricultural courses. This was extended in the George-Deen Act (1936) to include teacher education and training for certain other occupations. Vocational correspondence courses were formed in great numbers to meet the growing demand for training. However, these courses were often poorly designed and lacked value. Improvement for these courses came under the National Home Study Council (1926).

Significant advances in vocational education were made by the armed services during World War II. At this time, there was a great need for technicians. Special training methods stressing graphic presentation and work were used to meet this demand. Further impetus to vocational training resulted from the Servicemen's Readjustment Act of 1944 (otherwise known as the G. I. Bill of Rights) which allowed veterans to receive tuition and subsistence during extended vocational training. Subsequent bills provided funds for the vocational education of veterans of the Korean and Vietnam Wars. The Manpower Development Training Act (1962), Vocational Education Act (1963), Vocational Education Amendments (1968), and the Carl D. Perkins Vocational and Applied Technology Act (1984) have helped to upgrade the nation's workforce and ensure that vocational training is available for both physically challenged and economically challenged individuals (Calhoun & Finch, 1976; Wonacott, 2003).

The first community colleges were established in the 1920s and were locally funded until the legislature enacted the state's first junior colleges law in 1941. The law included a provision that specified career and technical education programs as part of the two-year college mission. The current system is framed in state law by the Community College Act of 1967 and the Technical College Act of 1991. The 1991 law merged the technical and community colleges and gave the State Board for Community and Technical Colleges (SBCTC) responsibility for adult basic education programs. Federal funding for career and technical education legislation began with the Smith Hughes Act of 1917. In 1976, the Vocational Education Act set aside funds to assist special populations, such as people with disabilities, the educationally disadvantaged, and single parents. The current law is the third reauthorization of a 1984 act. Known as Perkins IV, the act emphasizes career and technical education programs integrating academic and occupational education, technology use, teacher training, and distance learning (Rojewski, 2002).

Career and Technical Education in the Twenty-First Century

Career and technical education in the U.S. has gone through an extended evolutionary process. Formal vocational education began early in the twentieth century. Over the past hundred years, vocational education has evolved from its original inception to respond to changes in society, technology, education and educational philosophy, and work settings. Currently, vocational, or career and technical education goes well beyond the specific technical knowledge and skills required for particular occupations. Career and technical education is composed of not only technical preparation, but also academic foundations, higher-order thinking, and personal qualities needed in order to be successful in the workplace (Wonacott, 2003).

Until the end of the twentieth century, career and technical education focused on specific trades such as mechanics, plumbing, welding, or carpentry. The twenty-first century labor market has become much more specialized, and the workplace demands higher levels of skill. Career and technical education has diversified and now exists in industries such as retail, tourism, information technology, funeral services, and cosmetics, as well as in the traditional crafts and cottage industries. Many of these trades are highly paid and always in demand, making them particularly relevant for those seeking work in the twenty-first century (Wonacott, 2003).

CHARACTERISTICS DISTINGUISHING CAREER AND TECHNICAL PROGRAMS FROM THOSE OFFERED AT FOUR-YEAR COLLEGES/UNIVERSITIES

Higher education opens up a world of opportunities for individuals. It is possible for students to acquire postsecondary education in many different types of institutions: four-year, two-year, and certificate programs in the public, private not for profit, and private for profit sectors. Programs vary in the education they offer students and in the time students are expected to complete such programs (Gilmore & Bose, 2005). Career and technical education has provided many unique contributions to the field of education. It is important for counselors to be aware of what differentiates education geared toward a bachelor's degree and education intended to supply the skills necessary for career and technical occupations. The point is simple; differences *do* exist between the different types of education that are offered.

The main differences between career and technical education and other postsecondary options reside within the type of instruction provided and the way in which topics of study are addressed. One of the main distinctions between career and technical education programs and bachelor's degree programs is the program's main focus. Career and technical education exists as a very particular type of education.

Career and technical education is a modern alternative to the apprenticeships of the past but is executed much more quickly and efficiently. This is an alternative to the typical classroom education in which students are expected to learn information by listening and watching, rather than by doing and acting. Students who choose career and technical education programs will learn by participating in the specific activities that would be performed while in the workplace. The focus is on helping the student develop skills for a particular job market. This may be advantageous for these students over others who may have acquired a great deal of knowledge, but may not have direct, first-hand experiences. Additionally, career and technical education programs differ from bachelor's degree programs in the amount of general education courses offered. As opposed to students in bachelor's degree programs, students completing career and technical education programs will be required to complete far fewer general education courses.

The applied nature of career and technical education lends itself to more hands-on learning experiences than the liberal education provided in most bachelor's degree programs. The difference between the two types of education is that the liberal bachelor's degree programs are not necessarily preparing one for a specific work setting. At the postsecondary level, career and technical education courses enable students to develop marketable skills designed to meet the skill standards of an identified industry.

Class sizes also differ when comparing career and technical institutions with bachelor's degree institutions. Career and technical education classes are typically much smaller than those of their bachelor's degree-seeking counterparts. One of the primary reasons driving these small class sizes is the nature of the learning. Learning occurs as a hands-on process under the supervision of the instructor. These small class sizes allow the instructor to provide a greater amount of direct supervision to individual students for these types of activities.

The mission of career and technical education is *short-term training* for a *specific occupation.* This form of education is very practically oriented and focused on the outcome. The correlation between the training and education received and the actual world of work is much greater for those attending career and technical institutions. There is little homework assigned to students, as most education is performed at the institution in a hands-on, practical manner.

Degrees and Certificates Awarded

There are also considerable differences in the types of degrees awarded upon completion. The first degree that often comes to mind when thinking of postsecondary education is the traditional bachelor's degree. Students are typically conferred the baccalaureate degree or bachelor's degree in either the arts (BA) or the sciences (BS). Bachelor's degree programs provide a well-balanced education that include arts, sciences, and mathematics. Students in these programs emphasize a major field of study but are required to complete coursework in all of the major disciplines.

Pre-bachelor's degrees are awarded by postsecondary career and technical institutions and take three forms: associate degree in engineering technology (AET), associate degree of applied science (AAS), and certificate programs. An associate degree in engineering technology (AET) is considered to be very similar to a four-year technology degree, except that the AET programs do not include the general education or theory portions offered in bachelor's degree programs. The associate degree of applied science (AAS) is typically offered in areas not associated with engineering (e.g., health fields, food service, retail). AAS degrees are typically more applied and hands-on than AET degrees and require less advanced knowledge of mathematics and science. Career and technical institutions typically offer career development certificates (CDC) and technical certificates (TC). CDCs provide short-term programs for students who wish to develop competencies in a specific area. The programs are typically less than 30 semester credits in length. TC and AAS students complete their education in two years or less, which allows them to quickly enter the workforce. Finally, the associate of science degree programs include conceptual and technical skills training and prepare students for careers, career changes, and career advancement (Miller & Mupinga, 2006).

Characteristics of Career and Technical Education Students

The career and technical education curriculum appeals to a diverse group of students. Individuals from all racial and ethnic backgrounds and all levels of academic ability and socioeconomic status enroll in career and technical institutions. Knowing how career and technical education students differ from students enrolled in other institutions is important to counselors concerned with examining career development. Without knowledge of students' unique values, academic abilities, and future plans, appropriate career guidance cannot be administered (Echternacht, 1976).

Three different kinds of students typically make use of technical and trade schools (Gray & Herr, 2006). The first type of student is one who has a specific idea of the work he or she would like to engage in after completion of high school. For these types of students, a technical or trade school is an ideal choice because the curriculum is designed to teach real world job skills that will be required for specific occupations. For example, if an individual knew that he or she would like to become an automotive mechanic, he or she would enroll in a program such as automotive technology, which has a curriculum that ranges from 51 weeks for the core program to 63 weeks for a more specific program focused on a particular model of vehicle. Within the program, the student would be provided hands-on training in industry standard facilities by professionally trained staff including: learning how to diagnose, service, and repair domestic and foreign vehicles; troubleshooting problems using current equipment; building engines; learning essential business skills such as problem solving and math skills; and customer support skills.

The second type of student who enrolls in technical or trade schools is one who is just taking a class periodically in order to develop a particular skill or advance further in their current position. This is often referred to as adult education or continuing education. These individuals do not need to earn a full associate's degree, but rather need to complete specific courses to demonstrate that they have been trained and have sufficient knowledge in a specific area. Certificates may be offered for these students to obtain in order to demonstrate that they have acquired new skills necessary in a particular area.

The third type of student attending a technical or vocational school is a student who is planning to earn a bachelor's degree at a four-year college. In some cases, students may be unsure of their goals immediately upon leaving high school and are not ready to commit to a four-year education program. Career and technical education is a wonderful alternative for many students because many credits earned at technical or vocational schools can be transferred towards a bachelor's degree. This is particularly useful for students who may have had difficulty academically while in high school or need to increase their grade point average in order to be accepted to the college of their choice.

There are a variety of other students who pursue career and technical education (Colley, James, Tedder, & Diment, 2003; National Center for Education Statistics, 2008; Schuetze & Slowey, 2002). This may include high school dropouts with no occupational training; high school graduates of general education programs who lack any specific preparation for employment; individuals preparing for a licensable occupation; college dropouts or students desiring an otherwise unavailable course such as computer programming and individuals for whom the formal education requirements are eased because they have had several years of employment experience, but are currently unemployed or finding it difficult to remain in their present occupations (workers in transition).

Career and technical institutes have been the starting points for many successful careers and educations in the United States (Gray, 1999). The flexibility allowed by career and technical education institutions may allow students to gain an edge in the increasingly competitive workplace. At the postsecondary level, career and technical education plays an important role in advancing economic opportunity as well as social equity. Career and technical education results in students earning credentials or certificates that are important for career placement and career enhancement.

Since students are the major consumers at career and technical education institutions, it is necessary for counselors to adjust to student differences in age, educational attainment, ability, personality differences, differing backgrounds, and needs (Belitsky, 1970). The National Center for Education Statistics (NCES) reports demographic data of students seeking both credentials and associate's degrees from the year 2004. This data includes information such as sex, race, ethnicity, and age.

First, of all credential-seeking undergraduates in career education, 42% were male and 58% were female. The dispersement of students among certain concentrations differed significantly. Areas with the largest discrepancy between male and female students were education (80% female), engineering, architecture and science technologies (81% male), health sciences (83% female), consumer services (70% female), and public, legal, and social services (70% female). NCES also examined the category of race and ethnicity. White, non-Hispanic individuals composed 64% of those enrolled in career education. Black, non-Hispanic individuals represented 15% of the population. Hispanic individuals composed 12% of the population. Those in the Asian/Pacific Islander category made up 5% of the population. The category of Other (included American Indian, Alaska Native, those of more than one race, and those of other or unspecified race) composed 5% of the sample. Age was the final demographic category assessed by the NCES. The majority of career and technical education students were younger than 25 years of age. One fifth of the students were between the ages of 25 and 34. The remaining students were 35 years of age or older. The average age in years was 26. This data demonstrates the variety of students who are attending career and technical institutions.

Differences between Vocational Education at the Secondary and Postsecondary Levels

Secondary and postsecondary career and technical education differ with respect to basic goals. Secondary vocational education began with a fairly narrow mission. This mission was to provide students with specific occupational skills that can be used at work. However, over the years, other objectives have gained prominence. High school vocational programs may be designed to introduce careers, develop employment skills, prevent students from dropping out, provide a setting to accommodate alternative learning styles, teach specific occupational skills, help students secure employment, or provide a foundation for advanced training which takes place at the postsecondary level (Goodwin, 1989).

At the postsecondary level, vocational training is more advanced, technical, and focused on a single basic purpose. This purpose is to provide students with skills and knowledge needed to enter and progress in a chosen occupation. Nearly three fourths (72%) of career and technical education institutions rated preparation for specific occupations as the primary goal of the institution, compared to only 13% of secondary vocational programs (Goodwin, 1989).

Implications for Career Counseling

The implications for career counseling cannot be over emphasized. For one, productivity of the counselor is dependent upon competence. It is necessary for a counselor working with career and technical education students to be aware of the population. Statistics show that students in career and technical education below the bachelor's level consist of varying demography. Students of various age ranges are attending these institutions, and it is necessary that counselors working with this population are aware of the unique challenges associated with working with a diverse age range of students. For example, a young adult who has just recently graduated high school will have differing needs than an older adult who is in the process of a career change. Along with the existence of age differences, there is also the ethnic and diversity component. Compared to years gone by, the NCES shows an increasing number of Hispanics pursuing this form of education. This demonstrates that counselors must be aware of the multicultural implications suggested by a diverse student population. The gender variance also cannot be ignored. This awareness includes knowledge of the demographic characteristics of the student, personality characteristics, interests, aptitudes, and abilities.

An understanding of the developmental, personal, social, and cognitive assets is important when assessing students. This understanding implies that the counselor is a competent professional who utilizes pertinent information regarding the factors that affect individual and interpersonal relationships of the student. This leads to knowledge of self and others. This holds great importance because one of the problems that may lead to a crisis of confidence is a lack of knowledge of oneself and others.

American society is more multicultural and multiethnic, as well as technologically advanced. These advances impact counseling in a variety of ways. By gaining knowledge about personal and social information, the counselor will be able to assist the individual in a variety of ways. These may include developing a healthy sense of self and attitude toward others; acquiring skills in dealing with stress and frustrations including anxiety and depression; learning lifestyle practices that will enhance one's quality of life in general; and identifying career goals.

Another area in which the counselor must have knowledge is the institution itself. The counselor must be knowledgeable in the areas of course offerings, institutional policies, major areas of study, and resources for students who are nearing completion of their programs. In these terms, if a counselor is working with a career and technical student or in the community, he or she should be well-informed about career and technical education. This includes the manner in which career and technical institutions differ from other postsecondary options in order to best assist students seeking this type of education.

VOCATIONAL GUIDANCE OF CAREER
AND TECHNICAL STUDENTS

Theory of Career Development

The reference points for career counseling with career and technical education students rest on the known theories of vocational guidance. Each of the early career development theories addressed the areas of self-knowledge, information, and decision-making. Incorporating a holistic and lifelong approach to career development may allow career practitioners to assist clients even more effectively.

The most prominent career theories related to career and technical students include Super's Life-Span, Life-Space Approach (1980), Holland's Six-Factor Typology (1997), Parsons's Trait-and-Factor Theory (1909), and Hansen's Integrative Life Planning (1997). Due to the importance of knowing one's client base, it is necessary to utilize theories which provide information about development, personality, and interests in order to best assist clients. The following theories are practical and concrete, and thus lend themselves well to students who are enrolled in career and technical institutions. One important consideration for counselors is that these career development theories can be utilized in several ways to assist in the development of themes within an individual.

Super's Life-span, Life-Space Theory of Career Selection and Evolution

Super's (1980) Life-span, Life-Space theory of career selection and evolution proposes that each individual has a unique combination of abilities, personality traits, and values which make certain occupations more appealing to them as an outlet. This theory also states that particular occupations demand specific abilities and temperaments. Super notes that combinations of these abilities are usually so multifarious that people are suited to a wide spectrum of occupations. He also believes that the suitability of a person for a career and the satisfaction that an individual might feel in his or her career can be predicted by the parameters of their self-concept. Super contends that vocational development occurs in stages. He proposes that the growth of an individual in regards to work and career pass through the stages of growth, exploration, establishment, maintenance, and decline. These stages are primarily important when working with individuals in career and vocational education. Super's belief that career development is a continuous, life-long, and cyclical process lends itself well to those enrolled in career and technical institutions.

Parsons' Trait-and-Factor Theory

Parsons is regarded as the founder of the vocational guidance movement. Frank Parsons' book *Choosing a Vocation* (1909) is one of the most well known career development books ever published. His Trait-and-Factor theory operates under the idea that it is possible to measure both individual talents and the attributes required in particular occupations. It also holds the assumption that people may be matched to an occupation that is an appropriate match for the individual. This three-part theory is still highly relevant for the practice of career or vocational guidance. The three parts alluded to consist of the concept of the individual, the concept of work, and the concept of career choice.

Parsons maintains that there are seven stages for a career counselor to work through with clients: (1) personal data; (2) self-analysis; (3) client's own choice and decision; (4) counselor's analysis; (5) outlook on the vocational field; (6) induction and advice; (7) general helpfulness.

Personal data includes a statement of key facts about the individual, including all facts that have bearing on vocational issues. The self-analysis stage allows for self-examination to be completed with the assistance of a counselor. Each tendency and interest that might impact the choice of life work will be recorded during this analysis. Next, the counselor must keep in mind that the choice of vocation should be made by the client, with the counselor acting as a guide in the process. The client's choice and decision may be occurring throughout the first two stages as well. The counselor then provides his or her analysis to determine whether or not the client's decision matches with the career goals that were stated. After this stage, the counselor provides information regarding the outlook on the vocational field (e.g., lists and classifications of industries and vocations). In the sixth stage, induction and advice, the counselor needs to possess a broad-minded attitude along with logical and clear reasoning in order to provide this to the client. Finally, general helpfulness is the stage in which the counselor helps the client fit into the chosen area of work and reflect on the decision.

Holland's Six-Factor Typology/Holland Codes

John Holland's Six-Factor Typology (1997) is often used in assisting students to explore their careers choices. Holland's theory is grounded in a developmental process established through heredity and the individual's life history of reacting to environmental demands. This theory asserts that individuals are attracted to a particular occupation that meets their personal needs and provides them satisfaction. The six-factor typology is a set of personality types represented by Holland Codes. Holland's theory does not assume that an individual is simply one type, or that there are only six types of people. Rather, he asserted that any individual could be described as having interests associated with each of the six types in an order of preference. The six types are: realistic, investigative, artistic, social, enterprising, and conventional. These types are represented by a hexagonal model developed to illustrate the relationship between personality and the occupational environment. Holland's theory states that people search for environments that will allow them to exercise their skills and abilities, express their attitudes and values, and take on agreeable problems and roles.

Hansen's Integrative Life Planning (ILP)

The Integrative Life Planning (ILP) was created by Sunny Hansen (1997). This theory is one that is holistic in nature and departs from traditional career guidance approaches. It is argued that dramatic changes in society require individuals to examine how they make career decisions and how career counselors assist them in the process. This theory has a strong social justice emphasis and requires individuals to look at the context in which they live and grow to make career decisions. ILP suggests that there are six critical life themes or tasks which individuals need to address in their career planning. The following six themes are built around the theme of weaving lives into a meaningful whole. Theme one includes finding work that needs doing in changing global contexts. Theme two includes attending to the physical, mental, and emotional components of our overall health. The third theme is connecting family and work in relation to gender roles. The fourth ILP theme is valuing pluralism, diversity, and inclusion. Exploring spirituality and life meaning and purpose is the fifth theme. The final theme is managing personal transitions and organizational change.

Career Development Competencies

Career development is a lifelong process. It requires learning about oneself in relation to the world of work. Career counselors working with career and technical students should be aware of how these career development competencies pertain to them. The National Career Development Guidelines identify career development competencies for adult learners that include competencies in three areas: self-knowledge, educational and occupational exploration, and career planning.

For the adult learner, it is necessary that he or she develops self-knowledge. This includes the skills to maintain a positive self-concept and skills to maintain effective behaviors, as well as an understanding of developmental changes and transitions. Educational and occupational exploration competencies are also necessary for such students. These competencies cover a variety of different areas. Educational and exploration competencies include: skills to enter and participate in education and training; skills to participate in work and lifelong learning; skills to locate, evaluate, and interpret career information; skills to prepare to seek, obtain, maintain, and change jobs; and understanding how the needs and function of society influence the nature and structure of work. Finally, career planning competencies are necessary for students in order to make decisions, to understand the impact of work on individual and family life, to understand continuing changes in sex roles, and skills needed to make career changes.

One way to assess a student's career development status is to utilize the above competencies as well as the indicators used to assess the overall competency. There are many ways to assess a student's skills to maintain a positive self-concept. First, a student could be assessed on how competent he or she demonstrates a positive self-concept. Next, a student's identified skills, abilities, interests, experiences, values, and personality traits and their influence on career decisions may be assessed. Finally, the way in which the student identifies achievements related to work and demonstrates a realistic understanding of the self could be utilized to assess the self-concept the individual possesses. By rating competency in this manner, the counselor can assign ratings ranging from "very competent" to "not competent at all."

Tasks of the Counselor in Career and Technical Education Settings

Counselors working within career and technical institutions are involved with students in a variety of ways. A prerequisite for working with any student in the area of career development is awareness of the many possible determinants of careers. These determinants include interests, aptitudes, parental influence, salary, conditions of employment, and a desire for identity or status (Atherton & Mumphrey, 1969). Each of these factors plays an important role in career selection, and it is important for counselors to recognize these factors in order to work with students who are seeking career counseling in the career and technical institution setting.

One of the main roles of a counselor in this setting is to serve the unique needs and characteristics of the population he or she may be serving, as well as the unique differences of individuals. Student needs may be educational, social, or environmental and all are conceived as factors that hold influence on vocational choices. It is clear that students enrolled in career and technical institutions may have different needs than those enrolled in other postsecondary institutions. For example, a large number of students may have already determined their field of study and may be more interested in learning how they will be able to apply the learned skills in the real world. Additionally, students may be seeking reassurance that they have made the right choice as far as their field of study is concerned. Given that the demography of students in technical education has changed over the years, several factors come into play including the family, the media, and social interactions outside of the home. One area to be aware of is the student's family of origin and parental expectations. The effect of parental influence on the career selected is incredible. Parents can influence children to want to become lawyers, dentists, or doctors, and when this does not match the student's goals, a complete rebellion against parents' goals for children may occur (Atherton & Mumphrey, 1969).

The services of a trained counselor are invaluable in assisting the individual to assess academic and vocational strengths. Through the process of career advising or counseling, the counselor can significantly enhance appropriate career selection in career and technical education students (Atherton & Mumphrey, 1969). Career counseling can provide the student with knowledge about his or her characteristics and skills which would match with a chosen field. Although the counselor can provide knowledge, assistance in choosing a career, and assessments, it is necessary that the final decision rests on the student.

When entering into a program, all students are invited to meet with a counselor for career advising. During this process, students are assisted in determining their programs and career directions through a vocational assessment.

Vocational Assessment

Vocational assessment is concerned with determining an individual's interests, aptitudes, and skills to identify the particular work environment best suited for the individual. This assessment and evaluation involves a continuous process that may be both formal and informal. It is essential to follow-up and reassess as necessary. Formal methods include using standardized techniques (e.g., Holland's Codes, Self-Directed Search, 16 Personality Factors). Informal methods include using observation, interviews, work experiences, class tryouts, and other experiential means. Vocational assessment is part of the process used when counseling career and technical education and usually results in recommendations for training or employment, depending on the stage in which the student is.

Vocational assessment is often used for different purposes. The process of vocational assessment may be used to determine an individual's potential, the content of the career and technical education program, employability, or ability to adapt to different work environments. Many benefits may be gained by students participating in a vocational assessment. Through this process, students are provided assistance in making realistic job training and career choices based on personal characteristics. These characteristics include interests, aptitudes, and abilities. Students who are able to make realistic job training and career choices may become more productive workers in the workplace.

Vocational assessment is a frequent activity for counselors working in the career services centers in career and technical institutions. These are similar to the career services centers found in colleges/universities. The following list describes techniques and tools for counselors: gathering background information, conceptualizing students within a particular theory of career development, interviews with the individual, checklists, vocational exploration and counseling to clarify goals and help direct the process, paper and pencil standardized measures, situational assessment, and job tryouts.

Gathering background information may include receiving information about the academic programs an individual was involved in while obtaining secondary education. This could consist of general education, college-prep education, and technical/vocational education. These areas may provide information that is important in conceptualizing the knowledge someone has already obtained, and what areas in which they may be stronger. This non-standardized method of obtaining information may also include gathering prior inventories or information relating to disabilities the individual may have. Interviews may be structured or unstructured conversations with the intent to gather information from the individual through a question and answer format. Through the use of interviewing, the interviewer can gather key information about an individual and at the same time, build a trusting relationship and shared vision for the career planning process.

Choosing and using published tests and assessments are important components of the vocational assessment process. In order to gather sufficient information for career planning activities, the use of commercially published tests or instruments may be necessary. Assessments chosen should align with the ultimate goal of helping the individual. There are several factors that should be considered when choosing tests and assessments to utilize (Lowman, 1991).

First, the instrument should be one that is reliable, fair, and valid. The instruments should also be of appropriate length and well-matched to the qualifications of the test administrator. It is also important that these tests are easy to administer and provide appropriate, understandable results. Finally, and possibly most importantly, the instrument chosen to use must be appropriate to the individual's needs. After reviewing available records and conducting informal interviews, planning should determine some short-term and long-term goals. The formal testing process is used to assess seven areas that are related to career planning: academic performance or achievement; cognitive abilities; behavior, social, and emotional issues; vocational interests; vocational aptitudes; certification of occupational competencies; and physical and functional capacities. Students may need assessment in only some or many of these areas. Those who may most benefit from this are those who do not have clear vocational interests. The areas that will be of most importance for career and technical students are vocational interests, vocational aptitudes, and physical and functional capacities. Some of the most popular inventories in these areas include the Career Occupational Preference System Interest Inventory (COPS; Knapp-Lee, 1995), 16 PF, Self-Directed Search, Strong Interest Inventory, and the use of Holland codes. Individualized testing for non-traditional students, students with academic challenges, students with disabilities, and career transitioning students may require additional inventories. One such instrument for use with these students is the VALPAR 3000 system, which measures visual discrimination, motor coordination, and aptitudes. Another method of assessment is the use of computerized assessment. One final method of assessment is using work samples that simulate job tasks using tools that are more interactive and not as reliant on the client's ability to read.

Career Maturity

Career maturity reflects an individual's readiness to make appropriate career choices, including the requirements for making a career decision and the degree to which one's choices are both *realistic* and *consistent* over time (Crites, 1978; King, 1989). This concept has become well-established and is central to many career counseling and education programs in schools and colleges (Herr & Cramer, 1984). Career maturity has been changed to the concept of career adaptability in adulthood. This denotes the ability to cope with developmental and adaptation tasks, while recognizing that the ability to do so may have many peaks and valleys (Super, Osborne, Walsh, Brown, & Niles, 1992). Career maturity consists of five dimensions: planfulness, exploration, information gathering, decision making, and reality orientation. Career maturity has been associated with realistic self-appraisal, environmental experience, and several personal characteristics such as self-esteem and locus of control (King, 1989; Ohler, Levinson, & Sanders, 1995).

The notion of a comprehensive career guidance program for counselors requires a wide range of assessment strategies. When working with students enrolled in technical institutions, it is necessary to differentiate which strategies and tools are most appropriate for each individual student. There are many tests and inventories that may be used to shape the goals of the counseling relationship and define what is of importance for a client. More specifically, measures of career maturity may be used in many ways. These measures may be used to identify a client's ability or readiness to make career decisions and to identify areas a counselor may focus on with a client to enable the client to acquire the knowledge and skills that are required in order to make realistic and informed career decisions. Nurturing client readiness to make appropriate career decisions is the keystone of competent career counseling and can provide the basis for further analysis and exploration of interests, aptitudes, values, and personality traits related to work (Levinson, Ohler, Caswell, & Kiewra, 1998).

Assessment of Career Maturity

There are several inventories specifically designed to assess career maturity. The most pertinent to students in technical education include the Adult Career Concerns Inventory (Super, Thomspon, & Lindeman, 1988), the Assessment of Career Decision-Making (Buck & Daniels, 1985), the Career Decision Scale (Osipow, Carney, Winer, Yanico, & Koschier, 1976), the Career Beliefs Inventory (Krumboltz, 1994), and the Career Development Inventory (Super, Thompson, Lindeman, Jordaan, & Myers, 1988). Counselors working with technical education students may use these measures combined with insightful counseling to foster the process of career decision-making or provide evidence that the student has reached a certain level of career maturity.

Through this process, students attending career and technical institutions may be knowledgeable about the work involved in the career path they have chosen, but do not know of the different areas of practice or how to obtain their own career goals. By seeking counseling, individuals who are missing portions of knowledge necessary for career planning may be assisted in planning one of the most important aspects of their lives.

Assessment and student knowledge of self is simply the beginning of the career counseling journey for these students. Career assessment is not always a requirement whenever students enter into the career and technical institution. Those who engage in this process are assisted in determining their programs and career directions. This is accomplished through direct conversation, career interest inventories with follow-up consultations, and career planning courses.

Career counselors working in postsecondary career and technical institutions not only assist with career assessment, but also serve students in a variety of other ways. In many cases, counselors working in career and technical education settings work to aid students and graduates in taking responsibility for their own job search process. Most often, the career services/counseling portion of the institution does not serve as a placement agency. It is more common for counselors to provide general job search advice, information on preparing resumes and cover letters, resume review, preparation for interviewing (which may include mock interviews), skill building, job search classes, a job board on which advertisements or positions are posted, and also resume referrals upon request.

Career counseling has evolved and continues to grow in meeting the ever-changing world of education and technology. The roles and tasks of career counselors have also become increasingly demanding and complicated. While this process continues to unfold, the new and immediate tasks for the counselor include knowledge and competencies based on work application that involves the use of technology in meeting the needs of the current population of students that they serve. An additional requirement for career counseling is multicultural competency and adaptability. Career counselors can be expected to meet certain criteria and/or characteristics including a well-defined outline of professional practices, professional behavior, and acquisition of occupational information. While there is online availability and the library as a resource, the counselor can provide additional facts, conditions, and requirements about jobs, including training and benefits. Career counselors, however, take this a step further by assisting students in the combination of theory with practice. Students may be knowledgeable about job availability and benefits, but they may struggle with making sense of the work they are required to do while in school regarding jobs they may perceive as simple. Counselors assist clients in the process of identifying the link between performance (actual doing of the job or practice) and knowledge (theory) relating to work. This is important in strengthening the resolve to succeed in one's area of occupational choosing. Career counselors therefore act as verifiers of information "out there" to which everyone is privy. They are also engaging the students in how to use this information to achieve their goals. Essentially, the tasks of counselors include providing a database of occupational information for students and assisting students to evaluate the way in which factors such as gender, age, geography, psychology, and motivation influence their occupational choices. Counselors watch and explain occupational trends and changes including the nature and conditions of work, institution availability, training and qualifications for employment, job experience, and placements.

Career counselors also assist students with financial needs, given the fact that some students who enter into postsecondary and technical education are comprised of both young and older adult individuals with differing educational and socio-cultural backgrounds. These individuals may have different needs regarding finances that the counselor may assist with.

Additionally, counselors provide knowledge of and involvement with the future workforce to assist students in acquiring jobs and settling into the system. The goal is for this to be accomplished with a sense of pride and achievement. Career counselors sometimes go beyond working with clients within the school system to the community outside of the school system. This is because of counselors' knowledge of jobs and occupations and/or career opportunities within the outlying communities. Counselors may often incorporate the local workforce in efforts to assist the students for several reasons. One possibility is to help the students know of and learn about jobs before making choices regarding their future careers. Another reason involves assisting students in acquiring on-the-job placements in order to experience first-hand the environment of the position. Sometimes, counselors go as far as recommending their students to some of these organizations. They are able to achieve this due to the contacts they have established with these organizations. Since technical and vocational education students come from diverse backgrounds, the counselor also tends to organize activities around the student's needs. These activities are usually in collaboration with other staff and departments of the school's system. Examples of such activities include career day/week where different members of institutions and the workforce within the community are invited to come and speak with students, while sharing information about what they do. Visits to worksites are another alternative to gain contact with the work organizations.

REFERENCES

Apling, R. N. (2003). Vocational education: The Carl D. Perkins Vocational and Technical Education Act of 1998. In R. Nata (Ed.), *Vocational education: Current issues and prospects.* New York, NY: Nova Science.

Atherton, J. C., & Mumphrey, A. (1969). *Essential aspects of career planning and development.* Danville, IL: The Interstate.

Belitsky, H. A. (1970). *Private vocational schools: Their emerging role in postsecondary education.* Washington, DC: W.E. Upjohn.

Buck, J. N., & Daniels, M. G. (1985). *Assessment of career decision making manual.* Los Angeles, CA: Western Psychological Services.

Calhoun, C. C., & Finch, A. V. (1976). *Vocational and career education: Concepts and operations.* Belmont, CA: Wadsworth Publishing Company.

Colley, H., James, D., Tedder, M., & Diment, K. (2003). Learning as becoming in vocational education and training: Class, gender, and the role of vocational habits. *Journal of Vocational Education and Training, 55,* 471–496.

Crites, J. O. (1978). *Administration and use manual for the Career Maturity Inventory* (2nd ed.). Monterey, CA: McGraw-Hill

Echternacht, G. (1976). Characteristics distinguishing vocational education students from general and academic students. *Multivariate Behavioral Research, 11,* 477–491.

Gilmore, D. S., & Bose, J. (2005). Trends in postsecondary education: Participation within the vocational rehabilitation system. *Journal of Vocational Rehabilitation, 22,* 33–40.

Goodwin, D. (1989). *Postsecondary vocational education. National Assessment of Vocational Education: Volume IV.* Washington, DC: U. S. Department of Education.

Gray, K. (1999). *Getting real: Helping teens find their future.* Thousand Oaks, CA: Corwin Press.

Gray, K., & Herr, E. L. (2006). *Other ways to win: Creating alternatives for high school graduates* (3rd ed.). Thousand Oaks, CA: Sage Publications.

Hansen, S. L. (1997). *Integrative life planning: Critical tasks for career development and changing life patterns.* San Francisco, CA: Jossey-Bass Publishers.

Herr, E. L., & Cramer, S. H. (1984). *Career guidance and counseling through the life span* (3rd ed.). New York, NY: Scott, Foreman, and Company.

Holland, J. L. (1997). *Making vocational choices: A theory of vocational personalities and work environments.* Psychological Assessment Resources, Inc.

Hughey, K. F., & Hughey, J. K. (1999). Preparing students for the future: Making career development a priority. *Journal of Career Development, 25,* 203–216.

Husain, D. D. (1999). Good news on the horizon. *Techniques, 74,* 14–17.

King, S. (1989). Sex differences in a causal model of career maturity. *Journal of Counseling & Development, 68,* 208–215.

Knapp-Lee, L. J. (1995). Use of the COPSystem in career assessment. *Journal of Career Assessment, 3,* 411–428.

Krumboltz, J. D. (1994). The Career Beliefs Inventory. *Journal of Counseling & Development, 68,* 208–215.

Lakes, R. D. (2007). Four key themes in Perkins III Reauthorization: A political analysis. *Journal of Career and Technical Education, 23,* 109–120.

Levinson, E. M., Ohler, D. L., Caswell, S., & Kiewra, K. (1998). Six approaches to the assessment of career maturity. *Journal of Counseling & Development, 76,* 475–482.

Lowman, R. L. (1991). *The clinical practice of career assessment: Interests, abilities, and personality.* Washington, DC: APA Books.

Miller, D. K., & Mupinga, D. M. (2006). Similarities and differences between public and proprietary postsecondary two-year technical institutions. *Community College Journal of Research and Practice, 30,* 565–577.

National Center for Educational Statistics. (2008). *Statistical analysis: Career and technical education in the United States: 1990 to 2005.* Retrieved 2/17/2010, from http://nces.ed.gov/pubs2008/2008035.pdf

Ohler, D. L., Levinson, E. M., & Sanders, P. (1995). Career maturity in young adults with learning disabilities: What employment counselors should know. *Journal of Employment Counseling, 32,* 65–78.

Osipow, S. H., Carney, C. G., Winer, J., Yanico, B. J., & Koschier, M. (1976). *The Career Decision Scale* (3rd ed.). Columbus, OH: Marathon Consulting and Press.

Parsons, F. (1909). *Choosing a vocation.* Boston, MA: Houghton Mifflin.

Riegle, D. W. (1982). The psychological and social effects of unemployment. *American Psychologist, 37,* 1113–1115.

Rojewski, J. W. (2002). Preparing the workforce of tomorrow: A conceptual framework for Career and Technical Education. *Journal of Vocational Education Research, 27,* 7–35.

Schuetze, H. G., & Slowey, M. (2002). Participation and exclusion: A comparative analysis of non-traditional students and lifelong learners in higher education. *Higher Education, 44,* 309–327.

Snedden, D. (1910). The achievements and shortcomings of the American college. *The School Review, 18,* 369–383.

Super, D. E. (1980). A life-span, life-space approach to career development. *Journal of Vocational Behavior, 16,* 282–298.

Super, D. E., Osborne, L., Walsh, D. J., Brown, S. D., & Niles, S. G. (1992). Developmental career assessment and counseling: The C-DAC model. *Journal of Counseling & Development, 71,* 74–80.

Super, D. E., Thompson, A. S., & Lindeman, R. H. (1988). *Adult Career Concerns Inventory: Manual for research and exploratory use in counseling.* Palo Alto, CA: Consulting Psychologists Press

Super, D. E., Thompson, A. S., Lindeman, R. H., Jordaan, J. P., & Myers, R. A. (1988). *Manual for the Adult Career Concerns Inventory and the Career Development Inventory.* Palo Alto, CA: Consulting Psychologists Press.

U.S. Department of Labor, Bureau of Labor Statistics occupational outlook handbook. (2001). *Tomorrow's jobs.* Retrieved from http://stats.bls.gov/oco/oco2003.htm

Wonacott, M. E. (2000). Myths and realities series: Benefits of vocational education. *ERIC Clearinghouse, 71,* 3–4.

Wonacott, M. E. (2003). *History and evolution of vocational and career-technical education: A compilation.* Columbus, OH: Center on Education and Training for Employment.

CHAPTER 10

THE ROLE OF CAREER DEVELOPMENT IN TWO-YEAR AND COMMUNITY COLLEGES

Fred Redekop
Kutztown University of Pennsylvania

Chad Luke
Lehigh Carbon Community College

Cohen and Brawer (2008) describe the historical background and current trends that face contemporary two-year and community colleges. Among them are the ongoing tension between their college transfer function versus their vocational and other educational functions, how they operate conceptually and practically between secondary schooling and undergraduate and graduate education, as well as between more instrumental views of learning and views of learning as an end-in-itself. The authors describe the attempts to resolve other critical issues, such as the broad dichotomy between community colleges' role to enhance individual mobility versus its sanction to improve social welfare through the leveling of social class by improving access to education. Cohen and Brawer (2008) review arguments over whether community colleges divert certain segments of the population

Career Development in Higher Education, pages 211–236
Copyright © 2011 by Information Age Publishing
211

away from achieving higher educational, and presumably higher economic, statuses. This has been described as the "cooling out function" of higher education in general and community colleges in particular (Clark, 1960) and continues to be discussed as democratization versus diversion (Rouse, 1995) and as educational expansion versus cooling-out (Grubb, 1989).

Furthermore, Cohen and Brawer (2008) discuss whether there is an economic payoff to community college education, determining that "nearly all analysts conclude that community college attendance yields a net benefit. They only differ on the amount of gain" (p. 267–268). This position is echoed by Rouse (1998), who says that:

> researchers agree that community college students who complete an associate's degree earn significantly more than comparable high school graduates; many agree that even those students who complete only one or two semesters also earn significantly more than comparable high school graduates. (p. 615)

Grubb (1996) agrees in the main, saying that community colleges can give students substantial economic benefits if certain conditions are fulfilled; these conditions, which help to differentiate between what Grubb (2002) describes as the difference between "the naïve human capital perspective" (p. 299) and a more sophisticated understanding of when and how community college education and training is translated into higher earnings. Grubb (1996) describes how important it is for individuals to find employment related to his or her education, which might seem like an obvious caveat but one that is important nonetheless. He shows how important it is to take local conditions into account. For example, local labor markets with high unemployment might yield lower returns on any form of postsecondary education; periods of recession might also cut down on the numbers of community college students who are hired by local firms. In addition, finding a job with a local firm can be vital, as local companies are much more likely to have heard of the community colleges in their area; put another way, companies are less likely to value community colleges with which they are not familiar. Finally, "some fields of study, especially business and health occupations for women and business and technical subjects for men, have especially high returns" while "low-earning fields of study such as child care, agriculture, and horticulture, and many academic fields, have low or uncertain returns" (Grubb, 1996, p. 105). So, while there is an overall benefit to attending community colleges, these nuances must also be presented and discussed in order to gain a more rounded and sophisticated viewpoint.

These ongoing tensions inform this present inquiry into career development and community colleges (following Cohen & Brawer [2008], the focus in this chapter is on any regionally accredited institutions that can award the associate in science or the associate in arts degree as the highest degree) and the use of a variety of career development theories and approaches to help to focus and clarify the discussion. Community colleges, which serve as the major form of education for mid-skilled or sub-baccalaureate occupations (Grubb, 1996), are complex institutions that take on many different roles and attempt to help their students negotiate important transitions. They contend with varying, and at times contradictory, mandates, all the while "engaged with people on the cusp, people who could enter the mainstream or fall back into poverty and welfare" (Cohen & Brawer, 2008, p. 444) to a much greater degree than four-year institutions. This metaphor of being "on the cusp" is a useful one, as community college students may be on the cusp of many things—of gaining enough credits to transfer, of crystallizing a view of a possible career path, of gaining a terminal degree or certification which will hopefully prove to be their entry into the complex and often chaotic occupational marketplace. This chapter examines and redefines the tensions inherent in career development in community colleges, applies career theory, examines career development and special populations, and concludes with remarks on career counseling implications at contemporary community colleges.

CAREER DEVELOPMENT AND COMMUNITY COLLEGES: CREATIVE TENSIONS

A simple question might be posed: are community colleges actually concerned with career development over the lifespan? Are students? Or are they operating under what Cox (2009) describes as a highly utilitarian approach to learning—if a class doesn't help me to get a job in the short-term, why should I take it? Throughout many issues, there is a tension that reoccurs between short-term benefits versus long term investments. Students typically like the hands-on and applied classes or those that are tangentially related to the jobs that they see themselves getting and often dread the more theoretical classes. But as Grubb (1998) describes, there is a tension between the skills that may serve a prospective employee well to get a job and those that may help the employee to get promoted after securing that job. Employers want prospective employees to have the specific training needed for the job right now; they also want employees to have people skills, communication skills, motivation, common sense, and so on, that will benefit the company in the long term, and which will serve as criteria for promotion. The 2009 survey of the National Association of Colleges and Employers (NACE) reports communication skills, a strong work ethic, ability to work in a team, and initiative as the top qualities employers seek (NACE, 2009). Therefore, community colleges must balance their charge to prepare students for success by giving them access to the tools necessary to make them attractive to employers, while appealing to students' often short-term utilitarian approach to college.

In the complex, often chaotic, and changing occupational landscape, the specific skills that students crave and that employers demand can become obsolete overnight; Grubb (1996) describes how difficult it is for community colleges to provide the kind of current and up-to-date training that employers demand, due to the rapidity of change, as well as issues such as the expense of purchasing latest technologies. Grubb (1996) also indicates that "neglecting the more academic or higher-order competencies may not affect employment in the short run, but it is likely to be detrimental to the long-run prospects of the students" (p. 136). Grubb advocates for a return to a broader mission for community colleges as learning communities with a more holistic emphasis on flexible and coherent programming and innovative pedagogy.

But while this long-run approach may make sense to community college educators and theorists, students and prospective employers prove chronically difficult to convince. Why? For one, community college students are typically under financial constraints, and the need to compromise and perhaps forgo a desired career is particularly apparent among those with working-class backgrounds (Packard & Babineau, 2009). As Kane and Rouse (1999) demonstrate, forgone earnings are the biggest loss for those attending community college, outweighing tuition, and it may not be possible for some to recoup those losses, even taking into account the possibility of increased earnings due to more education. In addition, according to independent researchers and researchers at the National Center for Education Statistics (NCES), nontraditional community college students (those who are older, attend part-time, and commute to campus) tend to be more influenced by external variables and at a higher risk of attrition than younger, traditional four-year students (Bean & Metzner, 1985; Choy, 2002; Provasnik & Planty, 2008). Paying for tuition, forgoing earnings, finding themselves at risk for attrition—is it any wonder that community college students are concerned with knowing exactly how each class and each lesson is going to help get them a better-paying job? As some researchers have suggested, people with few financial resources may experience very little sense of volition in their career choices, and the very idea of a career may be a luxury that they very literally cannot afford (Blustein, McWhirter, & Perry, 2005). Thus, for many of those who attend community colleges, a long-term career assumes less importance in the face of the need to get a job in the short-term.

As these tensions are elaborated, it becomes obvious that the key lies in how community college students are productive rather than reductive. For example, as Cox's (2009) ethnographic study shows, students do want to learn and they are open, at least initially, to attempts to show how coursework out of their area of interest could be meaningful and important. At first, the tension between material that might serve a student's long-term interests (such as English composition, which could help to increase an employee's chances for promotion through more skill in effective communication), and his or her need to see the relevance of learning this material (the "How am I going to use this?" question) can be productive, if enhanced by the kind innovative teaching practices that Grubb and his associates (1999) promote. These practices can help draw the links between now and then, between job-specific skills and other highly-valued general job skills, between things the student needs to have to get the job and the things that he or she needs to have to get promoted. This represents a call to action for community colleges in meeting the perceived needs of their students (i.e., offering courses that provide technical, directly applicable training), while opening the door to opportunities to meet their other, perhaps unknown needs (i.e., transferable skills that promote advancement and career mobility).

However, these tensions can quickly become reductive, in the sense that without clear rationale and teaching practices, students, educators, and employers can make draconian distinctions between "book-learning" and "real-life experience," nearly always to the detriment of education. As Grubb (1996) points out, the irony is that community college students are in danger of getting neither—of not getting the most current and up-to-date technical training, since much training needs to be done on the job with particular machines, technologies, and protocols, and not getting much book-learning either, due to the student's inability to see what "theory" has to do with "practice." This observation reiterates the challenge for community colleges to work harder at selling students on the cumulative positive effects of higher education.

The Education Gospel, (New) Vocationalism, and HyperVoc

Community colleges operate within educational practices that are themselves informed by what Grubb and Lazerson (2004) term the "Education Gospel." This secular gospel, believed by many laypersons as well as by many policy makers and educators, says that revolutions in the modern, global, knowledge-based economy have rapidly shifted occupational needs from production-oriented ones to information- and service-oriented ones, which then creates a demand for higher-order cognitive and communication skills on the part of workers. In addition, the rapid pace of technology change renders many jobs and skills obsolete, so that workers must know how to learn in order to learn, since they will need to continually upgrade their skill sets and potentially change positions many times over the course of their working lives. The bar has been raised as the assumption continues to be that a college-educated person is more likely to have developed these necessary attributes. It is not necessarily our intention to argue the accuracy of this perception, but to acknowledge its reality in order to help community college students respond appropriately to it. Knowledge, both obtaining it and using it, is the currency of the new economy.

Grubb and Lazerson (2004) go on to describe the Education Gospel's clever sleight-of-hand in terms of how it addresses the tension between public and private uses of education:

> While much of the Gospel's rhetoric emphasizes national needs, it also incorporates the individual goal of 'getting ahead' and balances the public purposes of an expansive education system with the private intentions of using education for personal ends. The two are best combined... in the effort to make schooling more inclusive and equitable. (p. 3)

Thus the Gospel can simultaneously promote the idea that all U.S. citizens can benefit by becoming more competitive globally, while also acceding to the reality of the U.S.'s competitive, stratified socioeconomic system wherein, for example, there is an inverse relationship between educational attainment and unemployment, both in terms of rate and duration.

This vision of work and career as expansive and generative—the Education Gospel—is held in tension with the view of work and career as necessarily reductive to a particular job at a particular point in time, or vocationalism, "an educational system whose purposes are dominated by preparation for economic roles, one where there is sufficient access so that many individuals might have reasonable hope of more schooling, and one that is responsive to external demands" (Grubb & Lazerson, 2004, p. 3). Vocationalism, and new vocationalism, which "emphasizes career clusters or pathways that extend from the entry level to the professional level in career fields integral to the new economy" (Bragg, 2001, p. 7), highlight again the uneasy marriage between education that is "dominated by preparation for economic roles," and an understanding of vocations that views "occupations as careers rather than mere jobs, employment that provides personal meaning, economic benefits, continued development over the course of a life, social status, and connections to the greater society" (Grubb & Lazerson, 2004, p. 3).

These authors are well aware of the negative aspects of the Education Gospel and vocationalism, new or old. The Education Gospel exaggerates the rate of technological and occupational change, neglects history, oversimplifies and produces empty slogans, and overemphasizes the role of education in solving society's ills, among other things. American vocationalism has many good aspects (i.e., expands access to schooling, attempts to balance public and private gain, focuses on teaching skills and competencies, etc.), but negative ones as well. Vocationalism threatens to turn into what the authors term the world of HyperVoc, a place where employers care only about narrow employee skills to satisfy their specific company needs, where employees correspondingly seek education according to the narrowest set of criteria—no arts or music or poetry for them—and where educational institutions, community colleges and four-year institutions alike, must drop all courses that aren't directly related to workplace requirements (Grubb & Lazerson, 2004). HyperVoc is, in many ways, the logical outgrowth of the attitude voiced by the student in Cox's (2009) ethnography who provided the title for her study: "I would have rather paid for a class I wanted to take."

CAREER THEORY AND COMMUNITY COLLEGES

We have briefly investigated broad questions such as "Is the role of a community college utilitarian, ideological, personal, or social?" and "Are community colleges drawing students away from four-year institutions, enabling society to continue down a path of individuality and continued social stratification?" We turn now to career theory to help us formulate these kinds of questions in ways that can lead to strategies for intervention and assistance. For example, we might pose the following question: "Once students are in community college, what is being done to draw the attention of students to the fact that they now have greater access to and potential for success in their career pursuits, whether in furthering their education or in moving right into the work force?" There are multiple theories of career development and decision-making that can aid us in posing such questions and in formulating useful interventions.

Any theory of career development, and application thereof, must take into consideration population characteristics appropriate to that theory. Community college students represent a diverse cross-section of their wider community, with some distinctive characteristics. Compared with four-year college and university students, community college students are older (median age of 24 for community colleges and 21 for four-year), and are more financially independent (61% of community college students being financially independent, versus 35% of four-year students) (Provasnik & Planty, 2008). This financial independence contributes to 60% of community college students attending part-time, and of the 40% that attend full-time, more than one-third (36%) work 30 hours per week or more (Center for Community College Student Engagement [CCCSE], 2009). This may help explain community college students' motivations for attending classes: 51% intend to transfer to a four-year or other institution; 43% plan to complete an associate's degree; 17% plan to complete a certificate; 42% enroll to obtain job skills; and 46% enroll for personal interest (Provasnik & Planty, 2008). This distribution of overlapping motivations—survey respondents could select more than one option—highlights the uniqueness of community college students' motivations compared with students attending four-year institutions.

Social Cognitive Career Theory

One of the most useful theories of career development, especially for community college students, is Social Cognitive Career Theory (SCCT; Lent, Brown, & Hackett, 1994). Relevant especially to SCCT is the fact that almost 20% of community college students report feeling academically underprepared, further exacerbating the challenges for these students (CCCSE, 2009). The significance of this is pronounced given Social Cognitive Theory (SCT; Bandura, 1986), which describes students' perceptions of their abilities as important as the abilities themselves; abilities and self-efficacy together are far superior to abilities alone for predicting success (Bandura, 1986). SCCT offers a variety of ways to effectively address these needs.

SCCT is a well-researched approach to understanding career decisions. It is based primarily upon Bandura's Social Cognitive Theory (1986), and is comprised of four essential, interactive elements: self-efficacy, outcome expectations, goals, and perceived barriers. The theory posits that occupational interests are influenced by self-efficacy and outcome expectations. Because these two factors are based largely on perceptions, they may or may not accurately reflect actual abilities and potential outcomes (Lent & Brown, 1996). As a cognitive model, SCT rests on the premise that cognitive factors mediate the reciprocal influence of behaviors, environment, and individual characteristics (Bandura, 1986). In the case of career development, career-related behaviors (i.e., career exploration, interviewing) affect and are affected by personal characteristics (i.e., extroversion, intelligence) and the environment (i.e., job market, living situation). Each of these factors individually, and their mutual interactions, are filtered through the perspective of the individual, thereby influencing that perception.

Self-efficacy is the domain-specific belief a person has in his or her ability to succeed in a task, or set of tasks (Bandura, 1977), and is a key component of SCT. Put another way, "an efficacy expectation is the conviction that one can successfully execute the behavior required to produce the outcomes" (p. 193). Belief in ability to produce outcomes is more important than ability alone in determining behavior (Bandura, 1986). It is shaped or formed through four modes: personal mastery, vicarious learning or modeling, verbal persuasion or encouragement, and physiological arousal, as in reduction of anxiety associated with facing a task. In SCCT, self-efficacy describes the perception of an individual to accomplish specific career-related tasks. For example, Betz and Hackett's (1981) seminal study applied SCT to career decision-making among male and female college students. They found that women were less likely to express interest in traditionally male-oriented careers, despite having similar aptitude as the men in the study. The basis for this lack of interest was women's low self-efficacy regarding these careers. This study was the first to demonstrate the influence of self-efficacy beliefs on career interests and decision-making, and laid the foundation for subsequent work on career decision-making self-efficacy.

Outcome expectations include the beliefs that behaviors will have certain results. These beliefs serve to reinforce or diminish the likelihood that a given behavior will be repeated. An individual's belief that completing a two-year degree, for instance, will result in obtaining a satisfactory job, will increase the likelihood that they will complete the degree. Individual goals, "which relate to a person's determination to engage in certain activities to produce a particular outcome, also influence career behaviors in important ways. Goals help organize and guide behavior over long periods of time" (Niles & Hartung, 2000, p. 31). The last element of the theory includes barriers—real or perceived—that may negatively impact or influence the development of self-efficacy, outcome expectations, and goals.

It is important to distinguish SCCT from Social Learning Theory (SLT; Krumboltz, Mitchell, & Jones, 1976; Mitchell & Krumboltz, 1990). While SLT seeks to understand previous learning experiences, SCCT seeks to understand the mechanisms whereby individuals perceived those experiences:

> by specifying the cognitive mechanisms by which past history begets occupational interests, however, SCCT would suggest that (a) the client's processing of reinforcement information has led to the development of inaccurate self-efficacy beliefs, outcome expectations, or both, and (b) these occupations represent potentially foreclosed possibilities that deserve further discussions in counseling. (Lent & Brown, 1996, p. 356)

SCCT and Community College Students

Niles and Hartung (2000) discuss two of the major contributions of SCCT to career counseling with college students, which seem equally applicable to community college students: performance attainment and persistence in overcoming obstacles. They describe ability and performance as mutually reinforcing factors in the SCCT model. This increase in ability and performance increases self-efficacy beliefs and outcome expectations, thereby increasing persistence in overcoming obstacles.

One of the most significant impacts SCCT has on community college student career development can be seen in Betz's (2007) excellent review of recent research on the application of career self-efficacy. One of the findings most relevant to this discussion is the relationship of career self-efficacy to career interests, most notably that increases in career self-efficacy lead to increased career interests. As students come to increase their perceptions about their abilities to complete certain tasks, previously unconsidered career options emerge, facilitating the reflection on other possible skills and abilities, and so forth. Community colleges provide a place for opportunities to experience successes leading to increased self-efficacy, and SCCT demonstrates ways in which this can happen. Highlighting these successes early on can enhance this development of career self-efficacy.

It has been amply demonstrated that changing the way individuals think about their abilities and their career options increases their level of effort exerted and degree of interest expressed in occupational options (Hackett & Betz, 1981; Lent, Brown, & Hackett, 1994, 2002; Lent et al., 2005; Mitchell & Krumboltz, 1990; Rotberg, Brown, & Ware, 1987; Ryan, Solberg, & Brown, 1996). Working with community college students to increase their career self-efficacy—the perceived ability to accomplish career-related tasks—may ultimately impact their perceptions of the range of career options available to them, increase their expectations of the outcomes of attending college, and increase the likelihood of pursuing these newly discovered goals. In addition, self-efficacy can be a mediating factor in perceived barriers to choice actions and support, may predict outcome expectations and interests, and may also predict persistence among certain students (Lent et al., 2003).

Community college students experience a variety of barriers to making career choices and limited support for those choices. These students also often experience limited career interests and low outcome expectations. Applying the elements of SCCT to community colleges students can increase the likelihood of them exploring new and varied career options, expecting and achieving success, and persisting despite barriers to that success. SCCT suggests that as these students attend our nation's more than 1,000 community colleges, they are given the opportunity to reflect on previous successes and create new mastery experiences, observe others like them achieving success, experience encouragement from peers, faculty, and staff, and learn ways to reduce anxiety in the face of new challenges. Finally, elements of SCCT have been used effectively with a variety of underserved and under-represented groups, including women, African Americans, Native Americans, Latinos, and lower socioeconomic status (SES) and/or Appalachian youth (Betz, 2007).

Gottfredson's Theory of Circumscription and Compromise

Gottfredson's model, an elaboration of the person-environment fit model, is concerned with circumscription, or "the progressive elimination of unacceptable alternatives to create a social space (zone of acceptable alternatives)" and compromise, "the process by which youngsters begin to relinquish their most preferred alternatives for less compatible but more accessible ones" (Gottfredson, 1996, p. 187). As Gottfredson (2002) describes it, her original concern was to answer the following question: "Why do children seem to re-create the social inequalities of their elders long before they themselves experience any barriers to pursuing their dreams?" (p. 85). Accordingly she originated her theory of how children developmentally orient themselves to the world of work through narrowing unacceptable alternatives; her idea is that the process proceeds "by assessing the *compatibility* of different occupations with their images of themselves" (p. 91), from an initial orientation to size and power, proceeding to the realization of the gendered nature of occupations, to the recognition of how jobs differ in terms of prestige, and finally to a more in-depth understanding of one's own preferences and interests. These children move through four progressive stages of narrowing, or circumscription, moving from simplistic understandings of power and sex roles, through perceptions of prestige and social valuation, to ultimately internalize career options based on self-concept (Gottfredson, 1996).

Gottfredson (1981) describes how in stage three, orientation to social valuation (prestige), social class may lower the tolerable-level boundary of children. That is, a child's zone of acceptable alternatives is bounded at the top by what that child thinks they might be capable of, and at the bottom by what they would be willing to accept. Thus a child of low SES but high ability might think they could be a surgeon, but ultimately might accept a job of much lower status in a hospital, such as a lab technician; for a low ability, lower-SES child, it's worse, since they would not even aspire to jobs of higher status in the first place, and would be more likely to take anything they could get.

As one looks at the role of prestige in circumscription, and beyond that to the mechanisms of compromise, one might wonder whether there is more of a blurred line between the two processes than the author would have us believe. As Gottfredson (2002) describes it, "whereas circumscription is the process by which individuals reject alternatives they deem unacceptable, compromise is the process by which they abandon their most-preferred alternatives" (p. 100). Circumscription, then, apparently separates out the jobs I like from those I don't like (or slightly more technically those jobs which are compatible with my image of myself), while compromise sorts those remaining jobs I like. This description of the process as linear (progressive pruning) may also over-simplify the complexities involved in career development.

We wonder, however, whether Gottfredson's (2002) elaboration, in which she explicitly turns from between-group differences to within-group differences, may be a gloss on the thorny issue of how race/ethnicity (along with social class) drill down to the earliest formations of self-concept and consequent views of occupations. Fouad and Byars-Winston's (2005) meta-analysis on the cultural contextualization of career choice and development sets out the two related points that "race or ethnicity does not seem to contribute much to differences in career aspirations or decision making attitudes" but "there are, however, differences among racial/ethnic groups in perceptions of career opportunities and barriers" (p. 230). A significant racial gap between aspirations and expectations continues to exist, which is quite germane to any theory that attempts to explain how "if people see jobs in the same way, why don't they all want the same types of jobs?" (Gottfredson, 1981, p. 554).

We must question the idea that what they—the developing circumscribers—find unacceptable is what really matters; the point we are making is that this choice is not wholly in their hands. To paraphrase Blustein, McWhirter, and Perry's (2005) point, society itself circumscribes the circumscribers. Thus to call what they are doing "separating the unacceptable from the acceptable" before they go on to "sort acceptable occupations" may not be as accurate as to say that all along, as children become aware of occupations, the lens of race/ethnicity (along with the lens of socioeconomic class) directs their awareness, bringing some occupations into clearer focus, while leaving other occupations fuzzy. In other words, while the theory claims to be based on both psychological and sociological foundations, it limits its description of the impact of the more salient sociological factors.

Gottfredson's developmental theory is interesting and useful in many ways, providing, for example, a sophisticated way to understand how gender limits occupational choice. However, although some researchers have used the theory to look at the compromises that community college students make as they renegotiate their career choices (Packard & Babineau, 2009), it fails to clarify how race/ethnicity and social class operate in these choices. The gap between aspirations and expectations suggest that compromise is happening much earlier than Gottfredson's theory suggests— that all along, a child may not permit herself to "like" a choice or put it into the "acceptable occupations" category because of race and class, and that even as she might fantasize about her ideal occupation, she is preoccupied with those occupations she feels more likely to get. We are left wishing that Gottfredson would have spent more time showing how race/ethnicity and socioeconomic status help to answer her interesting question, "Why do children seem to re-create the social inequalities of their elders long before they themselves experience any barriers to pursuing their dreams?"

Super's Life-Span, Life-Space Career Theory

Donald Super's theorizing about careers evolved over six decades. In an early formulation, he described a theory of vocational choice and adjustment that contained twelve elements, which he then organized into ten related propositions (Super, 1953). These elements and propositions revealed his original functionalist, trait and factor approach to career choice and development, an approach that he never abandoned, but added to in his later formulations (i.e., Super, 1984; 1990; Super, Savickas, & Super, 1996). As Super and his colleagues state, "The benefits of adding a longitudinal view of careers to supplement the cross-sectional view of occupations was Super's single most important idea" (Super, Savickas, & Super, 1996, p. 122), and it is the longitudinal, developmental perspective which is most often referred to when his theory is referenced.

However, as Savickas (1997) outlines, Super's career itself developed as he continued to theorize. Super began as a trait and factor theorist, included the developmental component, formulated the self-concept segment, and finally added his final segment, the contextual component. The difficulty, however, with Super's various segments was how they fit together—as Savickas cogently argues, Super never was able to integrate and unify his disparate segments into a coherent whole. As Savickas (1997) describes it, Super was influenced by the functionalist tradition, which empirically investigated what people do, and why they do it; the trait-and-factor approach emerged as a data-driven method to identify key variables and find meaningful relationships among them, primary among these the relationship of person to his or her (vocational) environment. This method produced copious data, not theoretical constructs to organize the data, and Super struggled and ultimately failed to disengage from this "just-the-facts" methodology in order to gain a meta-perspective which could organize his results.

Savickas (1997), on the other hand, provides a convincing meta-theoretical perspective that accomplishes precisely that: career adaptability, which parsimoniously explains and unifies Super's segments. Adaptation organizes the objective status of the individual (the P-E fit) and his or her subjective perspective (the self-concept), and looks at these statuses and perspectives across the individual's entire life course (the life-span), which is set against the individual's historical and cultural context (the life-space). Viewed from the unifying perspective of adaptation, Super's segmental theory provides a great deal of insight into the career development of community college students. All learners are attempting to gain new knowledge and skill in order to be better equipped and more adaptable, but community college students may be especially in need of the ability to adapt. As we have shown, mid-skilled professions are prone to marketplace shifts, and employers consistently describe their ideal employee as one who is highly adaptable. The unifying concept of adaptation helps community college personnel to organize their efforts and succinctly answer the following question: What should be done to help community college students in their career development?—Help them adapt.

224 • F. REDEKOP and C. LUKE

Savickas' Career Construction and Social Construction/ Narrative Approaches

Savickas's modification of Super's segmental theory serves as a springboard to the author's own theory of career construction and constructivism (Savickas, 1995; 2002; 2005). As he states, "career construction theory, simply stated, asserts that individuals construct their careers by imposing the meaning on their vocational behavior and occupational experiences" and goes on to say that "career denotes a subjective construction that imposes personal meaning on past memories, present experiences, and future aspirations by weaving them into a life theme that patterns the individual's work life" (Savickas, 2005, p. 43). His theory is an outgrowth of the general movement in the social sciences toward epistemological theories that acknowledge the fact that what is regarded as true, valid, and so on is determined within human contexts—that reality is socially constructed, as Berger and Luckmann's (1966) text asserts. Savickas's theory of career construction, then, takes place within a historical context that has seen philosophical questions about "objective" reality (i.e., Rorty, 1979), as well as interesting applications to the field of psychology.

Some of these applications have come in the form of narrative approaches (i.e., Sarbin, 1986; White & Epston, 1990), wherein the adoption of a constructivist/constructionist viewpoint leads theorists and clinicians to pay attention to how a life story is constructed and understood by individuals. Savickas (2005) says that "in telling career stories about their work experiences, individuals selectively highlight particular experiences to produce a narrative truth by which they live. Counselors who use career construction theory listen to clients' narratives for the story lines of vocational personality type, career adaptability, and the life theme" (p. 43). This approach asserts the primacy of the individual's understanding of his or her own career history, while recognizing that an individual constructs meaning against the backdrop and within the constraints of the larger culture.

Since Savickas himself has modified and unified Super's approach and folded it into his own theory of career construction, one might continue this by saying that the narrative truth by which individuals live can and should be tales of successful adaptation. White and Epston's (1990) narrative theory provides a method of searching for "unique outcomes" that challenge the often pessimistic and failure-driven narratives that many people have. These unique outcomes are then used to provide evidence and support for the creation of an alternative story, one in which success, and, for the purposes of our discussion here, adaptation, are the major plot lines. Thus the work that remains for community college personnel is to help students identify concrete evidence that suggests plots of successful adaptation.

SPECIAL POPULATIONS

While scholars who write about special populations and community colleges typically lament the paucity of research done on their fields of interest (a lamentation common to many, if not most, fields of study), there does exist a variety of empirical research, theory, and meta-analytic reviews on race and ethnicity (i.e., Aragon, 2000; Maxwell & Shammas, 2007; Price, Hyle, & Jordan, 2009; Weissman, Bulakowski, & Jumisko, 1998); women and minorities (Gillett-Karam, Roueche, & Roueche, 1991; Laden & Turner, 1995; Perna, 2003; Teng, Morgan, & Anderson, 2001); women (Twombly, 1993) students with disabilities (Foote, 1998; Martz, 2003; McCleary-Jones, 2007; Quick, Lehmann, & Deniston, 2003); LGBTQ perspectives (Ivory, 2005; Leider, 2000); rural students and community colleges (Killacky & Valadez, 1995) and urban students and community colleges (Bowen & Muller, 1999); and reverse transfer students (Townsend & Dever, 1999), among other salient special student populations and community colleges.

A well-known debate between Booker T. Washington and W. E. B. Du Bois is a good beginning point to historically situate an overview of special populations in community college career development. Washington (1905) described the education at Tuskegee Normal and Industrial Institute as something "no longer to be regarded as an emotional impulse, a fetish made up of loosely jointed information, to be worshipped for its mere position," but instead as a "practical means to a definite end" (p. 7). In making the case to his critics, he said that

> Tuskegee emphasizes industrial training for the Negro, not with the thought that the Negro should be confined to industrialism, the plow, or the hoe, but because the undeveloped material resources of the South offer at this time a field peculiarly advantageous to the worker skilled in agriculture and the industries, and here are found the Negro's most inviting opportunities for taking on the rudimentary elements that ultimately make for a permanently progressive civilization. (pp. 10–11)

While critics such as Du Bois excoriated Washington for his "Atlanta Compromise" that placated Southern whites by surrendering black civil and political rights and concentrating on economic development, it is important to note that Washington wasn't blind to the dangers of focusing on industrial education, and said that "no one understanding the real needs of the race would advocate that industrial education should be given to every Negro to the exclusion of the professions and other branches of learning" (Washington, 1905, p. 8). His reasoning was that, if blacks in the South were to remain there and gain economically, they should be sensitive to local labor conditions, and that education should be situated in the South and be responsive to local labor needs. This reasoning on the basis of locale has a solid basis; as modern research has shown, the likelihood of attending college increases as geographical proximity increases (Rouse, 1995), and mid-skilled labor markets are "almost entirely local" phenomena (Grubb, 1996, p. 11). From Washington's perspective, it was important for black educators in the South to prepare black workers for the "peculiarly advantageous" local occupational fields that were growing at a rapid pace, which again anticipates researchers who have emphasized the need for educators of mid-skilled workers to forge close and responsive linkages to local labor markets (Grubb, 1996).

Du Bois (1903/2007) critiques Washington on both philosophical and practical grounds. Philosophically, he faults Washington for excessive materialism, saying that his program is in danger of "becoming a gospel of Work and Money to such an extent as apparently almost completely to overshadow the higher aims of life" (p. 25). Practically, he says that Washington's idea that economic advancement can happen without political power is a chimera. He makes the astute argument that without equality and civil rights through political enfranchisement, blacks will not be able to reap economic benefits: "it is utterly impossible, under modern competitive methods, for workingmen and property-owners to defend their rights and exist without the right of suffrage" (p. 26).

This early debate has resonance still, as we see in the charges that Cohen and Brawer (2008) enumerate against community colleges by critics who see them as subtle and not so subtle methods to cool out disproportionate numbers of minorities, a kind of educational disenfranchisement that echoes Du Bois's argument. Yet while these researchers say it remains in the last analysis unresolved whether community colleges are a net benefit to minority students, they also say that "for the minorities as for any other identifiable student group, the question should be put more broadly: 'The community college or what alternative?'" For most students in two-year institutions, "the choice is not between the community college and a senior residential institution, it is between the community college and nothing" (Cohen & Brawer, 2008, p. 58).

Thus the concern over whether vocationally-oriented education helps or harms special populations was present from the days of the Tuskegee Normal and Industrial Institute and still finds resonance today. While many commentators are convinced that the choice is between community college and nothing, as Du Bois reminds us it is essential to recognize the subtle and not so subtle linkages between educational structures and political, social, and economic enfranchisement. It is correct to say that community colleges cannot be expected to correct socioeconomic conditions that continue to disproportionately disfavor minority populations; however, career development researchers and counselors need to explicitly address issues of social justice and recognize that one of their roles includes social and political advocacy. This advocacy position, as certain researchers have pointed out, can be traced directly to Frank Parson's original vision of career counseling and development (Hartung & Blustein, 2002). This position is indeed reflected in Grubb and Lazerson's (2004) public policy recommendations that reference unfair and discriminatory practices (i.e., to discourage temporary and contingent work, which is often held by women and minority workers, by requiring that employers give equal pay and benefits for these jobs). While progress has been made, the problem of the twenty-first century remains the problem of the color line, to update Du Bois's famous statement. It is a line that continues to be drawn across college campuses; many predominantly white campuses may find similarities between themselves and the following campus: "Macro-aggressions were absent, and people came and went amicably. However, there was a huge disconnect between Black and White racial groups" (Price, Hyle, & Jordan, p. 20). This campus, where race was a problem that was invisible, yet pervasive and dominant, clearly illustrates the ongoing need for community college career theorists, administrators, and counselors to squarely talk about race and ethnicity.

As the growing body of research on special populations suggests, a general imperative exists to continue to look at the many visible and invisible characteristics of community colleges' diverse populations (for an application of the notion of invisibility and disabilities, see Martz, 2003), not the least of which is the continuing need to promote research on women and for women in community college settings (Quick, Lehmann, & Deniston, 2003). In addition, as time goes on, the very notion of "special populations in community colleges" and the allied notion of "traditional" versus "nontraditional" students may be increasingly unwieldy and perhaps even suspect categorizations. As Cohen and Brawer (2008) flatly state, variety defines community college students. Given the fact that the word "nontraditional" may accurately define more and more community colleges and more and more students that attend them, should there be an inversion of terms? Kim (2002) explores the "traditional" meanings of "nontraditional," and finds that in much of the literature, "nontraditional" identifies students 25 or older, but has also defined the background characteristics of the students, as well as the risk factors for attrition. The author ultimately questions the utility of the word: age may be a poor discriminator, and many (or most, depending on how one looks at attrition figures) students have at least one or more characteristics or risk factors. Choy (2002), in a report on nontraditional undergraduates, references another NCES study which defines the characteristics of nontraditional students—those who delay enrollment, attend part time, work full time, are financially independent, possess dependents other than a spouse, are single parents, and do not have a high school diploma—and indicates that 73% of all undergraduates met at least one of these criteria. Choy concludes that "the 'traditional' student is not typical" and that "the most highly nontraditional students (those with four or more nontraditional characteristics) were concentrated in public two-year institutions" (p. 19). If in fact the traditional college-age student is in the minority at community college campuses, are they not the new non-traditional? And who are the special populations? Appropriately enough, perhaps everyone.

COUNSELING APPLICATIONS

A major challenge is to address how students perceive community college. For example, community college is often viewed as the "13th grade," in which students errantly assume that college is simply a continuation of high school, rather than a completely new world of educational experiences and, more importantly, new expectations. As a result of such a view, many students lack the mindset needed to meet the challenges of college level work, while others minimize their successes in community college, because it is "only community college." These perceptions are significant in light of a theory such as SCCT because self-efficacy is tied directly to mastery experiences. Students who enter community college with a laissez-faire attitude and subsequently don't succeed miss a critical opportunity to demonstrate competency leading to increased self-efficacy. The view that community college is either easy or merely "plan B" is equally defeating in many ways, so any mastery experiences are minimized because of the perceived ease, again resulting in a missed opportunity to increase self-efficacy. On the other hand, students and even researchers can fail to distinguish between community colleges' distinct roles in the education of the individual, whether vocational—a two-year degree or certificate as an end in itself—or a means of meeting transfer requirements. Instead, they can be viewed as two-year commuter versions of four-year institutions. For example, some studies of self-efficacy in general and SCCT among community college students in particular fail to identify the distinctions between this population of students and other four-year college populations (Ryan, Solberg, & Brown, 1996; Tansley, Jome, Haase, & Martens, 2007).

There is also a very real risk of over- or under-emphasizing the differences between these students and students at four-year institutions. Over-emphasizing differences can mean treating community college students as so unique and idiosyncratic that no theory currently available can be applied appropriately; whereas, under-emphasizing differences treats community college students like any other college student and misses the nuances of theory necessary to work effectively with them.

Community college students are more likely to be first generation college students, are typically older, have a keener sense of trading work time (and money) for college time (credits), work more hours weekly, commute to campus, and are more likely to attend college part-time. These factors contribute to at least two important considerations when applying career theory to this population. The first is a utilitarian view of the college experience. These students tend to view college as next-job-training, rather than career development. They seek preparation for what is often a definition of work. Second, these students often view the connections between coursework and employment very concretely. As described earlier, these students have a "show me the money" approach to taking courses. As a consequence, they can fail to buy in to the career development models of career counseling. If the course does not appear to relate directly to the job they desire, they are unlikely to take it.

Lastly, these students, while they may have a sense of what they need to do in order to plan for their success, demonstrate resistance to taking these steps. More than half of community college students reported believing that career counseling is very important, yet only 5% reported using it often, and 21% not at all. The same is true for academic advising/planning: 62% think it is very important, yet only 13% reported availing themselves of this resource often, while 10% didn't use it at all (CCCSE, 2009). Persevering without asking for assistance can be deeply embedded in the cultural unconscious of this group of students. Given these considerations, it may seem overwhelming to provide assistance to these students; however, the theories outlined in this chapter provide some clear, useful direction. The key may be to meet the immediate perceived need of the student, find courses that translate overtly to job procurement while gaining access to students in order to meet their actual needs, and help them to develop a vocational narrative that equips them for the distant future as well as the immediate future.

As we've suggested, Savickas's (1997) elaboration of Super, Savickas, & Super's (1996) model should prove to be quite user-friendly for students. Given the current global economic conditions, community college students, many of whom are returning to college after being displaced from employment, may view adaptability as highly relevant. These students recognize as well as anyone how unpredictable the labor market can be, and given their pragmatic approach to college, focusing on the predictable factors in career development can assist in getting them to buy in to career development as adaptation. These conditions allow access into discussions about the components of adaptability: strategic attitudes, self- and environmental exploration, and informed decision-making (Savickas, 1997). Career interventions that focus on what Savickas calls a "concern for tomorrow" (p. 256) can direct students to be future oriented. The challenge with this, then, is identifying the factors which undergird these three components.

Despite the limitations of Gottfredson's (1996) theory of circumscription and compromise, the theory holds promise for working with the community college student population in at least one primary way. As a sociological and developmental model, it describes the individual and environmental factors that contribute to the elimination of possible career options. Many of these individual factors are strongly influenced by family and community, as well as wider cultural considerations (i.e., sex-roles, prestige, etc.). Understanding the influence of these factors can guide counselors to the source of prematurely foreclosed career options with these students. For instance, use of a career genogram (i.e., Brott, 2005) can move beyond client defenses to highlight familial patterns of employment and attitudes toward education. This method can assist students in becoming open to challenging these patterns by questioning their own limited thinking about issues related to career development. Gottfredson (1996) suggests developmental criteria for use with other career approaches: identifying occupational alternatives and being satisfied with those alternatives, matching appropriate abilities and interests to a chosen occupation, not unnecessarily restricting alternatives, and having a realistic understanding of obstacles. While helpful conceptually, this approach still lacks the concreteness offered by SCCT, which can serve to unify elements of these theories.

While the specific application of SCCT to community college students is limited, there are elements of the theory applied to these students, as well as applications of SCCT to related populations. Tansley and colleagues' (2007) study of 138 freshmen and sophomores at a large community college found that written statements projecting success significantly affected career decision-making outcome expectations and goals. The study demonstrates the power of theoretically written essays to influence career related thoughts, as a form of verbal persuasion, the third mode of developing self-efficacy (Bandura, 1986). Often, community college students lack the social support needed to persevere in overcoming barriers to academic success. Therefore, guiding them through activities that allow them to visualize their own success can be a type of verbal persuasion.

Albert and Luzzo (1999) outlined a series of approaches to dealing with barriers to self-efficacy, outcome expectations, and goals. They first suggest helping students distinguish between barriers for which personal control and responsibility are appropriate and which are not. Community college students face many types of barriers, so assisting them to discern which ones exist at systemic levels can take the pressure off of overcoming likely insurmountable barriers. More of their energy can then be devoted to addressing barriers for which they can exert a modicum of control. For example, a student facing institutional racism need not take personal responsibility for overcoming such a barrier at the system level; however, a non-native English speaking student may learn that taking ESL courses will help him or her take control of their academic development. Albert and Luzzo also suggest directing students to address skills and abilities before dealing with barriers. Attempts to improve career decision-making should focus on areas for which the student has the skills and abilities to overcome the barriers, but lacks the belief in that ability. The challenge in implementing this is agreeing with the student what skills are essential. For instance, as previously described, in addition to task-specific skills, employers seek employees with transferable skills—skills that transcend the specific job and relate more to the quality of the person (NACE, 2009). One of the most practical ways to implement this is through informational interviewing, the process of talking with hiring managers in desired fields of employment for a list of the qualities, skills, and characteristics for which they are looking. Community college students are less likely to lean on the authority of the counselors for this information, but hearing directly from employers can motivate them to consider a broader definition of skill development.

Albert and Luzzo (1990) also recommend using structured lists of potential barriers because these lists lead to identification of more barriers than does free association. Counselors can also emphasize increasing coping self-efficacy related to the four modes of learning: mastery—helping students review past success in overcoming barriers; directing them to keep a notebook of future potential barriers; vicarious learning and verbal persuasion—recommending mentor relationships with professionals; and physiological arousal—teaching techniques for reducing anxiety, or in obtaining accurate information about the career decision-making process.

CONCLUSION

Community college students, when all is said and written, are college students. They have the same needs any college student has: to feel connected, to fit in, to relate to the material in courses, and to access resources when necessary. But these students require some of these to a greater extent than other college students. Community college students are ultimately consumers, who want a clear understanding of the return on their investment of time, money, energy, and lost wages. Community colleges and counselors have an obligation, however, to help move these complex students away from a simplistic human capital approach to higher education, and to embrace the tension between college as utilitarian and college as utopian. These students require guidance toward a new educational and vocational narrative, one that paints for them a picture of overcoming barriers, and increased expectations of career options. They need a greater understanding of the role education plays—without overstating it—in creating previously unconsidered career options which mediate the influence of socioeconomic status, family culture, and prior educational experiences. The theories described in this chapter point the way to assisting community college students to understand the limits in their thinking about career (circumscription and compromise), uncover and believe in their abilities, raise their expectations about the outcomes of their behavior (SCCT), and write their own informed story of adaptability and success in their vocational journey (constructivism).

REFERENCES

Albert, K. A., & Luzzo, D. A. (1999). The role of perceived barriers in career development: A social cognitive perspective. *Journal of Counseling and Development, 77*, 431–436.

Aragon, S. R. (2000). Editor's notes. *New Directions for Community Colleges, 112*, 1–6.

Bandura, A. (1977). Self-efficacy: Toward a unifying theory of behavioral change. *Psychological Review, 84*, 191–215.

Bandura, A. (1986). *Social foundations of thought and action: A social cognitive theory.* Englewood Cliffs, NJ: Prentice-Hall, Inc.

Bean, J. P., & Metzner, B. S. (1985). A conceptual model of nontraditional undergraduate student attrition. *Review of Educational Research, 55*, 485–540.

Berger, P. L & Luckmann, T. (1966). *The social construction of reality: A treatise on the sociology of knowledge.* Garden City, NY: Doubleday.

Betz, N. E. (2007). Career self-efficacy: Exemplary recent research and emerging directions. *Journal of Career Assessment, 15*, 403–422.

Betz, N. E., & Hackett, G. (1981). The relationship of career-related self-efficacy to perceived career options in college women and men. *Journal of Counseling Psychology, 28*, 399–410.

Blustein, D. L., McWhirter, E. H., & Perry, J. C. (2005). An emancipatory communitarian approach to vocational development theory, research, and practice. *The Counseling Psychologist, 33*, 141–179.

Bowen, R. C., & Muller, G. H. (1999). *Gateways to democracy: Six urban community college systems.* San Francisco: Jossey-Bass.

Bragg, D. D. (2001). Opportunities and challenges for the new vocationalism. *New Directions for Community Colleges, 30*, 5–15.

Brott, P. (2005). A constructivist look at life roles. *Career Development Quarterly, 54*, 138–149.

Center for Community College Student Engagement. (2009). *Making connections: Dimensions of student engagement (2009 CCSSE findings).* Austin, TX: The University of Texas at Austin, Community College Leadership Program.

Choy, A. (2002). *Nontraditional undergraduates.* (NCES 2002-012). Washington, DC: National Center for Education Statistics.

Clark, B. R. (1960). The "cooling-out" function in higher education. *The American Journal of Sociology, 65*, 569–576.

Cohen, A. M., & Brawer, F. B. (2008). *The American community college.* San Francisco, CA: John Wiley & Sons.

Cox, R. (2009). "I would have rather paid for a class I wanted to take": Utilitarian approaches at a community college. *The Review of Higher Education, 32*, 353–382.

Du Bois, W. E. B. (2007). *The souls of black folk.* In H. Gates (Ed.), *The Oxford W.E.B. Du Bois.* Oxford: Oxford University Press. (Original work published 1903)

Foote, E. (1998). Disability support services for community college students. *Community College Journal of Research & Practice,* 297–301.

Fouad, N. A., & Byars-Winston, A. M. (2005). Cultural context of career choice: Meta-analysis of race/ethnicity differences. *The Career Development Quarterly, 53,* 223–233.

Gillet-Karam, R., Roueche, S. D., & Roueche, J. E. (1991). *Underrepresentation and the question of diversity: Women and minorities in the community college.* Washington, DC: Community College Press.

Gottfredson, L. S. (1981). Circumscription and compromise: A developmental theory of occupational aspirations. *Journal of Counseling Psychology, 28,* 545–579.

Gottfredson, L. S. (1996). Gottfredson's theory of circumscription and compromise. In S. Brown, & L. Brooks (Eds.), *Career choice and development* (3rd ed.). San Francisco, CA: Jossey-Bass.

Gottfredson, L. S. (2002). Gottfredson's theory of circumscription, compromise, and self-creation. In S. Brown & Associates (Eds.), *Career choice and development* (4th ed., pp. 85–148). San Francisco, CA: Jossey-Bass.

Grubb, W. N. (1989). The effects of differentiation on educational attainment: The case of community colleges. *Review of Higher Education, 12,* 349–374.

Grubb, W. N. (1996). *Working in the middle: Strengthening education and training for the mid-skilled labor force.* San Francisco, CA: Jossey-Bass.

Grubb, W. N. (2002). Learning and earning in the middle, part I: National studies of pre-baccalaureate education. *Economics of Education Review, 21,* 299–321.

Grubb, W. N., Worthen, H., Byrd, B., Webb, E., Badway, N., Case, C., et al. (1999). *Honored but invisible: An inside look at teaching in community colleges.* New York: Routlege.

Grubb, W. N, & Lazerson, M. (2004). *The education gospel: The economic power of schooling.* Cambridge, MA: Harvard.

Hackett, G., & Betz, N. E. (1981). A self-efficacy approach to the career development of women. *Journal of Vocational Behavior, 18,* 326–339.

Hartung, P. J., & Blustein, D. L. (2002). Reason, intuition, and social justice: Elaborating on Parson's career decision-making model. *Journal of Counseling & Development, 80,* 41–47.

Ivory, B. T. (2005). LGBT students in community college: Characteristics, challenges, and recommendations. *New Directions for Student Services, 111,* 61–69.

Kane, T. J., & Rouse, C. E. (1999). The community college: Educating students at the margin between college and work. *Journal of Economic Perspectives, 13,* 63–84.

Killacky, J., & Valadez, J. R. (1995). *Portrait of the rural community college.* San Francisco: Jossey-Bass.

Kim, K. A. (2002). Exploring the meaning of "nontraditional" at the community college. *Community College Review, 30,* 74–89.

Krumboltz, J. D., Mitchell, A. M., & Jones, G. B. (1976). A social learning theory of career selection. *The Counseling Psychologist, 6,* 71–81.

Laden, B. V., & Turner, C. S. V. (1995). Viewing community college students through the lenses of gender and color. *New Directions for Community Colleges, 89,* 15–27.

Leider, S. (2000). Sexual minorities on community college campuses. Los Angeles: ERIC Clearinghouse for Community Colleges. (ED 447841).

Lent, R. W., & Brown, S. D. (1996). Social cognitive approach to career development: An overview. *Career Development Quarterly, 44*, 310–321.

Lent, R. W., Brown, S. D., & Hackett, G. (1994). Toward a unifying social cognitive theory of career and academic interest, choice, and performance. *Journal of Vocational Behavior, 45*, 79–122.

Lent, R. W., Brown, S. D., & Hackett, G. (2002). Social cognitive career theory. In D. Brown and Associates (Eds.), *Career choice and development* (4th ed., pp. 255–311). San Francisco, CA: Jossey-Bass.

Lent, R. W., Brown, S. D., Sheu, H-B., Schmidt, J., Brenner, B., Gloster, C. S., et al. (2005). Social cognitive predictors of academic interests and goals in engineering: Utility for women and students at historically Black universities. *Journal of Counseling Psychology, 52*, 84–92.

Lent, R. W., Brown, S. D., Schmidt, J., Brenner, B., Lyons, H., & Treistman, D. (2003). Relation of contextual supports and barriers to choice behavior in engineering majors: Test of alternative social cognitive models. *Journal of Counseling Psychology, 50*, 458–465.

Martz, E. (2003). Invisibility of disability and work experience as predictors of employment among community college students with disabilities. *Journal of Vocational Rehabilitation, 18*, 153–161.

Maxwell, W., & Shammas, D. (2007). Research on race and ethnic relations among community college students. *Community College Review, 34*, 344–361.

McCleary-Jones, V. (2007). Learning disabilities in the community college and the role of disability services departments. *Journal of Cultural Diversity, 14*, 43–47.

Mitchell, L. K., & Krumboltz, J. D. (1990). Social learning approach to career decision choice and development: Krumboltz's theory. In D. Brown, L. Brooks, & Associates (Eds.), *Career choice and development: Applying contemporary theories to practice* (2nd ed., pp. 145–196). San Francisco, CA: Jossey-Bass.

National Association of Colleges and Employers (2010). *Job outlook: Verbal communication skills most sought by employers* (Spotlight Online for Career Services Professionals, December 8, 2010). Retrieved from http://www.naceweb.org/so12082010/college_skills/?referal=.

Niles, S. G., & Hartung, P. J. (2000). Emerging career theories. In D. A. Luzzo, (Ed.), *Career counseling of college students* (pp. 23–42). Washington, DC: American Psychological Association.

Packard, B. W., & Babineau, M. E. (2009). From drafter to engineer, doctor to nurse: An examination of career compromise as renegotiated by working-class adults over time. *Journal of Career Development, 35*, 207–227.

Perna, L. W. (2003). The status of women and minorities among community college faculty. *Research in Higher Education, 44*, 205–240.

Provasnik, S., & Planty, M. (2008). *Community colleges: Special supplement to the Condition of Education 2008 Statistical Analysis Report.* (NCES 2008-033). Washington, DC: National Center for Education Statistics.

Price, D. B., Hyle, A. E., & Jordan, K. V. (2009). Ties that blind: Perpetuation of racial comfort and discomfort at a community college. *Community College Review, 37*(1), 3–33.

Quick, D., Lehmann, J., & Deniston, T. (2003). Opening doors for students with disabilities on community college campuses: What have we learned? What do we still need to know? *Community College Journal of Research and Practice, 27,* 815–827.

Rouse, C. E. (1995). Democratization or diversion? The effect of community colleges on educational attainment. *Journal of Business & Economic Statistics, 13,* 217–224.

Rouse, C. E. (1998). Do two-year colleges increase overall educational attainment? Evidence from the states. *Journal of Policy Analysis and Management, 17,* 595–620.

Rorty, R. (1979). *Philosophy and the mirror of nature.* Princeton, NJ: Princeton University Press.

Rotberg, H. L., Brown, D., & Ware, W. B. (1987). Career self-efficacy expectations and perceived range of career options in community college students. *Journal of Counseling Psychology, 34,* 164–170.

Ryan, N. E., Solberg, V. S., & Brown, S. D. (1996). Family dysfunction, parental attachment, and career search self-efficacy among community college students. *Journal of Counseling Psychology, 43,* 84–89.

Sarbin, T. R. (1986). *Narrative psychology: The storied nature of human conduct.* New York, NY: Praeger.

Savickas, M. L. (1995). Constructivist counseling for career indecision. *The Career Development Quarterly, 43,* 363–373.

Savickas, M. L. (1997). Career adaptability: An integrative construct for life-span, life-space theory. *The Career Development Quarterly, 45,* 247–259.

Savickas, M. (2002). Career construction: A developmental theory of vocational behavior. In S. Brown & Associates (Eds.), *Career choice and development* (4th ed., pp. 149–205). San Francisco, CA: Jossey-Bass.

Savickas M. (2005). The theory and practice of career construction. In S. Brown and R. Lent (Eds.), *Career development and counseling: Putting theory and research to work* (pp. 42–70). New York, NY: Wiley.

Super, D. E. (1953). A theory of vocational development. *American Psychologist, 8,* 185–190.

Super, D. E. (1984). Career and life development. In D. Brown & L. Brooks (Eds.), *Career choice and development* (pp. 192–234). San Francisco, CA: Jossey-Bass.

Super, D. E. (1990). A life-span, life-space approach to career development. In D. Brown, L. Brooks, & Associates (Eds.), *Career choice and development: Applying contemporary theories to practice* (2nd ed., pp. 197–267). San Francisco: Jossey-Bass.

Super, D. E., Savickas, M. L., & Super, C. M. (1996). The life-span, life-space approach to careers. In D. Brown & L. Brooks & Associates (Eds.), *Career choice and development* (3rd ed., pp. 121–178). San Francisco, CA: Jossey-Bass.

Tansley, D. P., Jome, L. M., Haase, R. F., & Martens, M. P. (2007). The effects of message framing on college students' career decision making. *Journal of Career Assessment, 15,* 301–316.

Teng, L. Y., Morgan, G. A., & Anderson, S. K. (2001). Career development among ethnic and age groups of community college students. *Journal of Career Development, 28,* 115–127.

Townsend, B. K., & Dever, J. T. (1999). What do we know about reverse transfer students? *New Directions for Community Colleges 106*, 5–13.

Twombly, S. B. (1993). What we know about women in community colleges: An examination of the literature using feminist phase theory. *The Journal of Higher Education, 64*, 186–210.

Washington, B. T. (1905). *Tuskegee & its peoples: Their ideals and achievements.* New York: D. Appleton.

Weissman, J. Bulakowski, C., & Jumisko, M. (1998). Study of White, Black, and Hispanic students' transition to a community college. *Community College Review, 26*, 19–42.

White, M., & Epston, D. (1990). *Narrative means to therapeutic ends.* New York, NY: Norton.

SECTION V

CONTEMPORARY TOPICS IN CAREER DEVELOPMENT

CHAPTER 11

THE EVOLUTION OF THE VIRTUAL LEARNING ENVIRONMENT AND THE INTERNET

Ray Feroz and Marissa Fenwick

Technology has changed everything in our society and education is no exception. Charles Handy (1989) noted that technology was one of the *Great Discomforters* (along with wars, economics, values and demographics) that are responsible for the relentless and unstoppable change that occurs whether we like it or not. Since the advent of the personal computer around 1982, information availability and dissemination have been revolutionized. And the ability of people to interact and communicate has made quantum leaps, making commonplace what was previously unimaginable, for example, wireless connections, instant messaging, social networks, Teleseminars, smart phones, and so on. Our particular interest here is in educational applications.

The purpose of this chapter is to discuss the development of the virtual learning environment as it pertains to career development in higher education. The march of various technologies, most especially the use of the Internet, is key.

Career Development in Higher Education, pages 239–252
239

EARLY HISTORY

Until around 50 years ago, all career assessment, counseling and exploration was done by individuals taking paper-and-pencil tests, reading related career information, and meeting with a guidance or career counselor to interpret, sort things out and come to decisions about career development and job selection. Basic informational resources were found primarily in the library of the career counselor, although standard resources such as the Dictionary of Occupational Titles (U.S. Department of Labor, 2010) and the Occupational Outlook Handbook (U.S. Department of Labor, 2010) could always be found in guidance offices and on reserve shelves in public libraries. More recently, or about 40 years ago, career occupational systems were computerized and the consumer could sit at the computer station and respond to scripted messages as if in an interview. These systems were limited because of lack of memory and storage space, slow response time, and little or no capacity for audio, video, and graphics (Harris-Bowlsbey & Sampson, 2005). They did, however, free the user from the need to work one on one with a specialist for basic vocational assessment. Using these information sources, the newly enlightened career seeker would determine whether education or employment (or both) was the best choice. If education was the goal, a guidance or career counselor could be helpful with recommendations for advanced education, whether technical skill training or perhaps higher education at a community college or university. In both cases, the student would have to enroll and take classes part-time or full time depending upon their physical availability. If a job was the searcher's focus, then perusing local newspapers to find want-ads and/or finding employment through talking to friends, neighbors and individual resources could yield success. Employment agencies could be helpful if all else failed.

As the World Wide Web grew and the capacities and features of hardware and software increased simultaneously with decreasing costs, individual consumers could sit at their own home computer and perform basic vocational assessments and receive access to a myriad of resources to follow up on educational and vocational planning. The number of web site resources can be expected to proliferate. Harris-Bowlsbey & Sampson (2005) have noted some issues related to such growth of Internet resources:

- Quality of content
- Inability of counselors to know all of these sites or judge their quality
- Potential for information overload or confusion for clients
- Lack of support for clients to process information they need, and
- Lack of coordination or consistency in the information and services provided by the various pieces of this vast smorgasbord of assessments and information.

There were some unique specialty programs in the 1970s, too, such as *Job Clubs* as described by Azrin & Besalel (1980) that utilized behavioral approaches and positive group influence to provide a "can-do" structure to the amorphous task of finding and landing a job. What these early career development processes required was the need to devote face time with experts who could carry out initial assessments, interpret them, provide counseling, and assist with strategies to carry out a plan. Indeed, common to these early efforts was the need for individuals to make a serious investment of time, money and professional help.

THE SELF-HELP MOVEMENT

Careers and jobs are ubiquitous things; that is, everyone is familiar with them and everyone (with few exceptions) is cognizant with the need to "earn a living." Thus, the concepts are not so esoteric as to make students and adults fearful and feeling helpless, requiring them to find an expert to help them navigate. Unlike occupational specialties such as air conditioning repair or plumbing, everyone knows what a job is and many have firsthand experience and ideas on how to find and keep them. So job-seeking and career finding are areas that lend themselves to do-it-yourself methodology. The major drawback was that information was concentrated in the hands of experts, and finding the time and money to invest could be difficult.

Richard Nelson Bolles first published *What Color is Your Parachute* in 1970, and has published annual updates every year since. The book's new editions benefit from feedback from the prior year; the latest (2010) edition has a subtitle that mirrors the difficult US economy and affirms its contemporary nature as advertised with a 2010 *Hard Times Edition*. This book and others like it provide a career-seeker with information and hands-on ideas to use in finding a job. These books are important in that they provide an avenue for people to do career planning without need for a career counselor. In addition, many web-based resources are available for career development on the Internet (e.g., see Beutler, 2008; Jacobs, 2003; Malone, Miller & Hargraves, 2001) to include finding a job and advancing in one's career (McKay, n.d.).

DISCOVER (www.act.org/discover) is one of the oldest self-help systems available to career planners, and it has evolved from a clunky computerized software program to an Internet-based program that is very easy to use and draws upon a sophisticated data base to provide the user with plenty of available information regarding assessment, career ideas, educational information and job data and career planning. With the passage of years, it now features sophisticated links and intuitive direction from assessment information to potential career paths. Indeed, one can use the web to "Sign up for a free 30-day trial!" and the website encourages the reader to "Find Us on Facebook" (DISCOVER, n.d.).

VIRTUAL TECHNOLOGY

There are three focal areas of interest as we discuss the use of the Internet in career counseling applications. First, there is an available body of information that includes history, theories, application of theory, career and jobs data, as well as job openings and contact information. The second area is the individual vocational work to include completing assessments, developing self-awareness and a personal plan, implementing the plan (to include getting the word out to employers about your skill set and availability), and finally, monitoring success. A third area involves counseling, which is, being able to talk to an expert about one's journey through the jungle of career development and job acquisition.

In practical use, computer-assisted assessment and information gathering is done in conjunction with face-to-face career counseling, but there has been growth in virtual career guidance from start to finish, such as used at the Career Center at EM LYON, a business school located in Ecully, France (Virtual Career Guidance, 2005).

Computer-Assisted Career Guidance Systems

There has been steady expansion in the use of the Internet for career exploration and planning. The Internet "is used not only for gathering information but also for self-help" (Kleiman & Gati, 2004, p. 41). This growth has been so extensive that some have noted the danger of marginalization of the career counseling profession (Savikas, 2003; Tang, 2003; Tinsley, 2001).

At the outset of this discussion, the question needs to be answered regarding how computer and Internet applications compare to standard paper-and-pencil career assessment. Lumsden, Sampson, Reardon, Lenz & Peterson (2004) carried out a comparison study of paper-and-pencil, computer and Internet versions of Holland's Self-Directed-Search and their results suggested "that there are no statistically significant differences in the scores of the SDS Form R regardless of the version administered. These findings are consistent with the findings of 11 studies reported earlier" (p. 90–91). In addition, they "found a strong computer preference effect in general. Participants preferred taking the SDS on the computer (either on a stand-alone personal computer or a computer that was connected to the Internet) to taking the SDS on paper" (p. 91). Moreover, the administration time was much less for the Internet version, which was abridged; however, keep in mind that the scores of all three can be considered equivalent.

Kleiman & Gati (2004) have noted particular advantages and disadvantages of Internet assessment. Advantages for users include 24/7 availability and immediate feedback. Disadvantages include lack of preparation and prescreening, information overload, difficulty interpreting information, and varying quality of sites and potential for misuse and even harm (see discussion later in this chapter).

Building upon work done by Sampson (2004), Harris-Bowlsbey & Sampson (2005) have described factors that can be related to ineffective use of computer-based career development systems and services. These include:

- Personal characteristics (e.g., acute and disabling thoughts and feelings, chronic and disabling thoughts and feelings, limited verbal aptitude, limited language proficiency, and limited computer literacy)
- Personal circumstances (e.g., disabling family, social, economic, or organizational factors that influence decision making and difficulty adjusting to a recent behavioral/emotional, cognitive, physical, or sensory disability)
- Knowledge of self, options, and decision making (e.g., limited life experience, limited inclination to reflect on self-knowledge gained from life experience; limited knowledge of occupations, educational/training providers, or employers; and limited knowledge about the decision-making process)
- Prior experience with career resources and services (e.g., limited prior experience with career resources, inappropriate expectations about career choice and career services, and negative prior experience with career resources and services (p. 51–52).

Addressing these problems, and the likelihood that "individuals with low readiness for effective use of career resources and services are more likely to avoid using, or make poor use of, computer based career guidance systems" (Harris Bowlsbey & Sampson, 2005, p. 52) implies a need for effective strategies to train users. McCarthy, Moller & Beard (2003) developed an intervention by which graduate students trained and mentored undergraduates in order to develop proficiency with using the Internet technology, including search engines. Moreover, they observed that once students were trained to use the Internet for career development purposes, "the chance that a client will continue to use it for his or her career needs…seems greatly enhanced" (p. 377).

Bobek, Robbins, Gore, and colleagues (Bobek et al., 2005) suggested a model curriculum for training graduate-level counselors to use career-assisted career guidance systems (CAGC) effectively with clients. Their curriculum was developed using best practices and previous research. It included didactic training, practical experience, and opportunity for graduate students to process their experiences with fellow counselor trainees, and with counselor educators. The actual four components of the training curriculum were: (1) education regarding the role of CACG systems and relevant professional and ethical standards, (2) training to "master" a particular CACG system, (3) skill building—to include role play, and (4) service learning. They piloted their four module training program in four different institutions and reported positive efficacy and beneficial outcomes.

Given the earlier concern regarding marginalization of the counseling profession, it is more likely that technology will continue to enhance and improve the profession and not harm it. As Tang (2003) noted:

> Technology should become the career counselors' best assistant, not their competitor. Computers will accomplish much of the tedious and labor-intensive work, such as record-keeping, the management of assessment data, and searching for information. Discussion and consultation regarding cases can be done using multimedia technologies. I envision that technology will enhance career counselors' performance by being an extension to what they are doing but not replacing their jobs. Computer technologies cannot substitute for the counselor's role in facilitating self-awareness, self-exploration, and the construction of an individual's journey in a career path. (p. 67)

Similarly, McCarthy, Moller & Beard (2003) have observed "the services of career counselors may become ever more important as the amount of information available online expands exponentially" (p. 369).

Counseling

Research has shown that Internet counseling can be equally effective as traditional face to face counseling (Sutton, 2010). Virtual applications can include media such as e-mail, web pages, virtual bulletin boards, discussion boards, chat rooms (some are leader-led, others may be peer-self-help type) and video-streaming. Of course, counselor training also utilizes and benefits from the influence of the Internet through the use of teleconferences, virtual classrooms and web-based learning platforms such as *Blackboard* and *Desire To Learn*, commonplace throughout higher education.

Astramovich, Jones and Coker (2004) carried out two quasi-experimental studies comparing the effectiveness of counseling consultation using telephone and text chat, with and without adding a streaming video component. "The results from both studies suggest that (both) telephone consultation and text chat, especially when accompanied by video stream, are viable alternatives to face-to-face consultation" (p. 72).

The use of the Internet for psychological cybercounseling appears to be more prevalent in South America (Garcia, Ahumada, Hinkelman, Munoz & Quezada, 2004) and South Korea (Maples & Han, 2008) than it is in the United States. Perhaps this is due to shortages of counselors in those geographical areas, as has been experienced in states in the western U.S. where telemedicine has taken root in rural areas that are short of physicians and psychiatrists. It may also be that professionals in those areas are more technology-savvy and find it easier to adapt the technology into practice in the absence of past practices. These are only hypotheses; research needs to be done to verify these ideas.

Mentoring

Mentoring has been shown to be an important facilitator of career success, associated with advancement, pay increases and career satisfaction (Dreher & Cox, 1996; Reid, 1994). The Internet has enabled virtual mentoring to take this component of career development to a new level. One reason why many workers do not obtain mentors is difficulty in locating one, and this is particularly true for women and minorities (Knouse, 2001). Executing good mentor–protégé matches could be difficult, especially in smaller companies. Moreover, finding mentors who have a desired background and understand and appreciate the problems of women and minorities (gender issues, access to information and decision-maker issues, institutional pattern discrimination, etc.) makes the development of mentor–mentee relationships difficult. In addition, where mentors may be available, sometimes staff avoids mentorship development due to confidentiality fears and concerns about possible ramifications in terms of advancement and such.

Virtual mentoring can solve these key impediments to developing mentoring relationships. This "telementoring" presents an alternative to traditional face-to-face mentoring. Moreover, problems noted above are neutralized in terms of finding qualified mentors who would not be in a dual role relationship inside the same company. Knouse (2001) notes some advantages of virtual mentoring, including: 1) immediate access to lots of information, 24/7; 2) immediate access to mentor feedback, including that pertaining to job-related problems; 3) relative anonymity of the Internet ensures a degree of privacy not possible in traditional face-to-face mentorships and mentees would be more apt to discuss sensitive issues or personal problems; 4) from an organizational perspective, such mentoring is almost certainly cost-effective; finally, 5) mentoring can be done not just with the traditional one mentor and mentee, but with more than one mentor and multiple protégés. The advantage to this type of multiple-member group mentoring would be that protégés can receive varied feedback from different mentor perspectives (Knouse, 2001).

THE FUTURE

As stated at the outset of this chapter, the march of technology cannot be impeded. Our society has been transformed successively from agriculture to manufacturing to service to information-based economies, and there is no reason to doubt that the transformations will continue.

Dangers, Cautions and Ethical Concerns

Harris-Bowlsbey and Sampson (2005) noted ethical issues arising from the use of the Internet in career counseling:

- The quality of assessment and information resources
- The availability of interventions by practitioners when needed, including services specifically designed for individuals with a low readiness for career choice
- The quality of services provided at a distance in terms of practitioners' awareness of local conditions, events, and cultural issues
- Inappropriate access to information about an individual because of problems of confidentiality and security
- Auditory and visual privacy while using a system
- The equality of access to the Internet (p. 53).

Given the newness of the technology and the likelihood of its growth, Harris-Bowlsbey and Sampson (2005) suggested that a credential in distance counseling be created to guarantee that the holder has met the minimum criteria needed for competent practice. This could be a subspecialty under the state counselor licensure or under a national certification credential such as National Certified Counselor (www.NBCC.org) or the Certified Rehabilitation Counselor (www.crccertification.com).

Privacy and confidentiality is a serious concern with all Internet applications. Part of the march of technology is the ability of Internet companies to track the activities of their customers, capturing personal preferences and details about the interests of those customers. A recent Wall Street Journal investigative series highlighted the surveillance technology that companies are using on Internet users. This involves "Tracking Technology" that represents "a sea change in the way our industry works" as advertisers are buying access to people.

- Tracking technology is getting smarter and more intrusive. Monitoring used to be limited mainly to "cookie" files that record websites people visit. But the Journal found new tools that scan in real time what people are doing on a web page, then instantly assess location, income, shopping interests and even medical conditions. Some tools surreptitiously re-spawn themselves even after users try to delete them.
- These profiles of individuals, constantly refreshed, are bought and sold on stock-market-like exchanges that have sprung up in the past 18 months. (The Web's new Gold Mine: Your Secrets, 2010)

To put it more succinctly, when a person visits a website, tiny tracking files watch what they do online and develop a behavioral profile that is sold directly to advertisers and/or sold to a data exchange which can combine it with other sources of personal data to be sold to advertisers who target such consumers. These applications applied to career and job software certainly represent a privacy and confidentiality risk. There is a blurring between legitimate business data collection and the rights of individuals to privacy and confidentiality. It is not hard to imagine how such sophisticated behavioral tracking could be used to provide information that could be described as discriminatory or hurtful to individuals. When it involves a job or career, the potential long term damage to the individuals could be pervasive and detrimental.

The good news is that just as there has been progress in surveillance technology, there has also been progress in detecting and eliminating such snooping. This can be done by deleting cookies, adjusting browser settings, installing privacy "plug ins" and blocking or limiting ads. Realistically, though, the average user of the Internet, including career development websites, puts themselves at risk for loss of privacy as the vendors are becoming smarter and more intrusive in their pursuit of customers and profit. Be forewarned.

Though pursuing further education through virtual means may serve advantageous, certain cautions must be taken into careful consideration. As in any counseling relationship, counselors and clients alike must be advised of the ethical and legal implications that may arise when engaging in such activities. In 1995, the National Board for Certified Counselors (NBCC) was the first to address the practice of counseling via the Internet (www.nbcc.org). As the use of the Internet emerged, The American Counseling Association (ACA) approved the Ethical Standards for Internet Online Counseling in October of 1999 (www.counseling.org). Later, both organizations went on to revise statements of principles and ethical codes to encompass the many implications that may arise through technology-based counseling.

The Practice of Internet Counseling (NBCC, 2009) outlines standards for ethical practice of technology-based counseling. Forms of such counseling may include telecounseling, email-based counseling, chat-based counseling, and videoconferencing. The primary focus of this type of practice is placed on the Internet counseling relationship, confidentiality in Internet counseling, and legal considerations, licensure, and certification.

The ACA 2005 Code of Ethics provides professional counselors with a list of standard procedures to follow when practicing counseling in any type of environment (www.counseling.org). The eight main sections listed in the code include: the counseling relationship; confidentiality, privileged communication, and privacy; professional responsibility; relationships with other professionals; evaluation, assessment, and interpretation; supervision, training, and teaching; research and publication; and resolving ethical issues. Each of these topics is divided into subsections, providing even more detailed guidelines regarding ethical counseling practice.

Section A.12. of the ACA Code of Ethics outlines standards of counseling practice with specific regard to Technology Applications (ACA, 2005). According to the code, counselors are ethically obligated to "inform clients of the benefits and limitations of using technology applications in the counseling process" (ACA, 2005, p. 6). Counselors must also determine that clients are capable of using the most appropriate application (deemed by the counselor) that would best meet the clients' needs. Counselors are also obligated to abide by any laws or statutes relevant to the use of technology in the counseling process.

A counselor's main responsibility is to ensure no harm is done. When faced with an ethical dilemma that may be difficult to resolve, counselors are expected to "engage in a carefully considered ethical decision-making process" (ACA, 2005, p. 3). "Through a chosen ethical decision-making process and evaluation of the context of the situation, counselors are empowered to make decisions that help expand the capacity of people to grow and develop" (ACA, 2005, p. 3). Though an entire subsection of the ACA Code of Ethics (2005) is dedicated to technology-specific applications, the entire code applies to any form of counseling practice. It is necessary that counselors build and maintain a trusting counseling relationship with clients by adopting and adhering to a set of such standards. Failure to do so may result in the development of a negative stigma clouding potential clients' considerations to seek counseling services, technology-based or otherwise.

THE FUTURE OF LEARNING

Virtual Learning Environments

The ever-changing economy and job market continually present challenges to job and career transition seekers across the U.S. This may allow employers the opportunity to become extremely particular in their selection of job candidates and employees. As such, job seekers must present themselves as the most qualified and best fit of candidate for their target job. The demand of qualified employees may call for high school students, college students, or those currently engaged in the world of work to pursue further and/or more specific education. With the expanding use of technology has come the means to obtain further education.

Though many (if not all) colleges and universities now offer online courses as part of their core curriculum, strictly online institutions such as the University of Phoenix, Strayer University, and Capella University have emerged as some of the most widely used sources to obtain degrees from Associate's through Doctoral levels. Such programs provide college students and working adults with an opportunity to pursue further education without the demand of being present in a specific location (i.e., on campus) at a certain time. Rather, students have the convenience of logging in from their home, work, or any other computer with access to the Internet to complete their required coursework.

Student Services

As part of being enrolled or having already obtained further education, certain services are offered to endorse student and graduate success. The University of Phoenix (UOPX) assigns each student with a *Graduation Team*; a group of three advisors who support students from enrollment to graduation (University of Phoenix, 2010). The enrollment advisor aids student with requirements, educational goals, and questions they may have regarding student life or the university in general. The finance advisor provides students with information regarding academic funding, which may include grants, scholarships, and/or loans. Lastly, the academic advisor advises students on their program of choice, schedule, and degree requirements.

At Strayer University (Strayer Univerisity, 2007), admissions officers help students submit application materials, transfer credits from other institutions, or obtain credit for life experiences. The business office aids students regarding academic financing, and academic advisors help students create their course of study. The career development center specializes in assisting students with tasks such as resume writing, polishing interviewing skills, and capitalizing on network opportunities. The career development center also provides students with career fairs and job postings to connect students with local employers.

Capella University (www.capella.edu) academic advisors provide students with ongoing coursework planning and degree requirements support. Enrollment counselors guide students through the admissions and enrollment processes, while the financial aid team helps students explore options for financing their education. Capella students and graduates also have access to career counselors who are "experts who hold advanced degrees and have years of career counseling experience" (Capella University, 2010, p. 1). The career counselors are responsible for assisting students and graduates with their career planning and development needs.

SUMMARY AND CONCLUSION

The march of technology has been a driving force in redefining education, and the field of career management and development is no exception. We have come a long way from paper and pencil evaluations and face to face meetings with guidance counselors to the Internet-based assessment and career planning available today. Web-based applications that include peer support, information-sharing, virtual learning coursework and even counseling are a fact of life. These can be done entirely stand-alone or in conjunction with the traditional one on one vocational counselor. The quality and utility of these applications today, like in the past, depends upon not just information made available but the perspective, support and guidance of experts, through technology or in person.

There are also ethical issues inherent in the use of the technology and the Internet. These include issues of quality, access and privacy. Professional associations are addressing these concerns in the development of revised ethics policies and related recommendations.

Technological changes can be a blessing and curse. Self awareness is a necessary prerequisite for career planning decisions. Although technical progress brings with it new needs for safeguards, career planning has been and will continue to be served well by the ascendency of the virtual learning environment.

REFERENCES

American Counseling Association. (2005). Code of Ethics. Alexandria, VA: Author.

Astramovich, R. L., Jones, W. P., & Coker, J. K. (2004). Technology-enhanced Consultation in counseling: A comparative study. *Guidance and Counseling, 19*(2), 72–80.

Azrin, N. H., & Besalel, V. A. (1980). *Job Club Counselor's Manual: A behavioral approach to vocational counseling.* Baltimore, MD: University Park Press.

Beutler, S. (2008, May). Introducing students to career exploration. *Techniques,* 50–52.

Bobek, B. L., Robbins, S. B., Gore, P. A., Harris-Bowlsbey, J., Lapan, R. T., Dahir, C. A., & Jepsen, D.A. (2005). Training counselors to use computer-assisted guidance systems more effectively: A model curriculum. *The Career Development Quarterly, 53,* 363–371.

Bolles, R. N. (2010). *What color is your parachute?* Berkely, CA: Ten Speed Press.

Capella University. (2010). Career Center Services. Minneapolis, MN: Author.

DISCOVER. (n.d.) Retrieved from http://www.act.org/discover

Dreher, G. F., & Cox, T. H. (1996). Race, gender and opportunity: A study of compensation attainment and the establishment of mentoring relationships. *Journal of Applied Psychology, 81,* 162–169.

Garcia, V., Ahumada, L., Hinkelman, J., Munoz, R. F., & Quezada, J. (2004). Conference summary: Psychology over the Internet: On-line experiences. *CyberPsychology and Behavior, 7*(1) 29–33.

Handy, C. (1989). *The Age of Unreason.* Boston, MA: Harvard University Press.

Harris-Bowlsbey, J., & Sampson, J. P. Jr. (2005). Use of technology in delivering career services worldwide. *The Career Development Quarterly, 54,* 56.

Jacobs, R. (2003). Career and employment guide for job seekers and employees with disabilities. Retrieved from http://spot.pcc.edu/~rjacobs/career/index.htm

Kleiman, T., & Gati, I. (2004, April). Challenges of Internet-based assessment: Measuring career decision-making difficulties *Measurement and evaluation in counseling and development, 37,* 41–55.

Knouse, S. B. (2001, December). Virtual mentors: Mentoring on the Internet. *Journal of Employment Counseling, 38,* 162–168.

Lumsden, J. A., Sampson Jr., J. P., Reardon, R. C., Lenz, J. G., & Peterson, G. W. (2004, June). A comparison study of the paper-and-pencil, personal computer, and Internet versions of Holland's Self-Directed Search. *Measurement and Evaluation in Counseling and Development, 37,* 85–94.

Malone, J. F., Miller, R. M., & Hargraves, K. (2001, November) *USA Today.* 52–53.

Maples, M. F., & Han, S. (2008, Spring). Cybercounseling in the United States and South Korea: Implications for counseling college students of the millennial generation and the networked generation. *Journal of Counseling and Development, 86*(2), 178–183.

McCarthy, C. J., Moller, N., & Beard, L. M. (2003, June). Suggestions for training students in using the Internet for career counseling. *The Career Development Quarterly, 51,* 368–382.

McKay, D. R. (n.d.) Top books about career choice. Retrieved from http://career-planning.about.com/od/workplacesurvival/u/career_advancement.htm#s1.

National Board for Certified Counselors. (2009). The Practice of Internet Counseling. Greensboro, NC: Author.

Reid, B. A. (1994). Mentorships ensure equal opportunity. *Personnel Journal, 73*(11), 122–123.

Sampson Jr., J. P. (2004, June). Readiness for effective use of computer-assisted career guidance systems: A preliminary multidimensional model. In *International perspectives on career development.* Symposium conducted at a joint meeting of the International Association for Educational and Vocational Guidance and the National Career Development Association, San Francisco, CA.

Savickas, M. L. (2003). Advancing the career counseling profession: objectives and strategies for the next decade. *The Career Development Quarterly, 52,* 87–96.

Strayer University. *(2007)*. *Support*. Retrieved October 23, 2010 from http://www.strayer.edu/about#support

Sutton, D. (2010). What is Internet counseling? Retrieved from http://careerplanning.about.com/od/selfassessment/tp/assess_books.htm.

Tang, M. (2003). Career counseling in the future: constructing, collaborating, Advocating. *The Career Development Quarterly, 52,* 61–69.

The Web's new gold mine: Your secrets (July 31–Aug 1, 2010). *Wall Street Journal,* W1-3.

Tinsley, H. E. A. (2001). Marginalization of vocational psychology. *Journal of Vocational Behavior. 59,* 243–251.

University of Phoenix. (2010). *Graduation team*. Retrieved October 23, 2010 from http://www.phoenix.edu/students/how-it-works/your-graduation-team.html

U.S. Department of Labor. Dictionary of Occupational Titles. Retrieved from http://www.occupationalinfo.org/

U.S. Department of Labor (2010). Occupational outlook handbook, 2010–2011. Washington, DC. Bureau of Labor Statistics.

Virtual Career Guidance. (2005, January/February). *BizEd*. 51.

CHAPTER 12

MULTI-CULTURAL ISSUES IN CAREER DEVELOPMENT

Demond Bledsoe and Eric Owens
Duquesne University

INTRODUCTION

The United States is a rapidly changing society, but the theories behind career development have not been as quick to adapt to changing demographics. A report from the U.S. Census Bureau suggests that by the middle of the 21st Century, the United States will no longer be a predominately white society (U.S. Census Bureau, 2004). Instead, the United States will likely be a global society, in which half of all Americans will identify with one of four ethnic groups: Asian Americans, African Americans, Hispanic Americans, or Native Americans. This changing landscape of the collective American culture will pose significant challenges, most notably for counselors and others in the helping professions.

This shift in population growth will not only affect society in general, but higher education in particular. College communities are becoming increasingly diverse, which has posed significant challenges to those who provide helping services on the nation's campuses (Choy, 2002; Kitzrow, 2003; Levine & Cureton, 1998). Issues of culture and race have long been

Career Development in Higher Education, pages 253–274
Copyright © 2011 by Information Age Publishing
All rights of reproduction in any form reserved.

challenges for higher education but have become increasingly important in recent decades. The role of college counseling centers has continued to evolve in the face of changing social, political, and economic factors (Council for the Advancement of Standards in Higher Education, 1999). This evolution is also a result of the changing demographics among collegiate communities, which is represented by a growing heterogeneity in the race, gender, ethnic background, sexual orientation, and age of today's students.

Career counselors on college campuses are responsible for developing programs and interventions that will assist students from all backgrounds, part of which involves overcoming the various obstacles that can be present when cultural differences exist. Cultural barriers may include prejudice, language differences, cultural isolation, and cultural expectations and differences (Zunker, 2002). As a result of the changes in society, career counselors are challenged with developing cultural awareness, evaluating their own biases and perceptions, and appreciating the validity in others' perspectives (Sue & Sue, 1990). It is also critical that career counselors understand the needs of various populations, as well as theories and intervention strategies that are appropriate in a multicultural campus climate.

It is also important that helping professionals recognize that the worlds of work and education are far from equal.

> Black teachers if they are in the school [a contemporary school in the South] at all are teaching for the most part remedial courses that are all black. Very few blacks are teaching courses that you would value: literature, history or social studies. They are teaching remedial reading for blacks or home-ec. Schools are segregated within. In one high school that so-called has all the wealthy kids they city high school as such, they've got one black teacher. She teaches home-ec or gym or something like that....Well, initially especially, they didn't want any black principals down there and they trumped up charges against a lot of them and that sort of thing. And then the coaches. And it's not too subtle. (Foster, 1993, p. 284)

This chapter will begin with a discussion of culture and its meaning in relation to career counseling. The authors will also discuss changing demographics, both in society at-large as well as in higher education communities. Cultural factors that can have an impact on the workplace will be examined, as well as the career development process. Finally, the importance of cultural competence in career counseling will be discussed, and a theoretical framework for multicultural career counseling in higher education will be provided.

CULTURE DEFINED

Cultural diversity is an important consideration for anyone working in the helping professions, but it has been too often limited to the single, traditional course in multicultural awareness found in most preparation programs (Zunker, 2002). The literature is sparse with descriptions of techniques, intervention strategies, and assessments for specific cultural groups; most career counseling has been normed and focused on the majority culture (Betz & Fitzgerald, 1995). As the United States becomes progressively heterogeneous, the challenge of providing career development services for students will increase; however, this does not absolve the helping professions of focusing on these concerns and working toward resolution.

There are many definitions of culture found throughout the literature. The definitions of culture may include references to variables and customs related to culture; descriptions might include activities, rules, norms, heritage and traditions. There are many factors that comprise our collective understanding of culture, which makes definitions especially difficult. Matsumoto (1996) defines culture "as the set of attitudes, beliefs, and behaviors shared by a group of people, but different for each individual, communicated from one generation to the next" (p. 16) Marsella (2003) also posits that while culture is represented both internally and externally, it undergoes a continuous process of change that promotes growth and adjustment for the individuals and the population as a whole. While these definitions are not perfect, they incorporate a number of important elements for career counseling.

Ogbu's (1990) definition of culture is also helpful, as it approaches culture from a phenomenological perspective, that is, culture is defined through the lived experience of human beings:

> Culture is an understanding that a people have of their universe—social, physical, or both—as well as their understanding of their behavior in that universe. The cultural model of a population serves its members as a guide in their interpretation of events and elements within their universe; it also serves as a guide to their expectations and actions in that universe or environment. (p. 523)

While these definitions are hardly inclusive of all aspects of culture, they are helpful for career counselors and their use of culture in their work. These definitions focus on the shared experience of individuals who find connection and commonality through culture, including attitudes, values, behaviors, beliefs, and social norms. These definitions also focus on the cognitive processes that are associated with understanding and identifying with a particular culture. While there are many aspects to culture, Okun, Fried, and Okun (1999) have found agreement that environment, languages, family dynamics, and traditions are of significant importance in identifying with a particular culture and recognizing cultural differences. The most important aspect of defining culture comes from the understanding that culture is a means of identifying with others who have similar life experiences. It is *not*, however, a method of stereotyping and making assumptions. Each individual is unique, regardless of culture, and should be treated as such in the helping relationship. Identification with a particular culture is a learned behavior, and like any learned behavior, each person will learn in a different manner and identify with various elements of the environment.

To further understand culture and its impact on clients, several points tend to reappear in the literature:

- Culture includes all aspects of being human and is a process by which groups of people order and find meaning in their experiences (Erchak, 1992).
- An understanding of how language is used in a culture is critical to understanding the language itself. Language helps to shape experience (Agar, 1994; Goodenough, 1981; Sapir, 1958).
- The method most often used to understand one's culture is to compare it to the cultures of others. This process requires a perception of the various systems that are embedded in the cultures of others, and comparison to one's own cultural systems (Gibson & Mitchell, 2006).
- Culture is verbal, visual, spatial, temporal, symbolic, and auditory (Agar, 1994). It involves sensory interactions that are recognizable by others in the culture, even though this recognition may not be conscious.
- Members of a culture typically do not perceive their culture as socially constructed. Culture is considered a common sense experience, a belief that things are the way they are, the way they should be, and have always been (Geertz, 1983). This phenomenon is called ethnocentrism, and while individuals within a culture may experience things as normal within the social construction of their culture, other cultures may view the same experience as taboo or unacceptable (Okun et al., 1999).

DEMOGRAPHIC CHANGES

The U.S. Census Bureau has identified a number of cultural groups for the purpose of collecting data about the changing population in the country. While these groups are in no way inclusive of the wide range of cultures present in the United States, they have informed the research in the field of career counseling and are often used as a basis for understanding cultural changes among the population. For the purpose of our discussion, we will examine the changing cultural demographics in the United States in terms of four cultural classifications: African Americans (often referred to as black), Asian and Pacific Islanders (often referred to as Asian and Pacific Americans), Hispanic (often referred to as Latino/Latina), and Native Americans.

Figure 12.1 represents significant population changes in the United States over the next 40 years. What is most significant is that the U.S. Census Bureau estimates that by the year 2040, almost 50% of the population of the United States will be from groups that have historically been considered minorities. Other data estimates are also important to consider. The Hispanic population in this country is estimated to grow from 9% in 1990 to more than 30% by 2050, while the African American population is expected to stay relatively stable at approximately 13%. The Asian American/Pacific Islander population is also expected to grow significantly, from 3% in 1990 to more than 8% by 2050.

It can be assumed that with the significant changes in the cultural composition of the nation as a whole, similar changes would be found on college campuses. The data prove this assumption correct. In 1976, 16% of all college students were from underrepresented groups; by 1999 28% of students were people of color (Anderson, 2003). Hispanics and Asian Americans accounted for the majority of this increase. The number of Asian Americans in college increased by 360%, and the number of Hispanic students grew 243%. During the same period, the number of African Americans attending colleges and universities increased by 59% (Anderson, 2003). The number of Native Americans increased by 360%, although this statistic is somewhat skewed due to the disproportionately small number of Native

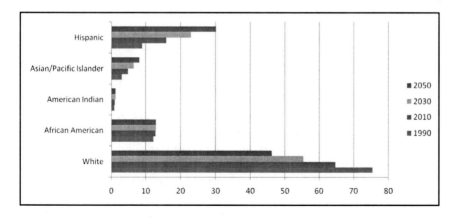

Figure 12.1   Population data collected from the U.S. Census Bureau (1996, 2004).

Americans attending higher education institutions. As the population of the United States continues to become more diverse, the heterogeneity of our campuses will likely increase as well.

What do these data mean? In short, the demographics of the United States are changing, as are the demographics on college and university campuses. The profession must continue—or perhaps even begin—to reconsider the theories, interventions, assessments, and models used in counseling students in the area of career development. The models used by the helping professions simply won't meet the needs of changing student populations. It is critical to meet the needs of this changing demographic, one that is becoming increasingly diverse, at an exponential rate.

Before entering the discussion of how to better work with an increasingly diverse population, the current state of career counseling—and counseling in general—with people from historically underrepresented communities must be considered. Ridley (1995) suggested that clients from minority groups frequently experience a lower quality of care than white clients. Specifically, minority clients tend to be misdiagnosed, usually involving inappropriately severe psychopathology, although underdiagnosis also occurs. Minority clients tend to be assigned to less experienced counselors, or even paraprofessional or nonprofessional helpers. Minority clients tend to receive low-cost, brief treatment, rather than appropriate levels of psychotherapy. Clients from different cultures are typically over-represented in public mental health treatment facilities and under-represented in private facilities. Minority clients have been found to have a higher rate of premature termination, and typically report more dissatisfaction and unfavorable impressions of counseling.

ISSUES IN MULTICULTURAL CAREER COUNSELING

Work Motivation

One issue cited in the career counseling literature regarding the world of work is that of work motivation. "Embedded within the historic core of the traditional theories of career choice and development is the notion of people having options and choices in their lives about the sorts of work that they could pursue" (Blustein, 2006, pp. 116–117). Dating back to the historic work of Frank Parsons (1909), the notions of choice and motivation have been a hallmark of traditional career development theory. However, cultural issues can have a significant impact on motivation and choice; choices are often restricted by factors such as gender, race, ethnicity, religion, sexual orientation, disability, and so forth. One assumption made in traditional career theories is that choices and options are available and known to the client. This is not always the case.

Triandis (2002) has described a culturally informed perspective on work motivation, which is centered on the conflicting values of individualism and collectivism:

> Individualism and collectivism are reflected in the goals of members of the culture. People in individualist cultures tend to have self-actualizing goals; those from collectivist cultures are oriented in achieving for the sake of others. As goals have important implications for work motivation, culture too has implications for work motivation. (p. 110)

The duality between individualism and collectivism, as these concepts relate to culture, has significant implications related to work motivation. Traditionally, Asian, African, and Latin American cultures tend to have a collectivist orientation with emphasis on "cooperation, endurance, persistence, obedience, duty, in-group harmony, personalized relationships, order, and self-control" (Triandis, 2002, p. 112). In these cultures, individuals are focused on the welfare of the group for their collective survival and well-being. Individual uniqueness is accepted and honored, but emphasis is placed on the social group. The needs of the whole are of greater importance than the needs of the one. In the career development milieu, a collectivist orientation may cause a person to consider a career choice in terms of family or community rather than individual gain.

The individualist perspective, often found in North America and Europe, takes the opposite perspective. The emphasis is on "self-realization, self-glory, pleasure, competition, and fair exchange" (Triandis, 2002, p. 112). In these cultures, individuals traditionally place their own needs and wants before any collective needs such as family, community, or society; career success is an individual goal and accomplishment. Career choice is a function of determining what is best for the individual, and decisions are made accordingly. People typically will choose the career that is best for them, with less regard for what is best for those around them.

Many of the career development theories found in the literature have been constructed around the individualist assumptions about life and work. Because these theories have been developed in individualist societies, they have typically followed individualist ways of thinking about work and career. However, recent innovations in motivational career theory have suggested the importance of shifting from individualist to collectivist thinking. Grantham (2000), for example, suggests that successful organizations affirm the importance of a collectivist approach to work and success. The successful workplace Grantham describes is one that focuses on collectivist values and interpersonal relationships. One goal of Grantham's approach is to restore an important piece of work motivation that has been lost in individualist work theory.

Work as a Function of Survival and Power

When the many purposes of work and career are considered, two significant reasons people engage in the career development process prevail: (1) to provide the goods and services necessary for their own survival and the well-being of their families and others, and (2) to enhance their social and socioeconomic status. People work because of the need to earn money; in turn they exchange money for the things that they need to survive. As people gain access to greater resources, many use them to improve their social station, which in turn provides them with the sense of safety and security that comes with economic power.

However, an element of this assumption cannot be overlooked, specifically, that access to the world of work is far from equal. The inequities are well documented and commonly discussed. Gender, race, religion, sexual orientation, age, and other factors often create an uneven playing field in the workplace. Smith (1983) examined issues of inequality in work as those inequalities related to concepts of survival and power. Smith took issue with the notion that there is dignity in all forms of work. Specifically, she argued that clear hierarchies in the world of work exist that value certain careers over others. While there may be dignity in providing for self and family, there is hardly equal value placed on the myriad of careers available to people. "For both the minority and majority of Americans, work may simply help to mark the passage of time" (Smith, 1983, p. 187).

The myth of the American Dream suggests that the American worker has unlimited options available and that one should choose wisely and then identify with that career. One of the most common openings to any conversation with someone new is, "So, what do you do [for a living?]" The reality, eloquently described by Smith (1983) and others, is that work is not always something that enhances self-esteem, and the notion of unlimited options is a farce for many Americans. Carter and Cook (1992) described the limits inherent in the traditional choice-based theories of career development. These limits result directly from the inequities in the workplace for many cultural groups. Helms and Cook (1999) argued that socioeconomic factors function to limit access to education and career options, most commonly affecting people of color in North America. In countries with a history of oppression (e.g., racism, sexism, etc.), being part of an underrepresented group plays a significant role in one's access to the world of work, and consequently, to the resources necessary for survival and power.

Flores and Heppner (2002) outline factors that are often overlooked in the career decision-making process of individuals from minority and underrepresented populations. These factors include, but are not limited to, culturally different individuals who define career, in which careers individuals are over- or underrepresented culturally, and what a person of a particular culture may experience in a specific career path. The ever present possibility that minorities will experience racism or discrimination in the workplace is an issue that may be minimized by providing specific skills and strategies of coping. Career choice and satisfaction may benefit from an exploration of careers that may have been excluded due to minimal exposure or support from family and community.

In short, access to education, skills, knowledge, and other key elements of career development have long been absent for many Americans. As more people from minority cultures enter higher education, this access is slowly increasing. However, access does not mean an immediate shift in the culture of the work world. The exponential growth of Hispanic, Asian, and African American students in colleges and universities does not necessarily change the experiences (and thus the worldviews) of these students, their parents, or their grandparents. Nor does it change the worldviews of employers and coworkers. Changes in culture typically occur slowly and require major paradigm shifts. This leads us to greater investigation into worldviews and their influence on career development.

The Personal Worldview and Career Development

The term worldview refers to a person's perception and understanding of the world around them (Sue & Sue, 1990). Okun and colleagues (1999) suggest that an individual's worldview is a function of many factors, including one's view of human nature, interpersonal relationships, the role of the family, work values and activities, orientation of time, and locus of control. In this context, one's worldview is both individually and socially constructed. Socially constructed, shared experiences reflect worldviews that are common to most or all members of a particular culture; individually constructed aspects of one's worldview typically account for the variations found within cultures.

College students are often still in the process of constructing their own worldviews. The literature on college student development describes the multitude of ways that students may construct their perceptions of the world: cognitively, morally, and socially. This is a process that many students are just beginning, and therefore, their worldviews may not be as fully developed as those of mature adults. When counseling students from different cultural groups, counselors should evaluate the degree of acculturation on the part of the client, as well as the nature of that acculturation, and how one's worldview may be affected.

Axelson (1999) suggests that some cultural values diminish as younger generations assimilate the values of the dominant culture. It is not unusual for some clients to attempt to reconcile their own culture with the dominant culture, and even other cultures to which they have been exposed. However, this can lead to internal and external conflict, as previous generations challenge the assimilation and attempt to maintain the elements of their own culture. This is often seen in the challenges between collectivist and individualist worldviews in Western countries; as younger generations assimilate an individualist worldview, they may make career choices that are incongruent with the collectivist culture that previous generations have come to expect. Younger members of the culture wish to make career choices based on their own needs and self-interests, while the collectivist nature of their culture is not accepting of this individualist approach to career development.

Different orientations to time may also present challenges in career planning and counseling. Western cultures, especially in the United States, have a strong orientation toward time and being "on time." Punctuality is considered a value and lateness is "often misunderstood as a symptom of indifference or a lack of basic work skills" (Zunker, 2002, p. 290). Other cultures are not as oriented toward time, and punctuality is not given the value that it is in the United States. Time orientation can have significant implications for career development. First, counselors should be aware of their own biases and consider the assumptions they may make when a client is late to a counseling appointment. Also, counselors should consider time orientation when working with students from other cultures. For example, a student from a minority culture that does not place value on punctuality might not be suited for a career where timeliness is an essential work function.

The importance of worldviews in the career development process does not end there. Perspectives on human nature are essential elements of one's worldview and of career development as well. Some cultures view human beings as essentially good, a view often characterized by Asian, Hispanic, and Native Americans. Members of these communities may be considered naïve or gullible among peers in the classroom and the workplace. Also, careers that involve moral and ethical evaluations of others can be challenging for members of these cultures. It is important for helpers to recognize and work with an individual's perspective on human nature when engaging in the career development process.

Privacy and personal space are other cultural elements that can be challenging when counseling members from non-dominant cultures. An example of this is eye contact: American and Arabic cultures value eye contact, while Asian cultures consider direct eye contact to be an insult. Physical proximity is also viewed differently among cultures, with many cultures having greater degrees of physical contact, such as hugging and kissing, or closer physical proximity while conversing. These are all traits that, if misunderstood in the counseling or work environments, can be extremely detrimental to a student's career development.

Cultural Differences in the Workplace

Traditional career development theories have long centered on values in the world of work; it is safe to say that most people bring different values to their careers. Cultural differences play a significant role in value differences, and it is important to note that value orientations can result in serious conflicts in working environments. Hofstede (1984) conducted a research study related to values and culture in the workplace that included 50 countries, 20 languages, and seven different levels or types of occupations. The goal of the study was to determine and examine how cultural differences impact work-related values.

Four of the most significant results of the study are provided here. First, Hofstede (1984) found significant differences in how power is perceived in the workplace. Specifically, this dimension of workplace value focused on the relationship and hierarchical tendencies between supervisors and subordinates. In some countries (e.g., the Philippines, Mexico, Venezuela, and India), significant hierarchies were found between employees and supervisors, with strong differences in status. In other countries, such as New Zealand, Denmark, Israel, and Australia, status differences were minimal. Research findings showed the United States falls in the middle of this continuum between strict hierarchy and a more communal atmosphere.

Another area of focus was the difference between individualist and collectivist attitudes towards work and the workplace. In this study, the United States, Australia, Great Britain, and Canada scored highest in measures of individualism. Latin American nations such as Peru, Venezuela, and Colombia scored highest on measures of collectivism. Employees in collectivist countries were more emotionally invested in their company and workplace, looked down on individual initiative, aspired to conformity and order from managers, and considered group decisions superior to individual decisions. People in countries that value individualism placed more importance on employees' lifestyles, were emotionally detached from their employer, were more attracted to small companies, and placed great value on autonomy and personal challenge in their work.

Another result of the study was an examination of how employees cope with uncertainty and stress. Using a questionnaire specifically designed for the study, significant differences were found between cultures in issues related to the anxiety caused by uncertainty. In cultures with lower scores, employees had less job-related stress, greater orientation to the present, stronger ambition related to advancement, and less resistance to change. Higher uncertainty scores were marked by fear of failure, higher levels of job-related stress and anxiety, a future orientation marked by distress, and less risk taking behavior.

The fourth significant finding in this study related to gender orientation and culture. Specifically, the study sought to identify which cultures would highlight and maintain gender differences in the workplace. Cultures that emphasized masculinity in the workplace valued independent decision-making, high aspiration for recognition, and stronger motivation for achievement. Cultures with less emphasis on masculinity valued collective decision-making, preferred shorter working hours, experienced lower levels of job stress, and emphasized security in the workplace.

These results suggest culture and workplace values are certainly related, if not intrinsically intertwined. Employees' perceptions of their workplaces and work roles are influenced by their value systems, which are in turn influenced by culture. Cultural differences may be used to help understand the attitudes, beliefs, behaviors, and group dynamics found in the workplace. It is also helpful when counseling students through career development to remember that culture can impact values, and values are an integral part of the career development process. Aligning values with work is important to healthy career development, and culture should certainly be part of the conversation.

CULTURAL COMPETENCE IN CAREER COUNSELING

Understanding how different cultures view and make sense of the world of work is important, but how can we become more competent when working with students from different cultures? Sue, Arredondo, and McDavis (1992) finalized the Multicultural Counseling Competencies (MCC), which are now considered necessary for counselors to practice in a culturally competent manner (Tomlinson-Clarke, 2000; Sammons & Speight, 2008). The perceived deficit in counselors' competency related to culture was the impetus for the development of the MCC (Sue, Arredondo, & McDavis, 1992). Though the focus of counseling is often on individuals, the MCC reinforce the concepts that all people are multicultural beings and thus all interactions will be affected by the various perceptions of culture by those involved (Bernard & Goodyear, 1992/2004). Today it is recognized and accepted that clinicians must attend to the client's cultural needs and demonstrate the competency to work with multicultural populations in order to practice ethically and effectively (Vasquez, 2010).

Arrendondo and colleagues (1996) operationalized the MCC by developing a matrix of counselor characteristics and cross-cultural counseling skills. The counselor characteristics include beliefs and attitudes, knowledge, and skills. The cross-cultural counselor skills include the awareness of the counselor's own values and biases, the client's worldview, and culturally appropriate intervention strategies.

According to Cross, Barzon, Dennis, and Isaacs (1989), self-awareness refers to the therapist's ability to be cognizant of personal biases, prejudices, and perceptions of people from dissimilar cultures. To better understand the cultural differences of others, therapists must be aware of how culture has influenced thinking, perception, values, behaviors, and so forth. They must understand how their own culture has directed their development, as well as how culture may have limited them. Just as it is ethically necessary to acknowledge limitations in skill, education, and expertise, it is just as important to understand cultural limitations and blind-spots.

Awareness and acceptance of differences is an essential component of becoming a culturally competent helper and must be addressed before any of the other skills can fully develop (Cross et al., 1989). The process of understanding and accepting differences consists of more than just knowing people are different. Each client will bring a different cultural background and perspective; however, it is also imperative to understand that differences extend beyond what can be seen and experienced through the senses. Cultural differences extend to worldviews, which incorporate collective understanding of the world and how it works. This includes the world of work.

A key factor in counselors' multicultural development is knowledge of the client's culture, which encourages helpers to learn as much as possible about a student's culture prior to engaging in the career counseling relationship (Cross et al., 1989). Factors such as a student's country of origin, language, religion, and sociopolitical situation should be considered. Additionally, it is preferable to learn as much as possible about a student's cultural identity through factors such as gender roles, family roles, behavioral expectations, values, work roles, customs, traditions, power relationships, and cultural ideologies.

Understanding the dynamics of difference is related to self-awareness. Developing this skill involves understanding the subtle differences in communication styles between cultures (Cross et al., 1989). As mentioned previously, eye contact is understood differently in various cultures; for some, eye contact is valued and respected, while for others it is considered disrespectful. Personal space is another area where differences in personal dynamics can be critical. Counselors can communicate awareness by adopting techniques appropriate to the differences in a client's culture of communication.

Therapeutic alliance, the quality of the interactions between the therapist and the client with regard to teamwork and rapport, is perhaps the most integral factor in attaining positive outcomes in a counseling relationship, and it can be critically affected by the multicultural competency of the counselor (Vasquez, 2010; Pope-Davis et al., 2002). Increased trust and decreased defensiveness are characteristics of clients who receive culturally competent counseling services (Hays & Erford, 2010). While generic counseling skills play a role in the efficacy of the counseling, Constantine (2002) found that clients' rating of the multicultural competence of the counselor was related to the overall satisfaction of the counseling services provided.

Sue and Sue (1990) argue that counseling interventions cannot be applied universally to culturally diverse populations without recognizing the cultural implications. They suggest that counselors who fail to consider differences in worldview have rendered themselves ineffective. Sue (1978) argues that counselors must recognize their own biases about human behavior and how those biases are culturally shaped. They must also be aware of the universalities in counseling theory, regardless of culture or theoretical orientation. Counselors must also understand and accept that racism and other forms of oppression exist and significantly influence the identities and perspectives of people from minority cultures. Counselors must be able to share their clients' worldviews and avoid negating the legitimacy of others' perspectives. Finally, counselors must be truly eclectic and integrated in their orientation and interventions.

Sue and Sue (1990) suggest that counselors need not limit their interventions, skills, or theories because of cultural differences. Instead, they encourage counselors to be aware that others' worldviews and perceptions will be different from their own. More important than changing tactics or theories is to avoid imposing values on clients and maintaining an awareness of the influence of culture on perceptions of the helping relationship, of the world of work, and of worldviews, in general.

Counselors' ability to adapt their intervention strategies is an important skill. This process involves altering or adapting one's intervention strategies, means of assessment, theoretical orientation, and so forth to better fit clients and their unique cultural perspectives (Cross et al., 1989). In order to successfully manage this skill, counselors must have the prerequisite skill of developing knowledge of the client's culture. If counselors are to adapt their techniques to the client's culture, it is necessary to first understand that client's culture. For example, clients from individualist cultures may expect to navigate the career development process on their own, while clients from collectivist cultures may ask family or other community members to be part of the process. It is critical that helpers evaluate their own processes to be sure that those helping systems are congruent with a client's needs and cultural expectations.

A THEORETICAL APPROACH
TO CULTURAL CAREER DEVELOPMENT

Throughout this chapter the need to adapt skills, techniques, and assessments to better meet the career development needs of students from different cultures has been discussed. This section will outline a theory that is designed to meet the needs of today's changing population. In seeking a theoretical framework in which to conceptualize multicultural career development in higher education, an approach that was flexible enough to meet the needs of heterogeneous campus populations, yet practical in working with the variety of students who seek career assistance was considered. The theory that best accomplishes these goals, while remaining congruent with the elements discussed earlier in this chapter is the Systems Theory Framework (STF; McMahon, 2002; McMahon & Patton, 1995; Patton & McMahon, 1997, 1999).

The STF accommodates the needs of specific cultural groups, as well as the universal views of cultural diversity. The STF encourages career counselors to examine cultural influences in career development by helping clients understand their position within and between the many systems in which they interact (Arthur & McMahon, 2005). As a multicultural career counseling theory, the STF allows the helper to assume a variety of roles,and encourages advocacy on the part of counselors (Arthur & McMahon, 2005). This theory also suggests counselors recognize their own influence on the client's systems, as well as how systems influence and impact the client.

Systems theories emphasize the individual elements of a system, but also suggest the entire system is greater than the sum of its parts. Systems theories examine the interconnected nature between the internal and external variables that influence students' career development processes (Arthur & McMahon, 2005). The STF has demonstrated application across countries, cultures, and training programs (Association for Counselor Education and Supervision and National Career Development Association, 2000). While other theories may be equally applicable, the STF is congruent with many of the concepts outlined previously in the chapter, and has proven utility in multicultural career counseling.

In the STF, the individual is central to the career development process, but the various systems that influence the individual are considered critical (Arthur & McMahon, 2005). The STF is appropriate for students from both individualistic or collectivist cultures, and while the STF assumes no particular cultural influences, it does address the aspects of culture that are relevant to the client. "Essentially, the STF provides a map to guide career counselors, and clients are encouraged to fill in the details and reality of the map through telling their career stories" (Arthur & McMahon, 2005, p. 211). The STF provides a means of connecting to people and groups who have traditionally been ignored in the career development literature, as well as exploring the influence of cultural context.

The STF provides a method of conceptualizing the influence systems have on career development (Arthur & McMahon, 2005). The STF examines both content and process variables as they relate to the career development process. Content influences are the intrapersonal, such as personality and age; social variables, such as family; and environmental influences, such as geography. Process influences include the interactions of the individual within their social context, as well as between individual and social context. Process influences also include the process of decision-making itself, as well as change over time. Finally, process influences include the variable of chance.

At the center of the STF is the individual system, which includes a range of intrapersonal influences such as age, gender, interests, abilities, values, personality, and sexual orientation (Arthur & McMahon, 2005). The person, however, does not exist isolated from other systems, but is instead part of many other interacting systems, specifically the social system and the environmental system (Arthur & McMahon, 2005). Thus, career counselors must not only consider the student in terms of the individual, but also how the individual interacts within these larger systems, as well as the reciprocal influence these systems have on the individual. In short, it is a recursive process of the individual exerting control over larger systems, and those systems influencing the individual, as well.

The social system includes the other individual systems with which the person interacts, such as family, campus institutions, peers, faculty, and so forth. Media has also been included as an often overlooked part of the social system (Arthur & McMahon, 2005). The values, attitudes, and beliefs of the individual can be profoundly influenced by the social systems with which he or she interacts. These factors (e.g., attitudes, beliefs, and values) are the core elements to the career development and decision-making processes. Also, these influences may be direct or indirect, so at times, it's possible that the individual is not even aware that these social systems are influencing them. Yet, there is a great deal of research (Bronfenbrenner, 1979, 2005) indicating that social systems can have considerable influence on the individual.

Finally, the environmental system includes larger influences such as geography, history, and globalization (Arthur & McMahon, 2005). While this system may seem less influential in the career development process, the globalization of world economies and trade systems has increased the importance of the environmental system. Additionally, historical issues such as racism, sexism, heterosexism, ageism, and other biases can be significantly influential on an individual's career development processes. When using the STF in multicultural career counseling, it is critical that helpers work with the individual to identify the systemic influences that have shaped their own career development and "elaborate their own stories and meaning around these environmental/societal factors" (Arthur & McMahon, 2005, p. 213).

The STF suggests that the multiple systems influencing the individual are dynamic and constantly interacting with and on each other. The three major processes involved are recursiveness, change over time, and chance (Arthur & McMahon, 2005). Recursiveness is the recurring interactions between systems; its use in the STF involves having clients discuss not only their own influences, but the recursiveness between influences. By doing so, students can elaborate on their own cultural development. Change over time involves an individual's past, present, and future influences. "The past is inextricably entwined with the present, and together past and present shape the future. Career counselors may have a role in assisting individuals to recognize the influence of past experience on present life and future ambition" (Arthur & McMahon, 2005, p. 214).

Finally, the influence of chance must be considered. People are influenced by unexpected events; chance may be positive or it may present difficult challenges. When someone wins a large lottery jackpot, it was certainly unexpected and will profoundly influence their career development process. Likewise, the loss of a job, or for the college student, a parent's sudden unemployment, may significantly influence the individual's career narrative. However, chance may have cultural implications, as well. For example, an unexpected accident may render an individual physically challenged, which will certainly have an impact on career development. Migration or immigration, sometimes based on the availability of employment, may also have a significant impact on the individual system.

Patton and McMahon (1997, 1999) suggest a number of potential benefits to using the STF in multicultural career counseling. First, the STF attempts to integrate aspects of multiple theories of career development through the use of systems theory. This allows career counselors to draw from multiple career and student development theories while incorporating cultural factors as well. The STF provides a guide for helpers while also drawing from culturally appropriate career and student development theories.

The STF is a multidisciplinary approach, incorporating principles from family therapy, economics, sociology, and psychology. These multiple perspectives may be used to better understand the many influences on a student's career development, as well as opening the possibility that career development is both an interpersonal and intrapersonal process. The STF integrates theory with practice; the theory allows helpers to work with students to explore the various systems that influence them, while the practical focuses on the basic principle of systems theory. This principle states that a change in one system will inevitably create change in other systems, as well.

The STF also places emphasis on the helper or career counselor as a system that will influence the systems of the students with whom one works. Counselors come to the helping relationship with their own cultural values, attitudes, beliefs, and so forth. The STF places emphasis on counselor self-awareness, an element of multicultural counseling discussed throughout this chapter. In order to be effective, counselors must have a sense of who they are, what biases they bring to the relationship, and how they will influence the various systems that comprise the student's world. The STF allows a process of analyzing the career counseling relationship between helper and student.

When using the STF, one must assume that culture is influential and pervasive through each of the various systems and subsystems in an individual's life; this occurs through the recursive process described previously (Patton & McMahon, 1999). In practice, the STF allows clients to create their career narratives using various dimensions of culture. Issues such as support from family and others, obstacles from family or peers, media messages, and so forth may all be considered in the student's career narrative. Additionally, environmental factors such as geography, cultural bias, governmental legislation, and economic circumstances can be taken into account. By incorporating the various systems in a student's life, career counselors have a fuller picture of the client, as well as their strengths and challenges. "The STF provides career counselors with a theoretical foundation from which to consider the salience of culture as experienced by clients in the context of their lives" (Arthur & McMahon, 2005, p. 217).

The STF encourages helpers to view client concerns as something that has been experienced, rather than a problem that is internal to the individual (Arthur & McMahon, 2005). This perspective removes the pathology that can be associated with experience; experience is simply something that has happened, while internalizing experience can create obstacles that may overwhelm and frustrate clients. Also, rather than encouraging students to adapt to difficult or unfair situations, the STF encourages advocacy in an effort to change social conditions (Arthur & McMahon, 2005). "Consequently, multicultural career counseling approaches imply that career counselors take a stand on issues that adversely affect the development and growth of individuals and client groups" (Arthur & McMahon, 2005, p. 218). Systems theory provides a structure and means for counselors to advocate for social and systemic change.

CONCLUSION

As the demographic of the population within the United States changes to a more globally-diverse representation of cultures, the profession of counseling will struggle to meet the evolving needs of the growing numbers of minority and underrepresented populations. Institutions of higher education will not be immune to the struggles and adversity that will no doubt accompany the impending socio-cultural changes as the enrollment of culturally diverse students increase. The discipline of career counseling will play a pivotal role in the acceptance, integration, and success of the changing face of colleges and universities across the country.

The collectivist orientation of many of the cultures that will be increasingly represented will pose challenges for counselors as students select majors and make decisions about future career choices. Assessing and understanding the work motivation of students from minority and underrepresented populations will benefit career counselors as they work with a diverse population of students. Counselors will be a resource to help students define career and navigate their future world of work, including assisting with the development of strategies for coping with discrimination as well as racism.

Along with increasing the counselor's multicultural competence by emphasizing the Multicultural Counseling Competencies, instituting a theoretical model such as Systems Theory Framework will provide consistent services across cultural lines and deliver the services necessary to successfully meet the needs of the students. The dynamic nature of STF can guide counselors' attempts to integrate factors from the individual, social, and environmental systems of the students to increase the academic and career success. The inclusive nature of STF will accommodate the needs of students of different cultures that will begin with successful completion at colleges and universities and eventually share increased representation in the workplace.

If the projected demographic change within the United States over the next 30 to 40 years is accurate, the need for culturally competent counselors will increase rapidly. Counselors will need to continually adapt their strategies to achieve successful outcomes with clients who represent adapting cultural groups. Focusing on counselor education and a Systems Theory Framework can guide counselors as they journey through the changing cultural landscape of higher education.

REFERENCES

Agar, M. (1994). *Language shock: Understanding the culture of conversation.* New York, NY: Morrow.

Anderson, E. L. (2003). Changing U.S. demographics and American higher education. In J. E. King, E. L. Anderson, & M. E. Corrigan (Eds.), *New Directions for Higher Education, 2003*(121), 3–12.

Arredondo, P., Toporek, R., Brown, S., Jones, J., Locke, D., Sanchez, J., & Stadler, H. (1996). Operationalization of the multicultural counseling competencies. *Journal of Multicultural Counseling & Development, 24*(1), 42–78.

Arthur, N., & McMahon, M. (2005). Multicultural career counseling: Theoretical applications of the systems theory framework. *The Career Development Quarterly, 53,* 208–222.

Association for Counselor Education and Supervision and National Career Development Association. (2000). *Preparing counselors for career development in the new millennium: ACES/NCDA position paper.* Retrieved from http://association-database.com/aws/NCDA/asset_manager/get_file/3405

Axelson, J. A. (1993). *Counseling and development in a multicultural society* (2nd ed.). Pacific Grove, CA: Brooks-Cole.

Axelson, J. A. (1999). *Counseling and development in a multicultural society* (4th ed.). Pacific Grove, CA: Brooks-Cole.

Bernard, J., & Goodyear, R. (2004). *Fundamentals of clinical supervision* (3rd ed.). Boston, MA: Pearson Education, Inc. (Original work published 1992)

Betz, N. E., & Fitzgerald, L. F. (1995). Career assessment and intervention with racial and ethnic minorities. In Frederick T. L. Leong (Ed.), *Career development and vocational behavior of racial and ethnic minorities* (pp. 263–277). Mahwah, NJ: Erlbaum.

Blustein, D. L. (2006). *The psychology of working: A new perspective for career development, counseling, and public policy.* Mahwah, NJ: Lawrence Erlbaum Associates.

Bronfenbrenner, U. (1979). *The ecology of human development: Experiments by nature and design.* Cambridge, MA: Harvard University Press.

Bronfenbrenner, U. (2005). *Making human beings human.* Thousand Oaks, CA: Sage.

Carter, R. T., & Cook, D. A. (1992). A culturally relevant perspective for understanding the career paths of visible racial/ethnic group people. In H. D. Lea & Z. B. Leibowitz (Eds.), *Adult career development: Concepts, issues, and practice* (pp. 192–217). Alexandria, VA: National Career Development Association.

Choy, S. (2002). *Access and persistence: Findings from 10 years of longitudinal research on students.* Washington, DC: American Council on Education.

Constantine, M. (2002). Predictors of satisfaction with counseling: Racial and ethnic minority clients' attitudes toward counseling and ratings of their counselors' general and multicultural counseling competence. *Journal of Counseling Psychology, 49*(2), 255–263.

Council for the Advancement of Standards in Higher Education (CAS). (1999). The role of counseling programs: CAS standards contextual statement. Washington, DC: CAS.

Cross, T. L., Barzon, B. J., Dennis, K. W., & Isaacs, M. R. (1989). *Towards a culturally competent system of care.* Washington, DC: Georgetown University Child Development Center.

Erchak, G. (1992). *The anthropology of self and mind.* New Brunswick, NJ: Rutgers University Press.

Flores, L., & Heppner, N. (2002). Multicultural career counseling: Ten essentials for training. *Journal of Career Development, 28*(3), 181–202.

Foster, M. (1993). Resisting racism. In L. Weiss & M. Fine (Eds.), *Beyond silenced voices: Class, race, and gender in the United States schools* (pp. 273–288). Albany, NY: State University of New York Press.

Geertz, C. (1983). *Local knowledge.* New York, NY: Basic Books.

Gibson, R. L., & Mitchell, M. H. (2006). *Introduction to career counseling for the 21st century.* Upper Saddle River, NJ: Pearson.

Goodenough, W. H. (1981). *Culture, language, and society.* Reading, MA: Benjamin Cummings.

Grantham, C. (2000). *The future of work: The promise of the new digital work society.* New York, NY: McGraw-Hill.

Hays, D., & Erford, B. (2010). *Developing multicultural competence: A systems approach* (1st ed.). Upper Saddle River, NJ: Pearson Education, Inc.

Helms, J. E., & Cook, D. A. (1999). *Using race and culture in counseling and psychotherapy: Theory and process.* Boston, MA: Allyn & Bacon.

Hofstede, G. (1984). *Culture's consequences: International differences in work-related values.* Newbury Park, CA: Sage.

Kitzrow, M. A. (2003). The mental health needs of today's college students: Challenges and recommendations. *NASPA Journal, 41,*165–179.

Levine, A., & Cureton, J. S. (1998). What we know about today's college students. *About Campus, 3,*4–9.

Marsella, A. (2003). Cultural aspects of depressive experience and disorders. In W. J. Lonner, D. L. Dinnel, S. A. Hayes, & D. N. Sattler (Eds.), *Online readings in psychology and culture.* Retrieved from http://www.ac.wwu.edu/~culture/Marsella.htm

Matsumoto, D. (1996). *Culture and psychology.* Pacific Grove, CA: Brooks-Cole.

McMahon, M. (2002). The systems theory framework of career development: History and future directions. *Australian Journal of Career Development, 11,* 63–68.

McMahon, M & Patton, W. (1995). Development of a systems theory of career development. *Australian Journal of Career Development, 4,* 15–20.

Ogbu, J. (1990). Cultural model, identity, and literacy. In J. Stigler, R. Shweder & G. Herdt (Eds.), *Cultural Psychology* (pp. 520–541). New York, NY: Cambridge University Press.

Okun, B. F., Fried, J., & Okun, M. L. (1999). *Understanding diversity: A learning practice primer.* Pacific Grove, CA: Brooks-Cole.

Parsons, F. (1909). *Choosing a vocation.* Boston, MA: Houghton Mifflin.

Patton, W., & McMahon, M. (Eds.). (1997). *Career development in practice: A systems theory perspective.* Sydney, New South Wales: New Hobson Press.

Patton, W., & McMahon, M. (Eds.). (1999). *Career development and systems theory: A new relationship.* Pacific Grove, CA: Brooks-Cole.

Pope-Davis, D., Toporek, R., Ortega-Villalobos, L., Ligiero, D., Brittan-Powell, C., Liu, W., Bashshur, M.,...Liang, C. (2002). Client perspectives of multicultural counseling competence: A qualitative examination. *The Counseling Psychologist, 30*(3), 355–393.

Ridley, C. R. (1995). *Overcoming unintentional racism in counseling and therapy: A practitioner's guide to intervention.* Thousand Oaks, CA: Sage.

Sammons, C., & Speight, S. (2008). A qualitative investigation of graduate-student changes associated with multicultural counseling courses. *The Counseling Psychologist, 36*(6), 814–838.

Sapir, E. (1958). *Culture, language, and personality.* Berkeley, CA: University of California Press.

Smith, E. J. (1983). Issues in racial minorities' career behavior. In W. B. Walsh & S. H. Osipow (Eds.), *Handbook of Vocational Psychology: Vol. 1. Foundations* (pp. 161–222). Hillsdale, NJ: Lawrence Erlbaum Associates.

Sue, D. W. (1978). Counseling across cultures. *Personnel and Guidance Journal, 56,* 451.

Sue, D., Arredondo, P., & McDavis, R. (1992). Multicultural counseling competencies and standards: A call to the profession. *Journal of Counseling & Development, 70*(4), 478–486.

Sue, D. W., Carter, R. T., Casa, J. M., Fouad, N. A., Ivey, A. E., Jensen, M., . . . Vazquez-Nutall, E. (1998). *Multicultural counseling competencies: Individual and organizational development.* Thousand Oaks, CA: Sage.

Sue, D. W., & Sue, D. (1990). *Counseling the culturally different: Theory and practice* (2nd ed.). New York: Wiley.

Tomlinson-Clarke, S. (2000). Assessing outcomes in a multicultural training course: A qualitative study. *Counselling Psychology Quarterly, 13*(2), 221–231.

Triandis, H. C. (2002). Motivation to work in cross-cultural perspective. In J. M. Brett & F. Drasgow (Eds.), *The psychology of work: Theoretically based empirical research* (pp. 101–117). Mahwah, NJ: Lawrence Erlbaum Associates.

U.S. Census Bureau. (1996). *Projected population change by race: 1990, 2000, 2025, 2050.* Washington, DC: U.S. Government Printing Office.

U.S. Census Bureau. (2004). *U.S. interim projections by age, sex, race, and Hispanic origin.* Retrieved from http://www.census.gov/population/www/projections/usinterimproj/natprojtab01b.pdf

Vasquez, M. (2010). Ethics in multicultural counseling practice. In J. Ponterotto, J. Cass, L. Suzuki, & C. Alexander (Eds.), *Handbook of multicultural counseling* (3rd ed., pp. 127–145). Thousand Oaks, CA: Sage Publications, Inc.

Zunker, V. G. (2002). *Career counseling: Applied concepts of life planning* (6th ed.). Pacific Grove, CA: Brooks-Cole.

CHAPTER 13

CAREER DEVELOPMENT AND THE INTERNATIONAL STUDENT

**Lourens Human, Ilse Ruane, Vicky Timm,
and Nkateko Ndala-Magoro**
University of Pretoria

INTRODUCTION

Studying in a foreign country can be an enriching experience, although it is not always an easy endeavour. International students who embark on this journey will be confronted with an array of experiences while in the host country. The face of institutions of higher education has drastically changed since their inception as many of these institutions of higher education now boast a great diversity of students, including international students. This diversity in terms of age, culture, ethnicity, gender, language, race and religion constitutes the multi-cultural nature of today's higher education institutions (Barletta & Kobayashi, 2007; Ruane, Kasayira & Shino, in press).

The term "international student," refers to students who temporarily reside in a foreign country, with the purpose of studying at an educational institution outside of their home country (Arthur, 2005; Barletta & Kobayashi, 2007; Lin & Yi, 1997). International students can face many issues when studying in a foreign country, such as living away from home, select-

Career Development in Higher Education, pages 275–299
Copyright © 2011 by Information Age Publishing
275

ing and registering for a specific academic program, adjusting to a new academic environment and making new friends (Abe, Talbot & Geelhoed, 1998; Al-Sharideh & Goe, 1998; Hayes & Lin, 1994; Lin & Yi, 1997; Mori, 2000; Popadiuk & Arthur, 2004; Shih & Brown, 2000; Smith, Chin, Inman & Findling, 1999; Toyokawa & Toyokawa, 2002; Yang, Wong, Hwang & Heppner, 2002). The top five adjustment problems experienced by international students in the U.S. are: lack of language (English) proficiency, inadequate financial resources, problems in social adjustment, dilemmas in daily living, and loneliness (Shih & Brown, 2000).

The facilitation of career development services for international students can be divided into three phases. The first phase entails exploring the possibility of studying in a foreign country (pre-career development phase), the second phase focuses on studying in a foreign country (career development phase), while the third phase emphasizes the importance of transferring acquired skills into the work context (post-career development phase) (Arthur, 2008; Barletta & Kobayashi, 2007; Harman, 2003). This chapter will be structured along these three phases to assist counselors who conduct career development services with international students. The University of Pretoria (UP), in South Africa (SA), will be used as a case study throughout this chapter.

The UP (SA) is a residential university situated in the city of Pretoria, which is the capital of SA. The UP (SA) originated in 1908 as the Pretoria branch of the Transvaal University College, with four professors, three lecturers, and 32 students. In 2008, the university celebrated its centenary year and has grown to an institution of higher education with nine academic faculties and one business school. The UP (SA) offers 181 academic qualifications, with 450 undergraduate and 1500 postgraduate programs. In the centenary year, there were 57,000 students enrolled at the UP, of which 2,800 were international students. Fifty percent of these students came from the Southern African Developing Community (SADC), which includes Angola, Namibia, Seychelles, Swaziland, Tanzania, Zambia, and Zimbabwe (University of Pretoria [UP], 2009).

PHASE 1: PRE-CAREER DEVELOPMENT PROCESS

This phase of the career development process involves investigating study opportunities in a foreign country; for example, enrolling at a higher education institution, selecting an academic program, as well as establishing living arrangements in the host country. This phase generally occurs within the home country prior to leaving to study abroad. However, within the host country, counselors can explore international students' reasons behind (1) studying within a foreign country, and (2) the chosen field of study (Arthur,

2008). The pre-career development phase of this chapter corresponds with the "pre-arrival stage," as well as the "adjustment stage," as seen by Lin and Yi (1997).

Information

The dissemination of information occurs when prospective international students are still living in their home country and exploring opportunities of studying in a foreign country. Therefore, one of the most important aspects pertaining to international students is preparing them through providing information on the host country in general, as well as the academic context specifically. Living and studying in a foreign country can be an anxiety-provoking experience, and it is therefore important that prospective international students receive adequate information on areas such as the adjustment process, the education system, financial requirements and housing arrangements. This information can assist international students in dealing with anxiety they might be experiencing regarding the unknown of the foreign country and academic context (Lin & Yi, 1997). For example, the UP (SA) has a booklet, "University of Pretoria: International Information Guide," that contains relevant information for international students on SA and the UP. This booklet can be obtained from the UP (SA) by international students while still in their home country to assist them in their decision-making and planning process regarding studying in a foreign country (University of Pretoria [UP], 2010).

Orientation Programs

Besides the dissemination of information to international students about the host country, the academic context and accommodation, orientation programs can also be presented by counselors to assist international students in adapting to the host country. These orientation programs are usually run when they are in the host country and have arrived at the institution of higher education. Research has indicated that international students who participate in orientation programs adjust better within an institution of higher education than international students who don't participate in orientation programs (Abe et al., 1998).

In an orientation program presented to international students in Turkey, the following modules are addressed. The first module focuses on creating awareness among international students on the role of culture in the adjustment process. The second module addresses the aspect of culture shock, when international students come into contact with the host country's culture. This usually results in physical, personal, and social changes as international students attempt to adapt to the host country's culture. The third module explains the psychological adaptation process as a result of culture shock experienced by international students. This psychological adaptation process usually has five phases: (1) encountering the host country's culture; (2) assigning meaning to encountering the host country's culture; (3) employing various strategies to deal with the stress caused in [1] and [2]; (4) experiencing the affects of the stress due to [1] through [3]; and (4) adapting to the culture of the host country (Bektas, 2008).

Counselors who participate in orientation programs and who interact informally with international students are likely to be seen as more approachable by international students (Arthur, 2008; Bektas, 2008). For example, the UP (SA) has an orientation week for all new students at the beginning of the academic year, as well as orientation camps sponsored by various religious organizations to assist all new students with their adjustment process (UP, 2009, 2010). Offering outreach programs for international students away from counseling centers has been found to be beneficial to the adjustment process (Smith et al., 1999).

PHASE 2: CAREER DEVELOPMENT PROCESS

Once international students have left their home country to pursue their academic experience in a foreign country, they are confronted with the unknown of the host country's culture, as well as the uncertainty surrounding the academic endeavour. On the one hand, some international students may adapt, integrate, and participate in the host country's culture and academic context without experiencing any problems; on the other hand, others may find this process difficult and even traumatic. This is often the point at which international students seek assistance through counseling services for mainly personal problems, as well as guidance for academic-related issues via career development services (Arthur, 2008). The career development phase of this chapter corresponds with the "initial adjustment stage" as well as the "on-going adjustment stage," as seen by Lin and Yi (1997).

Counseling Services

Institutions of higher education have a responsibility towards international students in providing them with appropriate counseling services while living and studying in the host country. Unfortunately, these counseling services are often under-utilized by international students. First, international students may be unaware of the counseling services; second, cultural inhibitions may prevent them from utilizing counselling services; third, they may not understand that the counseling process can enhance their experience of living in a foreign country and academic endeavour; while fourth, there might not be any professional counseling roles that correspond to counselors in their home country, which often makes utilizing counseling services difficult (Arthur, 2004; Luzio-Lockett, 1998; Mori, 2000; Yang et al., 2002). However, it has been found that the higher the level of acculturation of Asian international students into a white culture, such as that of the U.S., the greater the possibility is of these international students seeking professional psychological assistance (Zhang & Dixon, 2003).

Counseling services can play an important role in assisting international students to adapt to the host country, as well as integrating and participating in the academic context. Counseling of international students can be divided into two types: proactive counseling and reactive counseling. In proactive counseling, the counselor anticipates and addresses international students' potential problems before they become actual problems, thereby enhancing their educational experience. With reactive counseling, the counselor focuses on actual problems, such as academic problems (e.g., study methods, time management) and personal problems (e.g., depression, anxiety) (Butcher & McGrath, 2004).

The American Psychological Association has a set of multicultural guidelines which may be used by a psychologist or counselor when working with international students whose cultural background differs from their own. These multicultural guidelines pertain to awareness, education, research, practice, and policy (American Psychological Association, 2003):

1. Awareness:
   a. "Psychologists [counselors] are encouraged to recognize that, as cultural beings, they may hold attitudes and beliefs that can detrimentally influence their perceptions of and interactions with individuals who are ethnically and racially different from themselves" (p. 382), such as international students.
   b. "Psychologists [counselors] are encouraged to recognize the importance of multicultural sensitivity/responsiveness, knowledge, and understanding about ethnically and racially different individuals" (p. 385), such as international students.
2. Education: "As educators, psychologists [counselors] are encouraged to employ the constructs of multiculturalism and diversity in psychological education" (p. 386), with international students.
3. Research: "Culturally sensitive psychological researchers are encouraged to recognize the importance of conducting culture-centered and ethical psychological research among persons from

ethnic, linguistic, and racial minority backgrounds" (p. 388), such as international students.

4. Practice: "Psychologists [counselors] strive to apply culturally appropriate skills in clinical and other applied psychological practices" (p. 390), when working with international students.

5. Policy: "Psychologists [counselors] are encouraged to use organizational change processes to support culturally informed organizational (policy) development and practices" (p. 392), such as student support centers, when working with international students.

Multicultural guidelines for working with international students have also been depicted by Alexander, Klein, Workneh & Miller (1981), as well as Pedersen (1987, 1991).

Providing counseling within an organizational context, such as institutions of higher education, includes building networks and developing a database of resources. Working with other personnel facilitates an integrated approach to addressing the personal and academic needs of international students. Counselors can work with academic staff, residence advisors. and medical staff to better understand the international students' needs and provide a holistic approach. It is also important that counselors liaise with staff from the International Student Office (Bektas, 2008). Furthermore, counselors are often called upon to intervene on behalf of international students with other members of campus staff and the community (McLeod, 2007).

Research has shown that international students are unlikely to use counseling services beyond a single session. In light of this research, it is important that counselors build a relationship with both the international student population and with the academic support staff, such as student advisors, who have initial contact with international students. It is the responsibility of the counselors to be proactive in making students aware of the facilities and purpose of their services. The counselor should also consider whether students understand what is being offered through counseling and whether they have the option to refuse counseling services (Arthur, 2004, 2008; Sandhu, 1994).

At the UP (SA), counseling services, as well as life-skills programs, are offered to both local and international students through "Student Support Services." These services are free of charge to all UP registered students and facilitated by counselors (e.g., clinical psychologists, counseling psychologists, and social workers) on a full-time, as well as part-time, basis. The problems experienced by both local and international students are often related to personal issues and interpersonal difficulties that can all influence the academic experience of these students (UP, 2009, 2010).

Career Development Services

Besides the counseling services that student support centers offer international students at institutions of higher education, it is also important that career development services are offered to them. The apparent lack of attention paid to the academic and career planning of international students is surprising, considering that the choice of studying and working in another country is an important part of their career development process (Arthur, 2005; Shih & Brown, 2000).

Counselors need to be aware of the influence of choosing an academic program and subsequent career on the life of international students. Choosing an academic program and engaging in career planning is one of the primary reasons for which international students seek career development services. The everyday questions that they ask themselves about their studies and careers can be answered with appropriate guidance by counselors who are qualified to facilitate a career development process (Carney & Savitz, 1980; Holland, 1992).

Career Development Process

A basic career development process will entail (1) a holistic, culturally sensitive assessment pertaining to possible academic programs and career paths; (2) supplying international students with relevant information regarding academic programs and possible career opportunities based on their academic studies; and (3) assisting them in making decisions regarding academic programs and career paths based on (1) and (2) (Arthur, 2004; UP, 2010).

Assessment

International students, like local students, are often uncertain about their academic programs and career plans. It is therefore important that a thorough, holistic, culturally sensitive academic and career assessment of international students who engage in a career development process is conducted and entails a combination of quantitative and qualitative assessments (Arthur, 2004, 2008; Yang et al., 2002).

A quantitative assessment will, for example, entail an in-depth interview with an international student to form a detailed picture of who the international student is. Furthermore, such an assessment may also make use of any collateral information regarding the international student, such as previous academic results, part-time work, and personal hobbies. This information serves the purpose of enhancing the counselor's understanding.

Qualitative assessments will, for example, make use of culture-fair psychometric testing in support of the assessment. In this regard, psychometric testing can be used to measure intellectual functioning (e.g., Wechsler Adult Individual Scale (WAIS)), career interests (e.g., 19-Field Interest Inventory (19-FII)), personal aptitude (e.g., Differential Aptitude Test (DAT)), and personality type (e.g., Myers-Briggs Type Indicator (MBTI)).

The combination of a qualitative and quantitative assessment establishes a comprehensive assessment that can assist international students in making decisions regarding academic programs and their possible career paths. A quantitative assessment alone cannot yield the final answer, but needs to be supported by a qualitative assessment (Ruane et al., in press). For example, the UP (SA) career assessment services, as part of a career development process, are offered by "Student Support Services" to local and international students (UP, 2009, 2010).

Information

Once international students have participated in a holistic and culturally sensitive assessment, it is important that they be supplied with relevant information regarding possible academic programs and career opportunities. Supplying them with appropriate academic and career-related information will allow these students to make informed decisions about their studies and careers. For example, at the UP (SA) this academic and career-related information can be distributed via brochures, pamphlets, and yearbooks. Furthermore, international students can obtain information by attending open days at institutions of higher education or visiting potential organizations that offer career opportunities in their chosen field of study (UP, 2009, 2010).

Development

It is important that international students make informed academic and career choices so as to maximize the opportunity of studying and working in a foreign country. Making uninformed career choices can lead to wasted opportunities, resulting in potential personal problems and unnecessary financial costs on the part of international students. Various researchers stress that the academic and career needs of undergraduate and graduate students differ due to the stage of focus and specialization in their academic and career planning (Mallinckrodt & Leong, 1992; Shen & Herr, 2004). It is also important that counselors take note of cultural and gender differences in career decision-making (Zhou & Santos, 2007).

As indicated above, career development with international students should be based on a thorough, holistic, and culturally sensitive assessment and should supply these students with relevant academic and career information in assisting them to make informed academic and career choices.

However, a career development process does not only entail a holistic and culturally sensitive assessment and the dissemination of academic and career information. It also involves developing strategies for academic success, such as reading skills, study methods, and time management (Arthur, 2004; Shih & Brown, 2000). At the UP (SA), reading skills, time management, and study methods are delivered by counselors at "Student Support Services" to local and international students to assist them in enhancing their academic experience (UP, 2009, 2010).

Three aspects can influence the success of an individual's career development process: vocational identity problems, insufficient information and/or education regarding career choice, as well as personal and/or contextual barriers (Holland, Gottfredson, & Power, 1980; Shih & Brown, 2000). Counselors also need to be prepared to deal with the more serious mental health issues associated with transition and adjustment that can be detrimental to the academic experience of international students. Therefore, counselors need to be able to fulfill multiple roles (Barletta & Kobayashi, 2007; Watson, 2006).

Career Development Counselors.

Counselors providing career development guidance with international students need to be aware of the influence of their own culture, as well as the culture of the international student, on the career development process (Pedersen, 1988; Yoon & Portman, 2004). According to Cushman (1995):

> Culture is not indigenous 'clothing' that covers the universal human; rather, it is an integral part of each individual's psychological flesh and bones...the material objects we create, the ideas we hold, and the actions we take are shaped in a fundamental way by the social framework we have been raised in. (p. 17–18)

Being unaware of one's own culture as a counselor and insensitive to and uninformed about the culture of international students can be detrimental to the career development process.

Due to the cultural diversity of the international student group, counselors need to be prepared with culturally appropriate and culturally sensitive intervention plans. Arthur (2008) identifies five key areas in which counselors can enhance their cultural responsiveness in counseling international students:

1. Increase knowledge about emerging theories and models of cross-cultural transitions.

2. Gain knowledge about the common demands faced by international students.
3. Enhance multicultural competencies, including self-awareness, knowledge, and skills.
4. Learn ways to be proactive about engaging international students in counseling programs and services.
5. Expand counseling roles to include advocacy for addressing systemic barriers and improving institutional policies and practices that affect international students.

Popadiuk and Arthur (2004) offer several questions that can serve as pointers for counselors to work in a culturally sensitive manner with international students:

1. How do international students negotiate the transition from living/ studying in their home country to living/studying in a foreign country?
2. How can (career) counseling services be best organized, structured, and delivered to meet the needs of the international student in transition?
3. How can the needs of international students, especially those from non-Western or emerging countries, be met in a manner that is relevant, effective, and ethical?
4. How can the adaptation of international students experiencing cross-cultural transition be facilitated in a positive and proactive fashion?
5. How can a network be established that will enhance collaborative service delivery and referral processes?
6. How can the strategic planning of educational organizations be structured and aligned to assist in the adaptation process of international students?

Career Development Contexts

Counselors who engage in a career development process with international students need to be knowledgeable about contextual influences that might influence the academic experience of international students, while also facilitating a career development process (Luzio-Lockett, 1998).

Research has shown that contextual influences can be a greater predictor of international students' successful adjustment to their new environment than personal factors (Fouad, 1991; Yoon & Portman, 2004). Some of these contextual influences are adjusting to a new culture, academic differences, language problems, cross-cultural male-female relationships and financial difficulties (Barletta & Kobayashi, 2007). Perceived prejudice and discrimination (Barletta & Kobayashi, 2007; Sodowsky & Plake, 1992; Surdam & Collins, 1984; Yoon & Portman, 2004), as well as the lack of contact with host citizens (Alexander et al., 1981; Hayes & Lin, 1994; Yoon & Portman, 2004) are also two primary contextual factors which affect the academic experience of international students. However, it has been found that perceived prejudice and discrimination by the host country's students towards international students may lead to the construction of a minority group identity among these students (Schmitt, Spears, & Branscombe, 2003). Another study suggested that international students are psychologically better adjusted if they have more social ties with other international students (Kashima & Loh, 2006).

The following problems have been identified as the most important problems experienced by international students (Wedding, McCartney, & Currey, 2009):

1. Experiencing financial difficulties pertaining to academic and living costs, as well as high health care costs in the host country.
2. Experiencing difficulties when applying and acquiring the necessary documentation, such as the correct visa, for studying in the host country.
3. Experiencing difficulties with bureaucratic government officials when trying to acquire, for example, a motor driver's license.
4. Experiencing problems in establishing a way of living in the host country, which entails finding a place to stay, as well as locating shopping centers to buy living necessities.
5. Experiencing limited employment opportunities due to various factors, such as lack of proficiency in the host country's language, visa requirements for employment, as well as the limited hours that international students are permitted to work in the host country.
6. Experiencing anti-international attitudes from staff at institutions of higher education, as well as from the larger community.
7. Experiencing that many staff members at institutions of higher education treat international students in a very impersonal and unprofessional manner.
8. Experiencing additional employment conditions at institutions for higher education for international students when applying for work, such as teaching assistants.
9. Experiencing hostility from international students on campus and in the classroom due to international students' lack of proficiency in the host country's language, despite being knowledgeable in the subject area.

10. Experiencing that often the religious practices of international students are not understood by local students and therefore a lack of respect is shown towards these religious practices.
11. Experiencing family problems even when international students are away from home and trying to assist families long-distance to resolve these problems.
12. Experiencing dilemmas in decision-making when trying to decide whether to stay in the host country or to return home after international students have completed their studies in the host country.

Thus, it is important that counselors understand contextual influences such as culture, academics, finances, wellbeing, extramural activities, and accommodation on the academic experience of the international students, while engaging in a career development process. Cultural Context.

Many international students experience a culture shock resulting from the transition from one culture to another. This transition usually happens in three stages. First, there is the honeymoon stage, in which students experience excitement about their new academic endeavor. Second, there is the crisis stage. This occurs when international students find some of their own cultural values being incompatible with the host country's cultural values. The social norms and cultural values which exist at their new host institution and country might be different from their own social norms and cultural values. Many international students have lost significant social relationships, such as the support of parents, former schoolmates, and their friends, and might experience homesickness as a result. Third, there is the recovery stage. This stage is characterized by international students developing an appreciation for the culture of the foreign country. When they immerse themselves into the host culture by making new friends and using the host language, international students adjust well to the host culture and avoid isolation and loneliness (Barletta & Kobayashi, 2007; Ruane, Kasayira et al., in press; Wedding et al., 2009).

However, these opportunities to establish such networks of social support might not always materialize (Kagan & Cohen, 1990). Pedersen (1995), as well as Shih and Brown (2000), mentions three outcomes of acculturation, namely, assimilation, resistance to assimilation, and biculturalism. The ideal strategy is assisting international students in becoming bicultural. This allows international students to explore ways of incorporating the cultures of both their home and host countries. To achieve such an identity, they need guidance by a multiculturally competent counselor.

Cross-cultural transition involves a process over time through which individuals experience a shift in personal assumptions about themselves, others, and the world around them. International students find themselves in the position of experiencing new foods, transportation, living arrangements, climates, entertainment, social relationships, and academic curriculum. These new experiences require international students to shed their usual ways of conducting themselves and learn new ways of interacting (Arthur, 2005; Ellis, Sawyer, Gill, & Medlin, 2005; Poyrazili, Kavanaugh, Baker & Al-Timimi, 2004). Difficulties in adjustment arise when there is a great difference in practice between the culture of the home and host countries. This is especially true for the career environment as different countries have a different approach or "culture" regarding careers.

The complex diversity of the labor market further complicates the provision of culturally appropriate counseling and career development to international students (Pedersen, 1991). For example, international students may enter into the host country under the assumption that a particular career is sought after based on its popularity within their home country. These, along with other assumptions, can often lead to the international student feeling even more alienated within this unfamiliar cultural environment. Adjusting to this change can be a time-consuming process and requires a culturally sensitive career development process.

Although international students may experience problems in making a cultural transition, "they have unique strengths, including bilingualism, biculturalism, and having different perspectives that are based on diverse cultural and academic backgrounds... they are very select and resourceful students" (Yoon & Portman, 2004, p. 38). Furthermore, Yoon and Portman (2004) state that these unique skills, strengths, knowledge, and resources that international students possess can enrich the educational environment of the host campuses and simultaneously empower the international students proactively to become involved in their new environment. Mentorship has also shown to have a positive influence on different areas of adjustment for international students (Abe et al., 1998).

Academic Context

The academic context can also have a profound influence on international students. Choosing an academic program, attending classes, and preparing for tests and exams in the unknown of a foreign country can be difficult for them (Barletta & Kobayashi, 2007; Wedding et al., 2009). The following are some of the challenges that international students studying in a foreign country, such as the UP (SA), face (Ruane et al., in press).

First, international students can experience themselves as lost on the campus of the educational institution where they are studying, which can have a negative influence on their academic experience. For example, they can struggle to locate the administration building used for registration purposes; they can have difficulty in finding lecture halls where they attend classes, or even be disoriented with reference to the residences of the educational institution. This may influence the academic experience of international students in that it can distract them from focusing on their studies. In this regard, counselors facilitating the career development process with international students can arrange campus tours, set up meeting points where they can meet before lectures, and provide them with campus maps.

Second, the academic context in which international students find themselves in the host country may be highly competitive and stressful, which may affect their overall academic experience. Once international students have decided on an academic program to follow, they might have to go through a rigorous selection process in which they need to compete against local students, as well as other international students. For example, at the UP (SA), many undergraduate courses require a selection process, such as medicine, dentistry, physiotherapy, engineering, and architecture. Furthermore, there are also courses that have a rigorous selection process for postgraduate studies, such as psychology, accounting, and medicine. As part of a career development process, counselors can assist international students in preparing for a selection process through assisting them with completing their application forms, brainstorming questions that might be asked during a selection process, or even role-playing possible selection interviews. In this way, counselors conducting career development processes with international students can assist them in promoting their chances of being selected into specific courses of their own choice, thereby enhancing their academic experience.

Third, the content of some courses might focus specifically on issues relevant to the host country, often leaving international students marginalized in such courses while they attempt to form an understanding of these local issues. For example, in the Department of Psychology at the UP (SA), courses in community psychology focus on the diverse needs of the South African society (e.g., HIV/AIDS). International students could find that the focus of the courses in community psychology are far removed from their reality of their home country. The lack of understanding by international students regarding the content of specific courses might have a negative impact on the academic experience of international students. Counselors who facilitate a career development process can assist international students to look beyond the content of these courses and try to understand the underlying principles being lectured and practiced in these courses, and how these underlying principles can be applied in other settings, giving them a universal character.

Fourth, the academic experience of international students can also be influenced by the mode of delivery of courses, as this can differ from the mode of delivery of courses in their home countries. For example, at the UP (SA), courses can be delivered in a variety of ways. These include formal teaching, online education, practicum, and tutor sessions. During formal teaching, PowerPoint® presentations and overhead transparencies are often used during lectures, while online education and tutor classes often complement the material. International students can often be overwhelmed by the various modes through which the courses are delivered. This can contribute to a negative academic experience in that international students can experience themselves as lost among the different modes of course delivery. During a career development process, counselors can assist international students in grasping these various ways in which courses are delivered, thereby enhancing their academic experience.

Fifth, language can have a profound influence on the academic experience of international students. Some international students may only possess rudimentary language skills of the host country. This can lead to international students not understanding lecturers and therefore being disempowered. For example, a student from Germany (Europe) or Cameroon (Africa) might have difficulties with English and/or Afrikaans, which is used in a number of Southern African universities, such as the UP (SA). This may lead to international students doubting their own abilities to learn, leaving them with feelings of incompetence and inferiority, as well as confused and less willing to communicate with others. This could result in poor academic performance and ultimately impede their career paths. However, there are also international students who have the same mother tongue as the host country, or are able to communicate sufficiently to continue studying unimpeded. It is important that counselors conducting a career development process with international students explore the influence of language on their academic experience and refer them to language laboratories to assist them in overcoming this barrier.

Financial Context

Another context that can have a profound influence on the academic experience of international students is the financial context. The academic endeavor of international students can be affected when they worry about the payment of their tuition fees, or have to work on a part-time basis to earn money to pay for their studies (Barletta & Kobayashi, 2007; Wedding et al., 2009).

It is often the case that the studies of international students are not subsidized by the government of the host country. Due to the lack of government subsidies by the host country, tuition fees are usually higher for international students than is the case with subsidized local students. Institutions of higher education would therefore lose financially if international students were placed on the same fee structure as subsidized local students (Arthur,

2004; Butcher & McGrath, 2004; Wedding et al., 2009). For example, international students who study at the UP (SA) and do not come from countries forming part of the Southern African Developing Community (SADC) (Angola, Namibia, Seychelles, Swaziland, Tanzania, Zambia, Zimbabwe and South Africa (SA)) pay double the tuition fee that South African students pay. Therefore, recruitment drives by institutions of higher education are often levelled at those who can afford to finance the full cost of their education (Arthur, 2004).

As with every other aspect regarding international students, they also vary in their financial status. Some enjoy generous financial support, while others have only limited support. They often have to supplement their income with part-time employment and/or sponsorships. Some tuition fees and living expenses are paid for by parents and/or other family members, some are paid for by companies and/or aid grants, while others are sponsored by the home country's government and/or through university scholarships (Barletta & Kobayashi, 2007; Butcher & McGrath, 2004; Harman, 2003). For example, the UP (SA), does not award scholarships to undergraduate international students. Scholarships, such as the University of Pretoria Doctoral Scholarship, are awarded to post-graduate students on a competitive basis. Legally, international students are prevented from acquiring full-time employment in SA. Part-time employment of 20 hours per week can be secured on a study permit (UP, 2010). However, it is often the case that any money earned from part-time employment in the host country may have to be sent home to the payee and/or to help support the family (Butcher & McGrath, 2004).

Butcher and McGrath (2004) indicate that international students' finances are often influenced by:

1. Students not being able to draft and work according to a financial budget;
2. Students participating in unnecessary money-wasting activities, such as gambling;
3. Students who need to circumvent various immigration requirements that place financial demands on them;
4. Students who have responsibilities towards family members and/or whose lives are affected by unforeseen altered family circumstances;
5. Students facing unexpected needs arising from incidents such as theft, accidents, fines and/or tenancy requirements.

The difference in currencies of the home country and host country can also have a influence on the financial status of international students, making studying in a foreign country inexpensive for some, while for others it can cause a major financial burden. Counselors facilitating a career development process with international students need to recognize this influence on the academic experience of international students. They can assist these students by referring them to the appropriate people who can assist them in not just obtaining money to pay for their tuition, but also help them budget for academic expenses.

Wellness Context

The adjustment that international students need to make from their home country to the host country may have a profound influence on their physical, personal-social, and/or spiritual wellness.

First, the physical well being of international students plays a major role in their overall academic experience, as this may impact optimal functioning in many areas of their academic life (Harper & Quaye, 2009). On the one hand, international students may experience actual physical illness that can influence their ability to attend classes and/or focus on their studies. On the other hand, physical illness can often be somatic in nature and therefore a manifestation of personal struggles, adjustment issues, and/or academic problems. It is important that counselors explore the nature of the physical illness with the purpose of referring these international students to a medical doctor and/or a counselor dealing with personal problems that manifest as physical illnesses (Mori, 2000). Although the UP (SA), has a medical center for the treatment of physical illness as well as a student support center for meeting the emotional and/or academic needs of these students, it is still a prerequisite for international students to have medical insurance. In spite of this, some medical procedures might not be covered by basic medical insurance which most international students purchase. This may lead to added stress and anxiety as these students often do not have alternative support, such as limited part-time employment opportunities and/or financial support from relatives. Options such as going to a public hospital seem to be out of the question for most international students due to the ill-treatment of patients and possible discrimination (UP, 2010).

Second, it is paramount that counselors conducting a career development process also be sensitive to the personal-social wellness of international students, as it can have a profound impact on their academic experience (Barletta & Kobayashi, 2007; Poyrazili et al., 2004; Wedding et al., 2009). International students are often challenged on more levels than local students. They often experience various personal-social difficulties, such as prejudice and discrimination as seen in xenophobic attacks. They can also be exploited by various government organizations, such as the police force and/or home affairs through blackmailing. Furthermore, international students often experience difficulties, such as finding appropriate accommodations, and dealing with homesickness and ineffective support systems that can often lead to anxiety, depression, suicide, and other forms of mental illness (Barletta & Kobayashi, 2007; Lin & Yi, 1997; Mori, 2000). The "Department of Student Affairs" at the UP (SA), is positioned and structured to assist international students who are experiencing difficulties with their personal-social wellness. This is usually done though psychological counseling services and/or psychological education services. Whereas the psychological counseling services are more geared for one-on-one work, the acquiring of life skills is facilitated through psychological education services. Workshops are conducted in a group format on areas such as time management, stress management, and dealing with various relationships. Although these workshops are usually more didactic in nature, they can be seen as an opportunity to make contact with international students to identify their psychological counseling needs (UP, 2010).

Third, the spiritual wellness of international students also requires the attention of counselors conducting a career development process. The spiritual wellness of international students is enhanced through their spiritual involvement, due largely to the fact that their spiritual engagement is seen as a support structure and increases a sense of belonging. Being in the spiritual wilderness could have a negative influence on the academic experience of international students. It is therefore important that when a counselor becomes aware of this, the counselor will assist the international students in joining an organization that can fulfill their spiritual needs (Andrade, 2008). The UP (SA) assists in addressing the spiritual wellness of international students through various religious organizations. For example, certain religious groups conduct first-year camps for all new local and international students to assist in the adjustment process (University of Pretoria [UP], 2008a; UP, 2010).

Counselors engaging in a career development process with international students need to be aware of the influence of the wellness context on the academic experience of international students. If their physical, personal-social and/or spiritual wellness is being affected for whatever reason, it is important that counselors refer international students to the appropriate people to assist them.

Extramural Context

It can be beneficial for international students to participate in various extramural activities while studying in a foreign country. This participation can assist them in getting to know the host country, as well as its people (Harper & Quaye, 2009). Furthermore, the participation in extramural activities can allow international students to meet local students, as well as other international students. This in itself can enhance the academic experience of international students.

First, international students can become involved in social activities in the host country, as their adjustment process is enhanced through interaction with local students and people (Jacob & Greggo, 2001; Poyrazili et al., 2004; Toyokawa & Toyokawa, 2002). Most institutions of higher education have social organizations open to anyone who is a registered student of that particular institution (Lacina, 2002). For example, at the UP (SA), the "University of Pretoria International Students Association" (UPI) is such an organization. Some of the benefits of being a member include participation in all the events arranged by UPI and the International Students Division (ISD), interaction with other local student organizations, engagements with student organizations at other South African universities, as well as excursions to various places (UP, 2008a; 2010).

Second, it is not only important for international students to have exposure to the host country's culture, but that they also have the opportunity to experience other international students' cultures, while also participating in events through which they can showcase their own culture to local students and other international students. For example, at the UP (SA), this is done by means of an "International Student Day," as well as a "Mr. University of Pretoria International Contestants" and "Ms. University of Pretoria International Contestants" competitions. International students are given an opportunity to exhibit their traditional clothes, ornaments, foods, and various activities. When students from the host nation, as well as international students, take part in such an event, they are able to learn about each other cultures and this may lead to the reduction of discrimination and prejudice, while enhancing appreciation and understanding for one another (UP, 2010).

Third, the participation in athletics by international students can also assist these students in their adjustment process, thereby enhancing their academic experience. Furthermore, international students who participate in sports learn social skills, are able to make new friends, exhibit higher levels of tolerance, display high self-discipline and determination, as well as flexibility and assertiveness (Toyokawa & Toyokawa, 2002). For example, at the UP (SA), athletics run through "TuksSport" that has more than 30 clubs and ten academies with sports like rugby, cricket, football, athletics, hockey, netball, tennis, squash, swimming, rowing, canoeing, water polo, underwater hockey, cycling, golf, and gymnastics. Participation in sports is open to all students, local and international, and can be practiced on performance and recreational levels (University of Pretoria [UP], 2008b).

On the one hand, it is important that counselors are aware of the extramural activities that international students are involved in, as the participation in extramural activities can influence the academic experience of international students. On the other hand, it is important that counselors make international students aware of various extramural activities they can become involved in, with the purpose of enhancing their academic experience (Lin & Yi, 1997).

Accommodation Context

Counselors who engage in a career development process with international students need to consider the accommodation arrangements of these students (Jacob & Greggo, 2001). Appropriate accommodations can enhance the academic experience of international students as they don't have any concerns regarding this aspect of their academic endeavor; however, international students who struggle with their accommodations might miss valuable lecture time and practical sessions while trying to sort out their accommodations, which may be detrimental to their academic experience (Wedding et al., 2009). Research has indicated that international students who have more social ties with local students, as well as other international students, are psychologically better adjusted (Kashima & Loh, 2006; Poyrazili et al., 2004). The residence environment of institutions of higher education can be a meeting place for both local and international students, thereby assisting in the adjustment process. However, the cost of accommodation can be another concern that might influence the academic experience (Harman, 2003). International students can often choose to either make use of private accommodations or accommodations supplied by the institution of higher education where they plan to study.

For example, UP (SA) offers a variety of accommodation options to international students. There are eight men's residences, ten ladies residences, and eight mixed residences that accommodate 8,000 students. These residences are all managed according to eight values, namely respect, integrity, accountability, fairness, commitment, excellence, pride and relevance. These residences provide a safe environment where local and international students study, as well as participate in student life (e.g., culture, athletics) through the formal UP structure (UP, 2009, 2010). As previously mentioned, mentorship programs have also shown to have a positive influence on different areas of adjustment for international students (Abe et al., 1998). Many of the residences at the UP (SA) run mentorship programs to assist local and international students in adjusting to academic demands and residence life.

PHASE 3: POST-CAREER DEVELOPMENT PROCESS

Post-career development issues may emerge when international students approach the end of their international studies (Arthur, 2008; Barletta

& Kobayashi, 2007; Harman, 2003). The post-career development phase of this chapter corresponds with the "return-home stage," as seen by Lin and Yi (1997). It seems that international students fall into one of three groups at the end of their academic journey in the foreign country (Shen & Herr, 2004).

First, many international students may explore employment opportunities within the host country and therefore post-career development should assist them in this process, exploring employment opportunities within the host country. Some of the reasons that international students choose to stay in the home country and seek employment are: professional opportunities, competitive employment salaries, attractive working (and living) environment, and experiencing job dignity. Furthermore, there may not be any employment opportunities in the home country.

Second, some international students experience uncertainty as to whether to stay in the host country or return to their home country. The reason for their uncertainty often pertains to finding appropriate employment in the home or host country, which country their work experience will be valued most, the career promotion in the home and host country, marriage relationships, and family obligations.

Third, for those international students who choose to return home, they may need post-career development assistance in learning ways to transfer their foreign education to the local setting and re-entering the work context of their home country. The reasons that inform international students' decisions to return to their home country include a sense of security, career promotion, and family obligations.

Those international students who choose to immediately return to their home country after completion of their studies may even experience reverse culture shock when they return to their home country (Barletta & Kobayashi, 2007; Pedersen, 1991). Reverse culture shock is defined as when "the adjustment process focuses on the difficulties of readapting and readjusting to one's own home culture after one has sojourned or lived in another cultural environment" (Gaw, 2000, p. 83). These international students have changed their lifestyles and even become biculturally oriented, while on returning home their family and friends might harbor the expectation that they have not changed and are still who they were before studying in a foreign country (Pedersen, 1991).

According to Shen and Herr (2004), it would seem that international students' career plans after completing their studies in a foreign country are on the one hand affected by individualism (e.g., the individual's career possibilities), while on the other hand influenced by collectivism (e.g., the home country's needs). Whatever the choice of international students, counselors may be required to assist them with tasks such as the writing of curriculum vitae, seeking employment, and preparing for job interviews. In order for international students to make well-informed decisions and have the best possible opportunity at success, counselors need to be abreast of global trends within the job market and be aware of the economic conditions of both the home and host country.

CONCLUSION

Career development of international students at higher education institutions is not an off-on event, but rather a process. This process entails three phases; namely, the pre-career development phase, the career development phase, and the post-career development phase.

The pre-career development phase entails providing international students with relevant information on institutions of higher education, as well as running orientation programs for them, with the objective of empowering them within their new academic and living environment.

The career development phase focuses on conducting a holistic and culturally sensitive career development process by counselors who are adequately trained to work with international students. These counselors also need to consider the various contexts (e.g., culture differences, academic difficulties, financial problems, personal wellness, extramural activities, student accommodation) that can influence the academic experience of international students.

The post-career development phase entails assisting international students who are approaching the end of their academic endeavor. Some international students want to return to their home country after completing their studies, another group of international students is unsure whether to return to their home country or to remain in the host country, while yet another group desires to remain in the host country. Counselors need to assist all three of these groups of international students in their decision-making processes.

Seeing the career development of international students as not just an on-off event, but as a process, implies the continuous involvement of counselors in the lives and studies of international students.

REFERENCES

Abe, J., Talbot, D. M., & Geelhoed, R. J. (1998). Effects of a peer program on international student adjustment. *Journal of College Student Development, 39*, 539–547.

Alexander, A., Klein, M., Workneh, F., & Miller, M. (1981). Psychotherapy and the foreign student. In P. Pederson, J. Dragons, & J. Trimble (Eds.), *Counselling across cultures* (2nd ed., pp. 227–243). Honolulu, HI: University of Hawaii Press.

Al-Sharideh, K. A., & Goe, W. R. (1998). Ethnic communities within the university: An examination of factors influencing the personal adjustment of international students. *Research in Higher Education, 39,* 699–725.

American Psychological Association. (2003). Guidelines on multicultural education, training, research, practice, and organizational change for psychologists. *American Psychologist, 58,* 377–402.

Andrade, M. S. (2008). International student persistence at a faith-based institution. *Christian Higher Education, 7,* 434–451.

Arthur, N. (2004). *Counseling international students: Clients from around the world.* New York, NY: Kluwer Academic/Plenum Publishers.

Arthur, N. (2005). Counseling international students. In N. Arthur & S. Collins (Eds.), *Culture-infused counselling: Celebrating the Canadian mosaic* (pp. 483–509). Calgary, Canada: Counseling Concepts.

Arthur, N. (2008). Counseling international students. In P. Pederson, J. G. Draguns, W. J. Lonner & J. E. Trimble (Eds.), *Counseling across cultures* (6th ed., pp. 275–290). Los Angeles, CA: Sage.

Barletta, J., & Kobayashi, Y. (2007). Cross-cultural counselling with international students. *Australian Journal of Guidance & Counselling, 17,* 182–194.

Bektas, D. Y. (2008). Counselling international students in Turkish universities: Current status and recommendations. *International Journal for the Advancement of Counselling, 30*(4), 268–278.

Butcher, A., & McGrath, T. (2004). International students in New Zealand: Needs and responses. *International Educational Journal, 5,* 540–551.

Carney, C. G., & Savitz, C. J. (1980). Student and faculty perception of student needs and the services of a university counseling center: Difference that makes a difference. *Journal of Counseling Psychology, 27,* 597–604.

Cushman, P. (1995). *Constructing the self, constructing America: A cultural history of psychotherapy.* Reading, MA: Addison-Wesley.

Ellis, B., Sawyer, J., Gill, R., & Medlin, J. (2005). Influences of the learning environment of a regional university campus on its international graduates. *The Australian Educational Researcher, 32,* 65–85.

Fouad, N. A. (1991). Training counsellors to counsel international students: Are we ready? *Counseling Psychologist, 19,* 66–71.

Gaw, K. F. (2000). Reverse culture shock in students returning from overseas. *International Journal of Intercultural Relations, 24,* 83–104.

Harman, G. (2003). International PhD students in Australian universities: Financial support, course experience and career plans. *International Journal of Educational Development, 23,* 339–351.

Harper, S. R., & Quaye, S. J. (2009). Beyond sameness, with engagement and outcomes for all: An introduction. In S. R. Harper & S. J. Quaye (Eds.), *Student engagement in higher education: Theoretical perspectives and practical approaches for diverse populations* (pp. 1–16). New York, NY: Taylor & Francis.

Hayes, R. L., & Lin, H. (1994). Coming to America: Developing social support systems for international students. *Journal of Multicultural Counseling and Development, 22,* 7–16.

Holland, J. L. (1992). *Making vocational choices: A theory of vocational personalities and work environments.* (2nd ed.). Odessa, FL: Psychological Assessment Resources.

Holland, J. L., Gottfredson, D. C., & Power, P. G. (1980). Some diagnostic scales for research in decision making and personality: Identity, information and barriers. *Journal of Personality and Social Psychology, 39,* 1191–1200.

Jacob, E. J., & Greggo, J. W. (2001). Using counselor training and collaborative programming strategies in working with international students. *Journal of Multicultural Counseling and Development, 29,* 73–88.

Kagan, H., & Cohen, J. (1990). Cultural adjustment of international students. *Psychological Science, 1,* 33–137.

Kashima, E. S., & Loh, E. (2006). International students' acculturation: Effects of international, conational, and local ties and need for closure. *International Journal of Intercultural Relations, 30,* 471–485.

Lacina, J. G. (2002). Preparing international students for a successful social experience in higher education. *New Directions for Higher Education, 117,* 21–27.

Lin, J. G., & Yi, J. K. (1997). Asian international students' adjustment: issues and program suggestions. *College Student Journal, 31,* 473–480.

Luzio-Lockett, A. (1998). The squeezing effect: The cross-cultural experience of international students. *British Journal of Guidance and Counselling, 26,* 209–223.

Mallinckrodt, B., & Leong, F. T. (1992). International graduate students, stress and social support. *Journal of College Student Development, 33,* 71–78.

McLeod, J. (2007). *Counselling Skill.* Berkshire, England: Open University Press.

Mori, S. C. (2000). Addressing the mental health concerns of international students. *Journal of Counseling & Development, 78,* 137–144.

Pedersen, P. (1987). Ten frequent assumptions of cultural bias in counseling. *Journal of Multicultural Counseling and Development, 15,* 16–24.

Pedersen, P. (1988). *A handbook of developing multicultural awareness.* Alexandria, VA: American Counseling Association.

Pedersen, P. (1991). Counseling international students. *The Counseling Psychologist, 19,* 10–58.

Pedersen, P. (1995). *The five stages of culture shock.* Westport, CT: Greenwood.

Popadiuk, N., & Arthur, N. (2004). Counseling international students in Canadian schools. *International Journal of the Advancement of Counseling, 26,* 125–145.

Poyrazili, S., Kavanaugh, P. R., Baker, A., & Al-Timimi, N. (2004). Social support and demographic correlates of acculturative stress in international students. *Journal of College Counseling, 7,* 73–82.

Ruane, I., Kasayira, J. M., & Shino, E. N. (in press). Counseling students at tertiary institutions. In E. Mphufo (Ed.), *Counselling people of African ancestry.*

Sandhu, D. S. (1994). An examination of the psychological needs of students: Implications for counselling and psychotherapy. *International Journal for the Advancement of Counselling, 17,* 229–239.

Schmitt, M. T., Spears, R., & Branscombe, N. R. (2003). Constructing a minority group identity out of shared rejection: The case of international students. *European Journal of Social Psychology, 33,* 1–12.

Shen, Y., & Herr, E. L. (2004). Career placement concerns of international graduate students: A qualitative study. *Journal of Career Development, 31,* 522–530.

Shih, S., & Brown, C. (2000). Taiwanese international students: Acculturation level and vocational identity. *Journal of Career Development, 27,* 35–47.

Smith, T. B., Chin, L., Inman, A. G., & Findling, J. H. (1999). An outreach support group for international students. *Journal of College Counseling, 2,* 188–190.

Sodowsky, G. R., & Plake, B. S. (1992). A study of acculturation differences among international students and suggestions for sensitivity to within-group differences. *Journal of College Student Development, 33,* 53–59.

Surdam, J. C., & Collins, J. R. (1984). Adaptation of international students: A cause for concern. *Journal of College Student Personnel, 25,* 240–244.

Toyokawa, T., & Toyokawa, N. (2002). Extracurricular activities and the adjustment of Asian international students: A study of Japanese students. *International Journal of Intercultural Relations, 26,* 363–379.

University of Pretoria (UP). (2008a). *University of Pretoria International Students Association* (UPI). Retrieved from http://www.up.ac.za

University of Pretoria (UP). (2008b). *TuksSport Clubs.* Retrieved from http://www.up.ac.za

University of Pretoria (UP). (2009). *UP in a Nutshell.* Pretoria, SA: University of Pretoria.

University of Pretoria (UP). (2010). *University of Pretoria: International Information Guide.* Pretoria, SA: University of Pretoria.

Watson, M. (2006). Voices off: Reconstructing career theory and practice for cultural diversity. *Australian Journal of Career Development, 15,* 47–53.

Wedding, D., McCartney, J. L., & Currey, D. E. (2009). Lessons relevant to psychologists who serve as mentors for international students. *Professional Psychology: Research and Practice, 40,* 189–193.

Yang, E., Wong, S.vC., Hwang, M., & Heppner, M.vJ. (2002). Widening our global view: The development of career counseling services for international students. *Journal of Career Development, 8,* 203–213.

Yoon, E., & Portman, T. A. (2004). Critical issues of literature on counseling international students. *Journal of Multicultural Counseling and Development, 32,* 33–44.

Zhang, N., & Dixon, D. N. (2003). Acculturation and attitudes of Asian international students toward seeking psychological help. *Multicultural Counseling and Development, 31,* 205–222.

Zhou, D., & Santos, A. (2007). Career decision-making difficulties of British and Chinese international university students. *British Journal of Guidance & Counselling, 35,* 219–235.

CHAPTER 14

CAREER DEVELOPMENT OF SPECIAL NEEDS STUDENTS AND STUDENTS WITH DISABILITIES

Helen S. Hamlet, PhD
Kutztown University of Pennsylvania

Theodore R. Burnes, PhD
Alliant International University, Los Angeles

Although always present on college campuses, students with disabilities are becoming an identified part of college and university communities at a rapidly increasing rate. Current statistics report that 15.5 percent of enrolled college students nationwide have a disability (Rehabilitation Research and Training Center on Disability Statistics and Demographics, 2009). Students with disabilities are in 98 percent of public two-year and four-year post-secondary institutions, 63 percent of private four-year institutions, and 47 percent of private two-year institutions (National Council on Disabilities, 2003). Due to the increasing number of students with disabilities on higher education campuses, the need for culturally competent services for these

Career Development in Higher Education, pages 301–326
Copyright © 2011 by Information Age Publishing
All rights of reproduction in any form reserved.

students continues to rise. Further, the mandate to provide accommodations to students with disabilities challenges student services professionals on higher education campuses to generate a continually increasing range of services (Palmer & Roessler, 2000).

When addressing different types of institutional support for this growing population, the need for competent services is imperative when considering the career and employment implications of attaining a college degree. Although earning a college degree improves the employment outcome of individuals with disabilities (Madaus, 2006), when compared with peers graduating from institutions of higher learning, college graduates with disabilities have less positive career outcomes (Roessler, Hennessey, & Rumrill, 2007). Thomas (2008) reported that the percentage of college students with disabilities completing degrees dropped from 19 percent in 1986 to 12 percent in 2001. In order to achieve academically and vocationally and repel such statistics, Ochs & Roessler (2001) wrote that students with disabilities must acquire skills that would facilitate success. Such skills include self-confidence, self-identity, educational and social skills, and career maturity (Ochs & Roessler, 2001).

Scholars have further noted that acquisition of these skills is a developmental process. Career counselors cannot assume that students entering higher education arrive proficient in these skills; rather effective career counseling with the students with disabilities begins by focusing on the skill level of the individual student and applying traditional theories of career development using a culturally competent lens. Using such a lens (Mpofu & Harley, 2006), scholars have written best practice guidelines that recommend: focusing on the individual, using a collaborative approach to the postsecondary or high-school-to-college transition, continuing the transition process through the integration of student support services on the college campus, and culminating in the transition from higher education to the workplace. These guidelines highlight the importance of career counseling in higher education having a comprehensive, collaborative approach with an awareness of the academic, cultural, social, and psychological factors affecting the development of students with disabilities.

The National Career Development Association (2007) defines career development as "the total constellation of psychological, sociological, educational, physical, economic, and chance factors that combine to influence the nature and significance of work in the total lifespan of any given individuals" (n.p.). Although this definition addresses the needs of all students, it is particularly applicable to individuals with disabilities. As students' college years are a time of significant career and professional development (Arnett & Tanner, 2006; Lippincott & Lippincott, 2006), career development of all students is a critical part of many university life offices. The career development needs for college students with disabilities is no exception; however, career development specialists must take into account the students' multi-faceted developmental and cultural contexts (Peterson & Gonzalez, 2000).

Using the social-cognitive career framework, culturally competent counselors assist clients in identifying how their self-efficacy may be affecting their career development (Brown & Lentz, 1996). For example, are there occupations the client has eliminated due to faulty self-efficacy and outcome expectation beliefs? What support systems are in the client's life? What barriers does the client see to potential careers? If clients perceive significant barriers, they are less likely to pursue careers that may be of interest to them. Modifying faulty self-efficacy and outcome expectations can expand career options, improve the career decision-making process, and identify the complexities of the career process.

The synthesized writings above highlight the importance of analyzing traditional career development services in institutions of higher education to see how they can provide modified services for students with disabilities while concurrently providing innovative theory and practice recommendations for career counselors who work with this growing population of students. In response to these calls from the literature, this chapter will identify who students with special needs are, provide information on how educational and civil rights laws affects students with disabilities, review developmental and theoretical perspectives guiding the provision of services to students with disabilities, and provide an overview of the K–12 career development curriculum. Additionally, the authors will present a two-stage process of career development for students with disabilities in higher education: 1) the high-school-to-college transition for students with disabilities; and 2) comprehensive career counseling in higher education.

WHO ARE STUDENTS WITH DISABILITIES

ADA/ADAA

Students with special needs and/or with physical, sensory, developmental, cognitive, and neurological disabilities make up an incredibly diverse group of students. The Americans with Disabilities Act (ADA) of 1990 defined individuals with disabilities and set standards for the accommodation provided to these individuals. The original definition of a disability was "impairment that substantially limits one or more major life activities, a record of such an impairment, or being regarded as having such an impairment" (ADA, 1990). The Americans with Disabilities Amendments Act (ADAAA), which became effective in January 1, 2009, retains the original ADA basic definition of a disability while broadening the scope of that definition. The

ADAAA broadens this definition by modifying key terms of the original definition by:

- expanding the definition of "major life activities,"
- redefining who is "regarded as" having a disability,
- modifying the regulatory definition of "substantially limits,"
- specifying that "disability" includes any impairment that is episodic or in remission if it would substantially limit a major life activity when active, and
- prohibiting consideration of the ameliorative effects of "mitigating measures" when assessing whether an impairment substantially limits a person's major life activities, with one exception (ADAAA, 2008).

Because of these modifications, the ADAAA identifies and prohibits discrimination against three categories of individuals qualified with disabilities. These three categories are: 1) individuals with disabilities; 2) individuals who may not actually have a mental or physical disorder but who, based on fear, myth, or stereotype, are regarded as disabled; and 3) individuals with a record of disability. The third category protects individuals who have a history of, or have been misdiagnosed as having, a disability (United States Department of Labor, 2009).

The ADAAA's broadening of the definition of disability is particularly salient to institutions of higher education. It will likely have a significant impact on career development centers because the number of students who qualify as having a disability may greatly increase, causing a higher demand for support and career services. Although this change in definition will require an expansion of service provision from offices such as career services, this federal mandate may be unfunded because many offices of disability services are state-funded (Hermes, 2008). Thus, career counselors may require training and resources but are unable to find the institutional financial and structural support necessary to do so. Although ADAAA defines who "qualifies" legally as a student with disability, self-identification and identity development as an individual with a disability is another matter.

Identity Development

Concurrent with culturally competent career development theory, an understanding of identity development and the role the disability plays in that development is essential to working with students with special needs. Interestingly, one aspect of career development often overlooked when addressing the needs of this minority population is identity development.

While there are models of identity development for other marginalized minority groups, models of identity development have yet to play a part in the development of research and scholarship for individuals with disabilities. However, Mpofu and Harley (2006) have identified four potential constructs that may be fundamental to disability identity development. These constructs may provide a culturally competent conceptual framework that career counselors can use when working with students with disabilities. The constructs are:

a. Perception of disability status as salient to defining self;
b. An individual's perception of the need to accept a disability-related identity to achieve superior psychosocial functioning;
c. The individual's perception of whether owning to a disability identity would lead to a greater consciousness of disability-related discrimination, marginalization, and prejudice from having a disability; and
d. The individual's perception of whether having a strong disability identity may be a resource for countering disability-related stigma.

Cultural competency requires counselors to have awareness, knowledge, and skills when working with minority populations (ACA, 1991). An awareness of identity development with this population, in general, and with clients, in particular, is fundamental to effective culturally competent career counseling.

Developmental and Theoretical Perspectives

Competent career counseling professionals must also take into consideration how the developmental issues and needs of college students with disabilities intersect with their own career development. As scholars (Luzzo, 2000; Shearer, 2009) have noted, the age bracket of 18–30 years, an age bracket that contains many young adults who are members of higher education communities, is filled with social, cognitive, and relational challenges. Erikson (1968) conceptualized young adulthood as a time of relational conflict. He proposed that young adults were in a conflict between their desires to achieve true intimacy in their relationships versus isolation and the lack of deepening intimate relationships. Erikson believed that during this age bracket, young adults are beginning to develop cooperative social and work relationships. Further, he proposed that this is the first time that individuals believe that they can achieve an intimate relationship with another person. In their empirical investigations of constructs involved with young adult development, Arnett and Tanner (2006) found that young adults believed that establishing such an intimate relationship and finding a fulfilling career were of primary importance to young adults as they evolved through their development.

These various developmental processes may interact and impact a student's identity development in various ways. Young adults with disabilities who believe that finding a job will result in their developmental maturation but are met with oppressive and/or hostile industry and career climates may feel "developmentally delayed," as though they have not fully matured in comparison with their peers. Similarly, those young adults with disabilities who are not able to find mentors or trusted colleagues in the workplace may find that they are not able to achieve satisfactory intimate relationships, and consequently isolate themselves in line with Erikson's (1968) stage of development.

In addition to the social and relational considerations reviewed above, Perry (1999) proposed additional cognitive developmental processes that can also help career counselors to conceptualize their work with this population. Perry proposed that adolescents often enter the young adult stage of their development with dualistic thought processes. They may employ dichotomous thought structures that provide rigid thoughts with little ability to see alternative perspectives or to recognize that one issue can have multiple perspectives or viewpoints. Perry argued that young adults might reach stages of relativistic thinking and recognize that knowledge is often contextual. There may not always be "one right answer," and an individual might form personal commitments (values, self-referential labels of identity) from a relativistic frame of reference, allowing for recognition of diverse and fluid ideas and themes.

Perry's notion that students often struggle with the move from dualism to relativism can be seen in many examples of college student thinking as they explore and talk about their career plans. For many college students, the idea of finding "the right job" or "the 'real' job I'll have for the rest of my life" often plagues students. This sets an impossible objective that can frighten them from using career services due to occupational stress. Students often think that there may be only one trajectory to a certain professional position and they may be convinced that they cannot endure the financial, social, cultural, and/or familial pressures necessary to achieve their goal. Further, students' multiple identities that intersect with their identities as persons with disabilities may also impact their career development. For example, Noonan and colleagues (2004) found that contextual factors strongly influenced the career development of women with disabilities in terms of their perception of possible workplace climate and their career self-efficacy. Therefore, students with disabilities may experience heightened dualistic thoughts.

Combining students' cultural identity development and developmental life span issues with the many social, cultural, and cognitive messages that individuals with disabilities receive can either greatly support or impede their career development. When considering the complexities of this population, grounding career counseling practice in a culturally and developmentally-relevant theoretical approach is particularly important. Specifically, the three fundamental concepts of Brown and Lentz' (1996) social cognitive framework for career counseling are prevalent in research focusing on the career development of individuals with disabilities. These three concepts are: 1) self–efficacy, an individual's belief about one's ability to succeed; 2) outcome expectations, an individual's perception of the probability of an outcome; and 3) contextual factors, which includes contextual barriers to and support for obtaining specific career goals. Low career self-efficacy, a characteristic identified in some members of this minority population, is detrimental to optimal career choice and may impede an individual's development. Vocational outcome expectations of students with disabilities were lower than those of students without them (Panagos & DuBois, 1999). Further, the contextual message students with disabilities receive may lead to a lack of career maturity and confidence in decision-making (Hitchings et al., 2001).

STAGE 1: HIGH SCHOOL
TO COLLEGE TRANSITION PLANNING

The Foundation: K–12 Career Development Curriculum

Although the career development needs are unique for young adults with disabilities, it is important to note that professional organizations (National Career Development Association, 2007) emphasize that career development takes place throughout all stages of a person's life. Fouad and colleagues (2010) note the importance of attending to career development early in an individual's life and actively recognizing children's strengths and interests to help the individual self-examine possible careers and interests throughout the developmental process. The National Career Development Guidelines (NCDG), developed for the U.S. Department of Education by the National Career Development Association (NCDA), identify three domains as critical to the lifelong career development process: 1) social development; 2) educational achievement and lifelong learning; and 3) career management.

These three fundamental domains provide the foundation for lifespan career development and are especially salient to students with disabilities as they move through the stages of career development. Individuals with disabilities progress through the normal career developmental phases of awareness, exploration, and preparation. Career development for these students is a developmental process built on the career education and career awareness established during the elementary, middle, and secondary school years (Beale, 1999). However, Ochs and Roessler (2001) identified a "developmental differential" for students with disabilities, indicating the need for an individualized approach to career education and counseling for these students. This developmental differential is of particular importance when a student reaches higher education and is in the process of exploring and narrowing their vocational choices.

Consistent with NCDG's guidelines, career development theorists have provided information about the need for career counseling interventions for clients across different lifespan stages. Career exploration in the elementary school years focuses on acquisition of basic skill development, career awareness through exposure to a wide variety of careers, and early identification of the connection between education and occupational success. Building on these constructs, career counselors working with middle school-age students often use guidance curricula that emphasize increased self-understanding through career exploration for the student and the identification of tentative occupational choices. As the career development process continues into high school, NCDA calls for counselors to help all students make quality decisions regarding postsecondary educational and career planning (NCDA, 2007). Postsecondary transition planning takes on additional significance for students with disabilities due to the variability and fluidity of skill development within this population of students.

Although there are documented curriculum interventions for career counselors to use to ensure that individuals engage with career development to prepare them for their college years, acquisition of specific skills in this population are not a given due to the diverse needs of this specific population. In an attempt to support students who may experience a disparity in skill development due to a disability, the Individuals with Disabilities Education Improvement Act (IDEA, 2004) mandates postsecondary or transition planning. Despite this mandate, empirical research has found evidence that students with disabilities still face challenges transitioning into higher education that college-bound students without disabilities do not. The National Longitudinal Transition Study found that students with disabilities were not transitioning successfully into postsecondary life. A summative statement of the IDEA and the NLTS highlights a call for postsecondary transition planning for students with disabilities as an educational forefront. IDEA notes that "Improving educational results for children with disabilities is an essential element of our national policy of ensuring equality of opportunity, full participation, independent living, and economic self-sufficiency for individuals with disabilities" (IDEA, 2004, n.p.; Wagner, Newman, Cameto, Garza, & Levine, 2005).

The Law: IDEA

Understanding the legal aspects of services mandated in high schools versus the laws regulating services for students with disabilities in higher education is essential to providing support services and career counseling to students with disabilities as they prepare to enter higher education institutions. There is a significant difference in the regulatory laws in high school versus higher education in the areas of documentation requirement, systemic intervention and procedures, and student responsibilities in the processes. IDEA and Title II of the Higher Education Opportunity Act regulate the procedures, standards, and accommodations at the high school level and in the postsecondary transition.

IDEA and Title II of the Higher Education Act (HEOA, 2008) under the No Child Left Behind Act (NCLB) have supported curricular changes focusing on improving academic achievement and mandating postsecondary planning or transition services for student with disabilities. The Office of Special Education and Rehabilitative Services (United States Department of Education, 2000) defines transition services as a coordinated set of activities for a child with a disability that:

- Is designed to be within a results-oriented process that is focused on improving the academic and functional achievement of the child with a disability to facilitate the child's movement from school to post-school activities, including postsecondary education; vocational education; integrated employment (including supported employment); continuing and adult education; adult services; independent living or community participation; and [602(34)(A)]
- Is based on the individual child's needs, and takes into account the child's strengths, preferences, and interests [602(34)(B)].

The Council for Exceptional Children focuses on the developmental aspects of the high-school-to-college transition and defines it as a change in status from behaving primarily as a student to assuming emergent adult roles in the community. These roles include employment, participating in postsecondary education, maintaining a home, and becoming appropriately involved in the community (Boyer-Stephens et al., 1999). A major goal of these initiatives is to increase the access to higher education for students with disabilities ultimately resulting in positive career outcomes and success (Wilson, Hoffman, & McLaughlin, 2009).

Implementation of career counseling at the high school level varies from school district to school district. However, for students with disabilities, the IDEA mandated postsecondary transition planning formally begins when students with an Individualized Education Plan (IEP) turn 16 years of age.

The initial IEP process begins when a student is first identified with a disability. The focus of the IEP prior to the age of 16 is providing appropriate educational accommodations to facilitate a student's academic success. At or before the age of 16, the focus of the IEP broadens to include career and postsecondary planning. Postsecondary or career planning for students with disabilities takes place during the annual IEP meeting and focuses specifically on planning and goal setting in order to prepare the student for the postsecondary transition. The student's strengths, weaknesses, academic coursework, experience, community service, and vocational interests are components to consider. The individuals who attend IEP transition meetings are the student, the student's teachers, counselors, school representatives, and parents.

Students are encouraged to participate in Individual Transition Planning (ITP), which is the postsecondary transition portion of their IEP, in order to facilitate the development of self-advocacy skills (Martin, VanDycke, Greene, Gardner, Christensen, Woods et al., 2006). As a student with disabilities prepares to graduate from high school, IDEA 2004 requires a written summary of performance (SOP) to support student transition (Madaus & Shaw, 2006). IDEA 2004 states that "... a local educational agency shall provide the child with a summary of the his or her academic achievement and functional performance, which shall include recommendations on how to assist the child in meeting the child's postsecondary goals" (§300.305(e)(3)).

Essential to student career development and success during this transition is a carefully and proactively designed transition plan. The National Center on Secondary Education and Transition recommends the following seven points as fundamental to effective transition planning:

1. Student involvement in developing his or her IEP and in transition planning;
2. Opportunities to develop self-determination, self-advocacy, communication, and independent living skills;
3. Students' interests, goals, and strengths guide the planning process;
4. Interagency collaboration;
5. Obtain assessment and disability documentation that is acceptable to postsecondary institutions;
6. Obtain and use information about the requirements for entering postsecondary institutions to plan students' secondary coursework. Classes should meet requirements for graduation from secondary school and for entering postsecondary school; and
7. Identify and explore the types of supports and accommodations that students will need in postsecondary environments and plan for ways

to prepare students to transition to the postsecondary environment (HEATH, 2006, p. 4).

Transition Models for College-Bound Students with Disabilities

In order to provide culturally competent career counseling services for students with disabilities, the need for transition planning before the student with a disability enters the university system is essential. An understanding of this transition plan and the skills associated with it are fundamental aspects of career counseling on a college campus. As previously noted, Ochs and Roessler (2001) identified a "developmental differential" for students with disabilities in career maturity, career development, and skill acquisition. This "developmental differential" identified in skill development for students with disabilities requires counselors to not only understand the skill development and transition planning processes, but also to assess their students' awareness and level of skill. As Rothman, Maldonado, and Rothman (2008) stated, assessment of skills, such as self-advocacy, is pivotal of the career counseling process. In addition, the familial, school, and larger systems influencing student career development inform the counseling process.

Kohler's Taxonomy of Transition Programming (1996) presents a model for skill development and transitional planning. This model addresses student-focused planning, student development, family involvement, program structure, and interagency collaboration. The student-focused planning section of Kohler's taxonomy specifically addresses IEP planning, student participation, and planning strategies. Self-determination and self-advocacy, as part of this taxonomy, encourages the student to identify key components necessary for transition programming, including life skills instruction, work skills instruction, career and vocational curricula, support services, assessment, and the role of structured work experience. Family involvement, a contextual aspect of this model, supports significant family participation in the postsecondary transition process (e.g., program policy development, student assessment, decision-making, IEP meetings). Family empowerment and training are also recommended through promoting self-determination, advocacy, support, the transition planning process, agencies and services, and legal issues.

The Taxonomy of Transition Programming (Kohler, 1996) also addresses the need for systemic involvement, a critical area in which career counselors can assist and help the student and the student's family as they prepare to enter a university system and continue to develop the student's career decision-making process. The taxonomy addresses program structure through a variety of components, including human resource development (e.g., transition practices resource materials available to personnel, families, and employers; pre-service training; transition-related technical assistance), and resource allocation (e.g., sufficient allocation of resources, creative use of resources). Interagency collaboration targets communication, cooperation and coordination of service delivery and a collaborative framework, including structures such as an interagency coordinating body, established methods of communication among service providers, and management systems.

This taxonomy highlights self-determination as one of its core tenets. Scholars (e.g., Martin, Huber Marshall & Sale, 2004) have found this to be a strong predictor of successful career decision-making outcome (Martin, Kohler, & Osmani, 2009). Based on a framework of self-determination, Martin and his colleagues developed the "Student-Directed Transition Planning" (SDTP) model that recommends seven steps for transition planning. The model uses a team approach involving the student, family, and educators (Sylvester, Woods, Martin, & Poolaw, 2007):

1. Student involvement in the transition planning process,
2. Completion of a three-part transition assessment process,
3. Writing the present level of academic achievement and functional performance,
4. Developing a course of study,
5. Developing post school linkages,
6. Students work on attaining IEP and personal goals, and
7. Families and students build a student-directed summary of performance.

Both the Kohler Taxonomy of Transition Programming and the SDTP incorporate active student engagement in the transition process, student skill development, family involvement, systemic intervention, and interagency collaboration in their postsecondary transition models. Developing these student strengths and skills while improving systemic and interagency collaboration will increase the likelihood of educational success leading to positive vocational outcomes (Janiga & Costenbader, 2002). Recommendations for intervention specifically focus on self-advocacy skills through student-led transition meetings, knowledge of disabilities and legal issues, self-determination, social skill development, and collaboration between secondary and postsecondary institutions (Foley, 2006; Janiga & Costenbader, 2002; Oesterreich & Knight, 2008). The transition to college begins during a student's high school career; best practice recommends that outreach between the two educational systems occur and support systems continue into the higher education setting facilitating student academic success, career development, and successful career outcomes.

STAGE 2: COMPREHENSIVE CAREER COUNSELING IN HIGHER EDUCATION

Higher Education: The Law–ADA and Section 504 of the Rehabilitation Act

For college students with disabilities, having a working knowledge of the disability laws is considered essential to completion of a college degree, successful career outcomes, and competent career counseling. Milsom and Hartley (2005) stated,

> While one could argue that students can successfully complete high school ignorant of the laws that help them, the same cannot be said for students in college. Because the ADA and Section 504 mandate that postsecondary institutions provide support services only for individuals who request them, provided those individuals possess the appropriate documentation, students with learning disabilities must be aware of their rights and responsibilities.

However, the transition from the laws and procedures in the Individuals with Disabilities Education Act (IDEA) presents a major developmental and procedural shift for students with disabilities entering higher education.

Special education and IDEA provide a formalized, structured approach for accessing educational accommodations. Adults in the student's life implement the K–12 special education system and do not require action from the student in order to receive services. Special education provided under IDEA is an entitlement program, which guarantees an individual access to services. Higher education institutions are not required to comply with IDEA. Postsecondary institutions must comply with the Americans with Disabilities Act and Section 504 of the Rehabilitation Act of 1973 (Sitlington, Clark, & Kolstoe, 2000). These regulations are civil rights protections which require colleges and universities to provide appropriate academic adjustments to ensure that they do not discriminate on the basis of a disability (Wilson, Hoffman, & McLaughlin, 2009; Rothman, Maldonado, & Rothman, 2008; U.S. Department of Education, Office for Civil Rights, 2010). Thomas (2000) stated that "with respect to postsecondary education, a qualified student with a disability is one who is able to meet a program's admission, academic, and technical standards (e.g., all essential nonacademic admissions criteria) either with or without accommodation" (p. 250). Specifically, Section 504 states:

No otherwise qualified individual with a disability in the United States… shall, solely by reason of her or his disability, be excluded from participation in, be denied the benefits of, or be subjected to discrimination under any program or activity receiving Federal financial assistance. (U.S. Department of Education, Office for Civil Rights, 2010, n.p.)

Table 14.1 presents the notable differences in legal protection between high school and college; Table 14.2 presents the differences in advocacy and access between high school and college. Think College, a project of

TABLE 14.1   Differences in Legal Protection Between High School and College

High School	College
Individuals with Disabilities Education Act (IDEA)	Americans with Disabilities Act (ADA) and Section 504 of the Rehabilitation Act
IDEA is about success.	ADA and Section 504 are about access.
Education is a RIGHT and must be accessible to you.	Education is NOT a right. Students must apply to attend.
Core modifications of classes and materials are required.	NO modifications are required–only accommodations.
School district develops Individual Education Plans (IEPs) and must follow this legal document in the provision of educational services.	Student must identify needs and ask for services. No IEP exists and is not considered legal documentation.

Source: University of Massachusetts Boston (2010). *Think college.*

TABLE 14.2   Differences in Advocacy and Access Between High School and College

High School	College
Student is helped by parents and teachers, even without asking directly.	Students must request accommodations from Disability Services Office.
School is responsible for arranging for accommodations and modifications.	Student must self-advocate and arrange for accommodations.
Parent has access to student records.	Parent has no access to student records without student's written consent.
Parent advocates for student.	Student advocates for self.
Teachers meet regularly with parents to discuss their child's educational progress.	College faculty members seldom, if ever, interact with parents and expect the students to address issues with them directly.
Students need parental permission to participate in most activities.	Student is an adult and gives own permission.

Source: University of Massachusetts Boston (2010). *Think college.*

the Institute for Community Inclusion at the University of Massachusetts Boston, developed these tables. Grants from the National Institute on Disability and Rehabilitation Research, the Administration on Developmental Disabilities, and the Office of Special Education Programs fund the Think College initiatives. The major differences in the educational systems require college students with disabilities to understand their legal rights and to advocate for themselves.

Bridges: Initiatives Bridging the High-School-to-College Gap

As previously noted, best practice for career counseling of students with special needs in higher education begins with a collaborative relationship between the secondary and postsecondary institutions (National Council on Disabilities, 2003). Although collaboration and coordination often exists between local high schools and colleges, there is no formal structure for a coordination of services for students with disabilities. Roessler, Hennessey, and Rumrill (2007) recommend that institutions of higher education consider adopting transition education practices that would support the high school level transition initiatives, provide a cohesive interagency transition to a successful college experience, and help students develop the competencies needed in this new environment. Building on the postsecondary transition programming that took place in high school, Dukes and Shaw (1999) noted that more and more higher education institutions are developing programs and providing support for students with disabilities to facilitate successful completion of a college degree and successful career outcomes.

Outreach from High School to Higher Education: Summary of Performance

In addition to dealing with such agencies and institutional infrastructure, students must present documentation that they qualify for those services in order to receive services at the higher education level. Thus, a major initiative to bridge the transition process from high school to college has focused on the documentation process in order to improve students' access to disability services in higher education (Madaus & Shaw, 2006). This initiative has focused on using the current IDEA 2004 mandated documentation system, the Summary of Performance, and developing uniformity in the information provided in order to meet the needs of students in both high school and college. Madaus and Shaw (2006) state that "representatives from key national organizations involved in the education of students with disabilities worked collaboratively to develop an SOP that would bridge the gap between IDEA and 504/ADA" (p. 16). The National Transition Documentation Summit (2005) developed the following sections for the SOP template:

1. Background information: identifying student's disability, the date of the most recent IEP or 504 plan, copies of most recent assessment reports that diagnose and clearly identify the student's disability or functional limitations that will assist in postsecondary planning;
2. Student's postsecondary goals: indicating postsecondary environment(s) the student intends to transition;
3. Summary of performance: academic, cognitive, and functional levels of performance, the accommodations, modifications, and assistive technologies that were essential in high school to assist the student in achieving progress, and why they were needed;
4. Recommendations to assist the student in meeting postsecondary goals: suggestions for accommodations, adaptive devices and services, compensatory strategies, and support services to enhance access to post-high school environments; and
5. Student input: the student's perspective on how the disability affects schoolwork and school activities, past supports, accommodations that have been helpful to the student, and the student's strengths and needs.

Effective transfer of information is essential for a successful transition from high school to higher education. Hence, developing a common language among all stakeholders is in the best interest of the student's academic and future career success. Specifically, Madaus and Shaw (2006) reported that

> Postsecondary education is targeted as an important transition outcome for students with disabilities because of the impact of a college degree on future adult outcomes. Students with disabilities who graduate from college exhibit similar employment rates and annual salaries compared to their counterparts without disabilities.

Outreach from Higher Education to High Schools: ACT Now

ACT Now is a program designed to bridge the transition between high school and college through training and curriculum for students, parents, and high school educators. Northampton Community College, in collaboration with the Bethlehem Area School District and the Colonial Intermediate Unit 20, and funded in part by United States Department of Education's

Fund for the Improvement of Postsecondary Education (FIPSE), developed this Pennsylvania program. The ACT Now curriculum:

1. Delivers training to secondary educators, who hold much influence over the educational preparation of students;
2. Prepares students for their transition to postsecondary education through a process of self discovery, knowledge, and self advocacy; and
3. Provides the parents of these students with needed information and understanding to support their sons and daughters as they move into adulthood (NCC, 2010).

An important characteristic of this program is that it addresses the needs of all the stakeholders involved in the high school to college transition.

Higher Education-Based Transition Programs

The State University of New York (SUNY) Albany offers a pre-college summer experience for students with disabilities. The SUNY Albany Disability Resources Center's Pre-college Experience Program Web site indicated,

> This program is run in conjunction with the New York State Commission for the Blind and the Visually Handicapped (CBVH) and Vocational Educational Services for Individuals with Disabilities (VESID), and Hudson Valley Community College (HVCC). High school juniors or seniors who are residents of the state and who are blind or visually handicapped can come for this seven day intensive orientation program to college life for students with disabilities. Participants attend colleges all over New York State and not just the University at Albany. (SUNY Albany, 2010, n.p.)

This program began in 1988 and focuses on developing skills, such as self-advocacy, communication, social networking, and self-determination. Rothman, Maldonado, and Rothman (2008) examined participants' perception of the influence of this one-week residential transition program. Results indicated that attending a program, such as the SUNY program, increased the likelihood of college degree completion and career success.

Transition/orientation programs take many forms. The Disabilities Resource Center of the University of Florida offers three options for orientation and transition programs: 1) an orientation session focusing on the specific concerns of students with disabilities, such as how to speak to your instructor about accommodations, getting a note-supplier in class, and utilizing assistive technology; 2) weekly transition groups focusing on specific academic and success strategies; and 3) the Disabilities Resource Center

Mentoring Program (University of Florida, 2010). Multiple options provide students the opportunity to select the option that best meets their need and also to self-select and determine their level of participation.

College and university web sites vary greatly in the information available. The web site of Pennsylvania State University's Office of Disabilities is a wealth of information and resource for students, families, high school educators, and higher education faculty. This web site provides information about resources on campus, such as academic adjustment, auxiliary aids, and services; rights and responsibilities for students with disabilities; confidentiality and release of information; policies and procedures for testing adjustment; establishing eligibility for ODS services; and procedures for requesting academic adjustments, auxiliary aids, and/or services. Resources are also made available through links to educational and governmental organizations, such as publications from the Office for Civil Rights; the laws impacting higher education and disability; ETS's Web page on test-taking for individuals with disabilities; and the Pennsylvania Office of Vocational Rehabilitation (PSU, 2010).

CAREER COUNSELING: A COLLABORATIVE MODEL

When synthesizing the multiple identities of students with disabilities and the stages of career counseling for these students, the result is a series of counseling strategies that necessitate an individualized approach along with the use of a collaborative model across the various offices in a university setting. In particular, career counselors must first assess a student's identity development and the role that disability has in his or her development, as well as high school transition planning and experience, academic background, contextual background, and level of development with skills, such as self-advocacy and self-determination.

In addition to getting to know the client, an essential aspect of career counseling with students with disabilities often includes coordination of services with the various offices serving this population. Although the structure of student support services offices varies from campus to campus, the offices most often involved in providing career support services for students with disabilities are the career counseling center, the center for counseling and psychological services, and the office of disability services. The U.S. Department of Education notes the importance of coordinating services for students with disabilities and states that it occurs when (a) there is linkage among each of the component activities that comprise the services, and (b) an inter-relationship exists among the various agencies that provide services. Specifically, career counselors are able to take a leadership role in this collaborative endeavor.

Office of Disability Services

Disability services offices originated in response to the ADA and Section 504 to provide accommodations to students with disabilities on college and university campuses (McCleary-Jones, 2007). The offices of disability services offer a range of accommodations and services that vary from school to school. Services may include alternative exam formats, tutors, readers and note-takers, registration assistance, adaptive equipment and technology, textbooks on tape, sign language and oral interpreters, course substitution, disability benefits counseling, special college orientation programs, disability resource handbooks, placement services, adaptive physical education or sports, and paratransit for campus mobility (PACER, 2010).

Hitchings and colleagues state that "a major attribute for personal success among highly successful adults with learning disabilities is a strong sense of control over career-related events and a conscious decision to take charge of one's life. Other factors include the ability to reframe the learning disability experience and a goal-oriented perspective" (2001, p. 9). Offices of disability services facilitate equal access to educational opportunity and participation for persons with disabilities. As students access appropriate accommodations and begin to gain a sense of their own academic self-efficacy and their ability to achieve goals, they gain a sense of control over their academic progress, ultimately leading to successful career outcomes. In addition to such testing and accommodation services, it is important for these offices to provide a variety of needed mentoring for students about their career options. Having conversations with students about careers related to student course tracks and assignments (as well as having appropriate referral sources in career centers and academic department advising staff) can help students to gain a greater sense of career self-efficacy throughout their matriculation at the university.

Counseling and Psychological Services

The American College Counseling Association (ACCA), as part of the 20/20 Commission, defines counseling as *"a professional relationship that empowers diverse individuals, families, and groups to accomplish mental health, wellness, education, and career goals"* (ACCA, 2010). Counseling centers on college and university campuses focus on student development, interpersonal skills, identity development, self-awareness, conflict resolution, educational and vocational goal clarification, drug and alcohol awareness, and provide psychological and psychiatric services (Lippincott & Lippincott, 2006). In essence, counseling centers provide services consistent with the potential needs of all college students. Counseling services for students with disabilities may assist students to address the role of disability in their identity development and their interpersonal relationships.

Career Counseling Centers

Career counseling centers provide services which focus on clarification of educational and vocational goals; career exploration; occupational trends; self-determination; assessment of career interests, values, and goals; self-awareness; assessment of personality traits; self-advocacy; networking skills; communication skills; resume building; resume writing; and interviewing skills. Career counselors may also help students with disabilities answer questions, such as: should students disclose their disability status during interviews, job training, and/or performance reviews; what are employee rights under ADA at the company or career track of interest; and what is a reasonable accommodation for the student/new employee's status.

A Narrative Approach.

Taking a narrative approach (Sharf, 2006) to career counseling when working with students with disabilities provides the opportunity to hear the student's story. Having a space for the student to deconstruct his or her own journey is particularly important for students with disabilities. The story of a student with one or multiple disabilities may well include aspects of life that are unfamiliar to many professionals: experiences of oppression and discrimination; messages the student has received about his or her ability to succeed; and internalized family, community, and societal messages. For example, for some students, the age when they became aware of their disability is particularly relevant to their narrative and can influence their perception of future career opportunities. Further, assessing whether the student believes that his or her disability is relevant to the issue for which he or she has come to the career counseling center is essential to developing a counseling relationship. As a career counselor, professionals should let the student speak about his or her disability and how, if at all, the disability impacts the student's lifestyle. Establishing a helping relationship and developing rapport is essential with any client; however, it is much more essential with a marginalized population, such as individuals with disabilities (Sue & Sue, 2008). Once the helping relationship is established, career counselors should focus on the presenting goals of the student.

One critical goal for the majority of college students is degree completion. Because students may feel overwhelmed by impending graduation requirements, career exploration, and the concurrent job search process, low retention, along with reduced graduation rates of students with disabilities, often occurs (Getzel, Stodden, & Briel, 2001). Thus, providing support to facilitate future career success and, potentially, degree completion is fundamental to the career counseling process. Collaboration with the office of disabilities, with student consent and/or participation, may facilitate the student's ability to become a self-advocate and request the necessary and appropriate accommodations needed to be successful. Self-advocacy skills are essential for student success in higher education (Chickering & Reisser, 1993; Phinney, 2006) and become paramount for students with disabilities (Beale, 2005). Previous research has found that students with disabilities, as a product of social marginalization, may have underdeveloped communication skills and a lack of belief in their ability to achieve. Self-advocacy and conflict resolution training, focusing on both communication and negotiation, improve students' understanding of their rights and responsibilities and their ability to self-advocate (Palmer & Roessler, 2000). These self-advocacy skills, which are important to a successful college experience, are the same skills identified as essential to positive career development.

The development of a sound sense of self-determination is a competency essential to student success and is a potential point of intervention for students with disabilities. A self-determined person is one who sets goals, makes decisions, sees options, solves problems, self-advocates, and understands what one needs to accomplish successful outcomes (Martin & Marshall, 1996). Wehmeyer, Palmer, Argan, Mithaug, and Martin (2000) developed the Self-Determined Learning Model of Instruction to teach self-determination skills to students with disabilities. This model is a three-phase instructional: 1) set a goal; 2) take action; and, 3) adjust plan. Following implementation of this intervention model, results indicated that it enhanced student self-regulation and self-determination (Webb, Patterson, Syverud, Seabrooks-Blackmore, 2008).

Traditional career counseling incorporates assessment of traits, values, and interest inventories. The counselor should consider if the assessment instrument is appropriate for the client before it is used. Hence, the counselor should use mainstream career inventories with caution and interpret with even greater care. Career assessment of students with disabilities may provide information that is more valid when gathered through a personal narrative approach. This also provides the opportunities to investigate life and work experiences potentially leading to a discussion about internships and cooperative educational possibilities. Burgstahler (2001) reports that "students with disabilities benefit from work-based learning activities as much as, if not more than, their non-disabled peers" (p. 209). Career counseling for students with disabilities also provides information on what is happening in the current zeitgeist; trends in occupations; how ADA may impact their access and role in the workplace; disclosure of disability status; resume building and writing; appropriate interview conduct and attire; and current communication etiquette.

Career counseling with students with disabilities in higher education requires the counselor to step out of the box and the office, and enter the world of the client. Working with this minority population requires in-depth knowledge of disability and education law, minority identity development, available accommodations, state-of-the-art assistive technology, and inter-agency collaboration. It also requires a heightened sensitivity and ability to understand the individuals experiences and narrative.

REFERENCES

American College Counseling Association. (2010). *20/20 Commission*. Retrieved from http://www.collegecounseling.org

American Counseling Association. (1991). *Multicultural Counseling Competencies*. Retrieved from http://www.counseling.org/Resources/Competencies/Multcul-tural_Competencies.pdf

Americans with Disabilities Act of 1990, Pub. L. No. 101-336, §12101-12213, 42 (1991).

Americans with Disabilities Amendments Act of 2008, Pub. L. No. 110-325, §4(a), 122 Stat. 3553, 355 (2008).

Arnett, J. J., & Tanner, J. L. (Eds.). (2006). *Emerging adults in America: Coming of age in the 21st century*. Washington, DC: American Psychological Association.

Beale, A. (1999). Career planning guidelines for parents of students with mild *disabilities*. *Clearing House, 72*(3), 179–183.

Beale, A. (2005). Preparing students with learning disabilities for postsecondary education: Their rights and responsibilities. *Techniques Connecting Education and Careers, 80*(3), 24–27.

Boyer-Stephens, A., Corbey, S., Jones, B., Miller, R., Sarkees-Winceski, M., & West, L. (1999). *Integrating transition planning into the IEP process* (2nd ed.). Reston, VA: Council for Exceptional Children.

Brown, S., & Lentz, R. (1996). A social cognitive framework for career choice counseling. *The Career Development Quarterly, 44*, 355–367.

Burgstahler, S. (2001). A collaborative model to promote career success for students with disabilities. *Journal of Vocational Rehabilitation, 16*, 209–215.

Chickering, A. W., & Reisser, L. (1993). *Education and identity* (2nd ed). San Francisco, CA: Jossey-Bass.

Dukes III, L. L., & Shaw, S. F. (1999). Postsecondary disability personnel: Professional standards and staff development. *Journal of Developmental Education, 23*(1), 26–31.

Erickson, E. (1968). *Identity: Youth and crisis*. New York, NY: Norton.

Foley, N. E. (2006). Preparing for college: Improving the odds for students with learning disabilities. *College Student Journal, 40*(3), 641–645.

Fouad, N. A., Cotter, E. W., Fitzpatrick, M. E., Kantamneni, N., Carter, L., & Bernfeld, S. (2010). Development and validation of the family influence scale. *Journal of Career Assessment, 18*(3), 276–291.

Getzel, E. E., Stodden, R. A., & Briel, L. W. (2001). Pursuing postsecondary education opportunities for individuals with disabilities. In P. Wehman (Ed.), *Life beyond the classroom: Transition strategies for young people with disabilities*. Baltimore, MD: Paul H. Brookes Publishing Co.

HEATH Resource Center. (2006). *Guidelines and career counselor's toolkit: Advising high school students with disabilities on postsecondary options*. Washington, DC:

The George Washington University National Clearinghouse on Postsecondary Education for Individuals with Disabilities. Retrieved from http://www.heath.gwu.edu

Hermes, J. J. (2008). Bill to broaden Disabilities Act concerns some colleges. *Chronicle of Higher Education, 54*(40), A23.

Higher Education Opportunity Act. (2008). Pub. L. No. 110-315 (2008). Retrieved from http://ed.gov/policy/highered/leg/hea08/index.html

Hitchings, W. E., Luzzo, D. A., Ristow, R., Horvath, M., Retish, P., & Tanners, A. (2001). The career development needs of college students with learning disabilities: In their own words. *Learning Disabilities Research and Practice. 16*(1), 8–17.

Individuals with Disabilities Education Improvement Act, §108-446, 20 U.S.C. 1400. (2004). Retrieved from: http://idea.ed.gov

Individuals with Disabilities Education Act Amendments of 1997, Pub. L. No. 105–17, §1400 et seq., 104 (1997).

Janiga, S. J., & Costenbader, V. (2002). The transition from high school to postsecondary education for students with learning disabilities: A survey of college service coordinators. *Journal of Learning Disabilities, 36*(5), 462–479.

Kohler, P. (1996). *Taxonomy for transition programming.* Champaign, IL: University of Illinois.

Lippincott, J. A., & Lippincott, R. A. (2006). *Special populations in college counseling: A handbook for mental health professionals.* Alexandria, VA: American Counseling Association.

Luzzo, D. A. (2000). *Career counseling of college students: Empirical strategies that work.* Washington, DC: American Psychological Association.

Madaus, J. W. (2006). Employment outcomes of university graduates with learning disabilities. *Learning Disablties Quarterly, 29,* 19–31.

Madaus, J. W., & Shaw, S. (2006). Disabilities services in postsecondary education: Impact of IDEA 2004. *Journal of Developmental Education, 30*(1), 12–21.

Martin, J. E., Huber Marshall, L., & Sale, P. (2004). A 3-year study of middle, junior high, and high school IEP meetings. *Exceptional Children, 70,* 285–297.

Martin, J. E., & Marshall, L. H. (1996). Infusing self-determination instruction into the IEP and transition process. In D. J. Sands & M. L. Wehmeyer (Eds.), *Self-determination across the lifespan: Independence and choice for people with disabilities* (pp. 215–236). Baltimore, MD: Paul H. Brookes.

Martin, J. E., Van Dycke, J. L., Greene, B. A., Gardner, J. E., Christensen, W. R., Woods, L. L., & Lovett, D. L. (2006). Direct observation of teacher-directed IEP meetings: Establishing the need for student IEP meeting instruction. *Exceptional Children, 72,* 187–200.

Martin, J. E., Kohler, P. D., & Osmani, K. (2009). *Transition education and self-determination course: A complete higher education class.* Norman, OK: OU's Zarrow Center for Learning Enrichment.

McCleary-Jones, V. (2007). Learning disabilities in the community college and the role of disability services departments. *Journal of Cultural Diversity, 14*(1), 43–47.

Milsom, A., & Hartley, M. T. (2005). Assisting students with learning disabilities transitioning to college: What school counselors should know. *Professional School Counseling, 8*(5), 436–441.

Mpofu, E., & Harley, D. (2006). Racial and disability identity. *Rehabilitation Counseling Bulletin, 50*(10), 14–23.

National Career Development Association. (2007). *Career development: A policy statement of the National Career Development Association Board of Directors.* Retrieved from http://associationdatabase.com/aws/NCDA/pt/sp/Home_Page

National Council on Disability. (2003). *People with disabilities and postsecondary education.* Retrieved from http://www.ncd.gov/newsroom/publications/2003/education.htm

National Transition Documentation Summit. (2005). *Summary of performance model template.* Retrieved from http://www.cec.sped.org

Noonan, B. M., Gallor, S. M., Hensler-McGinnis, N. F., Fassinger, R. E., Wang, S., & Goodman, J. (2004). Challenge and success: A qualitative study of the career development of highly achieving women with physical and sensory disabilities. *Journal of Counseling Psychology, 51*(1), 68–80.

Northampton Community College. (2010). *ACT Curriculum.* Retrieved from http://www.northampton.edu/Student-Resources/Disability-Services/Special-Projects/ACT-Now/Curriculum.htm

Ochs, L. A., & Roessler, R. T. (2001). Students with disabilities: How ready are they for the 21st century? *Rehabilitation Counseling Bulletin, 44*(3), 170–176.

Oesterreich, H. A., & Knight, M. G. (2008). Facilitating transitions to college for students with disabilities from culturally and linguistically diverse backgrounds. *Intervention in School and Clinic, 43*(5), 300–304.

PACER. (2010). *Minnesota Parent Training and Information Center.* Retrieved from http://www.pacer.org/tatra/legislation/IDEAtransition.asp

Panagos, R. J., & DuBois, D. L. (1999). Career self-efficacy development and students with learning disabilities. *Learning Disabilities Research and Practice, 14*(1), 25–34.

Palmer, D., & Roessler, R. T. (2000). Requesting classroom accommodations: Self-advocacy and conflict resolution training for college students with disabilities. *Journal of Rehabilitation, 66*(3), 38–43.

Pennsylvania State University. (2010). *Office of Disabilities Services.* Retrieved from http://www.equity.psu.edu/ods/site.asp

Perry, W. G. (1999). Forms of intellectual and ethical development in the college years: A schema. *Higher and Adult Education Series.* New York, NY: Jossey-Bass.

Peterson, N., & Gonzalez, R. C. (2000). *The role of work in people's lives: Applied career and vocational psychology.* Pacific Grove, CA: Brooks/Cole-Wadsworth.

Phinney, J. S. (2006). Ethnic identity exploration in emerging adulthood. In J. J. Arnett & J. L. Tanner (Eds.), *Emerging adults in America: Coming of age in the 21st century* (pp. 117–134). Washington, DC: American Psychological Association.

Rehabilitation Research and Training Center on Disability Statistics and Demographics. (2009). *Annual Compendium of Disability Statistics Compendium: 2009.* Rehabilitation Research and Training Center on Disability Demographics and Statistics, Hunter College. Retrieved from http://www.disabilitycompendium.org

Roessler, R. T., Hennessey, M. L., & Rumrill, P. D. (2007). Strategies for improving career services for postsecondary students with disabilities: Results of a focus group study of key stakeholders. *Career Development of Exceptional Individuals, 30*(3), 158–170.

Rothman, T., Maldonado, J. M., & Rothman, H. (2008). Building self-confidence and future career success through a pre-college transition program for individuals with disabilities. *Journal of Vocational Rehabilitation, 28,* 73–83.

Sharf, R. S. (2006). *Applying career development theory to counseling.* Belmont, CA: Brooks/Cole-Wadsworth.

Section 504 of the Rehabilitation Act of 1973, §504, 29 U.S.C. 794 et seq. (1973). Retrieved from http://www.dol.gov

Shearer, C. B. (2009)._Exploring the relationship between intrapersonal intelligence and university students' career confusion: Implications for counseling, academic success, and school-to-career transition. *Journal of Employment Counseling, 46*(2), 52–61.

Sitlington, P. L., Clark, G. M., & Kolstoe, O. P. (2000). *Transition education and services for students with disabilities* (3rd ed.). Boston, MA: Allyn & Bacon.

State University of New York Albany. (2010). *Program Success.* Retrieved from http://www.albany.edu/disability/programs.shtml

Sue, D. W., & Sue, D. (2008). *Counseling the culturally diverse* (5th ed.). New York, NY: Wiley.

Sylvester, L., Woods, L. L., Martin, J. E., & Poolaw, S. (2007). *Student-directed transition planning.* Retrieved from http://www.ou.edu/zarrow/SDTP

Thomas, B. T. (2000). College students and disability law. *The Journal of Special Education, 33*(4), 248–257.

Thomas, E. E. (2008). Experience of college students with disabilities and the importance of self-determination in higher education settings. *Career Development for Exceptional Individuals, 31*(2), 77–84.

University of Florida. (2010). *Disabilities Resource Center Mentoring Program.* Retrieved from http://www.ufl.edu/disability

University of Massachusetts Boston. (2010). *Think college.* Retrieved from http://www.thinkcollege.net

United States Department of Education, Office of Special Education and Rehabilitative Services. (2000). *IDEA lessons for all.* Retrieved from http://www.ed.gov/offices/OSERS/IDEA25th

United States Department of Education, Office for Civil Rights. (2010). Rehabilitation Act of 1973, Section 504, Pub. L. No. 93-112, §791–794, 29. Retrieved from http://www2.ed.gov/about/offices/list/ocr/transitionguide.html

United States Department of Labor. (2009). *American with Disabilities Amendment Act 2008.* Retrieved from http://www.dol.gov/ofccp/regs/compliance/faqs/ADAfaqs.htm#Q1

Wagner, M., Newman, L., Cameto, R., Garza, N., & Levine, P. (2005). After high school: A first look at the post school experiences of youth with disabilities. *A Report from the National Longitudinal Transition Study-2 (NLTS2).* Retrieved from www.nlts2.org/reports/2005_04/nlts2_report_2005_04_complete.pdf

Webb, K., Patterson, K. B., Syverud, S. M., & Seabrooks-Blackmore, J. J. (2008). Evidence based practices that promote transition to postsecondary education: Listening to a decade of expert voices. *Exceptionality, 16,* 192–206.

Wehmeyer, M., Palmer, S., Argan, M., Mithaug, D., & Martin, J. (2000). Promoting casual agency: The self-determined learning model of instruction. *Exceptional Children, 66,* 439–453.

Wilson, M. G., Hoffman, A. V., & McLaughlin, M. J. (2009). Preparing youth with disabilities for college: How research can inform transition policy. *Focus on Exceptional Children, 41*(7), 3-10.

FURTHER INTERNET RESOURCES

ACT Now, N. Northampton Community College:
http://www.northampton.edu/Student

Association for Higher Education and Disability (AHEAD):
http://www.ahead.org

Council for Exceptional Children:
www.cec.sped.org

Center for Self-Determination:
www.selfdetermination.com

HEATH Resource Center:
www.heath.gwu.edu

LD On-Line:
www.ldonline.orgl1d_indepth/postsecondary/index.html

National Center on Secondary Education and Transition:
www.ncset.org

PACER, Minnesota Parent Training and Information Center:
http://www.pacer.org

Pennsylvania State University, Office of Disabilities:
http://www.equity.psu.edu/ods/site.asp

Recordings for the Blind and Dyslexic (RFB&D):
www.rfbd.org

University of Washington, DO-IT CAREER:
www.washington.edu/doit

Zarrow Center of the University of Oklahoma:
http://education.ou.edu/zarrow

CHAPTER 15

CAREER DEVELOPMENT IN THE MILITARY

Col George T. Williams
Brig Gen Michael B. Barrett
Lt Col Charles H. Graham
The Citadel, the Military College of South Carolina

There is a wealth of information to be learned about the military through pamphlets/brochures, speaking to recruiters, and accessing by electronic means on the Internet. The co-authors of this chapter are currently employed at The Citadel, the Military College of South Carolina. We thought it might be helpful to initially share some simple terms. The military is known as the U.S. Armed Forces and is composed of five branches including the Air Force, Army, Coast Guard, Marine Corps, and Navy. Three general categories of military people include: (a) active duty (full-time soldiers and sailors); (b) reserve and guard forces (usually work a civilian job, but can be called to full-time military duty); (c) and veterans and retirees (past members of the military).

ORGANIZATION AND STRUCTURE OF THE U.S. MILITARY

The President of the United States of America is the Commander in Chief, in charge of the military and responsible for all final decisions. The Secretary

Career Development in Higher Education, pages 327–341
Copyright © 2011 by Information Age Publishing
327

of the Department of Defense (DOD) has control over the military and each branch, with the exception of the Coast Guard (CG), which resides under the Department of Homeland Security. In time of war, the CG reports to the Navy command and control, whereby reservists may be called to active duty for one to two years, just as the other services' reserve components.

Each branch of the military has a specific mission within the overall mission of U.S. security and peace (Military Advantage, 2010).

- *Air Force and Air Force Reserve:* The mission of the Unites States Air Force (USAF) is to deliver sovereign options for the defense of the United States of America and its global interests—to fly and fight in air, space, and cyberspace.
- *Air National Guard:* The Air National Guard is a separate reserve component of the USAF and is under the control of the Governor of the state in which the base is located. In times of national emergency, the Air National Guard can be federalized and then fall under the command of the USAF.
- *Army and Army Reserve:* The Army and Army Reserve is the dominant land power. The Army's mission is to fight and win our nation's wars by providing prompt, sustained land dominance across the full range of military operations and across the spectrum of conflict.
- *Army National Guard:* The Army National Guard is comprised of citizen soldiers who dedicate a portion of their time to serving their nation. Each state has its own Guard, as required by the Constitution. It is the only branch of the military required by the Constitution. The Army National Guard is normally under the control of the Governor of the state in which the base is located. In times of national need the Army National Guard can be federalized and then fall under the command of the U.S. Army.
- *Coast Guard and Coast Guard Reserve:* The Coast Guard's mission is primarily patrolling domestic waterways, performing rescue operations at sea, assisting with homeland security, law enforcement, drug smuggling prevention, and keeping waterways navigable. Overseas, the Coast Guard helps protect U.S. ships in foreign ports.
- *Marine Corps and Marine Corps Reserve:* The Marine Corps is the U.S.'s rapid-reaction force trained to fight in the air, land, and sea. The Marine Corps are usually the first "boots on the ground when conflict arises." The Marines also guard all U.S. Embassies worldwide.
- *Navy and Navy Reserve:* The mission of the United States Navy is to protect and defend the right of the United States and its allies to move freely on the oceans, and to protect the country against her enemies.

Joining the Military

While there are several pathways for joining the military, a succinct 10-step process is highlighted below (Military Advantage, 2010):

Step 1: Learn about the military (military basics, what they do, where they go, who they are).

Step 2: Decide if you're ready (eligibility requirements for joining, benefits information, and branch missions).

Step 3: Choose the proper path (finding best point of entry, comparing services, considering guard and reserve services, comparing enlisted vs. officer options, examining job choices).

Step 4: Meet the recruiter (how and where to meet, questions and answers, suggestions for visiting a recruiter, documents you'll need, incentives).

Step 5: Excel on the Armed Services Vocational Aptitude Battery (ASVAB) (earn an excellent score on ASVAB for best possible options).

Step 6: Get the best job (make sure you will be doing what you enjoy, find an interest matcher, learn how to find the appropriate job, and study all jobs in each branch).

Step 7: Complete the process (eliminate the fear and confusion about the military entrance processing station [MEPS], learn about medical conditions, waivers, and legal problems).

Step 8: Raise your right hand (preparation to swear in, learn about the oaths applicants take, general orders needed to learn, and military ranks).

Step 9: Prepare for boot camp (getting ready for the challenge, preparing mentally and physically).

Step 10: Entrance and maximizing success (sequence of events after boot camp, experiencing success; wisdom and advice from mentors who have been there).

COMMON TERMS

Three terms connoting authority and responsibility in the military include: (a) rank, (b) rate, and (c) grade. A military member's "rank" determines member status and authority in comparison to other military members. The Navy/Coast Guard uses the term "rate" for enlisted sailors. The other services refer to it as "rank."

The term "grade" describes personnel and pay functions. Military personnel across the services receive the same base pay, based on rank and time-in-service. Although the "ranks" are named differently in each service, to save confusion, the term "grade" is used.

Three general categories of rank/rate include: (a) enlisted personnel, (b) warrant officers, and (c) commissioned officers (Powers, 2010). All commissioned officers "out-rank" all warrant officers and enlisted members, while all warrant officers "out-rank" all enlisted members. "Insignia" are the stripes and bars worn on the shoulders of the military uniform and denote a person's rank/rate.

ENLISTED ENTRANCE INTO THE MILITARY

The goal of initial enlisted military career counseling is not to make the career decision for the individual, but to present all options and facilitate the recipient's exploration of their qualifications, abilities, interests, desires, and long-term goals so they can make an informed decision. This may sound elementary, but the number of enlisted Military Occupational Specialties (MOS) available in today's military are impressive and many find it difficult to choose. Normally recruits develop a "wish list" after counseling by selecting several MOSs compatible with their Armed Services Vocational Aptitude Battery (ASVAB) scores.

The ASVAB test scores are the initial evaluation tool for recruiters and counselors to evaluate a recruit's potential success both academically and technically. Prospective enlistment candidates may request guaranteed specific career field training and/or an enlistment bonus prior to enlistment. To do so, he or she must meet the minimum qualifications for that specific training on the ASVAB. The ASVAB is a battery of tests that assess the basic knowledge and skills of high school graduates aspiring to enter the military. The four subareas of the ASVAB are Arithmetic Reasoning, Word Knowledge, Paragraph Comprehension, and Mathematics Knowledge. To qualify for specific MOS training, the individuals must achieve the minimum score for that MOS in all necessary areas. The ASVAB can be further broken down into additional subcategories of Science, Mechanical Aptitude, Word Association, Auto/Shop, Paragraph Comprehension, Numerical Operations, Coding, and Electronics.

The difficult part of military performance and career counseling is the role of conveying information to the recipient that he/she does not desire to hear. The most productive and comfortable method to do this is to look at them directly in the eyes and speak directly and honestly. For example, "your ASVAB score is _____ and the threshold for the career field you have selected is _____." The reality is that the recipient either met the required criterion and made the cut or did not.

Another consideration when providing career counseling to a prospective enlistment candidate is determining if the parameters of the career choice are in harmony with the long term goals of the individual. Several MOSs such as infantry and artillery are military specific, and the skills obtained by the training are not readily compatible for continuation into civilian careers. In contrast, most MOS training and skills are easily marketed in the private sector. For example, logistics, military police, mechanical, communication, and flight training are easily sought after and transitioned to the private or public sectors when a person leaves military service. If a particular person has no desire to complete 20 years on active duty, then it may be wise for him or her to choose an MOS that will provide training and skills compatible with one's civilian goals and job markets vice his or her military aspirations. It is worthy to keep this in mind because eventually everyone leaves active duty and most will seek a second career.

In the military, the desires and goals of the individual are also taken into account and balanced with the ASVAB scores and then positions are filled with all these factors taken into consideration. Ultimately however, it is the needs of the service that outweigh all else.

OFFICER COMMISSIONING PROGRAMS

The most prestigious means to obtain a college education and a commission as an officer into one of the five services is to obtain an appointment to one of the four military academies:

- Air Force: Air Force Academy, Colorado Springs, Colorado
- Army: U.S. Military Academy, West Point, New York
- Coast Guard: U.S. Coast Guard Academy, New London, Connecticut
- Navy/Marines: U.S. Naval Academy, Annapolis, Maryland

Other pathways to earn a degree and a commission are:

Military College Tuition Assistance Programs: All U.S. Military Services offer college degree assistance programs for service men or women already on active duty. There are variations within each service branch; however, the general programs are the same. Civilians willing to enter the service upon graduation, as well as current active duty enlisted service members and reserve-enlisted personnel may qualify for one of the many programs.

There is a required service obligation upon graduation for all programs. Brief overviews of these programs are:

Baccalaureate Degree Completion Program (BDCP): The BDCP is for current military enlisted members who have some college credit. It offers up to $169,700 of financial support to finish a degree while also providing a regular monthly salary for up to three years prior to graduation. This program also requires a service obligation upon graduation.

Marine Enlisted Commissioning Education Program (MECEP): The MECEP is an enlisted to officer commissioning program. It is designed to provide competitively selected enlisted Marines the opportunity to earn college degrees and then serve as Marine Corps officers. Marines selected for MECEP who successfully complete Officer Candidate School and graduate with a Bachelor's Degree are commissioned as a Second Lieutenant in the U.S. Marine Corps. These individuals are literally assigned to attend college during the normal workday.

Reserve Officers Training Corps (ROTC): The ROTC program is for incoming college students. It is an elective curriculum taken along with normal degree-specific required college classes. ROTC offers up to $180,000 to cover the cost of earning a degree for up to five years. It provides funding for tuition, lab fees, textbooks, and a monthly spending allowance. Students may apply while in high school or as a current college student. Students may attend any of more than 160 major colleges and universities.

Other related specialized military educational programs include but are not limited to:

Officer Candidate Schools: Current or soon to be college graduates may also apply for acceptance into Officer Candidate School (OCS). This is a program that recruits recent college graduates and those too far along in their academic careers to qualify for ROTC programs. They will receive no financial assistance, but upon successful completion of the program, the candidate will be commissioned a 2nd Lieutenant or Ensign in the Reserve Component of the particular service.

Civil Engineer Collegiate Program (CECP): This program includes applying for OCS up to three years before earning one's bachelor's degree or up to one year before completing a master's degree. Applicants selected are placed on active reserve duty as a Baccalaureate Degree Completion Program or Civil Engineer Corps collegiate and receive more than $1,600 per month while completing a program of study. Applicants may earn up to $60,000 during their sophomore, junior, and senior years while receiving many benefits granted to regular Navy personnel, including 30 days vacation earned each year. Following college graduation, candidates receive military training at the OCS in Pensacola, Florida and earn commission as a naval officer.

Military Reserve: Many members of the Reserves attend college using the Montgomery GI Bill or the Post 911 GI Bill. These individuals attend any accredited and participating Institution of Higher Learning while drilling in the reserves. The advantage here is that they receive financial support while working towards a degree, and they receive pay for their reserve participation. There is no obligation for continued military service as this benefit has already been earned with prior military service.

Nuclear Propulsion Officer Candidate Program (NUPOC): This program offers qualified persons unique technical training, exceptional benefits, and the opportunity to join the elite group of Naval Officers responsible for the operation of the Navy's nuclear propelled submarines and aircraft carriers. Program benefits include serving aboard submarines or surface ships, serving as an instructor at the Navy's Nuclear Power School in Charleston, South Carolina, or as an engineer on staff at Naval Reactors in Washington, DC. Qualified college students can earn a substantial signing bonus and receive a salary of more than $2,500 a month for up to 30 months prior to graduation for some programs. For more information, refer to http://www.cnrc.navy.mil/nucfield.

Nurse Candidate Program (NCP): This program provides a monthly stipend for full-time students in accredited Bachelor of Science in Nursing programs. Applicants can enroll after their sophomore year and receive an initial grant of $10,000 (paid in two installments of $5,000 each) plus $1,000 a month for up to 24 months. After graduation, participants join the Navy, Air Force, or Army Nurse Corps as an officer, while earning a competitive salary, regular promotions, comprehensive medical and dental coverage, low cost travel opportunities, retirement and educational benefits, further training, and a rewarding clinical practice. For more information, refer to http://www.med.navy.mil/sites/navmedmpte.

MENTORING, LEADERSHIP, AND CAREER DEVELOPMENT

The military occupation specialty (MOS) is a major component of career development in the military. For eligible young adults (ages 17–27) who enlist in the military, there is a wide range of expectations and maturity levels concerning career development. Havighurst's (1964) developmental tasks theory model of vocational development identifies six stages of vocational development. Stage three (ages 15–25) is where the young person acquires identity as a worker in the occupational structure, chooses, and prepares for an occupation, while getting work experience as a basis for occupational choice and for assurance of economic independence. Stage four (ages 25–40) in vocational development, according to Havighurst (1964), is characterized by becoming a productive person, mastering the skills of one's occupation, and moving up the ladder with one's occupation. Some young people, when enlisting, have no preference for a military occupation specialty (MOS) or career field, and in such instances, the needs of the service and the results of the enlistee's performance on the Armed Service Vocational Aptitude Battery (ASVAB) test will determine the individual's MOS.

For those who do have a specific MOS in mind, attaining a certain score on the ASVAB will usually guarantee training in that field. After completion of Basic Combat Training (BCT), enlistees next attend a career-specific school where the soldier receives training at a specified level in the MOS career field. Upon graduation, the soldier reports to a unit and begins work in that specific MOS.

Up to this point, there will be no career guidance per se, the emphasis being on attaining minimal proficiency in the MOS. All the services specify a minimum time the serviceman/woman must complete before being eligible for promotion to the next higher grade or rank. Up to pay grade E-3 (corresponds to Army—Private First Class [PFC]; Navy/Coast Guard—Seaman [SN]; Air Force—[Airman First Class]; and Marine Corps—Lance Corporal [LCpl]), the soldier needs only to meet specified requirements for promotion, usually related to time in service and the avoidance of disciplinary issues. Promotion to the next grade, E-4 or Specialist, is slightly different. At this point (and for the remainder of a soldier's career), not only must specific proficiency and time in service be met, but also there must be a vacant position on the unit's personnel authorization table for the soldier's specific MOS. The corresponding enlisted rank for each branch at grade E-4 is: Army—Corporal (CPL) 1; Navy/Coast Guard—Petty Officer Third Class (PO3); Air Force—Senior Airman (SrA); and Marine Corps—Corporal (Cpl) (Hall, 2008, p. 292). There are two types of E-4s in the Army: corporals and specialists. A corporal is a noncommissioned officer and a specialist is not.

Most soldiers will end their military careers at this level and will leave the service at the end of their initial enlistment obligation. For those who stay on and re-enlist for another four to six years, their status unofficially changes to what is considered "careerist." Depending on the needs of the service and the qualifications of the soldier, a potential re-enlistee can negotiate and change career fields (MOS) at this point. It is not common, but it can be done and involves attending another MOS training course. Soldiers effect this change because of personal interest ("I always wanted to be a bulldozer operator.") or the perception that certain MOS fields offer better promotion opportunity ("There are a lot more infantrymen than cooks.").

Regardless of MOS area, the next promotion to pay grade E-5 involves a jump to noncommissioned officer (NCO) status, which means that with promotion comes the new ranks including: Army—Sergeant (SGT), Navy/Coast Guard—Petty Officer Second Class (PO2), Air Force—Staff Sergeant (SSgt), and Marine Corps—Sergeant (Sgt). Not only must minimum time in service requirements be met as well as the necessity of a vacancy in the unit to which the soldier is assigned, but also because the soldier will become a NCO if promoted, the army begins to look for evidence of leadership ability. The Army provides formal training in leadership (e.g., the specialist attends the basic level non-commissioned officer course, called BNOC, of several weeks in duration). (*Please note:* The Army is used as a generic example because it is the largest service and its ranks the most familiar, but the other branches generally adhere to the same career pattern and guidance.)

After graduation, the specialist must appear at a promotion board, held on the post of assignment, and if deemed qualified, is placed on a list for promotion. A point system is used; points are awarded for education, time in service, distinctions, weapons qualification, physical fitness, and so on. The unit commander can award a certain number of points based on the soldier's performance in the unit, as can the board, and vacancies/promotions are filled in order of one's total number of points.

Promotion to higher grades, Staff Sergeant (E-6), Sergeant First Class (E-7), Master or First Sergeant (E-8) and Sergeant Major (E-9) are handled in a similar manner, except instead of a local promotion board, the board is centralized in Washington, DC. Personal appearance at these boards is not authorized. At each higher level of pay grade, the soldier assumes greater leadership responsibilities, roughly corresponding to expectations similar to those of supervisor or team leader in the civilian world. The military does provide formal, resident instruction at the Sergeant First Class level (Advanced Noncommissioned Officer Course or ANCOC) and Sergeant Major level (Sergeant Major Academy) which must be completed prior to promotion. Attendance at the ANCOC is offered to all; the Sergeant Major Academy attendees are selected as part of the promotion process and do not attend until selected for promotion. With the focus on increasingly higher and greater responsibilities for leadership, these NCO schools do not focus on the specific MOS of each soldier but rather on the leadership functions expected of noncommissioned officers, thus infantrymen, postal clerks, mechanics, and so on will attend BNCOC and ANCOC together.

At each of these levels of schooling, formal classes are held that offer career guidance, usually in the form of specialists from each MOS telling the soldiers of that MOS where there are vacancies in their area that offer potential opportunities for promotion. The great majority want to be stationed in Hawaii, so there are few if any openings there, but Korea or Fort Polk, Louisiana, may have openings for an ambitious soldier. If a particular MOS is shrinking—for example, new diagnostic equipment has resulted in a need for fewer x-ray technicians, the career guidance may be to encourage reclassification in a related field (e.g., ultrasound or CAT scans, with appropriate training).

Officer career patterns are similar. On the eve of being appointed an officer, the officer candidate requests an occupation specialty (MOS) that relates to his or her interest and academic preparation. Academic preparation is helpful in some career areas (e.g., engineering, medical service, finance). However, most prospective officers complete a form known as the "dream sheet," which supplements each application. The officer lists his or her preference, but the needs of the service come first, and once assigned to a branch, officers rarely change, although injury and occasionally desire have forced changes. (*Please note:* The Army is cited here as a generic example because it is the largest service and its ranks the most familiar. The other services do not have the easily identified branches, but all have MOS fields that correspond.)

Officer pay "grades" and "rank" range from second lieutenant to general, and the career trajectory has three levels much like the enlisted ranks: company grade (lieutenants, captains), field grade (majors to colonel), and general officers (brigadier to general). Paralleling the NCO world, schooling is provided at the entry to each of the three zones—company (officer basic course), field grade (command and general staff training), and general officer (War College). Promotions are based on the competitive principle of best qualified, which amounts to naked competition, and there are always far more potential officers in the pool hoping for promotion than there are open positions. Failure to be selected for promotion twice leads to dismissal from the service.

The Army provides a broad pamphlet that outlines the ideal career pattern. Initially, one masters a skill specialty (MOS) at the lieutenant and captain level, culminating with a tour of duty as a successful company commander. Branching out at mid-career level to acquire skills in additional fields is "de rigueur" because very few field grade officers will actually command units (only 10% of officers will command a battalion, and the other 90% needs to go somewhere) or even serve in their original MOS. There are only two majors in an infantry battalion; there are more majors in an ROTC detachment, and there are probably as many ROTC detachments as infantry battalions. Headquarters of all types need field grade officers as do service schools, recruiting units, garrisons, and the like. For the majority of officers, once they reach the field grade level, their service with soldiers in their specific MOS field is over. This is not malevolent. War is a young person's occupation; age and illness take a toll, and tossing unfit officers (many injured in the line of duty) is both heartless and unnecessary given the vast amount of work to accomplish elsewhere. The career guidance pamphlet outlines many possibilities, but it really does not discuss the virtues of each new career area. Instead, it leaves that to the officer who largely makes the choice based on interests, a perception of a strength in a certain field ("I'm good at public relations.") or a deliberate aiming of a trajectory for a post-military career ("If I go into procurement, I can get a good job with company X upon retirement.").

During the periodic formal schooling (officer basic and advanced courses, command and general staff, and the Army War College), the emphasis starts with MOS qualification in one's branch (e.g., infantry, artillery, flying) and gradually transitions to leading and commanding at the small unit level (the platoon and company) to much larger organizations, divisions, and corps. Technical skills are assumed once past the basic entry level and the emphasis transitions to leadership and staff work because the organizations are far more complex at higher levels.

The officer schools provide formal career counseling. It can range from a one-size-fits-all class about what one needs to do to prepare oneself for the next level of schooling, to admonitions to acquire a civilian advanced degree, and so on. However, the best career guidance comes from mentors. This system is unofficial and by no means systematic. A junior officer is indeed fortunate to find a mentor. Mentoring usually takes the form of advice and guidance on what positions to seek. All the services place the highest emphasis on commanding a unit or organization on the premise it covers everything and stresses the core focus of one's career field. An infantry officer commanding an infantry battalion is at the center of infantry action. A commander is responsible for all the unit does or fails to do; therefore he or she must master both the technical and leadership skills in order to succeed. However, one will not command an infantry unit forever, and one must give due thought to other positions and how these help attain job and personal satisfaction, prepare one for future jobs, or even prepare for a future career. Identifying these jobs is critical, and career guidance takes the form of a mentor, an officer (or noncommissioned officer for enlisted soldiers) senior in grade "who has been there."

There is no formal mentor identification or assignment. It usually takes the form of attracting the attention of a senior officer by virtue of outstanding job performance, and that senior leader then assumes the role of mentor, guiding the mentee in requesting certain duty assignments. The two will usually discuss career goals: does the mentee want to be a general officer or would the mentee be more satisfied with spending more time in the USA and with his or her family and be willing to settle for a military career ending as a lieutenant colonel, or is the mentee looking for a prosperous post-military career? The mentor will not always be attracted to the type of officer who will sacrifice all to become a general. The mentor will often have the candor to advise an officer that he or she is not general officer material and ought to pursue this or that. Let us cite some examples of career guidance that would emanate from a mentor.

For example, one is a captain for six to seven years. Command of a unit, ship, squadron of planes, and so on is highly stressful and intense and therefore limited to about two years. First, the mentor will advise that not all companies, battalions, or ships are created equal. For an infantry officer, an infantry company is a better assignment than a company that trains enlistees who have just entered the service; for a pilot, commanding an actual bomber squadron is far more valuable career wise than commanding a training squadron. The mentor has served on promotion boards and knows that commanding a destroyer on patrol duty is regarded as far more important than an officer who commands a tanker or supply ship. The Navy's job is to fight, not supply, and while the later is an intrinsic part of the service, commanding a fighting ship is deemed of higher importance. Second, and perhaps even more critical, the mentee will be a captain or lieutenant colonel for six to seven years, so what should he or she do when not in command? Here is where the mentor plays a vital role in career guidance. Some staff positions are valued more than others are. A captain or major usually has a two-three year stint with one of the 3 R's: reserve unit duty, ROTC, or recruiting duty. These might appear to be more or less equally worthy and on the same level, but the services expect a field grade officer who hopes to be a colonel to have an advanced degree from a civilian college. Of the three "R's," ROTC duty will place an officer on a college campus at which the opportunity to acquire a master's degree in evening programs is greater than serving as a recruiter or reserve advisor in a small town in the prairie states. The mentor will bring this to the officer's attention and tell him or her to apply for ROTC duty. At the field grade level, majors are ubiquitous at large headquarters of which there are many, and serving on the staff of one of these headquarters is the norm. Nevertheless, a mentor will provide guidance that not all headquarters are created equal, and certain ones are more equal than others. Within a headquarters, a promotion board will always see serving in operational areas where things "happen" as more significant than running the housing office, motor pool, or the education office. For a major, teaching prospective company commanders at a service school is a better assignment than serving as an assistant commissary officer.

Finally, the mentor will assist in what are called nominative assignments, for which officers must be nominated by name and are selected by a committee of one. For example, generals' aides are nominated to the general who needs the aide and that general will make the selection, as are executive officers for generals or senior civilian authorities in the Pentagon. Headquarters commanded by very senior generals (lieutenant general) will get to select whom they want, and mentors provide names. These are the positions where one meets future leaders and contacts, along with the officers already in the senior and important positions who will serve on selection boards for command positions and promotion boards. The mentor takes steps to position his or her mentee in the proper limelight.

The same process occurs at the enlisted ranks. A first sergeant and sergeant major will take under his or her wing a junior NCO and provide exactly the same sort of advice that senior officers do for junior officers. As with the officer mentors, these mentor NCOs have made it to the top and therefore know what the service values and wants. Like their officer counterparts, they cannot compel a promotion or selection board to make a certain choice, but they have served on these boards, know how they function, and most importantly, know what the board considers valuable and of significance.

RESOURCES

Numerous resources exist for learning more detailed information concerning career development in the military in the higher education environment. A partial listing of these helpful relevant resources:

- *Air Force:* http://www.af.mil
- *Air Force Reserve Command:* http://www.afrc.af.mil
- *Air National Guard:* http://www.ang.af.mil
- *Army:* http://www.army.mil
- *Army National Guard:* http://www.arng.army.mil
- *Army Reserve:* http://www.armyreserve.army.mil
- *Armed Services Vocational Aptitude Battery (ASVAB):* The ASVAB, introduced in 1968, is a battery of tests including 4 subareas (Arithmetic Reasoning, Word Knowledge, Paragraph Comprehension, and Mathematics Knowledge) that measures developed abilities and helps predict future academic and occupational success in the military. More than 40 million examinees have taken the ASVAB that is administered annually to over one million military applicants, high school, and post-secondary students. http://www.official-asvab.com/
- *Coast Guard:* http://www.uscg.mil
- *Marine Corps:* http://www.usmc.mil
- *Marine Forces Reserve:* http://www.marforres.usmc.mil
- *Military OneSource:* This organization offers no cost private counseling up to six visits in the local community, including couples counseling, parenting information, and issues related to deployment and reunion for active duty, Guardsmen, Reservists (regardless of activation status), and their families. http://www.militaryonesource.com
- *Naval Reserve Officer Training Corps (NROTC):* The NROTC is a college scholarship program that includes full tuition for 4 years (up to 5 years for some technical degrees), allowances for textbooks, monthly spending money, and coverage of related educational expenses. Specific eligibility requirements include: U.S. citizenship; 17 years old by September 1 of the year starting college, and no more than 23 years of age on June 30 of that year (exceptions for prior military service); must not have reached his or her 27th birthday by June 30 of year in which graduation and commissioning are antici-

pated; physically qualified by Navy or Marine Corps standards; and qualifying scores on Scholastic Aptitude Test (SAT) or American College Test (ACT), or be in top 10% of high school graduating class. There are more than 160 approved NROTC schools throughout the United States. http://www.nrotc.navy.com

- *Navy:* http://www.navy.mil
- *Navy Reserve:* http://www.navy.mil

MILITARY TERMINOLOGY

A very brief listing of military terms from a list of 12,000-plus terms and acronyms used in the United States Military that might be useful to the reader is included below (Military Terms, 2006).

- *Basic Combat Training (BCT):* fundamentals of soldiering.
- *Battalion:* a unit smaller than a brigade but larger than a company; there are two or three battalions in a brigade.
- *Brigade:* a unit smaller than a division but larger than a battalion; there are usually two or more brigades in a division.
- *Company:* a unit larger than a platoon but smaller than a battalion; there are usually three companies in a battalion.
- *Corps:* a unit larger than a division; there are only two corps in the Army.
- *Deployment:* a long-term assignment, usually to a combat or war zone.
- *Insignia:* the stripes and stars worn on the shoulders of the military uniform to denote a person's rank/rate.
- *Installation:* the military complex; *installation* is a generic word; *base* is used by the Army, *post* is used by the Air Force, *station* is used by the Navy.
- *Platoon:* a unit larger than a squad but smaller than a company; there are usually four platoons in a company.
- *ROTC (Reserve Officer Training Corps):* There are approximately 160 colleges and universities in the United States with ROTC programs on campus. Six senior military colleges/universities are: The Citadel (Charleston, South Carolina), Texas A&M University (College Station, Texas), Virginia Military Institute (Lexington, Virginia), Norwich University (Northfield, Vermont), North Georgia Military College (Dahlonega, Georgia), and Virginia Polytechnic Institute and State University (Blacksburg, Virginia).
- *Squad:* the smallest unit; there are usually four squads in a platoon.
- *Unit:* an organization title of a subdivision of a group or any military element whose structure is prescribed by competent authority.

- *U.S. military academies:* the federal government operates the following:
  - – Air Force: Air Force Academy, Colorado Springs, Colorado
  - – Army: U.S. Military Academy, West Point, New York
  - – Coast Guard: U.S. Coast Guard Academy, New London, Connecticut
  - – Navy/Marines: U.S. Naval Academy, Annapolis, Maryland

REFERENCES

Hall, L. K. (2008). *Counseling military families: What mental health professionals need to know.* New York, NY: Routledge.

Havighurst, R. J. (1964). Youth in exploration and man emergent. In H. Borow (Ed.), *Man in a world at work* (pp. 215–236). Alexandria, VA: National Career Development Association.

Military Terms. (2006). *Military terms.* Retrieved from http://www.militaryterms.info/

Military Advantage. (2010). Retrieved from http://www.military.com/Recruiting/Content/html

Powers, R. (2010). *U.S. Military 101: The "basics" of the United States Military.* Retrieved from http://usmilitary.about.com/cs/generalinfo/a/military101.htm

CHAPTER 16

RETRAINING AND SECOND CAREERS IN A DECLINING JOB MARKET

James K. Matta, Sr. Ed.D., LPC, NCC
Dana S. Matta, PhD, LMFT
Thomas F. Matta, PhD, LMFT

INTRODUCTION

Historically, those in the hallowed halls of higher education were buffered from the highs and lows of the broader economical reality. Traditionally, a college degree has been viewed as a ticket to, at the minimum, to a comfortable life, and for many, depending on how hard one worked or how creatively he or she used their knowledge, a path to status, prestige, and economic security and freedom. Today, while education still means a great deal, in light of the current economic downturn, just getting a college degree or advanced degree does not automatically provide the kind of fast track to the career or economic dreams that most Americans were raised to believe.

The current economic downturn, which has become known in the popular media, as the "Great Recession," began in December, 2007. According to the Wall Street Journal, the United States has lost over 8.4 million jobs (Izzo, 2010) and according to the Bureau of Labor Statistics (2010), 15 mil-

Career Development in Higher Education, pages 343–356
Copyright © 2011 by Information Age Publishing
All rights of reproduction in any form reserved.

343

lion people are (at the time of this writing) unemployed. In November of 2009 the unemployment rate rose above 10%. This is only the second time the unemployment rate has surpassed the 10% mark since World War II. Currently (late July 2010) the unemployment rate has dipped to 9.7% (Bureau of Labor Statistics, 2010).

Regarding the length of unemployment, as of February, 2010, it has been estimated that 6.3 million Americans have been unemployed for six months or longer. The current ratio of job seekers to job openings is at five to one nationwide (Skladany, 2009). A new vernacular has sprung up to describe the different types of unemployed, such as the discouraged worker (those no longer looking for work because they are dispirited), and the under employed worker (those that are working but not in the jobs that they are trained to do). This recession has also been nicknamed the "Mancession" because of the large number of men, and particularly middle aged white men, that have become jobless (Rampell, 2009).

While the unemployment rate for workers with a college degree has remained relatively low, new graduates coming out of college seeking employment are, on average, carrying a greater amount of student loan debt then previous generations, applying for and competing for fewer jobs, with more workers competing for these jobs, in an economic environment where companies are waiting to see whether the recession is going to take another dip before spending more money on new hiring. Consequently, older workers have lost a significant amount of money in their 401Ks and retirement accounts and many are postponing their retirement and delaying others the opportunity of getting their jobs. In this economic environment, with large sections of our population out of work, the notion of retraining and second careers, has taken on new meaning and importance.

LITERATURE REVIEW

The economic meltdown of 2007 is still so new that the fallout of this recession is still reverberating in all sectors of our economy. This economic debacle has been so huge and relatively recent that little scholarship and research has been done. This "Great Recession" has, in a brief period, radically changed how we perceive the value of a college education and the security of a good job, and has made us question the taken-for-granted assumptions that higher education was an assured pathway to a fulfilling career and financial security. Today, millions of workers will need to be retrained at a second career.

As a result of the economic downturn, the definitions for retraining and second careers have changed. Retraining was a term that surfaced during the Great Depression to refer to a person training for a different career that required a skill set that he/she did not possess.

With the advent of technology, it has also been applied to upgrading skills or developing new ones for a current career. As it relates to defining a second career, traditionally, it had been defined as a change or transition after retirement infused with many of the Erikson psychosocial dynamics of generativity for middle-aged and young-old adults.

In the past, the goals for a second career might include fulfilling a dream, giving something back to the community, passing on skills to the next generation, or the more general goal of helping others. The intent, in many cases, was to do this without necessarily looking for economic gain. The current economic circumstances have redefined previous notions of retraining and a second career from a luxury, something someone does after they have had a successful career, to a necessary process in order to adapt and survive in this current economic climate.

CHANGING EXPECTATIONS

These different definitions translate into a different expectation for both employers and employees alike. Employers are expecting employees to be more flexible. Many companies have cross-trained employees to ensure that if a worker is removed or replaced due to their own volition or company down-sizing, specialized skills are not lost and another worker can step in and fulfill the work responsibilities. Increases in job mobility require workers be able to adapt to multiple job shifts when compared to their more traditional counterparts from prior generations (Rosenfeld, 1992).

Upward job mobility during economic booms is usually the rule as workers become aware of better opportunities than their current employment. But lateral or downward job mobility occurs when economies struggle (Kahn, 2010; Rosenfeld, 1992). Unlike past generations, workers cannot assume to be in a single career during one's lifetime. Given the longer life expectancies of the average worker and the changing nature of the workplace due to globalization, mergers, outsourcing, and ever advancing technologies, most people will have several different careers over the course of their lifetime (Boldt, 1999). Corporations have replaced the paternalism of past generations for stockholders profit and outright impersonal disregard for their workers welfare. As a result, employee loyalty has virtually disappeared.

Consequences of the Economic Downturn on Higher Education

In many states the economic downturn and the negative impact on income and tax revenues has translated into crisis level budget deficits. As a result, states are in the unenviable position of lessening their monetary support for higher education. At the same time, people continue to buy into the common benefits of a college degree and either decide to ride out the recession by going straight into graduate school or make a career change or return to school due to job loss, underemployment or insufficient wages. Therefore, institutions of higher learning are expected to do more with less (Doyle & Delaney, 2009).

Breneman (2008) noted that colleges and universities weather recessions rather well, making several points that "student demand has remained strong through the vicissitudes of changing labor markets and shifting patterns of finance" (p. 112). In addition, colleges are both "adaptable" and "creative" in their collective responses to challenging financial times (p. 112). A third point is that college is seen as a private good with less governmental support for higher education. Individuals are expected to bear more of the costs, which may make remaining competitive in the global markets an ongoing challenge. The real changes however, may occur in how students reevaluate the value of a college degree. The price of tuition has increased so dramatically over the past few decades, for even third tier universities. Combine that with diminishing returns, and most students are coming to the realization that a college education does not appear to guarantee the return that it once had.

A second significant response by colleges during these difficult economic times is the trend or decline in "faculty members' circumstances" (p. 112). Breneman (2008) states that more and more colleges are relying on adjuncts and non-tenure track faculty. More recently, some institutions have done away with adjuncts and have required existing tenure-track faculty to increase their teaching workload. Breneman concludes that "... poor working conditions, dim employment prospects, and rising costs of graduate education" (p. 112) may gradually deplete the pool of qualified faculty.

Barriers to Getting Retrained

Potential re-trainees and those exploring second or third careers, in addition to the challenges they are facing with the economy and institutions of higher education, must take into consideration multi-faceted familial and personal obligations. For the younger generation, emancipation issues, school loans, and the cost of raising children must be factored in to the decision making process. For the older worker, these decisions must take into consideration existing obligations such as healthcare, college expenses for children, caring for aging parents and retirement, just to name a few.

Eby (1995) investigated the effect of financial resources, social support, and family flexibility on individuals' adaptation to job loss and later career growth as predicted by Latack & Dozier's (1986) model of career growth.

This model proposes factors that may moderate the stress of job loss and promote career growth for men and women. Men and women differ in social support and how they manage job losses. Eby's study included 515 participants that were involuntarily displaced professionals. Eby found that family flexibility was the greatest predictor of career growth for women, followed by financial resources, and low pre-job satisfaction. Other factors included avoiding financial hardship, emotional acceptance of a job loss, and opportunity to remove oneself from job loss.

Many academics in business and sociology have written about the impact of cyclical economic downturns on the general population of workers and the difficulty individuals have in deciding whether to re-skill, retrain, or transition to a new career in difficult circumstances (Douglass, 2008). Others have chronicled the current changing employment landscape by identifying how individual meaningfulness around the value of work and career identities have been negatively impacted as a result of multiple displacements (Koeber, 2002).

Boldt (1999) identified a number of significant issues facing workers, but viewed them as opportunities as well as dangers. He included globalization, merger mania, the electronic revolution, out-sourcing, and advent of mass retail, which removed many white-collar workers and careers. Boldt stated that the American workplace has been "radically and inexorably transformed" (p. xlviii) with new dangers and opportunities. The dangers include displacement to lower skilled jobs for less pay and a corresponding job environment that is far less secure with ever increasing demands.

The opportunities include most notably, the significant increase in self-employment. Staying with Boldt's (1999) overreaching theme of agency, this "requires them (the worker) to take greater responsibility for shaping their career destinies" (p. xlviii). Boldt was optimistic this greater freedom would translate into the potential for a "social transformation" (p. li) that has the individual working because he chooses it and locates him/herself in a career he/she loves, which "has the potential to make the world a more just, humane, and beautiful place" (p. li).

Koeber (2002) conducted a case study on unemployed IBM computer and Link aerospace workers in Binghamton, New York and as a result developed insights into worker "displacement as a process" (p. 220). He states, "By analyzing displacement as a process, it is possible to consider factors and outcomes present before and after job loss" (p. 221). Koeber's interviews with displaced workers "capture ways in which respondents experienced the decline of paternalism, with its internal labor markets, and the simultaneous rise of a contemporary market-mediated form of work relations, more despotic in character" (p. 231). According to Koeber, corporate paternalism is waning with the death of the traditional exchange of job security for worker loyalty. The process model Koeber articulated followed workers through their job loss through rather lengthy periods of unemployment to re-employment that included either underemployment or downward mobility, particularly for men over 50 years of age and female workers as a whole.

This ongoing employment instability effected personal epistemologies to include disillusionment with traditional meanings of work, family and community. For these displaced workers, the meaningfulness of work gravitated away from work valued as an expression of one's mastery and competence to solely a means to an end, such as economic survival. As it relates to higher education, those that did retrain found employment but it "did not necessarily result in higher earnings" (Koeber, 2002, p. 230) to justify the time and expense. The implied recommendation is for labor market structures and institutions to remain attuned to changing workforce needs rather than to focus solely on the "one-sided emphasis of individual characteristics" (p. 235).

Koeber (2002) discusses how the employment landscape has been forever changed with a person engaging in "serial employment" arrangements and in many instances a downward mobility trajectory when displaced due to economic circumstances. Koeber cites the U.S. Department of Labor's definition of a displaced worker as "persons who lost or left a job because their plant or company closed or moved, there was insufficient work for them to do, or their position or shift was abolished" (2002, p. 220). In the latter portion of the twentieth century this worker displacement was more common in the manufacturing sector, but as the economy transitioned from hard industry to service and information economies, the educated, professional class of workers, who usually reside in the middle to upper-middle class, were no longer shielded.

What can be seen from Koeber's research is that as the ever-changing marketplace generates increasing employment instability and displacement, vocational viability becomes a higher priority over career meaningfulness. The changes suggest younger workers must delay their dream career to meet their daily financial obligations such as large education debt, lower pay and longer periods of unemployment or underemployment. This would be particularly true during a recession. Therefore, the optimism of Boldt's notion of an individual living out their dream career must be recast in pragmatic terms.

Douglass (2008) identifies a number of systemic and structural issues in the higher education system for traditional students that must be addressed to ensure an educated workforce during these difficult economic times. He states, "Here is the gist of the problem: too few students who graduate from high school; too many part-time students; too high a proportion of students (nearly 50 percent) in two-year community colleges, most never getting a degree; too many part-time faculty; an absence of long-term goals at the national level and by state governments regarding higher education access and graduation rates; and to date no well-conceived funding models to ensure quality" (p. 4).

Douglass encourages the current Obama administration and "federal government, in partnership with state governments, . . . (to) . . . view higher education as a vital component for economic recovery and long-term prosperity—on par with new investments in infrastructure and stop-gap measures to stabilize housing and credit markets" (p. 5). In addition to recommendations for additional federal government foresight and involvement, Douglass cautions states not to be too hasty in cost-cutting in higher education or increasing fees for students as the country "will lose ground in the race to develop human capital suitable for the modern era" (p. 7).

Watching states like California, with ever increasing enrollments due to population growth, and the shrinking state budget resources, universities must raise tuition rates, which in turn discourages many from retraining for a second career (Woo, 2009). Those that pursue a second career, undaunted by the current increases in higher education costs, do so at their own financial peril as they face the possibility of being saddled with higher personal debt in the way of second mortgages on homes or large credit card debt. By the time the federal and state governments sort out the structural issues, others contemplating second careers will recognize they have a ceiling to their timeline to making the possible benefits to such a change significantly shorter. Those individuals exploring second careers are in the latter years of early adulthood or middle-age. This results in hesitation to pursue a second career due to the national economic downturn with an ensuing paralysis. As a result, a default "no-choice" option is decided for by those who are realistically worried about significant downward mobility and heightened debt.

INNOVATIVE TRENDS IN HIGHER EDUCATION

Although it appears that the economic downturn will continue well into the foreseeable future, there are some innovative ways for those looking to retrain or pursue that second career in these difficult labor market conditions to make it happen. Some of these options have been around for a very long time, other options are considered recent arrivals, and still others tend to be a blend of old and new. This section will review some of the more prevalent trends.

Community Colleges

A traditional and very popular option for many students in the past few years is seeing if a community college can fulfill ones educational needs. Recent enrollment rates at higher education institutions hit an all-time high. It is believed that the recent spike in enrollment was due to the upsurge of those deciding to attend a community college. The four year degree granting institutions at the same time showed almost a flat line in their rate of growth (Fry, 2009).

A report completed in 2006 by the National Center for Education Statistics (NCES) (Parsad & Lewis, 2008) stated that in 2006–07 there were 1,045 community colleges in existence throughout the United States. The overall enrollment rates at these institutions were projected at 6.2 million students, which is approximately 35 percent of all the students enrolled in postsecondary institutions. It has been estimated that in the last eight years alone the student growth rate for seniors enrolled in community colleges jumped from approximately 10% to the mid-teens (Supiano & Hoover, 2009). The current recession is often cited as the reason behind the increase in enrollment rates (Miller, 2010).

According to the NCES, the average annual tuition and fees for a full time, in-state student at a community college was half of that of a public 4-year college or university, and about a tenth of the average annual tuition and fees at a private 4-year college or university (Provasnik & Planty, 2008). Any person seeking to pursue retraining or a second career needs to seriously investigate this option to achieve their higher education goal(s), while limiting the overall debt that would be incurred.

Distance Learning

A second option that is a relatively recent phenomenon in higher education is the option of distance learning. It has only been in the last decade that distance learning has gained broader acceptance (Miller, 2010). The demand for distance learning has more than doubled in recent years (Instructional Technology Council, 2009).

In the NCES publication (Pardsadt & Lewis, 2008), this topic was investigated. It conducted a large national survey to estimate the number of degree-granting postsecondary institutions offering distance learning and it found the following findings for the 2006–07 academic years. Distance education in this study was defined as any formal educational process in which the student and the instructor were not in the same place and do the coursework online.

It has been estimated that there are approximately 11,200 college level programs in the Unites States. NCES mailed their questionnaires to over 1,600 out the 4,200 Title IV degree-granting postsecondary institutions in the 50 states and the District of Columbia. The response rate from these institutions was close to 90%. From this nationally represented sample it estimated that two-thirds (66%) of the two-year and four-year Title IV degree-granting post-secondary institutions offer some form of distance learning. It was estimated that two-thirds (66%) of these programs offered a degree, while one-third (34%) offered a certification.

According to Basu (2005), the age group that is most likely to utilize distance education is those individuals over age 24. He also reported that those individuals who are more likely to participate in distance learning are women, minorities, and those who are single parents. He predicted at the time that the median age of those enrolled in distance learning by 2009 would be 37.2. This would be up from the age 35.3 during the year 2000. If this is an age trend, he interprets it as an indication that a significant portion of the market share in higher education will shift from the traditional age undergraduate student to adults approaching middle-age.

According to the NCES (Provasnick & Planty, 2008), the most common factors cited for affecting the decision to choose distance learning were the following: allows for student demand for flexible schedules (68%), allows access to college for those individuals who would otherwise not have access (67%), have a greater increase in choice of classes (46%), and seeking to increase student enrollment (45%). These factors can be viewed as stemming from traditional and nontraditional students whose lifestyle changes are driving the demand for distance education (Basu, 2009). Also distance learning has the ability to eliminate various compelling economic issues as they relate to housing and transportation expenditures, which are normally associated with a "brick and mortar" school.

Integration of Both Trends

A final innovative area to be considered in this section is an obvious integration of both trends to gain retraining for a second career that combines attending a community college (lower cost) and the (convenience and time saver) of distance learning. It has been estimated that 46% of adults (92 million) have participated in some form of formal adult education (Kim, Hagedorn, Williamson, & Chapman, 2004). The enrollment rates in these blended type programs have mushroomed recently and there appears to be no slowing down (Miller, 2010). In one survey over 97% of public 2 year institutions offer some form of distance education (Provasnik & Planty, 2008). This happens to be the highest percentage for any postsecondary institutions offering distance learning.

And it appears that these postsecondary institutions are dramatically increasing the number of programs being offered. In one survey that was conducted during the academic 2007–08 years, community colleges showed a 22% growth rate in their distance education programs. This was up from an 11% growth rate the year before (ITC, 2009). During the same time the overall enrollment rate in higher education grew less than 2%. Obviously there is a strong demand during these tough economic times for educational programs that combine a low cost option with the most flexible schedule.

RECOMMENDATIONS

1. Keep higher education affordable for the masses. The only way that our economy is going to keep up with other developed countries is to maximize the use of human capital. If higher education becomes more expensive than the common person can manage, the economy will suffer irreparable harm.

2. Creating and strengthening existing community colleges could be a cost efficient way to meet a good portion of the cost challenge that confronts the American higher education system (Ramaswami, 2009).

3. To maximize income and job stability, students must consider majoring in STEM careers (Science, Technology, Engineering & Mathematics).

4. A liberal arts education still has high value. Given the likelihood of several very different careers over the lifecourse, the skills learned are easily transferrable to almost any employment. Students must obtain skills that are broad-based and valued across careers.

5. For displaced workers retraining in a new field, Colgan & Weidemann (1996) have a number of recommendations for colleges and universities to address this social issue. First is for institutions of higher education to recognize that they have a responsibility to create "appropriate programs" (p. 24) for the displaced workers in their communities. Second is for schools of higher education to develop long-term relationships that serve the displaced worker such as the U.S. Department of Labor, National Alliance of Business, and The National Association of Private Industry Councils. The authors argue that "such organizations working in partnership can help frame the current debate and provide leadership in shaping the future of national policy initiatives concerning the education and training of displaced professionals" (p. 24). Third is the importance of "appropriate counseling programs for displaced" (p. 24) workers. Not only could this offer support and pscyhoeducation to the displaced person, but it could be utilized as a tool to direct the displaced worker by exploring "existing and emerging occupations/professions" (p. 24). Other recommendations include encouraging colleges and universities to create certified programs that also have some degree

of portability. Certificate programs have at least minimum standards, while portability makes moving a career to another state less of a career or income disruption. Colgan & Weidemann (1996) encourage schools to work politically to give workers an independent voice in choosing programs that are in their best interest. Finally, schools of higher education should create programs that are built on collaboration of the institutions of "higher education, industry, and government" (p. 25).

6. A number of helpful resources are available if one is exploring occupations that require a college degree or are "college preferred" (Dohm & Wyatt, 2002). They include *The Occupational Outlook Handbook* (it is available online at www.bls.gov/oco/home.htm.) Second, one can explore job fairs in articles in *The Occupational Outlook Quarterly*. Explore these articles online at www.bls.gov.opub/ooq/ooqhome.htm. Third, for career perspectives from their corresponding industries go to www.bls.gov/oco/cg/home.htm. Fourth, for recent economic projections as well as "labor force, industry employment, and occupational employment," go to www.bls.gov/opubl/mlr/mlrhome.htm. The final online resource from the Bureau of Labor Statistics explores wage data, employment and other relevant data at www.bls.gov.

CONCLUSION

In summary, the current socio-historical context has redefined traditional assumptions about retraining and second careers. Over the past two decades, in the field of career development, there has been a revolution taking place. The prophets of this field have been raising the cry that we, as a society, need to change our ways of how we view the traditional trajectory of building a career. With the advent of the economic collapse and the rising cost of earning a degree, along with the time and energy investment that is required, community colleges and distance learning may be the solution for large number of men and women that need to retrain or pursue a second career.

REFERENCES

Basu, A. (2005). The Economics of Changing Demographics. Keynote address: Distance Education Management Pre-conference, Boston, MA: The Sage Policy Group.

Boldt, L. (1999) *Zen and the Art of Making a Living*. New York, NY: Penguin USA.

Breneman, D. (2008). What Colleges Can Learn from Recessions Past. *The Chronicle of Higher Education, 55*(7).

Bureau of Labor Statistics. (2010). Economic News Release, April 2, 2010.

Colgan, A., & Weidemann, C. (1996). Careers in transition: Higher education's role in serving displaced professionals. *Continuing Higher Education Review, 60*(1), 16–26.

Dohm, A & Wyatt, I. (2002). College at work: Outlook and earnings for college graduates, 2000–10. *Occupational Outlook Quarterly, 46*(3), 2–15.

Douglass, J. (2008). College vs. unemployment: Expanding access to *higher education* is the smart investment during *economic downturns.* Research & Occasional Paper Series. University of California, Berkeley, Center for Studies in Higher Education.

Doyle, W., & Delaney, J. (2009). Higher education funding: The new normal. *Change.* July/August, 60–62.

Eby, L. T. (1995). Job loss as career growth: Responses to involuntary career transitions. *The Career Development Quarterly, 44*, 26–42.

Fry, R. (2009). College enrollment hits all-time high, fueled college surge. Washington, DC: PEW Research Center. Retrieved from http://pewsocialtrends.org/assets/pdf/college-enrollment.pdf

Instructional Technology Council (ITC). (2009). Trends in eLearning: Tracking the Impact of eLearning at Community Colleges (Distance Education Survey Results). Retrieved from http://www.itcnetwork.org/file.php?file=%2F1%2FITCAnnualSurvey2009Results.pdf

Izzo. P. (2010, February 11). Economist Expecting Shifting Workforce. Wall Street Journal. Retrieved February 11, 2010, from http://online.wsj.com/article/NA_WSJ_PUB:SB10001424052748703382904575059424289353714.html

Kahn, L. (2009) The long term market consequences of graduating from college in a bad economy. *Labour Economics, 17*(2) 303–316.

Kim, K., Hagedorn, M., Williamson, J., & Chapman, C. (2004). Participation of Adult Education and Lifelong Learning: 2000–2001 (NCES No. 2004-050). U.S. Department of Education, National Center for Education Statistics. Washington, DC: U.S. Government Printing Office.

Koeber, C. (2002). Corporate Restructuring, Downsizing, and the Middle Class: The Process and Meaning of Worker Displacement in the "New" Economy. *Qualitative Sociology, 25*(2), 217–246.

Latack, J.C., & Dozier, J.B. (1986). After the ax falls: Job loss as a career transition. *Academy of Management Review, 11*(2), 375–392.

Miller, M. H. (2010). Distance Education's Rate of Growth Doubles at Community College. *The Chronicle of Higher Education.* Wired Campus, April 13, 2010.

Parsad, B., & Lewis, L. (2008). Distance Education at Degree-Granting Postsecondary Institutions: 2006–07 (NCES 2009-044). National Center for Education Statistics, Institute of Education Sciences, U.S. Department of Education. Washington, DC.

Provasnik, S., & Planty, M. (2008). Community Colleges: Special Supplement to The Condition of Education 2008 (NCES 2008-033). National Center for Education Statistics, Institute of Education Sciences, U.S. Department of Education. Washington, DC.

Ramaswami, R. (2009). The Three R's: Resourceful, Resilient, and Ready. Campus Technology, 22(7), pg. 29.

Rampell, C, (2009). The Mancession. Economix Blog, New York Times. Retreived February 11, 2010, from http://economix.blogs.nytimes.com/2009/08/10/the-mancession/

Rosenfeld, R. (1992). Job Mobility and Career Processes. *Annual Revue of Sociology, 18*, 39–51.

Skladany, B. (2009). Maybe Johnny Paycheck Was Right. From AARP.org. October 9, 2009. Retrieved from http://www.aarp.org/work/work-life/info-10-2009/skladany_johnnypaycheck_right.html

Supiano, B., & Hoover, E. (2009) Will the Economy Really Change Students' College Plans? Early Signs Say Yes. *Chronicles of Higher Education*, 00095982 20090424, *55*(33).

Woo, S. (2009, November 2009). California Raises University Fees 32% to Close Budget Gap. *The Wall Street Journal. 254*(121).

HOUSEHOLD DATA: SUMMARY TABLE A   Household Data, Seasonally Adjusted Numbers in Thousands

Category	March 2010
Employment status	
Civilian noninstitutional population	237,159
Civilian Labor Force	153,910
Participation Rate	64.9
Employed	138,905
Employment–Population Ratio	58.6
Unemployed	15,005
Unemployment Rate	9.7
Not in Labor Force	83,249
Unemployment Rates	
Total, 16 years and over	9.7
Adult men (20 years and over)	10.0
Adult women (20 years and over)	8.0
Teenagers (16 to 19 years)	26.1
White	8.8
Black or African-American	16.5
Asian (not seasonally-adjusted)	7.5
Hispanic or Latino Ethnicity	12.6
Total, 25 years and older	8.3
Less than a high school diploma	14.5
Some college or associate degree	10.8
High school graduates, no college	8.2
Bachelor's degree and higher	4.9
Reasons for unemployment	
Job losers and persons who completed temporary jobs	9,354
Job leavers	894
Reentrants	3,544
New entrants	1,197
Duration of Unemployment	
Less than 5 weeks	2,646
5 to 14 weeks	3,228
14 to 26 weeks	2,436
27 weeks and over	6,547
Employed persons at work part-time	
Part-time for economic reasons	9,054
Slack work or business conditions	6,177
Could only find part-time work	2,388
Part-time for noneconomic reasons	18,379
Persons not in the labor force (not seasonally adjusted)	
Marginally attached to the labor force	2,255
Discouraged workers	994

CHAPTER 17

CAREER DEVELOPMENT AND THE STUDENT-ATHLETE

Amy S. Walker, PhD, Licensed Psychologist
Taunya Marie Tinsley, PhD, NCC, LPC
California University of Pennsylvania

There are about 400,000 American undergraduate college and university students participating in intercollegiate athletics each year (United States General Accounting Office, 2001). Year after year, thousands of these college and university student-athletes dream about making it to the professional level and have been dreaming since high school. However, the National Collegiate Athletic Association (NCAA) (2010b) reports that only 1.2 percent of NCAA male senior basketball players will get drafted by a National Basketball Association team. The NCAA (2010b) further reports that less than one in 100 of NCAA female senior basketball players will get drafted by the Women's National Basketball Association. Only 5.7% of seniors playing football in high school will continue to play at the college level, while only 1.7 percent of NCAA senior football players will get drafted by a National Football League team (NCAA, 2010b). The statistics are consistent with non-revenue producing sports teams as well (NCAA, 2010b) and may suggest that many high school, college and university student-athletes will not often make their dream of reaching the professional level a reality.

Career Development in Higher Education, pages 357–376
Copyright © 2011 by Information Age Publishing
All rights of reproduction in any form reserved.

Furthermore, these alarming numbers give rise to questions regarding college student-athletes career development as "a number of intercollegiate athletes, particularly those in revenue-generating sports, lack a sense of career direction" (Petitpas & O'Brien, 2008, p. 133).

The purpose of this chapter is to highlight some of the key career development concepts related to collegiate student-athletes. The chapter will begin with a review of the literature that connects the intercollegiate student-athlete population as a unique cultural group, the role of helping professionals who work with intercollegiate student-athletes, and the multicultural sports counseling competencies. Human developmental theories, career development theories, assessment techniques and interventions are explained and applied to a case study with suggestions for working with student-athletes. Finally, we discuss recommendations and ethical issues for helping professionals in higher education who work with intercollegiate student-athletes as well as implications for professional development. For the purpose of this chapter, the term helping professional will be used interchangeably with the terms counselor, psychologist, and advisor, and will include the student affairs areas of clinical counseling, career counseling, academic advising and life skills development.

LITERATURE REVIEW

Multicultural Sports Counseling Competencies

The multicultural movement, the "fourth force in counseling" has transformed the thinking and practices of many helping practitioners and has contributed to the profession's greater and much needed understanding and appreciation of differences among racial, ethnic and cultural groups (D'Andrea & Heckman, 2008; Pedersen, 1991; Pope, Reynolds, & Mueller, 2004). For more than 20 years, the training of professionals who are able to meet the needs of an increasingly diverse population has presented challenges (Holcomb-McCoy, 2001; Pope et al., 2004; Pope-Davis, Coleman, Liu, & Toporek, 2003). By extending the principles of multicultural counseling to include the athlete population, counselors, psychologists, advisors and other helping professionals may be in a better position to receive formalized instruction beyond the basic counselor preparation, respond to the developmental needs of athletes, and enhance the quality of services they provide (Miller & Wooten, 1995; Pinkerton, 2009).

Like many cultural groups, athletes are confronted with a multitude of complex demands, challenges and stressors where they may be underserved by counseling services. Care must be taken to provide effective advising and counseling services (Etzel, 2009; Goldberg & Chandler, 1995; Valentine & Taub, 1999). Although the athletic environment may be alien to some counselors, psychologists, advisors, or other helping professionals, one who is open to learning and empathic could grasp the meaning to the [athlete] client (Heyman, 1986).

Helping professionals who work with the athlete population should be multicultural sport counseling competent and should have specialized knowledge and skills beyond their basic counselor preparation as well as an awareness of biases, misperceptions, and prejudices towards the athlete population (Cole, 2006; Edwards, 1991; Etzel, Ferrante, & Pinkney, 1996; Nejedlo, Arredondo, & Benjamin, 1985; Pinkerton, 2009; Tinsley, 2005). Tinsley (2005) developed the multicultural sports-counseling competencies that utilize statements and language from the Multicultural Counseling Inventory (Sodowsky, Taffee, Gutkin, & Wise, 1994) and have been modified to be more inclusive of the athlete population. The competencies consist of four dimensions and are defined as the extent to which a helping professional has developed an integrated awareness, knowledge and skills while maintaining a positive relationship necessary to work with the athlete population (Sodowsky et al., 1994; Tinsley, 2005).

Student-Athlete Population

For over twenty-five years, several authors have contended that student-athletes are a group of non-traditional students who create a culture of their own with special issues and unique developmental needs (Chartrand & Lent, 1987; Cole & Tinsley, 2009; Engstrom & Sedlacek, 1991; Goldberg & Chandler, 1995; Harris, Altekruse, & Engels, 2003; Jolly, 2008; Petitpas & Champagne, 2000; Sowa & Gressard, 1983; Valentine & Taub, 1999; Watson, 2003). Furthermore, "the athlete population is a group of people who appear to have a unique culture where norms of behavior and values are well defined, spend a great deal of time together, often have common goals generated by their experiences together as athletes, and have a set of experiences in life that differentiate them from others" (Cole & Tinsley, 2009, p. 523; Sedlacek, 1996). Further evidence that supports this group's status as a unique cultural group is based on the fact that student-athletes have faced prejudice and are a group that faces oppression, prejudice and discrimination, similar to racial and ethnic groups, women and disabled students (Baucom & Lantz, 2001; Engstrom & Sedlacek, 1991; Sedlacek, 1996; Simons, Bosworth, Fujita, & Jensen, 2007; Steinfeldt, Reed, & Steinfeldt, 2010).

There also is diversity among individuals who participate, as well as subgroups within the student-athletes population, with specific developmental needs (Chartrand & Lent, 1987; Cole & Tinsley, 2009; Hinkle, 1994). Racial, ethnic, and religious athletes, as well as women and other minorities differ in their goals and objectives for participating and competing in sports, which reflect individual developmental needs (Cole, 2006; Cole & Tinsley, 2009; Hinkle, 1994; Poinsett, 1996; Steinfeldt et al., 2010; Tinsley, 2005). High school, collegiate, professional and leisure athletes differ in their developmental needs (Hinkle, 1994).

College sport teams are typically categorized as revenue producing or non-revenue producing. At most Division I or II schools, revenue producting sports such as football as well as men's and women's basketball pay the bill in athletic departments (Sailes & Harrison, 2008; Steinfeldt et al., 2010; Upthegrove, Roscigno, & Zubrinsky, 1999). That is, these big money sports generate a great proportion of the that funds that support the organization. On the other hand, nonrevenue sports, also referred to as Olympic sports, are varsity teams that compete in the NCAA and conference competition but are not financially self-supportive (Cochrane, 2008). According to the NCAA, nonrevenue sports include all championship sports, with the exception of the revenue producing sports (e.g., soccer, golf, lacrosse, wrestling, and tennis) (NCAA, 2010c).

The business-minded mentality of athletic departments often creates a conflict with the academic mission of the university and places a huge demand on the athletes' time. This drain on the college student-athletes' time is in conflict and direct competition with the time demands including attending class, completing homework, studying for exams, and engaging in career planning and development (Sailes & Harrison, 2008). Helping professionals working with college student-athletes from nonrevenue sports can also assume that they too deal with a myriad of issues including those related to transitions, stress, identity, personal and clinical issues, athletic competition, psychosocial development, retirement from sport, injuries, and career planning and development (Cochrane 2008; Cole & Tinsley, 2009).

The developmental needs of student-athletes are also similar to their non student-athlete counterparts. Although "student-athletes constitute a unique college population because they have come into college through a different door than their classmates, and they have had experiences and challenges that are quite different from the traditional college student" (Howard-Hamilton & Villegas, 2008, p. 115), particular attention and services should given to their developmental needs including psychosocial, identity, cognitive, and person-environment concerns. "Similar to those [services] provided to other special populations on campus, such as minority groups, honors students, and students with disabilities, services should be tailored to meet the needs of student-athletes on college campuses" (Howard-Hamilton & Villegas, 2008, p. 112).

Career development needs are among other development concerns where student-athletes may need specific support. Collegiate student-athletes need supportive counselors, psychologists, and other student affairs staff to assist them with exploring career interests, vocational alternatives, and majors early as well as helping professionals who are knowledgeable of career development theories specific to the athlete population (Howard-Hamilton & Villegas, 2008; Pope & Miller, 1996). Additionally, helping professionals should develop programs that not only challenge college student-athletes' attitudes toward short term career development planning, but also eventually lead to long-term changes in motivation and behavior (Petitpas & O'Brien, 2008).

Career Development Theories and Research with Student-Athletes

A number of career development theories have been explained in previous chapters throughout this text. For this reason, the authors of this chapter have selected to highlight two important aforementioned frameworks and their related concepts that are germane to the student-athlete population. Particularly, Social Cognitive Career Theory (SCCT) and Super's Life Span, Life Space Theory will be reviewed. While these two theories are not exclusive to the student-athlete population, and while other theories, such as Holland's Person-Environment Fit Theory may be beneficial to use with student-athletes, SCCT and Super's have been examined the most within the student-athlete population. A brief overview of the SCCT and Super's Life Span Life Space theories is provided and particular elements of each theory and their relationship to the student-athlete population is explained.

SOCIAL COGNITIVE CAREER THEORY

Albert Bandura's (1986) social cognitive perspective of behavior and thought have impacted theories of career development over the years. Lent, Brown, and Hackett (1994) created Social Cognitive Career Theory which connects Bandura's (1986) perspective with concepts including self-efficacy beliefs, outcome expectations, and career goals. Self-efficacy beliefs is an area that continues to grow in popularity for researchers, specifically as it relates to career decision-making. In 1981, Betz and Hackett conducted trailblazing research regarding self-efficacy and its relation to women's career decisions and achievement. Their research also created a strong foundation for future studies that defined career decision-making self-efficacy and led to the creation of instruments to measure the construct (Cammack, 2007).

Career decision-making self-efficacy (CDMSE) research is limited within the collegiate student-athletes group. To date, only two published studies serve as the current research in the area of student-athletes and career decision-making self-efficacy. The results of these two studies indicate that higher levels of career decision-making self efficacy were negatively related to hours of sport activity, positively related to an internal career locus of control, and negatively related to low levels of career exploration activities (Brown, Glastetter-Fender, & Shelton, 2000; Korspan & Etzel, 2001).

In the first published study of CDMSE, Brown and colleagues (2000) administered the Career Decision-Making Self-Efficacy Scale-Short Form (CDMSES-F), along with other career measures, to 189 student-athletes. Factors including career locus of control, career decision-making self-efficacy, identity foreclosure, and athletic identity were examined. Other factors taken into consideration in the study were student-athletes' time in sport and expectations of sport participation. Their study suggests that students with lower career decision making self-efficacy beliefs also participated in more hours of the more hours sport activity. Moreover, results indicated that student-athletes who possessed a greater internal career locus of control appeared to have higher career decision-making self-efficacy scores. Students who did not participate in career exploration activities tended to report lower career decision making self-efficacy scores (Brown et al., 2000).

The second published study of CDMSE with student athletes was completed by Korspan and Etzel (2001). These researchers examined the effects of locus of control and self-efficacy on career maturity levels of male and female, junior college students. The results of the study concluded that career decision-making self-efficacy is related to career maturity.

In both Brown, Glastetter-Fender, and Shelton's (2000) and Korspan and Etzel's (2001) findings, career decision-making self-efficacy is important and beneficial to students' overall career development as noted in their research. Additionally, higher CDMSE scores were also related to higher levels of career locus of control.

Locus of Control (LOC)

Another concept that derived from social learning theory and is now examined within the career development field is locus of control. The construct was initially defined as generalized expectancies as a result of skill or chance (Lefcourt, 1981). Rotter (1966), the most prominent researcher in LOC theory suggests that, "a reinforcement acts to strengthen an expectancy that a particular behavior or event will be followed by that reinforcement in the future" (p. 2). The expectancy may or may not be contingent upon one's own behavior (Rotter, 1966).

Rotter (1966) proposed that there are two distinctions in the types of controllability—internal and external control. The internal locus of control orientation is defined as the belief that reinforcements are a result of personal effort; an external locus of control orientation is the belief that reinforcements are a result of outside forces that are beyond one's personal control (Rotter, 1966).

The study of locus of control within the college student-athlete population further warrants exploration and analysis. The extant research, however, concludes that college student-athletes have been found to possess a greater external locus of control orientation than their non-athlete peers (Etzel, 1990; Frederick, 2000; Korspan & Etzel, 2001; LeUnes & Nation, 1982). Moreover, higher levels of an internal locus of control were positively related to career decision making self-efficacy scores in Brown and colleagues' study (2000), accounted for variance in career attitudes and career skills in Korspan and Etzel's (2001), and were related to career maturity (Brown et al., 2000; Korspan & Etzel, 2001). In fact, career locus of control was the most significant predictor of career maturity scores (Korspan & Etzel, 2001).

Interestingly, career locus of control within the student-athlete population predicted significantly greater variance in career maturity than in the general college student population. This finding is in contrast to the Luzzo (1995) study and suggests that career locus of control may be a more important variable than career decision-making self-efficacy for college student-athletes when attempting to understand career maturity. College student-athletes who have higher levels of career locus of control have also been found to have higher CDMSE levels and higher levels of career maturity (Brown et al., 2000; Korspan & Etzel, 2001).

Career maturity is a concept that derived from the work of the most distinguished and published writer of the career development field—Donald Super. Super's developmental theory is known as the Life Span, Life Space Theory. The Life Span, Life Span Theory is briefly described below with particular emphasis on the importance of the self-concept in relation to identity and career maturity.

Super's Life Span, Life Space Theory

In their review of his work, Isaacson and Brown (2000) report that Super "often stated that his view is a 'segmented' theory consisting of several related propositions, out of which he hopes an integrated theory will ultimately emerge" (p. 29). His theory purports that an individual develops roles and specific tasks over his or her life time. These roles are child, student, citizen, leisurite, worker, spouse, homemaker, parent, and pensioner. Super's (1953) five stages of development also include Growth (birth–14), Exploration (15–24), Establishment (25–44), Maintenance (45–64) and Decline (65+).

Super hoped to one day consolidate his 14 propositions into one view, one theory. Perhaps his segmented view compelled other researchers to study his theory in parts. In keeping with this compartmentalized study, the examination of two of the concepts that evolved from Super's theory, career maturity and the self-concept, and their relation to the career development of student-athletes will be provided.

The Self-Concept and Career Maturity

Super defined the self-concept as one's view of self and his or her view of the environment or situation that one experiences (Super, 1953, 1980). This idea of the self-concept is closely related to identity phenomenon. That is, the development of an individual's identity and self-concept both require a person to examine his or her individuality and affiliation as it relates to a group. Specifically, for student-athletes, they have to examine two roles simultaneously—that of a student and that of an athlete.

Super's Life-Career Rainbow suggests that individuals will typically experience several roles as they develop along the continuum (Super, 1980). These roles begin with child and end with pensioner, with several roles in between. Student-athletes are required to carry out the task of both student and athlete, with some identifying the role of athlete as more salient than their student status, and vice versa. That is, one may devote more time and energy to his or her athletic status more than his or her academic duties such as studying, attending class, completing homework assignments, and participating in career development activities (Cammack, 2007).

Combining concepts of career and identity, the term career identity is defined as the developing structure of self-concepts in their relation to the (future) career role perceived by the individual himself (Law, Meijers, & Wijers, 2002). Overall, the research examining career development and college student-athletes warrants much further investigation.

Of the extant studies, we find that either the information is not-up-to-date or it is simply limited in number. Perhaps in some areas, such as career identity and career maturity, the current research does exist; however, most of it is conducted by graduate students who have not published their theses (Carswell, 2009; Clow, 2001; Finch, 2008; Heller, 2009; Hughes, 2006; Ihle-Helledy, 2006; Rivas Quinones, 2003) . Those very same dissertations may also include other valuable career information, such as career development interventions, that will benefit student-athletes.

From formal to informal, career development interventions can be creative ways to assist student-athletes to increase their knowledge of their own career interests, skills, and values. Various assessments help students identify who they are and who they would like to become in the world of work using paper-pencil techniques, computer assisted guidance programs, and counseling interventions. The following sections highlight several of these interventions and their use within the student-athlete population.

Career Development Interventions

The beginning of this chapter discussed the idea that the developmental needs of student-athletes are similar to the developmental needs of their non student-athlete counterparts. The same notion is true regarding the use of career interventions within the athlete group. That is, many of the career development assessments that students complete, either in their university counseling center or community based career center, to assess career interests, skills, and values, are applicable to the student-athlete population.

Career development interventions span the gamut and are involved in the career counseling process either as formal or informal assessments, job shadowing activities, informational interviews, and career research. Formal assessments are described as "inventories or tests, with no right or wrong answers, developed by experts according to scientific principles of test construction" (Career Assessment Goddess, 2010). Examples of formal assessments include the Self-Directed Search (SDS), Strong Interest Inventory (SII), My Vocational Situation (MVS), Campbell Interest and Skills Survey (CII), the Myers-Briggs Type Indicator, and the Transferrable Skills Inventory. A novel career assessment that specifically measures the career development of student-athletes is the Student-Athlete Career Situation Inventory (SACSI; Sandstedt, Cox, Martens, Ward, Webber & Ivey, 2004).

The SACSI is a career development instrument that measures the career related attitudes, beliefs, and interests of the student-athlete population (Sandstedt et al., 2004). Sandstedt and colleagues (2004) defined career situation as "the extent of one's career development and preparation characterized by the sophistication of one's career attitudes, beliefs, and interests" (p. 90). This 30-item assessment was normed in a Division I college student-athlete group. Five factors were found on the assessment: career decision-making self-efficacy, career versus sport identity, locus of control, barriers to career development, and sport to work relationship, which can also be translated into transferrable skills development (Sandstedt et al., 2004). The SACSI is fairly new measure introduced to the career domain and warrants further empirical investigation by researchers.

Transferable skills are a critical concept to explore with student-athletes (Petitpas & Schwartz, 1989; Petitpas & O'Brien, 2008). Due to time constraints including practice, academics, and game schedules, many student-athletes are not afforded the opportunity to engage in experiential learning activities such as internships or part-time/summer employment. These experiences are much more available to their non student-athlete peers where they are able to learn on-the-job training and translate their academic acknowledge into practical exercises. Fortunately, many athletic academic advising offices offer students the opportunity to participate in the NCAA CHAMPS (Challenging Athletes' Minds for Personal Success) Life

Skills program (Etzel, 2009; Leslie-Toogood & Gill, 2008, NCAA, 2010a). This program allows student-athletes to participate in activities where they can use the skills they learned on the field or court in another area of interests. In other words, students can practice their transferable skills such as leadership, teamwork, and strategic planning. The CHAMPS /Life Skills program is further explained in the next section. It may be important to explore the area of transferable skills through both formal assessments such as the Transferrable Skills Inventory or through informal assessments such as checklists.

Informal assessments are described as "simple questionnaires or exercises, like journal writing, creating a 'dream-job' collage of pictures, or brief essays about past experiences" (Career Assessment Goddess, 2010). One of the major benefits of completing activities such as these is that an individual can complete them independently or while in meeting with a career professional. Considering student-athletes' busy schedules, completing these activities on their own time allows them to reflect on thoughts, ideas, and experiences and conduct self-assessments at their own leisure. Additional interventions include attending face-to-face and on-line career courses (Wotten & Hinkle, 1994), career workshops and seminars, and information sessions hosted by various career professionals and/or industry professionals.

RECOMMENDATIONS FOR HELPING PROFESSIONALS

Many colleges and universities utilized specialized programs designed for the student-athletes in higher education, including the CHAMPS/Life Skills program. According to the NCAA:

> The mission of the NCAA is to maintain intercollegiate athletics as an integral part of the campus educational program and the student-athlete as an integral part of the student body. With this in mind, the CHAMPS/Life Skills Program was created to support the student-athlete development initiatives of NCAA member institutions and to enhance the quality of the student-athlete experience within the context of higher education. (NCAA, 2010a, n.p.)

This specialized program, that is designed to promote student-athletes' academic, athletic, personal, community, and career development may provide specific documentation of the multicultural sports counseling competence required for helping professionals (NCAA, 2010a; Tinsley, 2008). Additionally, the CHAMPS/Life Skills program may provide the necessary program components needed to be successful when providing career development services with college student-athletes. Thus, counselors, psychologists, advisors and other student affairs staff may want to consider the successful initiatives of the CHAMPS/Life Skills programs when working with college student-athletes.

In addition to the core knowledge base and skills required for all counselors, psychologists, advisors and student affairs staff, helping professionals who work with college student-athletes should also acquire advanced awareness, knowledge and skills to provide career counseling to student-athletes. They should be able to refer student-athletes to specialized community and professional resources that may not be available within the higher education environment, recruit and organize mentors, and facilitate communication among helping professionals, coaches, administrators and families (Cammack, 2007; Cole & Tinsley, 2009; Tinsley, 2008).

Counselors, psychologists, student affairs staff, and other helping professionals on college and university campuses should also consult and communicate with one another to provide awareness and knowledge of career planning and development services to the student-athletes population. This is especially true in that many intercollegiate student-athletes, given more time, would rather devote that extra time to athletics rather than academics and possibly career planning and development (NCAA, 2010a). Additionally, helping professionals on campus should understand their roles, coordinate their services and assist student-athletes with navigating the difficulties that accompany career development and intercollegiate athletics. Moreover, a systems approach that incorporates a multicultural sports counseling competency model may assist to build a transparent process that is clear to the student-athletes, the athletic department, campus helping professionals and university departments (Leslie-Toogood, Gill & Tinsley, 2009).

Ethical issues may arise from helping professionals' lack of multicultural sports-counseling competence, which may impact service delivery to the unique cultural group of intercollegiate student-athletes (Constantine & Ladany, 2001; Tinsley, 2005). It may behoove helping professionals to familiarize themselves with their appropriate professional organization's ethical codes and principles. Professional organizations have developed ethical codes to serve as guides for helping professionals' practice with clients and to increase the probability that counselors will not harm their clients and provide quality service (Kocet, 2006). For example, those who provide counseling services to intercollegiate athletes can use the American Counseling Association's (ACA, 2005) ACA Code of Ethics, the American Psychological Association's Ethical Principles of Psychologists and Code of Conduct, and the Multicultural Counseling Competencies for helping professionals (Arredondo et al., 1996; Pope et al., 2004). Other professional organizations' ethical standards that can serve as a guide for helping professionals who work with intercollegiate student-athletes include the National Association for Academic Advisors for Athletics (2010), the Association for

Applied Sport Psychology's (2010), the American College Personnel Association (2006), and the National Association of Student Personnel Administrators (NASPA, 2009).

CASE STUDY

Thus far, this chapter has provided theoretical frameworks, results of related research, and practical suggestions for helping professionals who assist student-athletes achieve their career development needs. To paint an even more pragmatic picture of these theories, research, and interventions, below is a case study that outlines how a helping professional might work with a student-athlete in need of career assistance. In thinking through this case, we recommend that you reflect on the following areas: (1) larger contextual issues related to intercollegiate athletics, (2) unique on-campus dynamics, (3) individual realities within the student-athlete culture, and (4) inclusion in one or more subpopulations or groupings (Leslie-Toogood & Gill, 2008).

David (pronounced Da-veed) is a Latino-American, 19 year-old sophomore at an eastern Division I institution. David is a basketball player. David is the oldest of five children, and his mother is a single parent. David is a first-generation college student who plans to major in kinesiology; however, he is undecided regarding his career plans.

David was referred to career counseling by his academic advisor. She noticed that while David reports interests in kinesiology, he also appears to have difficulty with core major classes, many which are science based. David scheduled an appointment to meet with a career counselor in the university career center and met for a total of eight sessions.

Sessions One through Three: The first session consisted of introductions of both the counselor and the client. David talked about his importance of his cultural heritage, growing up as the oldest child, and his journey to success as a Division I basketball player. The counselor explained limits to confidentiality, and a general discussion of the purpose of the career counseling was provided. David wrapped up the first session with questions about meeting times, expectations, and next steps. The second and third sessions included a description of computer assisted career guidance programs such as DISCOVER, and other formal interest, skills, and values assessments. During session three, David reported that he was interested in taking the Strong Interest Inventory and the Myers-Briggs Type Indicator. He was particularly interested in these assessments because he wanted to take a closer look at how he compared to others in his fields of interests. He was also attracted to these instruments because he could access them on-line at his leisure.

Sessions Four through Seven: Session four was the first of a two-session interpretation. David learned that math and science were not his strengths and also learned that his current major consists of mostly science based courses; clearly, his interests and skills were not congruent. He also learned that his strengths included working with others, organizing events, and teamwork. During sessions six and seven, David began to identify majors where he could exercise these strengths and later be able to parlay these areas into a meaningful career.

Session Eight. Session eight was David's last session with the counselor. The counselor summarized their work together and asked David about his thoughts regarding his experience in career counseling. David discussed what he felt worked, what didn't work, and his future career plans. The counselor provided career resources, both on campus and off campus, so that David would have tools in his career development tool belt. He was reminded that the work doesn't end at the termination of career counseling; instead, it was just the beginning of his journey on the road to career success.

Additional Case Study Reflection Questions

While thinking through the above case study regarding David, helping professionals should reflect on their particular role and the many people with whom to consult and collaborate with to best serve this student-athlete. Additional reflection questions modified from Leslie-Toogood, Gill & Tinsley (2009) are as follows:

1. What do you think may be the barriers to developing a relationship with David and how will you overcome them? (A variety of factors may impact your response to this question including your gender, race, ethnicity, socioeconomic status, etc.).
2. What are your attitudes, beliefs, biases, knowledge, and skills for working with culturally diverse students, specifically a Latino-American who is a member of the men's basketball team?
3. What knowledge do you possess regarding the development of students of color and of the athlete population?
4. What skills do you possess for working effectively with culturally diverse populations?
5. What additional information would you like to know about David?
6. What is the role and meaning of basketball in David's life?
7. What is a group intervention you could develop for other student-athletes similar to David?
8. How will you explain the implications of David's change of major and career development to important parties such as his coaches, the athletic department, including the compliance coordinator and

his academic advisor, and his family? What are you ethically and legally allowed to share?

9. What transitions do you think David will have as he furthers his career development at your college or university?

10. What training should you engage in to help you learn more about how to best serve the student-athlete population with their career development?

FUTURE DIRECTIONS FOR PROFESSIONAL DEVELOPMENT

The national attention given to the challenges of career planning and development of college student-athletes has generated much needed discussions regarding the career developmental needs of student-athletes. Future directions for career counseling with college student-athletes should include strengthened training programs and professionals' awareness of multicultural sports counseling competencies. Those offering programs to professional counselors, psychologists, athletic advisors, school counselors, student affairs or student development staff, as well as those designing programs for these professions, may want to consider implementing strategies to address the multicultural sports counseling competencies among helping professionals (Tinsley, 2008). Strengthening these competencies may increase helping professionals self-reported proficiency with providing career counseling and development programs to the student-athletes in higher education.

Helping professionals who work with student-athletes must recognized that they are a unique cultural group with specific career developmental needs. As a result, specialized training should be available to counselors, psychologists, student affairs professionals and other helping professionals in the areas of training after graduate school and continuing education workshops. Those designing counselor education programs may consider incorporating the athlete population as part of the multicultural-counseling course, the career counseling course, and the student affairs course curriculums. Those designing psychology or sport psychology programs may consider similar concepts including adding student-athletes, as a cultural group, into the study of the multicultural counseling context as well as studying the dynamics and developmental issues related to the population. Finally, counselor education, psychology, sport psychology, and student affairs programs may consider developing a complete course devoted to the career developmental needs of the athlete population across the life-span.

As previously stated, the published studies of career development and the student athlete population is scarce. Our final recommendation is that helping professionals who work with athletes on college/university campuses increase their research activities. More importantly, we encourage graduate students to publish their theses and/or dissertations which may contain important information regarding the student-athletes' career decision-making self-efficacy, career maturity, career identity, and overall career success.

CONCLUSION

Like many cultural groups, athletes are confronted with a multitude of complex demands, challenges and stressors where they may be underserved by career counseling services. Helping professionals who work with the athlete population should be multicultural sport counseling competent and should have specialized knowledge and skills beyond their basic counselor preparation. Helping professionals must also be aware of the developmental challenges facing the college student-athlete as well as be appropriately trained to provide effective career development interventions to the athlete population.

In this chapter, we highlighted some of the key career development concepts related to collegiate student-athletes. In addition, a review of the literature that connected the intercollegiate student-athlete population as a unique cultural group, the role of helping professionals who work with intercollegiate student-athletes, and the multicultural sports counseling competencies was provided. Human developmental theories, career development theories, assessment techniques and intervention were also explained and applied to a case study with suggestions for working with student-athletes. Finally, we discussed recommendations and ethical issues for helping professionals in higher education who work with intercollegiate student-athletes as well as implications for professional development.

APPENDIX: PENTA-SPORT DIAGRAM

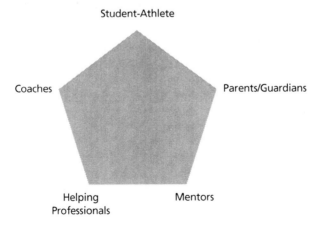

REFERENCES

American College Personnel Association. (2006). Statement of ethical principals and standards. Retrieved from http://www2.myacpa.org/ethics/statement. php

American Counseling Association. (2005). ACA code of ethics. Alexandria, VA: American Counseling Association.

Arredondo, P., Toporek, R., Brown, S. P., Jones, J., Locke, D. C., Sanchez, J., et al. (1996). Operationalization of the multicultural counseling competencies. *Journal of Multicultural Counseling and Development*, 24, 42–78.

Association for Applied Sport Psychology. (2010). AASP ethical principles and standards. Retrieved from http://appliedsportpsych.org/about/ethics/code

Bandura, A. (1986). *Social foundations of thought and action: A social cognitve theory*. Englewood Cliffs, NJ: Prentice Hall.

Baucom, C., Lantz, C. D. (2001). Faculty attitudes toward male division II student-athletes. *Journal of Sport Behavior, 24*(3), 265–276.

Betz, N.E., & Hackett, G. (1981). The relationship of career-related self-efficacy expectations to perceived career options in college women and men. *Journal of Counseling Psychology, 28*(5), 399–410.

Brown, C., Glastetter-Fender, C., & Shelton, M. (2000). Psychosocial identity and career control in college student-athletes. *Journal of Vocational Behavior, 56*(1), 53–62.

Cammack, A. S. (2007). *An examination of the career development of predominantly African-American inner-city high school student-athletes*. Unpublished doctoral dissertation. The Pennsylvania State University. Dissertation Abstracts International, 68 (10-B), 6996.

Career Assessment Goddess. (2010). Retrieved from http://www.assessmentgoddess.com/career_assessments.html.

Carswell, M. (2009). *Predictors of retirement distress among male former intercollegiate athletes*. Unpublished doctoral dissertation. Michigan State University. Dissertation Abstracts International, 70 (2-B), 1335.

Chartrand, J. M., & Lent, R. L. (1987). Sports counseling: Enhancing the development of the student-athlete. *Journal of Counseling and Development, 66*, 164–167.

Clow, C. (2001). *Student-athletes perceived value of education: Effects of a career exploration intervention*. Unpublished doctoral dissertation. Auburn University, AL. Dissertation Abstracts International, 61 (7-B), 3836.

Cochrane, K. (2008). Nonrevenue sport. In A. Leslie-Toogood and E. Gill (Eds.) *Advising student-athletes: A collaborative approach to success* (pp. 103–106). Manhattan, KS: NACADA, National Academic Advising Association.

Cole, K. W. (2006). An examination of school counselors' knowledge and perceptions of recruited student-athletes. Unpublished doctoral dissertation. University of Iowa. Dissertation Abstracts International, 67, 2891.

Cole, K. W., & Tinsley, T. M. (2009). Sports counseling. In American Counseling Association (Ed.), *The ACA encyclopedia of counseling* (pp. 522–524). Alexandria, VA: American Counseling Association.

Constantine, M. G., & Ladany, N. (2001). New visions for defining and assessing multicultural counseling competence. In J. G. Ponterotto, J. M. Casas, L. A. Suzuki, & C. M. Alexander (Eds.), *Handbook of multicultural counseling* (2nd ed.) (pp. 482–98). Thousand Oaks, CA: Sage.

D'Andrea, M., & Heckman, E. F. (2008). A 40-year review of multicultural counseling outcome research: Outlining a future research agenda for the multicultural counseling movement. *Journal of Counseling & Development, 86,* 356–363.

Edwards, H. (1991). Democratic pluralism: Placing African American student-athletes in the context of a new agenda for higher education. *National Academic Advising Association Journal, 11,* 228–122.

Engstrom, C. M., & Sedlacek, W. E. (1991). A study of prejudice toward university student-athletes. *Journal of Counseling & Development, 70,* 189–193.

Etzel, E. F. (1990). Life stress, locus of control, and sport competition anxiety patterns of college student-athletes. Dissertation Abstracts International, 50, B4205.

Etzel, E. F., Ferrante, A. P., & Pinkney, J. W. (1996). *Counseling college student-athletes: Issues and interventions.* Morgantown, WV: Fitness Information Technology, Inc.

Etzel, E. F. (2009). *Counseling and psychological services for college student-athletes.* Morgantown, WV: Fitness Information Technology.

Finch, B. (2008). Investigating college athletes' role identities and career development. Unpublished doctoral dissertation. Texas A&M University. Dissertation Abstracts International, 69(9-A), 3756.

Frederick, C. (2000). Competitiveness: Relations with GPA, locus of control, sex, and athletic status. *Perceptual and Motor Skills, 90*(2), 413–414.

Goldberg, A., & Chandler, T. (1995). Sports counseling: Enhancing the development of the high school student-athletes. *Journal of Counseling and Development, 74*(1), 39–44.

Hackett, G., & Betz, N. E. (1981). A self-efficacy approach to the career development of women. *Journal of Vocational Behavior, 18,* 326–339.

Harris, H. L., Altekruse, M. K., & Engels, D. W. (2003). Helping freshman student-athletes adjust to college life using psychoeducational groups. *Journal for Specialists in Group Work, 28*(1), 64–81.

Heller, T. (2009). Psychological predictors of career maturity in college student-athletes. Unpublished doctoral dissertation. The Florida State University. Dissertation Abstracts International, 70 (2-B), 1368.

Heyman, S. R. (1986). Psychological problem patterns found with athletes. *The Clinical Psychologist, 29,* 68–71.

Hinkle, J. (1994). Integrating sport psychology and sports counseling: Developmental programming, education, and research. *Journal of Sport Behavior, 17*(1), 52–49.

Holcomb-McCoy, C. C. (2001). Multicultural training, self-construals and multicultural competence of school counselors. *Professional School Counseling, 4,* 202–208.

Howard-Hamilton, M., & Villegas, H. (2008). Student development theory. In A. Leslie-Toogood and E. Gill (Eds.) *Advising student-athletes: A collaborative ap-*

proach to success (pp. 111–119). Manhattan, KS: NACADA, National Academic Advising Association.

Hughes, T. (2006). Factors that influence the career maturity of African-American athletes. Unpublished doctoral dissertation. University of South Carolina. Dissertation Abstracts International, 6(7-A), 2491.

Ihle Helledy, K. (2006). Exploration of the factors related to the career development of collegiate student-athletes. Unpublished doctoral dissertation. University of Wisconsin. Dissertation Abstract International, 67(3-A), 914.

Isaacson, L., & Brown, D. (2000). *Career information, career counseling, and career development.* Needham Heights, MA: Allyn and Bacon.

Jolly, J. C. (2008). Raising the question # 9: Is the student-athlete population unique? And why should we care? *Communication Education, 57*(1),145–151.

Korspan, A., & Etzel, E.F. (2001). The relationship of demographic and psychological variables to career maturity of junior college student-athletes. *Journal of Counseling Student Development, 42*(2), 122–132.

Kocet, M. M. (2006). Ethical challenges in a complex world: Highlights of the 2005 ACA code of ethics. *Journal of Counseling & Development, 84*, 228–234.

Law, B., Meijers, F., & Wijers, G. (2002). New perspectives on career and identity in the contemporary world. *British Journal of Guidance and Counselling, 30*(4), 431–449.

Lefcourt, H. M. (1981). *Research with the locus of control construct.* New York: Academic Press.

Lent, R. W., Brown, S. D., & Hackett, G. (1994). Toward a unifying social cognitive theory of career and academic interest, choice, and performance. *Journal of Vocational Behavior, 45*, 79–122.

Lent, R., Hackett, G., & Brown, S. (2000). Contextual supports and barriers to career choice: A social cognitive analysis. *Journal of Counseling Psychology, 47*(1), 36–49.

LeUnes, A., & Nation, J. (1982). Saturdays heroes: A psychological portrait of college football players. *Journal of Sport Behavior, 5*(3), 139–149.

Leslie-Toogood, L., & Gill, E. (2008). *Advising student-athletes: A collaborative approach to success* (Monography Series Number 18). Manhattan, KS: National Academic Advising Association.

Leslie-Toogood, A., Gill, E., & Tinsley, T. M. (2009). A case study of a student-athlete with learning issues: A professional development tool for athletic academic advisors. *Academic Athletic Journal, 20*(1), 69–97.

Luzzo, D. A. (1995). The relative contributions of self-efficacy and locus of control to the prediction of career maturity. *Journal of College Student Development, 36*(1), 61–66.

Miller, G., & Wooten, R. (1995). Sports counseling: A new counseling specialty area. *Journal of Counseling & Development, 74*, 172–173.

NASPA–Student Affairs Administrators in Higher Education. (2009). NASPA'S commitment to diversity, inclusion, and equity. Retrieved from http://www.naspa.org/about/diversity.cfm

National Association of Academic Advisors for Athletics. (2010). Code of ethics. Retrieved from http://nfoura.org/about/code-of-ethics.php.

National Collegiate Athletic Association. (2010a). CHAMPS Life Skills Program. Retrieved from http://www.ncaa.org/wps/portal/ncaahome?WCM_GLOB-AL_CONTEXT=/ncaa/NCAA/Academics+and+Athletes/CHAMPS+-+Life +Skills/Program

National Collegiate Athletic Association. (2010b, April 20). *Estimated probability of competing in athletics beyond the high school interscholastic level.* Retrieved from http://www.ncaa.org/wps/portal/ncaahome?WCM_GLOBAL_CONTEXT =/ncaa/ncaa/academics+and+athletes/education+and+research/ probability+of+competing/methodology+-+prob+of+competing.

National Collegiate Athletic Association. (2010c). Sports and programs. Retrieved from http://www.ncaa.org/wps/portal/ncaahome?WCM_GLOBAL_CON-TEXT=/ncaa/NCAA/

National Occupational Information Coordinating Committee (NOICC). (1992). The national career development guidelines. Washington, DC: Local Handbook.

Nejedlo, R. J., Arrendondo, P., & Benjamin, L. (1985). *Imagine: A visionary model for the counselors of tomorrow.* DeKalb, IL: George's Printing.

Pedersen, P. (1991). Multiculturalism as a generic approach to counseling. *Journal of Counseling & Development, 70,* 6–12.

Petitpas, A. J., & Champagne, D. E. (2000). Sport and social competence. In S. J. Danish & T. P. Gullotta (Eds.), *Developing competent youth and strong communities through afterschool programming* (pp. 115–137). Washington, DC: CWLA Press.

Petitpas, A., & O'Brien, K. (2008). A focus on career considerations. In A. Leslie-Toogood & E. Gill (Eds.), *Advising student-athletes: A collaborative approach to success.* Manhattan, KS: NACADA, National Academic Advising Association.

Petitpas, A., & Schwartz, H. (1989). Assisting student-athletes in understanding and identifying transferable skills. *The Academic Athletic Journal,* 37–42.

Pinkerton, R. (2009). Forward. In E. F. Etzel (Ed.), *Counseling and psychological services for college student-athletes* (pp. viiii-xi). Morgantown, WV: Fitness Information Technology.

Poinsett, A. (Ed.). (1996). *The role of sports in youth development: Report of a meeting.* New York, NY: Carnegie Corporation.

Pope, M. L., & Miller, M. T. (1996). *A review of the literature related to service for college student-athletes.* (ERIC Document Reproduction Service No. ED419477).

Pope, R. L., Reynolds, A. L., & Mueller, J. A. (2004). *Multicultural competence in student affairs.* San Francisco, CA: Jossey-Bass.

Pope-Davis, D. B., Coleman, H. L. K. , Liu, W. M., & Toporek, R. L. (Eds.) (2003), *Handbook of multicultural competence for counseling and psychology.* Thousand Oaks, CA: Sage Publications.

Rivas Quinones, L. (2003). Career maturity, exploration, and identity factors of student-athletes. Unpublished doctoral dissertation. Southern Illinois University Carbondale. Dissertation Abstracts International, 64(3-A), 811.

Rotter, J. B. (1966). Generalized expectancies for internal versus external locus of control of reinforcement. *Psychological Monographs: General and Applied, 80*(1), 1–28.

Sailes, G., & Harrison, L. (2008). Social issues of sport. In A. Leslie-Toogood and E. Gill (Eds.) *Advising student-athletes: A collaborative approach to success* (pp. 13–21). Manhattan, KS: NACADA, National Academic Advising Association.

Sandstedt, S. D., Cox, R. H., Martens, M. P., Ward, D. G., Webber, S. N., & Ivey, S. (2004). Development of the student-athlete career situation inventory (SAC-SI). *Journal of Career Development, 31*(2), 79–93.

Sedlacek, W. E. (1996). An empirical method of determining nontraditional group status. *Measurement and Evaluation in Counseling and Development, 28*, 200–210.

Simons, H. D., Bosworth, C., Fujita, S., & Jensen, M. (2007). The athlete stigma in higher education. *College Student Journal, 41*(2), 251–273.

Sodowsky, G. R., Taffe, R. C., Gutkin, T. B., & Wise, S. L. (1994). Development of the Multicultural Counseling Inventory: A self-report measure of multicultural competencies. *Journal of Counseling Psychology, 41*, 137–148.

Sowa, C. J., & Gressard, C. F. (1983). Athletic participation: It's relationship to student development. *Journal of College Student Personnel, 24*, 236–239.

Steinfeldt, J., Reed, C., & Steinfeldt, M. C. (2010). Racial and athletic identity of African American football players at historically black colleges and universities and predominantly white institutions. *Journal of Black Psychology, 36*(3), 3–24.

Super, D. E. (1953). A theory of vocational development. *American Psychologist, 8*(5), 185–190.

Super, D. E. (1980). A life span, life space approach to career development. *Journal of Vocational Behavior, 16*, 282–298.

Tinsley, T. M. (2005). The self-reported multicultural sports counseling competencies among professional school counselors and Play It Smart academic coaches. Unpublished doctoral dissertation. Duquesne University, PA. Dissertation Abstracts International, 66 (11), 3942. (UMI No. 3199518).

Tinsley, T. M. (2008). Advising and counseling high school student-athletes. In A. Leslie-Toogood and E. Gill (Eds.) *Advising student-athletes: A collaborative approach to success* (pp. 139–147). Manhattan, KS: NACADA, National Academic Advising Association.

Tinsley, H. E. A., & Tinsley, D. J. (1987). Uses of factor analysis in counseling psychology research. *Journal of Counseling Psychology, 34*, 414–424.

Upthegrove, T. R., Roscigno, V. J., & Zubrinsky, C. C. (1999). Big money collegiate sports: Racial concentration, contradictory pressures, and academic pressures. *Social Sciences Quarterly, 80*(4), 718–737.

Valentine, J. J., & Taub, D. J. (1999). Responding to the developmental needs of student-athletes. *Journal of College Counseling, 21*, 164–179.

Watson, J. C. (2003). *Overcoming the challenges of counseling college student athletes.* Greensboro, NC: Clearinghouse on Counseling and Student Services. (ERIC Document Reproduction Service No. ED475387).

CHAPTER 18

JOB SUPPORT SERVICES

Helping to Remove Barriers Facing College Graduates with Mental Illness

Mark Lepore, Ed.D, LPC, MSW, LCSW

The difficulties and challenges presented to individuals with mental illness to secure employment after completing a college degree are numerous. While the majority of persons with mental illness desire to work and express their desire for job services and support, today, with unemployment on the rise, individuals with disabilities are finding it ever more difficult to obtain employment. Finding employment and an occupational identity is especially important for those with chronic mental illness, who have often been defined by their illness (Seeman, 2009). The positive effects of employment foster pride and self-esteem, promote coping strategies and facilitate the process of recovery (Dunn, Wewiorski, and Rogers, 2008)

The focus of this chapter is on vocational counseling and support of young professionals with mental health issues, identifying the themes and issues individuals are facing, and supporting their efforts to become resilient in their approach. Much of the information contained in this chapter comes from lessons learned and experience gained in coordinating a

Career Development in Higher Education, pages 377–390
Copyright © 2011 by Information Age Publishing
All rights of reproduction in any form reserved.

program called Work-Able. Work-Able is designed to help professionally-oriented individuals dealing with mental health issues enter the workforce in a number of ways, providing holistic services in an atmosphere free of stigma. The program provides vocational counseling, resource coordination, as well as direct placement assistance, including leads and ideas for jobs/career paths. For those who have secured employment, ongoing contact with a counselor is provided for at least six months (http://www.careerdevelopmentcenter.org).

CHALLENGES FACED BY COLLEGE GRADUATES WITH MENTAL ILLNESS

Many of the individuals who have sought assistance through the Work-Able program have been able to find gainful employment. Over 100 individuals have been helped in the past three years. Over half of them have found professional employment. Many, however, remain underemployed or are in temporary or volunteer positions. The success rate of the Work-Able population is high compared to national statistics that show a majority of individuals with disabilities between the ages of 16 and 64 remain unemployed (Bond, et al., 2007).

Some of the individuals this author has worked with have had a difficult time making it through college, and most of their energy and resources have gone into the attainment of the degree. Less focus has been placed on planning for and obtaining a career beyond college. Other individuals have had a smoother time making it through college and have found the career market to be much more challenging and foreboding. In both cases work and the obtainment of a career has proven to be difficult, confusing, and frustrating at times.

The Work-Able program combines vocational and mental health services in a mainstream setting, allowing work to become the primary force in the recovery process. The program's goal of helping participants find appropriate and meaningful employment is rooted in best practices of the strength-based recovery model.

The goals and objectives of Work-Able are as follows:

Goals
1. To enable professionals and skilled workers with mental illness to recover their dignity and improve their mental health status through meaningful work experiences.
2. To provide the supports necessary for professionals/skilled workers to successfully retain employment.

3. Advocate on behalf of clients, and help clients advocate on their own behalf, to alleviate employer fears of hiring individuals with mental illness.

Objectives
1. To create an innovative, replicable, sustainable program model, using evidence-based practices.
2. To deliver services in a setting free of the stigma associated with mental health programs.
3. To work collaboratively with other similar minded providers, avoiding duplication and maximizing community resources available.
4. To provide outreach and education to referring mental health community as well as to employers as potential providers of internships and jobs for clients.

This program has clearly indentified and responded to a need that exists in many communities nationwide, as existing employment programs do not focus on helping this population of professionals feel and achieve the dignity so important in maintaining gainful employment. The clients served are educated and/or skilled who seek relevant jobs to their backgrounds through the use of services free of the stigma associated with mental health programs. Through entering the CDC as any other client, only the counselor knows the details of the services needed. Ultimately, these individuals find employment in settings assigned in some way with their professional background—an outcome that is far too often not achieved in traditional job programs.

One of the ways that Work-Able determines program success, in addition to placement rate and quantity, is via use of the Global Assessment of Functioning (GAF) Scale. The GAF Scale is a 100 point model used to consider psychological, social, and occupational functioning. GAF is a reliable, widely used, and well respected assessment instrument. Clients are evaluated upon entry to the program and again as their situation changes. Entry scores range from a low of 31 to a high of 65, with an average entry score of 55.8. In the most recent evaluations, the low was 54 and the high 85, with an average score at 67.2. Overall, Work-Able has seen an average of 12.4 points, a 23% improvement. Every client has seen gains in their score.

Work-Able Eligibility

Work-Able services are provided free of charge. Eligibility and acceptance are determined through an assessment process and criteria established for the program. Clients are first evaluated for appropriate and adequate treatment. In order for this program to be beneficial, clients must be receiving adequate treatment and be stable. If they are not, they are referred out for services. Once the client has worked through the necessary steps to become medially stable, they are welcome to participate in the program again.

In order to be admitted into the program, individuals must be dealing with challenges and meet eligibility criteria:

- Mental health impairment that affects the ability to attain or retain employment
- Educational or professional credentials (Bachelor's, or other formalized training and/or professional work experience).
- Unemployed or underemployed and seeking professional employment.
- Demonstrated motivation to work (compliance with appointments and attendance at workshops), as determined through the counselors assessment.

Work-Able model addresses many issues:

- Low self-esteem and incomplete self-concept
- Lack of opportunity to network
- How to develop emotional intelligence skills including resilience and problem solving
- Organizational and interviewing skills
- Managing anxiety about the job search process

Lack of Work Experience and Opportunity

Many of the clients in the Work-Able program have had considerably limited prior work experience. Not having work experience seems to have limited their outlook in regards to what careers may be available and increased worries and, in a few instances, unrealistic expectations. The effect of limited early vocational experiences is described by Holland (1985) as a precursor to the development of career related problems. Such problems include failure to develop a consistent and differentiated personality pattern, a clear vocational identity, and the establishment of a career in an incongruent occupation (Gysbers, Heppner, & Johnston, 2003).

Low Self-Esteem and Poorly Developed Self-Concept

Many clients have presented with very low self-esteem. Lack of success in vocational attainment is an ongoing theme that emerges. So much of who we are is reflected in the work that we do. Western European/American culture especially embodies this characteristic. We identify ourselves by the type of work that we do. Having not been very successful in this area, clients feel discouraged and unproductive. It has been this authors experience that clients more readily attribute their lack of successes to a personal failure or shortcoming, more so than the general population, who might be more inclined on which to blame a poor economy or job shortages. Help could include putting the job search into a perspective that is a realistic reflection of the overall vocational goal and outlook. It is essential to help the client maintain realistic optimism about how he or she could maximize his or her own strength to use toward finding and maintaining a career. Encouragement helps to restore self esteem development. A necessary ingredient to helping the client stay motivated is for the individual to begin to make progress toward their stated goals and objectives. Another useful strategy, to borrow a term used by Dr. Robert Brooks, is to help the client identify his or her "islands of competence" (Brooks & Goldstein, 2004). What tasks does the client feel he or she is good at? Clients should self-identify as many islands of competence as possible, even if the client does not believe they are or could be related to the job search. Themes and their related skills can be identified from the clients reported areas or islands of competence. These can be use to help the client see that he or she has legitimate skills applicable toward a vocational pursuit. For example, a new college graduate had a great deal of difficulty identifying islands of competence. Eventually, he was able to say that he was very good at several video games. We discussed how some branches of the military used some of those same games to train people. As we continued to discuss this, he began to concede that maybe he had very good dexterity, hand-eye coordination, decision-making, and other positive qualities that could have career and vocational merit. This approach is very much in keeping with the strength based approach to helping people (Tedeschi & Kilmer, 2005). Again, encouragement in helping clients to self-identify strengths is a critical factor to helping them form a more positive self-concept. The counseling relationship that is formed out of these experiences also goes a long way to helping a client improve his or her self-esteem. Eventually, progress in the pursuit of a career, such as first getting an interview, and then obtaining a job will increase self-esteem further. The adage that success breeds success is particularly applicable in this situation.

Lack of Opportunity to Network

A variety of factors emerge can lead to social isolation for clients. They often feel reluctant to share their mental health disability with other people. This could be partly due to the slowly changing yet still pervasive view that mental illness is something to be feared, as it is still more than a little misunderstood by the general public. I recently spoke to several law firms about the possibility of hiring an individual who has Asperger's syndrome. This individual had earned three associates degrees and was a trained paralegal. Some of the feedback I received was that if this client was physically disabled in some way, the firms could more readily see him fitting in to their system. They saw a social disability as something that would cause too much misunderstanding, and possibly create a problem in their system. It is rare to get such candid feedback; however, the attitude toward individuals with a mental disability can be seen in many non-verbal ways, such as excuse making as to why they could not be hired or avoidance.

Finding opportunities for clients to utilize can be advantageous. Identification of community service opportunities can be helpful. The agency that created Work-Able recently started a mentoring program whereby individuals can work alongside an established professional in the community for career experience and networking opportunities. When possible, making connections within the community that clients are able to utilize is very beneficial in creating networking opportunities and reducing problems wrought by isolation.

INCREASING EMOTIONAL INTELLIGENCE LEVELS, INCLUDING SKILL DEVELOPMENT IN RESILIENCY AND PROBLEM SOLVING

It seems to be a common misconception for people to believe that they may or may not be resilient, or may or may not have good problem solving skills. In fact, it is possible to develop and increase skills related to emotional intelligence. Emotional intelligence can be defined as the capacity to acquire and apply information of an emotional nature, to feel and to respond emotionally (Goleman, 1997). This capacity resides in the emotional brain/mind. Emotional literacy and emotional competence are used interchangeably to describe the relative ability to experience and productively manage emotions. Emotional competencies are skills and attributes—self awareness, empathy, impulse control, listening, decision making, and anger management—whose level of development determines the strength of our emotional intelligence and the degree of our emotional competence (Goleman, 1997).

It can be useful to open up a dialogue about these skills. Many clients have not talked about nor have been taught how to go about increasing their ability to utilize and increase emotional intelligence. Increasing skills in this area is useful in many, if not all, aspects of career preparation and maintenance. These skills can help clients rebound after the inevitable disappointments that are inherent in the job search process.

Client Vignettes*

Bill's Story

Bill, a 24 year old man referred to Work-Able by his therapist, had been looking unsuccessfully for a job for several months. He had earned a bachelor's degree in Sociology and Philosophy and earned a secondary teaching certification. Bill had spent some time as a substitute teacher before deciding not to continue his career as a teacher. Part of Bill's inability to find work related to several mental health challenges that complicated his ability to find and maintain employment. Bill had been diagnosed with Asperger's Syndrome, Major Depressive Disorder, and had also formerly struggled with substance abuse, a form of self-medication. Bill's many professional skills and talents were often overshadowed in interviews by his social challenges, which were part of his Asperger's diagnosis. Many months and numerous job rejections began to reduce his positive self-concept and he began to question his ability to be a provider for his family. In Work-Able he was given a chance to discuss these concerns and fears that he had in a supportive, non-judgmental environment. Through the program, he was able to make an honest account of his positive and negative qualities in terms of both his job search and his life. He also requested that we maintain an on-going communication with his therapist of seven years. This communication was helpful in providing direction for goal planning and problem solving. Bill's confidence and self-esteem improved, through practicing interview skills like maintaining eye-contact, and improving social skills, and by organizing a cohesive resume and cover letter. A job search campaign was conducted, and with the support he was able to connect with potential employers. When an employer contacted CDC to inquire about any potential candidates for a position as a Customer Service Representative or Manger, CDC suggested Bill. Several days after the interview, which resulted in his hiring, the employer called to thank CDC for sending such a qualified applicant. Bill is grateful for the help he received, and his enthusiasm and motivation continue to be high.

Jill's Story

Like many people with bi-polar disorder, Jill had struggled for years. She managed to get through college and get a degree and was working in social services. A couple of years later things began to unravel. Jill had multiple

---

* Names and all other identifying details have been changed to protect privacy.

hospitalizations and trouble with her medications and treatments. Simultaneously, problems at work (unrelated to her disability) began to spiral out of control. Finally, her mother died unexpectedly. Jill wanted to get better and kept trying to find the right help. Once she was connected to Work-Able, she went to every workshop offered. She followed up on her treatment and was open with her counselor. It was not an easy road, and even during this period, she was re-hospitalized for treatment. Eventually, through hard work with her therapy, medications, and Work-Able counselor, Jill got a job working as a therapeutic staff support, counseling clients who have been newly released from state hospitals and are living with severe diagnoses, and helping them to be independent. She opted to disclose her condition to her employers, and they are supportive of her continuing efforts to remain stable. Jill has held her job for nearly a year and anticipates remaining for many more to come.

James' Story

James is a 25 year old male. He began his college studies at a state university, but after a year and a half was unable to continue after experiencing a severe bout of depression and making a suicide attempt. He later transferred to another university and was able to complete his bachelor of arts degree. Unable to find a job, feeling discouraged, he had only worked part-time jobs and remained somewhat isolated. He continued to have problems with depression, obsessive-compulsive disorder, and anxiety. He sought out help through the Work-Able program. Initially, the discouragement was very evident by the reluctance to put forth effort and even to voice anything positive about the possibility of obtaining a job. It was important for him to build a working relationship with a counselor in the program before he could move forward. He then took weeks to get his resume to the place that he felt comfortable in presenting it to potential employers. After several months of supportive counseling, James developed a renewed enthusiasm for the job search. He found a position as a counselor for at-risk youth. He has been very successful, and the agency called to thank us for sending him to them. It was obvious that by obtaining this job and experiencing success, his attitude, demeanor, and confidence has dramatically improved. He is now living independently in his own apartment. He is able to express ideas about where he sees himself in five or ten years from now.

Fran's Story

Fran is a 24 year old female. Fran earned bachelor's and master's degrees in business and accounting. She always saw school and academics as her island of competence. She believed when she graduated she would earn her C.P.A. license and have a successful career as an accountant. Toward the end of her graduate studies she began to experience problems with overwhelming anxiety. For a couple of years she attempted to deal with her problems on her own. Eventually she sought mental health treatment for severe anxiety and was eventually diagnosed with an anxiety disorder. She continued to experience panic attacks and was not able to maintain employment. She was referred for help by her therapist to the Work-Able program. She initially felt shame and embarrassment about her condition and inability to find a job. After supportive counseling sessions, participation in workshops, resume development, and networking, her confidence began to improve. She also was able to put things into perspective and view her mental health issues as an illness that was not her fault. Paradoxically, this helped her to take responsibility for what she could do to get her life back on track. She found a position as an office manager and has been doing very well on the job despite still managing bouts of extreme anxiety. She also has plans to continue her career and she describes feeling more confident and optimistic.

ASSISTING CLIENTS TO THINK ABOUT AND TAKE ACCOUNT OF THEIR RESILIENCE STRENGTHS, DEFICIENCIES

Clients' identification of strengths, labeling, and categorizing these skills is often illuminating. They can rate their abilities in several areas of emotional intelligence. One such area is emotional regulation, which is defined as how good an individual is at understanding and managing feelings so that he or she may stay goal focused. Other areas of emotional intelligence are impulse control, the command they have over behaviors; self-efficacy, a person's belief in themselves and how he or she can handle problems; reaching out, which is defined as an indicator of how a client may look at taking on new challenges and opportunities. All of these skills can be discussed along with gaining a commitment from the client to attempt to utilize these skills to increase the effectiveness of his or her personal career development. Providing a forum to help clients understand and come to terms with their own decision making process is a crucial component of career development. With counseling support clients can examine factors that affect decision making, including taking a candid look at the values and value systems behind decisions that have been and will be made. In some instances persons with mental illness have historically not been in a position to make many decisions on their own and therefore can lack competence in this area. Many models exist for understanding and factoring the decision-making process. These skills can be rehearsed with clients to help them gain skill for making decisions.

Career Counseling Strategies for Helping Persons with Mental Health Disabilities

The Work-Able program embraces the philosophy that when a person is engaged in work and career they are also taking part in a very empowering and therapeutic process. This philosophy encompasses elements of the humanistic approach to counseling, which takes a view of human nature from a person centered perspective, which can be summarized as follows:

The degree of misery a person experiences is related to the discrepancy between what she is and what she is capable of becoming. The natural order of nature was for human beings to continue to develop and grow unless impeded by other things or the environment (Archer & McCarthy, 2007). In keeping with the humanistic perspective, the counselor is mindful of the frustration that individuals may bring to the career development process from years of struggling with impediments to their own personal and professional growth and development.

Career counselors can bring their own theoretical approaches to the process. The following three-stage implementation process is just an overview of some of the concepts and activities that can take place and have been effective in helping people find a chosen career path. It is valuable and important for each counselor to bring his or her own unique qualities and personality to the process as they build rapport and trust with clients in assisting them to make a very major step in their personal and professional development.

Initial Phase—Establishing a Foundation Built on Respect, Trust, and Safety

Whenever possible it is vital to the success of the career counseling process to devote as much time as is necessary to hear clients' stories about how they arrived at this place in their career path. Attempts to move along or hurry the process will most likely result in a delay on the client's part to trust that this is a safe environment for them to be open and honest. The counselor should not be another reflection of a society that has demeaned or devalued them by lack of respect for their personal points of view. Becoming knowledgeable about how culture has influenced the client is important, including what relevance and influence the client's disability has had on them. Ask for clarification when needed. Also ascertain other cultural influences such as the roles of poverty, sexism, racism, and disability. During this stage counselors should be genuine and use their counseling skills only as a means to demonstrate sincere concern for the client.

Empathy is important but it is valuable only if we have a way to convey to the client that we understand and that they have worth as a human being even when what they are expressing is something negative or problematic. Allowing time for a client to ventilate makes it more likely that they will begin to feel empowered enough to take positive risks later on toward achieving their goals. Counselors should encourage clients to give expression to feelings and attitudes, and make it clear that they can express these without judgment by the counselor. The technique known as the "one down" position can be helpful in the initial sessions (Turner, 1996). Clients will often bring to the career counseling session the belief that the counselor is an expert or authority, which could lead to defensiveness or guardedness in that situation. Career counseling from a "one down" position can be subtly expressed in a number of ways. The counselor can acknowledge that the questions asked of the client may seem very trivial. A counselor can emphasize that the client is really the expert about themselves. Also avoid the use of very definitive language and stay open-minded. This method reduces resistance and can prevent power struggles with the client.

In summary, this portion of the career counseling process can be the most crucial. The idea of a career with all of the expectations that come with that can be an enormous burden for some people. Clients will bring much of their emotional baggage with them to the session. They will react to perceived negative attitudes of the counselor. Pay close attention to your non-verbal communications, which are often more honest than verbal communications.

Middle Stage—Charting a Course

Counselors, in this stage, will concentrate on the inevitable highs and lows that come from the job search process. The utilization of aforementioned resilience-building strategies will be effective when helping clients stay focused on their goals. During this stage the rapport that has been built with the client in the preceding stage will be valuable. Job seekers are likely to experience a great deal of rejection. The rejection can lead to increased anxiety, making it difficult to achieve goals. Encouragement remains an effective tool in helping the clients maintain motivation. This stage will inevitably bring about some realism, tempering expectations on behalf of the client. Clients may for the first time be exposed to the realities of a career, including the salaries, hours, expectations, and more. In many instances clients may have to reevaluate the type of career they want. Career counselors can help by presenting options to the client. Role playing the interview process has proven to be very valuable for clients, including asking difficult questions for practice. All of the traditional career counseling techniques would be employed at this stage. The inevitable setbacks during this stage will continue to call for the counselor to stay tuned to the needs of the client and be prepared to help remove obstacles and barriers that may keep them from achieving their goals.

One of the decisions an individual must make is whether or not to disclose to an employer the fact that they have an identifiable disability (Marwaha & Johnson, 2005). If they choose to disclose that fact, employers sometimes have the option to have a portion of the salary they would pay reimbursed to them by various government incentive programs such as the Work Opportunity Tax Credit, the Disabled Access Credit, the Social Security Administration Employment Network Cash Provision, and others. It is important to research the current options and incentives available to employers who hire individuals who have a mental disability. A majority of individuals the author has worked with choose not to self identify as having a mental health diagnosis. The utilization of effective supportive counseling techniques seems to be the most efficacious way of helping individuals achieve their career goals (Corrigan & Kleinlein, 2005; Killackey, Jackson, Gleeson, Hickie, & Mcgorry, 2006)

Transition Stage—Support for Increased Competency

In the Work-Able program, a client still receives counseling for up to six months after they have found gainful employment. The career counselor can utilize what is called competency enhancement. This is an opportunity to build on the client's success and increase their skills and confidence. The approach in this phase is to support and enhance the growing competencies of the client through the work experience. Career counselors will help clients reduce perceived barriers to continued job success. Topics that may be covered include stress management, problem solving, utilization of effective communication skills, building personal networks and social supports, increasing hardiness, and other topics that are necessitated by the needs of the clients.

Szymanski and Hershenson (1998), indicated that the focus of career counseling should be eclectic and include supporting the client through his or her transition into work. Once clients are placed into positions of employment, support for their success can be enhanced by connections to and ease of access to community resources such as Jewish Family and Children's Services. Efforts will focus on enhancing the clients' self-resilience, and how to tap in to supportive workplace and community networks. Clients should ultimately transfer their personal empowerment beyond career enhancement to all areas of their lives (Kosciulek, 2003).

IN CLOSING

Career counseling with college graduates who have a mental health disability is a very challenging and rewarding task. The skills needed to be successful are rooted in the personal characteristics of the counselor combined with the willingness on the part of the counselor to seek out ongoing, relevant information about the career market, a market that is dynamic, constantly changing, and one that offers innovative opportunities for career enhancement. The possibilities embraced in career counseling are poignant, potentially life-changing, and can pave the way for a constructive and rewarding life for the client for the future in both their professional and personal lives.

REFERENCES

Archer Jr., J., & McCarthy, C. J. (2007) *Theories of counseling and psychotherapy: contemporary applications.* Upper Saddle River, NJ: Pearson.

Bond, G. R., Salyers, M. P., Dincin, J., Drake, R. E., Becker, D. R., Fraser, V. V., & Haines, M. (2007). A randomized controlled trial comparing two vocational models for persons with severe mental illness. *Journal of Consulting and Clinical Psychology, 75,* 6, 968–982.

Brooks, R. E., & Goldstein, S. (2004). *The power of resilience: achieving balance, confidence, and personal strength in your life.* New York, NY: McGraw Hill.

Corrigan, P. W., & Kleinlein, P. (2005). The impact of mental illness stigma. In P. W. Corrigan (Ed.), *On the stigma of mental illness:Practical strategies for research and social change* (pp. 11–44). Washington, DC: American Psychological Association.

Dunn, E. C., Wewiorski, N. J., & Rogers, E.S. (2008). The Meaning and Importance of Employment to People in Recovery from Serious Mental Illness: Results of a Qualitative Study. *Psychiatric Rehabilitation Journal, 32,* 1, 59- 62.

Goleman, D. (1997). *Emotional Intelligence: Why It Can Matter More Than IQ.* New York, NY: Bantam Books.

Gysbers, N. C., Heppner, M. J., & Johnston, J.A. (2003). *Career Counseling: Process, Issues, and Techniques* (2nd ed.). Boston, MA: Allyn and Bacon.

Holland, J. L. (1985). *Making vocational choices: a theory of vocational personalities and work environments* (2nd ed.) Englewood Cliffs, NJ: Prentice-Hall.

Killackey, E. J., Jackson, H. J., Gleeson, J., Hickie, I. B & Mcgorry, P. D. (2006). Exciting career opportunity beckons! Early intervention and vocational rehabilitation in first-episode psychosis: employing cautious optimism. *Australian and New Zealand Journal of Psychiatry 40,* 951–962

Kosciulek, J. F. (2003) An empowerment approach to career counseling with people with disabilities. In Gysbers, N. C., Heppner, M. J., Johnston, J. A., *Career Counseling: process, issues, and techniques* (2nd ed.) pp. 139–153. Boston, MA: Allyn and Bacon.

Marwaha, S., & Johnson, S. (2005). Views and experiences of employment among people with psychosis: A qualitative descriptive study. *International Journal of Social Psychiatry 51*, 302–316.

Seeman, M.E. (2009). Employment Discrimination Against Schizophrenia. *Psychiatric Quarterly, 80*, 9–16

Szymanski, E. M., & Hershenson, D. B. (1998). Career development of people with disabilities: an ecological model. In R. M. Parker & E. M Szymanski (Eds.), *Rehabilitation counseling: Basics and beyond* (3rd ed.). Austin, TX: Pro-Ed.

Tedeschi, R. G., & Kilmer, R. P. (2005). Assessing strengths, resilience, and growth to guide clinical interventions. *Professional Psychology: Research and Practice, 36*, 3, 230–237.

Turner, F. J. (Ed.). (1996). *Social work treatment: interlocking theoretical approaches* (4th ed.). New York, NY: Simon & Schuster.

ABOUT THE EDITORS

Jeff L. Samide is associate professor of Counselor Education at California University of Pennsylvania. His interest in Career Development has spanned thirty years and was renewed as he assisted his daughter, Rosie, as she made decisions about her path in life. Dr. Samide has published on diverse topics, including spirituality and counseling, and the fusion of art, science and technology into counselor education and folklore. Dr. Samide is a Licensed Professional Counselor (LPC), National Certified Counselor (NCC), Master Addictions Counselor (MAC), Approved Clinical Supervisor (ACS) and a past PA State Certified Elementary School Guidance Counselor. As a psychotherapist with over thirty years experience, he has expertise in working with individuals and families with a variety of problems, including addiction, sexual abuse, domestic violence and more. He has provided expert testimony in the Commonwealth of Pennsylvania courts well over two hundred times. Past positions include clinical director at a chemical dependency rehabilitation center, individual and group psychotherapist in a variety of settings, consultant, school counselor, and mental health emergency case worker specialist. He can be reached at samide@calu.edu.

Grafton T. Eliason is currently an associate professor in the department of Counselor Education at California University of Pennsylvania. He has taught and written numerous publications on theories, culture, career, school counseling, death, dying, and spirituality. He has a special interest in existential philosophy and religion. He received his Doctorate in Counselor Education and Supervision from Duquesne University. He has also earned an MDiv. from Princeton Theological Seminary and an MEd in School Counseling from Shippensburg University. He has numerous cer-

Career Development in Higher Education, pages 391–392
Copyright © 2011 by Information Age Publishing

tifications, including National Certified Counselor (NCC), Licensed Professional Counselor (LPC) in Pennsylvania, Certified School Counselor (K–12) in Pennsylvania, and he is an ordained Presbyterian minister. He has taught at Duquesne University, the Citadel, and Chatham University.

John Patrick is currently a professor in the department of Counselor Education at California University of Pennsylvania. Dr. Patrick has taught numerous courses in Career Counseling and has a special interest in using the creative arts in career counseling. He has published extensively on various career topics, including career assessment, curriculum development, and vocational rehabilitation. He has been a reviewer for several state and national journals and has held a variety of leadership positions within the American College Counseling Association, Alabama Counseling Association, and the Pennsylvania Counseling Association. Dr. Patrick is a professional artist, Certified Rehabilitation Counselor (CRC), National Certified Counselor (NCC), and a Licensed Professional Counselor (LPC) in Pennsylvania. He has also taught at The Pennsylvania State University, Minnesota State University-Moorhead, and Troy University Montgomery Campus. Past positions include serving as a vocational rehabilitation counselor, Job Corps counselor and counseling director, and various career and academic positions in higher education. He can be contacted at patrick@calu.edu.

ABOUT THE CONTRIBUTORS

Brigadier General Michael B. Barrett is professor in Department of History, School of Humanities and Social Sciences at The Citadel and earned his BA degree from The Citadel in 1968 with honors and a degree in Modern Languages (German). He was a Distinguished Military Graduate and earned his MA and PhD at the University of Massachusetts. He is author of *Operation Albion: The German Conquest of the Baltic Islands* (Indiana University Press, 2008) and co-author of *Clausewitz Reconsidered* (Praeger, 2009). He is a retired brigadier general in the US Army Reserve.

Demond E. Bledsoe, a Licensed Professional Counselor, is a Clinical Consultant with Wesley Spectrum Services and an Adjunct Instructor at Chatham University. Currently, Demond is a doctoral candidate at Duquesne University in Pittsburgh, PA. His research interests include multiculturalism, trauma, and supervision.

Theodore Burnes is an associate professor at the California School of Professional Psychology at Alliant International University in Los Angeles. His scholarly interests include multicultural counseling, social justice, young adult development inside and outside of university systems, qualitative methods, and LGBTQI mental health and wellness.

Kimberly J. Desmond, PhD, LPC, NCC is an associate professor in Counseling at Indiana University of Pennsylvania. She is a counselor educator teaching primarily in the school counseling program. She is also a practicing Licensed Professional Counselor and Certified School Counselor. Her

Career Development in Higher Education, pages 393–399
Copyright © 2011 by Information Age Publishing
All rights of reproduction in any form reserved.

scholarly interests include school counseling, career counseling, interventions, and mentoring.

Marissa (Betters) Fenwick is the Assistant Director of the CareerWorks department at Seton Hill University in Greensburg, Pennsylvania. She obtained her Master of Education degree in School Counseling from California University of Pennsylvania. She is a National Certified Counselor (NCC) and is currently working toward becoming a Pennsylvania Licensed Professional Counselor (LPC).

Dr. Ray Feroz is a professor of Special Education and Rehabilitative Sciences at Clarion University of Pennsylvania, where he has taught for 21 years. His doctoral degree is in Rehabilitation Counseling from the University of Pittsburgh. He is a Certified Rehabilitation Counselor (CRC), National Certified Counselor (NCC) and Pennsylvania Licensed Professional Counselor (LPC).

Nadine E. Garner, LPC is an associate professor in the Psychology Department at Millersville University of Pennsylvania and the Graduate Program Coordinator of the School Counseling Program. She is co-author of the book *A School with Solutions: Implementing a Solution-focused/Adlerian-based Comprehensive School Counseling Program*, published by ASCA.

Rhonda Gifford has worked in the field of career services for 17 years and is Director of Career Services at California University of Pennsylvania. Prior to coming to Cal U in 2002, Rhonda worked in Career Services at the University of Pittsburgh and at Saint Vincent College. She earned a BS in Business Administration/Marketing and an MA in Student Affairs in Higher Education from Indiana University of Pennsylvania.

Lt Colonel Charles H. Graham USMCR is the 1st Battalion Tactical Officer at The Citadel. He earned his BA degree from the University of South Carolina, an MA degree from Webster University, and a Master of Strategic Studies degree from the Air War College. His military career operational experience includes three reserve mobilizations and four combat operations tours.

Helen S. Hamlet is an assistant professor of Counseling & Human Services at Kutztown University and is a frequent lecturer at the University of Pennsylvania Graduate School of Education. Her scholarly interests focus on training, supervision and assessment in school counseling programs and multicultural counseling in the school setting.

Matt Ishler MEd, LPC, NCC is Assistant Director of Career Counseling and Planning at Penn State's Career Services Center. At Penn State, Matt provides career counseling and career education programs to undergraduate and graduate students. Matt is also pursuing a PhD in Counselor Education and Supervision, with a focus upon Career Counseling and Supervision.

Prof. Lourens Human is a registered Counseling Psychologist with the Health Professions Council of South Africa. He is an associate professor in the Department of Psychology at the University of Pretoria, South Africa, and coordinator of the MA (Counseling Psychology) program. He lectures at undergraduate and postgraduate levels, while his research interests primarily fall within the fields of health psychology and sport psychology.

Dr. Jonathan Lent is currently a visiting assistant professor at John Carroll University in University Heights, Ohio. He is licensed as both a professional counselor and school counselor. Additionally, Jonathan is employed by Psy-Care, Inc. in Austintown, Ohio where he sees both individual and group clients for a variety of clinical issues.

Mark Lepore has obtained a doctorate in Counselor Education and Supervision at Duquesne University. He holds an MA from Duquesne University and an MSW from West Virginia University. He also has a Clinical Social Work license and five education certifications. He has worked as a School Counselor and is currently a professor and Director of the University Counseling Center at Clarion University. Dr. Lepore has worked extensively in the field of trauma and grief and loss counseling. He is a mental health trainer for the American Red Cross, and he is a supervisor for National Disaster Response, having volunteered for assignments after the terrorist attack of September 11th, hurricane Katrina, California wildfires, and many others.

Chad Luke is the Associate Dean for Student Success at Lehigh Carbon Community College, where he oversees counseling, advising, career services, and first-year student success initiatives. He earned his doctorate from the University of Tennessee and is a Licensed Professional Counselor. He lives in Pennsylvania with his wife and daughter.

Ms. Nkateko Ndala-Magoro is an intern Counseling Psychologist with the Health Professions Council of South Africa and a junior lecturer in the Department of Psychology at the University of Pretoria, South Africa. She is involved in undergraduate and postgraduate education, and her research interest primarily lies in community psychology and HIV/AIDS.

Rebecca Roberts Martin, PhD, PCC-S has an extensive work history in counselor education as well as in clinical counseling and supervision. Dr. Roberts Martin is currently a counselor supervisor at Coleman Behavioral Health in Canton, Ohio and adjunct faculty at Kent State University, Stark Campus, and Walden University.

Dana Matta is an Advisory Editor for the journal *Family Process*. He is also a family and life consultant for the United States Military and is an adjunct instructor for Northcentral University. His doctorate is in Marital and Family Therapy from Loma Linda University.

James Matta is an associate professor in the Master of Arts in Counseling Program at Geneva College in Beaver Falls, Pennsylvania. He also is a Senior Research Principal at Western Psychiatric Institute and Clinic in Pittsburgh, where he works in research with adolescents and young adults. He earned his doctorate at Duquesne University in Counselor Education and Supervision.

Thomas Matta is a licensed marriage and family therapist in practice in Erie, Pennsylvania. His doctorate is in sociology from the University of Southern California, and he has taught at the undergraduate and graduate levels. Regulating the Marriage and Family profession in Pennsylvania and nationally has been a career focus.

Maryann O. Meniru is currently a doctoral student at The University of Akron in Akron, Ohio. Maryann is licensed as a professional counselor and is currently seeing clients in a community-based mental health center in Canton, Ohio. Additionally, Maryann is an adjunct professor at The University of Akron.

Eric W. Owens is a professional school counselor at Vincentian Academy in Pittsburgh, PA, as well as a doctoral candidate at Duquesne University. Prior to his work in the school setting, he worked in higher education for 12 years. Eric is a National Certified Counselor and an Approved Clinical Supervisor.

Caroline Perjessy is a Doctoral Candidate from Kent State University. She is a licensed professional counselor in the states of Ohio and Georgia and has previously taught Career Counseling at Youngstown State University. Her private practice includes work with career clients, utilizing a constructivist perspective.

Fred Redekop is an assistant professor in the Department of Counseling and Human Services at Kutztown University of Pennsylvania. His doctorate is from the University of Iowa, and he is a Licensed Professional Counselor.

Cathy Rintz received her undergraduate degree in Business Administration from Elizabethtown College and her graduate degree in School Counseling from Millersville University of Pennsylvania. She is employed by Franklin & Marshall College as an Admissions Counselor.

Ms. Ilse Ruane is a registered Counseling Psychologist with the Health Professions Council of South Africa and lecturer in the Department of Psychology at the University of Pretoria, South Africa. She is involved in undergraduate and postgraduate education, and her research interests are in the areas of multi-cultural therapeutic education of students in professional psychology programs, praxis of community psychology, local relevance and indigenous psychology, as well as multiculturalism.

Dr. William S. Rullo serves as the Director of Counseling Services at Upper St. Clair High School in Pittsburgh, Pennsylvania. He is an adjunct professor at California University of Pennsylvania, Point Park University, and Duquesne University, teaching both educational and school counseling courses. He obtained his Doctorate of Education degree in May of 1996, from the University of Pittsburgh through the Administrative and Policy Studies program. He received his Master of Education degree in Counselor Education from Indiana University of Pennsylvania in May of 1992. His Bachelor of Arts degree in Secondary Education was acquired in June, 1986, at Saint Vincent College in Latrobe, Pennsylvania.

Travis W. Schermer, PhD, LPC works as a counselor at Mercy Behavioral Health's East Liberty Center and as an instructor at Chatham University in Pittsburgh, PA. He is a Kent State University alumnus and has worked in research, university, and private practice settings. Travis enjoys actively constructing his career narrative.

Gene Sutton has worked in the field of career services for 13 years and is the Associate Director of Career Services at California University of Pennsylvania. Prior to coming to Cal U in June of 2006, Gene worked in Career Services at the University of Connecticut, Oregon State University and Marietta College. Gene earned a Bachelor of Science in Exercise and Sports Science and a Master of Arts in Student Affairs in Higher Education from Indiana University of Pennsylvania.

Kayla Snyder, MEd has a Master of Education in School Counseling and a Bachelor of Science in Elementary Education/minor in Educational Psychology from Indiana University of Pennsylvania. Her interests include school counseling, solution-focused counseling, and counseling school-aged children facing difficulties. She has professional experience implementing career education programming with school-aged populations.

Dr. Emily Sweitzer is an associate professor of Justice and Behavioral Crime and Director of the Justice Studies Division at California University of Pennsylvania. She has a doctoral degree in Educational Psychology, 39 post-doctoral credits in Educational Administration, an MS in School Psychology and a BA in Psychology. She is a nationally certified school psychologist, certified K–12 principal, and certified in Forensic Science and Law. Her interests include violence prevention, delinquency, and parent-child behavioral issues.

Ms. Vicky Timm is a registered Research Psychologists and Counseling Psychologist with the Health Professions Council of South Africa. She is also a lecturer in the Department of Psychology at the University of Pretoria, South Africa. Ms. Timm is involved in the teaching of both undergraduate and postgraduate programs. Her research interest areas include violence, family therapy, as well as qualitative research methods.

Dr. Taunya M. Tinsley completed her requirements and graduated with her PhD in December 2005 from Duquesne University's Executive Doctoral Program in Counselor Education and Supervision (ExCES). Dr. Tinsley is a counselor educator and assistant professor at California University of Pennsylvania. Additionally, she is the program coordinator for the Graduate Certificate in Sports Counseling.

Brielle Valle is a senior at Millersville University of Pennsylvania majoring in public relations. She will graduate with four co-op experiences varying in professions including admissions, event planning, and internal communication. She is employed by Linden Hall School and Susquehanna Bancshares. A career in special events and promotion will be pursued upon graduation.

Dr. Amy Sherell (Cammack) Walker is a licensed psychologist with special interests in topics related to vocational, sport, and multicultural psychology. She earned her Bachelor of Arts in Communications from the University of Pittsburgh and her Master of Arts in Community Counseling from the University of Maryland College Park. Dr. Walker completed her doctoral studies in Counseling Psychology at the Pennsylvania State University. Over the past 12 years, Amy has been committed to working with athletes on various levels from high school to the professional ranks. Dr. Walker spent the majority of her career counseling collegiate student-athletes from universities coast to coast including UCLA and the University of Maryland. Athletes represented sport teams such as football, men and women's basketball, track and field, tennis, and gymnastics.

Colonel George T. Williams is professor and Coordinator of Counselor Education Programs, School of Education, The Citadel. He earned his BA and MEd degrees at Kutztown University of Pennsylvania and EdD at the University of Cincinnati. He has held numerous professional organization leadership positions, including past president of South Carolina Counseling Association. He has been a K–12 school/college counselor, counselor educator and/or psychologist in the states of Pennsylvania, Ohio, Minnesota, Louisiana, California, and South Carolina.

CPSIA information can be obtained at www.ICGtesting.com
Printed in the USA
LVOW011340261111

256555LV00002B/67/P